D0132268

Preserving and Strengthening
Small Towns
and Rural Communities

Preserving and Strengthening Small Towns and Rural Communities

Iris B. Carlton-LaNey, Richard L. Edwards,
and
P. Nelson Reid, Editors

NASW PRESS

National Association of Social Workers
Washington, DC

Josephine A. V. Allen, PhD, ACSW, *President*
Josephine Nieves, MSW, PhD, *Executive Director*

Paula Delo, *Executive Editor*
Steph Selice, *Senior Editor*
William Schroeder, *Staff Editor*
Caroline Polk , C. G. Polk Editorial Services, *Copy Editor*
Pamela Murray, *Indexer*
Chanté Lampton, *Acquisitions Associate*
Heather Peters, *Editorial Secretary*

Cover by Jane Weber, Weber Design, Alexandria, Virginia
Typeset by Maryland Composition Company, Inc., Glen Burnie, Maryland
Printed and bound by Victor Graphics, Inc., Baltimore, Maryland

© 1999 by NASW Press

Library of Congress Cataloging-in-Publication Data

Preserving and strengthening small towns and rural communities / Iris
B. Carlton-LaNey, Richard L. Edwards, and P. Nelson Reid, editors.
    p. cm.
  Includes bibliographical references and index.
  ISBN 0-87101-310-X (alk. paper)
    1. Social service, Rural—United States Congresses.   2. Human
services—United States Congresses.   I. Carlton-LaNey, Iris B.
II. Edwards, Richard L.   III. Reid, P. Nelson.   IV. National
Institute on Social Work and Human Services in Rural Areas (23rd :
1998 : University of North Carolina)
HV91.P734   1999
361.973′09173′4—dc21   99-33081
                                     CIP

Printed in the United States of America

Dedication

We are pleased to dedicate this book to Drs. Janice Hough Schopler and Kermit B. Nash, Jr. Both Jan and Kermit were involved in the early stages of planning the 23rd Annual National Institute on Social Work and Human Services in Rural Areas, the conference at which the papers included in this volume were originally presented. Unfortunately, both Jan and Kermit, who were professors in the School of Social Work at the University of North Carolina at Chapel Hill, died in the months preceding the Institute. Jan grew up on a farm in Michigan and never forgot her rural roots. Kermit came from a small town in upstate New York and taught courses on rural health and social work in rural areas. They and their contributions to social work education are greatly missed.

Iris B. Carlton-LaNey, Richard L. Edwards, and P. Nelson Reid

Table of Contents

Acknowledgments

As with any edited book, this volume represents the contributions of many people. We wish first to thank the authors of the various chapters, whose efforts were critical to making this book possible. Second, we thank all who participated in the 23rd Annual National Institute on Social Work and Human Services in Rural Areas, held July 16–19, 1998, at the University of North Carolina at Chapel Hill School of Social Work. Their involvement in the Institute and their comments to the presenters whose papers were selected for inclusion in this book certainly contributed to strengthening the final product.

Others who deserve special thanks include the following individuals who were involved in planning and organizing the Institute: Dee Gamble, Sherry Megner, Daniel Lebold, Tricia Daisley, Anne-Linda Furstenberg, Maxcine Barnes, Audrey Burkes, Margaret Morse, Anne Marie Sullivan, Alice Richman, and Naomi Swinton. Also, we particularly want to express our gratitude to the staff at NASW Press who oversaw the coordination, production, and editing processes that resulted in the book's timely publication: Paula Delo, Steph Selice, William Schroeder, Chanté Lampton, and Heather Peters. Special thanks also go to Caroline Polk, who initially copyedited the manuscript, and Pam Murray, who indexed it.

Finally, we want to acknowledge all of our colleagues who labor in the many small towns and rural communities throughout the United States and Canada. They frequently are the unsung heroes who daily struggle to make communities better places for individuals and families to live and thrive, often against seemingly overwhelming odds.

SECTION I

INTRODUCTION AND OVERVIEW

This book is the product of the 23rd Annual National Institute on Social Work and Human Services in Rural Areas, which was held in the summer of 1998 at the University of North Carolina at Chapel Hill School of Social Work. The first National Institute took place in 1976 at the University of Tennessee School of Social Work, and the Institutes have been held annually since that time in a variety of locations across the United States. The 1976 institute spawned the National Rural Social Work Caucus and helped focus the attention of the social work profession on the particular needs of rural residents and the specific attributes and skills required of social workers who practice in rural areas.

Although evidence of interest in social work in rural areas can be seen in the literature of the 1920s and 1930s, such interest waned considerably in the wake of the increasing migration of the population from rural to urban areas. By the 1960s, the focus of the United States and of the social work profession was heavily oriented toward the growing problems of urban areas. To many observers, it appeared that there had developed "a distinct preoccupation with and bias toward urban areas by federal and state governments, private organizations, and the profession of social work" (Davenport & Davenport, 1995, p. 2083). However, this situation began to change a bit between 1969 and 1974, as sessions on rural social work issues began to appear on the programs of various national social work conferences (Green & Webster, 1977). Gradually, an increasing amount of published materials on rural social work practice began to appear. The 1976 National Institute on Social Work in Rural Areas in Knoxville, Tennessee, became the catalyst for the rural social work movement that has led, 23 years later, to the publication of this book.

In part, interest on social work in rural areas was reawakened by 1970 census data revealing that for the first time since the early 1900s, the rate of growth in nonmetropolitan areas (that is, small towns and rural communities) exceeded the rate of population growth in urban areas (Ginsberg, 1977). Although the urban population of the United States has continued to grow, small town and rural population has been increasing rapidly, to the point where more people live in rural areas now than at any other time in our nation's history (U.S. Bureau of the Census, 1991).

The population of small towns and rural areas is diverse. It includes people who were left behind when the great waves of urban migration occurred, those who left and are now coming back, and those who have decided that the presumed advantages of small towns and rural areas make them attractive places to retire. In addition, African Americans, Hispanics, and American Indians make up significant portions of the rural population. At the same time, rural areas tend to be characterized by poverty rates that are higher than those in urban areas (Morris, 1995). Suffice it to say that our small towns and rural areas are confronted with a range of problems that must be addressed, including such traditional issues as lack of services, transportation, and employment opportunities. The economy in small towns and rural areas is undergoing significant changes that encompass various types of economic restructuring and a concomitant steady decline in the numbers of small family farms.

The chapters included in this book represent an attempt to shed additional light on ways in which small towns and rural communities can be strengthened. Given that the chapters collected here were originally presentations at the 23rd Annual National Institute on Social Work and Human Services in Rural Areas, the editors wish to extend their thanks to and deep regard for the work of the many people who made presentations at that conference. To those who allowed us to consider including their papers in this volume, we extend our special thanks. Many excellent papers were submitted for our review, and space limitations made it impossible to include all of them. We are particularly indebted to those authors whose work is included here for their willingness to consider our editorial suggestions and for helping us meet our stringent production deadlines.

This book is dedicated to an important but currently debated proposition, namely, that life in small towns and rural communities is different from life in urban areas and that those differences have significance for social work practice and education. It is our belief that small town and rural life is certainly different from what it used to be, just as it is certainly different from life in urban or metropolitan areas. This book, which was developed around the 23rd Annual Institute's theme, "Preserving and Strengthening Rural Communities," explores those differences in a multitude of ways and contexts. The chapters not only make clear the resilient qualities and advantages of life in small towns and rural communities but also reflect the fragility and sense of threat that many such communities feel.

For the purposes of this book, we have not attempted to define "rural" and "small town" in any strict way, because no uniformity, beyond the U.S. Census Bureau's narrow definition, exists in how the terms are used by government agencies or social researchers. It is evident in the chapters in this book that there is considerable variability in the composition and life of the communities; thus, we allowed each author to operationalize the terms according to his or her work. Some authors elected to use the U.S. Census Bureau definition, but most elected to be more flexible and identify rural areas as places closer to the rural end of the rural–urban continuum. Although divisions and boundaries are necessary in some instances, as in the application of policy, it is critical for social workers to be aware that people's personal perceptions of place and their social interactions as they define their existence and their space are equally valid in these rural areas.

The chapters in this book are organized into eight sections. The first section focuses on some of the romantic notions about rural life and the harsh realities that too often confront residents of small towns and rural communities. It provides some demographic information and discusses a number of perspectives on rural life. The remaining sections of this book address many of the issues confronting small towns and rural communities, including recognizing the importance of families, developing exemplary services and programs, acknowledging and celebrating diversity, enhancing service delivery through technology, preparing social workers for rural practice, and organizing for social change. It is our hope that social work practitioners and students will find in these chapters material that will enable them to understand better and serve better those who are residing in small towns and rural communities.

Iris Carlton-LaNey, Richard L. Edwards, and P. Nelson Reid

REFERENCES

Davenport, J. A., & Davenport, J. (1995). Rural social work overview. In R. L. Edwards (Ed.-in-Chief), *Encyclopedia of social work* (19th ed., Vol. 3, pp. 2076–2085). Washington, DC: NASW Press.

Ginsberg, L. H. (1977). Social work in rural areas. In R. K. Green & S. A. Webster (Eds.), *Social work in rural areas: Preparation and practice*. Knoxville: University of Tennessee School of Social Work.

Green, R. K., & Webster, S. A. (Eds.). (1977). *Social work in rural areas: Preparation and practice*. Knoxville: University of Tennessee School of Social Work.

Morris, L. C. (1995). Rural poverty. In R. L. Edwards (Ed.-in-Chief), *Encyclopedia of social work* (19th ed., Vol. 3, pp. 2068–2075). Washington, DC: NASW Press.

U.S. Bureau of the Census. (1991). Poverty in the United States: 1990. *Current population reports* (Series P–60, No. 175). Washington, DC: U.S. Government Printing Office.

CHAPTER ONE

Small Towns and Rural Communities: From Romantic Notions to Harsh Realities

Iris B. Carlton-LaNey, Richard L. Edwards, and P. Nelson Reid

Hofstadter's observation that "the American mind was raised upon a sentimental attachment to rural living" (1955, p. 41), although made nearly 45 years ago, still rings true. Most of the U.S. population resides in urban areas, and many urban dwellers have idealized and romanticized views of rural life. The small town as a place of constancy in morals and relationships and a place where one's identity can find root and nourishment is a powerful cultural theme. Idealized notions of farms and farm families, from Montana ranches to southern plantations, all have held some sway over the imagination and often have been the subject of media portrayals. Television shows, ranging from "The Beverly Hillbillies" and "Green Acres" to "The Andy Griffith Show" and "The Waltons," and such movies as *Country, Deliverance, The Milagro Beanfield War,* and *The Bridges of Madison County* are examples of portrayals of rural people and rural life, although they are often grossly stereotypical or negative. Bluegrass and country music frequently portray life in small towns and rural communities. Furthermore, musical benefit performances, such as Willie Nelson's "Farm Aid" concerts, have focused attention on rural problems and raised money for the amelioration of problems facing rural areas.

Much of what we see in urban development or, more properly, suburban development clearly has its roots in rural idealization. For example, four-wheel drive vehicles are popular among city dwellers even though they were originally developed to fill the needs of rural users. Marketing approaches for "planned," often gated, communities promote "shared values," "shared public domain," and "common destiny," evoking powerful images and values (Blakely & Snyder, 1997). It is evident, however, that the character of small town and rural life has changed fundamentally as a result of the transformation of the agricultural economy from a labor-intensive, disaggregated one to an economy that employs relatively few and is organized around large corporations. Nevertheless, the sentiments regarding small town and rural life are very much alive.

CHARACTERISTICS OF RURAL COMMUNITIES

Many people are surprised to learn that more Americans live in rural areas now than at any time in our history. More than 62 million people are estimated by the U.S. Census Bureau to live in rural areas. For census purposes a rural area is defined as an unincorporated place of fewer than 2,500 inhabitants. A number of definitions of rural that are more liberal than the Census Bureau's suggest that the proportion of the population in small towns and rural areas is much greater than the Census Bureau's estimate (Davenport & Davenport, 1995). A very small portion of the rural population is engaged primarily in farm labor.

Families continue to be vitally important to life in rural communities. Farley, Griffiths, Skidmore, and Thackeray (1982) characterized rural families as traditional and conservative; family members spend a good deal of time together in work and recreation. They further noted that it is not unusual for rural families to have more than two generations living in the same household. The fact that families in rural areas have more children and elders and fewer young and middle-age adults than their urban counterparts contributes to the increased incidence of multigenerational households (Hofferth & Iceland, 1998). Although these elements are important to family stability, Fitchen (1991) found that the rural American family, like its urban counterpart, is increasingly insecure, particularly among low-income populations.

Rural poverty is a significant problem for families with young children. Just over 22 percent of rural children under age 18 were living in poverty in 1991. Morris (1995) indicated that rural African American married-couple families with young children are at the highest risk of poverty. Rural white families with young children have substantially higher poverty rates than do their urban counterparts, and Hispanic families with young children have high poverty rates regardless of location. Real wages in rural areas have declined over the past 15 years, contributing to the poverty of many rural families. Nearly three-fourths of young rural workers ages 16 to 24 and most women heads of households have wage earnings that are too low to move a family of four out of poverty.

Rural poverty is also a great concern of the elderly. Rural elders are over 50 percent more likely to be poor than are urban elders. The oldest-old, racial and ethnic minorities, women, widows, divorced and separated persons, and those with low educational attainment are likely to have the highest rates of poverty. Elders with multiple risk factors, such as grade school–educated African American women who are widows and among the oldest-old have the highest poverty rates of all (Glasgow & Brown, 1998).

Although some people may think of small town and rural areas as homogeneous, they actually are often characterized by significant heterogeneity. For example, African Americans in rural areas number nearly 4 million, 3.5 million of whom live in the South. In addition, a substantial migrant labor population in the United States has contributed to a new cultural diversity in many areas. Our tendency to romanticize rural and small town communities is accompanied by an inclination to ignore or minimize the racial tensions that are an enduring part of these communities' character (Snipp, 1996). Rural social workers must understand the importance of acknowledging and celebrating diversity in the areas they serve.

Snipp (1996) described three areas in which rural minority groups are concentrated: American Indian reservations, Latino *colonias* (settlements of Hispanic migrant workers throughout the rural West), and African American communities. In recent years tribal sovereignty has brought a modicum of self-sufficiency to American Indians on reserved lands; most Americans Indians who live on reservations, however, remain poor and isolated. Rural African American communities have no designated or specific name, yet they inhabit an easily identifiable section of the landscape in the South. Sometimes referred to as the "Black Belt," the "bottoms," or the "quarters," these communities are home to 90 percent of the African American population living in rural areas. The southern economic boom of the 1970s and 1980s has not rejuvenated these communities.

The three types of communities suffer from a lack of public services and from various health problems. Furthermore, they are subject to the whims of policy makers as public opinion about immigration vacillates. The three areas share several characteristics, including the fact that they all tend to be desperately poor. They typically are isolated from the mainstream society physically as well as because of racism and discrimination. These three distinctive communities are home to large numbers of rural people whom rural progress has ignored and to whom rural problems have gravitated.

PROBLEMS OF RURAL COMMUNITIES

Rural communities experience many of the same social problems as their urban counterparts. Nevertheless, some problems are specific to rural communities. Although the problems themselves may not differ greatly from those in urban centers, they are magnified by the rural communities' inability to target the needed resources in ways that alleviate suffering and ultimately eliminate the problems.

The list of problems with which rural and small town residents must cope includes poverty, lack of transportation, inadequate childcare, unemployment, substandard housing, and insufficient health care. Problems of access and adequacy, for example, remain critical issues that need to be addressed in rural social work practice. Krout (1994) noted that access problems add time and expense to service delivery efforts, ultimately discouraging both the development of new services and the expansion of existing services into rural areas. For example, rural homebound individuals who could benefit from home-delivered meals and thereby maintain independence are denied this service because it is too expensive. The cost of delivering meals to remote areas can significantly limit the amount of money available for the service itself.

Health care is another significant problem. Rural areas, particularly low-income areas, are underserved because of a lack of physicians and other healthcare providers. The South especially suffers from a maldistribution of health care professionals and facilities.

Fundamental to the problems of rural communities is the new growth that rural areas and small towns are experiencing. Although many rural communities continue to lose population, recent population data show a return to the "reverse migration" of the 1970s (Johnston & Beale, 1994). The March 1993 *Current Population Survey* showed that most internal migration involved people shifting from metropolitan to nonmetropolitan areas. Approximately one-quarter of all Americans—about 60 million people—lived in rural areas by 1990, and only about 6 percent lived on farms (McLaughlin & Jensen, 1998).

Bradshaw and Muller (1998) identified five factors that account for this new growth in rural America. Those factors are as follows:

1. Unique geographic resources are not as important to the location of industrial and corporate growth today as they have been in the past. Today the primary criteria for the location of most industries focus on such nongeographical factors as venture capital firms, proximity to universities, good business climates, and an attractive quality of life for executives and employees.
2. The continued decline in the real cost of transportation of manufactured products and the low cost of long-distance information transmission contribute to the decline of distance as a factor in business location.
3. Communities are more interdependent within regions, and the function of the central city is changing. The small town cluster, or "rural-plex," within a particular area is adopting a range of specialized regional roles.
4. Employment does not drive residential choices. People relocate to remote areas with the expectation that employment will follow and commutes will shorten.
5. Policy choices have a major influence on population growth trajectories. Essentially, policy decisions to fund roads, schools, and corporate ventures are also choices to accommodate or promote population growth.

A number of other reasons also account for the growth in rural areas, including return and retirement migration.

CHARACTERISTICS OF RURAL SERVICE DELIVERY

In the *Communist Manifesto,* Marx and Engels referred to the "idiocy of rural life" and described cities as places of rescue from such idiocy. The idiocy they refer to is the economic deprivation common to rural life (common then and now), the oppressive social organization of traditional rural life, and the boredom of it all. Perhaps for this reason it is worth noting that in the United States, public policy and associated services in rural areas have been concerned not so much with preserving the character of rural economy or culture but with extending urban amenities and economic development to rural areas (Reid, 1986). Similarly, other scholars (Davenport & Davenport, 1995; Fulton, Fuguitt, & Gibson, 1997) have indicated that although small towns highly value their autonomy and independence, they are, nonetheless, becoming increasingly dependent on and expressive of the larger economy and culture. It is evident from many of the contributions to this book that the desire to preserve and strengthen does not always coexist harmoniously in small towns and rural communities.

Historically, small towns and rural areas have been disadvantaged with regard to the availability and accessibility both of human services and of competent professionals to provide those services. Indeed, whether the issue is unemployment, poverty, high school completion, major health risks, or housing standards, nonmetropolitan areas tend to stand out in a negative way from urban areas. Increases in federally funded programs and services, along with greater mobility and telecommunications technology, have helped residents of small towns and rural communities have greater access to social services and social programs. Significant numbers of small town and rural areas, however, have nonetheless continued to be faced with persistent disadvantages. One factor in this ongoing problem may be that many rural programs and services are based on programs and policies designed for urban areas. The "scaled-down" versions implemented in rural areas have often not proved effective.

RURAL SOCIAL WORK PRACTICE

Over the past couple of decades, the social work profession has made increased efforts to prepare professionals for effective practice in rural areas. Both the Council on Social Work Education (CSWE) and the National Association of Social Workers (NASW) have published materials that focus on rural social work practice (see, for example, Davenport & Davenport, 1995; Ginsberg, 1977, 1993; Martinez-Brawley, 1990; Morris, 1995). Scholars who publish in this area may disagree over whether rural social work is distinct from urban social work practice, or they may identify the differences as subtle and unimportant. Others speak of a rural–urban continuum as they wrestle with defining exactly what constitutes a rural area and whether the residents are rural people or urbanites seeking some romanticized notion of life away from the city. Nonetheless, their scholarship has given rural social work a place within the ranks of the profession while contributing to the rich, yet limited, literature in this field. Major social work journals, such as *Social Work, Families in Society,* and *Health & Social Work* continue to publish articles that discuss specific social problems in rural areas along with practice strategies unique to those issues.

Farley and colleagues (1982) indicated that within the definition of rural practice are several elements that describe the strengths and limitations of rural communities. They identify three positive definitional elements:

1. *An open communication system.* Within an open communication system, news and information travel fast and people generally are aware of each other's comings and goings. This system has led rural life to be described as a sort of "fish bowl" existence. The skilled social worker recognizes and uses this open communication system as a resource to facilitate the helping process.

2. *Interagency cooperation.* The social agencies, which are usually public, work cooperatively. The recognition of a shortage of services and programs encourages
   practitioners to work together to meet the needs of the clients. These professionals usually know each other and reach out to each other regularly.
3. *A sense of community.* Community concern and compassion are critical elements
   that encourage communities to designate a safe place for all members including
   those who may be considered dysfunctional and isolated in more urban environs.
   The sense of community is a strength upon which the social worker must build.

Identifying and capitalizing on those strengths increase the informal network of service and support for the client.

Social workers who choose to practice in rural areas must be prepared not only
to use a wide range of skills and methods but also to work with a heterogeneous
client population. They must have some knowledge and awareness of the communities' history, customs, rituals, goals, plans, problems, and population heterogeneity. It is essential that social workers understand that diversity, rather than sameness,
characterizes the living circumstances of rural community residents. This understanding will not only focus best-practice strategies but also help social workers work
with increased enthusiasm and commitment.

According to Ginsberg (1977), rural social work practice is a generalist practice.
As generalists, practitioners in rural settings require skills in all the social work methods along with an ability to interact effectively with all social institutions. Essentially,
Ginsberg (1993) concluded that the unique quality of social work in rural areas lies
in the way in which it is *practiced.* Martinez-Brawley (1990) supported Ginsberg and
further noted that rural social work was built on the premise of locality-specific or
locality-relevant services.

According to Davenport and Davenport (1995), clients will evaluate the practitioner on the basis of help delivered and problems solved. The ability to cultivate
horizontal and vertical ties is also critical for effective practice. Horizontal ties consist of contacts and relationship with various local service providers and influential
people, and vertical ties are relationships outside the community on the state and
local organizational level.

Technology continues to enhance the quality of life in rural communities and
small towns. Telemedicine, for example, is a growing and promising way to redress
the imbalance in the availability of health care resources for rural residents.
Described as a wide range of telecommunications systems, including interactive
video and Internet-based communications, telemedicine promises to significantly
improve efficiency, quality, access to services, and equity of health care resource distribution while concurrently lowering health care cost in rural areas (Williams,
Ricketts, & Thompson, 1998). Interactive video and Internet capability likely will
continue to influence the access and quality of services that are available in rural
communities.

Farley and colleagues (1982) identified three limiting definitional elements in
rural social work practice: (1) geographic isolation, (2) personal isolation, and (3)
service isolation. Social workers in rural areas often are isolated from their clients

and from other professionals. Distance is crucial and limits the social worker's ability to meet regularly with clients and with colleagues alike. The social worker often must travel great distances to meet with clients and may find that she or he is one of only a few professionals in the area. Furthermore, few services are available within rural areas, and social workers often find that they must refer clients to agencies that are many miles from the clients' homes. Farley and colleagues (1982) cautioned that anyone who engages in rural social work must be prepared to understand and deal with geographic, personnel, and service isolation.

Rural social work practice can be quite rewarding. Ginsberg (1993) identified some of those rewards as the opportunity to work independently, advance rapidly, see tangible results, receive personal rewards, and receive recognition. In addition, we believe social work practice in small towns and rural communities empowers workers to develop practice that is creative and flexible, builds on history and culture, and constantly adjusts itself in response to clients' desires, feelings, and circumstances.

REFERENCES

Blakely, E., & Snyder, M. (1997). *Fortress America: Gated communities in the U.S.* Washington, DC: Brookings Institution Press.

Bradshaw, T., & Muller, B. (1998). Impacts of rapid urban growth on farmland conversion: Application of new regional land use policy models and geographical information systems. *Rural Sociology, 63,* 1–25.

Davenport, J., & Davenport, J. (1995). Rural social work overview. In R. L. Edwards (Ed.-in-Chief), *Encyclopedia of social work* (19th ed., Vol. 3, pp. 2076–2085). Washington, DC: NASW Press.

Farley, W., Griffiths, K., Skidmore, R., & Thackeray, M. (1982). *Rural social work practice.* New York: Free Press.

Fitchen, J. (1991). *Endangered spaces, enduring places: Change, identity, and survival in rural America.* Boulder, CO: Westview Press.

Fulton, J., Fuguitt, G., & Gibson, R. (1997). Recent changes in metropolitan–nonmetropolitan migration streams. *Rural Sociology, 62,* 363–384.

Ginsberg, L. (1977). Rural social work. In J. Turner (Ed.-in-Chief), *Encyclopedia of social work* (17th ed., Vol. 2, pp. 1228–1234). Washington, DC: National Association of Social Workers.

Ginsberg, L. (1993). *Social work in rural communities.* Alexandria, VA: Council on Social Work Education.

Glasgow, N., & Brown, D. (1998). Older, rural, and poor. In R. Coward & J. Krout (Eds.), *Aging in rural settings* (pp. 187–207). New York: Springer.

Hofferth, S., & Iceland, J. (1998). Social capital in rural and urban communities. *Rural Sociology, 63,* 575–598.

Hofstadter, R. (1955). *The age of reform: From Bryan to FDR.* New York: Knopf.

Johnston, K., & Beale, C. (1994). The recent revival of wide-spread population growth in non-metropolitan areas of the United States. *Rural Sociology, 59,* 655–667.

Krout, J. (1994). Community size differences in senior center resources, programming, and participation. *Research on Aging, 16,* 440–462.

Martinez-Brawley, M. (1990). *Perspectives on the small community: Humanistic views for practitioners.* Washington, DC: National Association of Social Workers.

McLaughlin, D., & Jensen, L. (1998). The rural elderly: A demographic portrait. In R. Coward and J. Krout (Eds.), *Aging in rural settings* (pp.15–43). New York: Springer.

Morris, L. (1995). Rural poverty. In R. L. Edwards (Ed.-in-Chief), *Encyclopedia of social work* (19th ed., Vol. 3, pp. 2068–2075). Washington, DC: NASW Press.

Reid, P. N. (1986). Social policy, social services and the rural way of life. In R. C. Wimberly, D. Jahr, and J. Johnson (Eds.), *New dimension in rural policy: Building upon our heritage* (pp. 353–360). Washington, DC: Joint Economic Committee, U.S. Congress.

Snipp, C. (1996). Understanding race and ethnicity in rural America. *Rural Sociology, 61,* 125–142.

Williams, M., Ricketts, T., & Thompson, B. (1998). Improving health care research for rural elderly people using advanced communications technologies. In W. Gesler, D. Rabiner, & G. DeFriese (Eds.), *Approaches to rural health and aging research: Theory, methods and practical application* (pp. 225–237). Amityville, NY: Baywood.

SECTION II

ISSUES CONFRONTING SMALL TOWNS AND RURAL COMMUNITIES

Small towns and rural communities face many problems that threaten their traditional way of life. These communities, however, also have a tradition of self-help, collaboration, and cooperative existence. When external or internal forces endanger them, the communities rely on those practices that have sustained them over the years. This section discusses specific strengths-based strategies and highlights ways in which communities have responded to crises such as welfare reform, funding cuts, and the growth of a controversial industry.

Ellen Russell Dunbar in chapter 2 focuses on "blended funding" as a promising strategy to help rural communities enhance their opportunities for providing effective social services. Blended funding is a fiscal strategy that involves the county leaders who control the funds. Using Stanislaus County, California, as an example, the author presents a picture of creative and innovative funding strategies. She also highlights a specific project, initiated with blended funds, that provided intensive services for selected families with serious difficulties as well as a framework for communitywide cooperation, communication, and collaboration.

In chapter 3, Craig White and Kathleen Marks discuss the "resourceful communities" approach to community development, which combines aspects of community organizing, economic development, and natural resource conservation to strengthen the cultures, economies, and environments of rural communities. According to the authors, the resourceful communities approach acknowledges the problems that exist in rural areas but focuses on strengths in an effort to promote feelings of hope and empowerment. This chapter presents two case studies to illustrate the process.

Patsy Dills Tracy, Joanne Chezem, and Martin Tracy provide a case illustration of Illinois's welfare reform efforts in chapter 4. The collaborative demonstration project that these authors present—the Federation of Community United Services (FoCUS)—took place in a section of southern Illinois called "Little Egypt." The project was the only rural, multicounty community collaborative in the state experiment and was instrumental in the statewide initiative to re-engineer the human services delivery system. The authors conclude that reform can be effective when there is co-operation among consumers, professional service providers, communities, and states.

In an effort to clarify the problems and issues of hog farming, Judith A. Davenport and Joseph Davenport present in chapter 5 an exploratory investigation of this rapidly growing industry. Their investigation is based on information from sources including personal interviews with farm advocates, environmentalists, social scientists, and politicians. The authors present arguments for and against corporate swine production and focus some attention on the resulting environmental problems. They conclude with a discussion of rural social work's response to the controversy surrounding the growth of this industry and encourage social work educators to devote more time and resources to this topic.

CHAPTER TWO

Strengthening Services in Rural Communities through Blended Funding

Ellen Russell Dunbar

Rural communities frequently suffer from inadequate services to meet health, mental health, and social services needs; their local resources are limited, and outside funding is scarce (Bhaerman, 1994). Rural economies often are limited to one industry and remain impoverished over time (Davenport & Davenport, 1995). Among the difficulties faced by counties responsible for providing services in rural communities are the inappropriate administrative, legal, and regulatory systems that serve as barriers to delivering appropriate services. Rural communities also experience a lack of planned coordination among the services.

Human services are funded through more than 100 federal agencies, numerous state and county agencies, and a variety of private foundations. Each agency is directed from a national or state perspective according to regulations and requirements that have the effect of compartmentalizing human problems. This arrangement can be especially difficult for rural communities for two reasons. First, the communities may actually see the benefits of few funding programs. Second, many of the benefits rural communities do receive are fragmented and unrelated to their needs (Hadley, 1996; Hagebak, 1980).

Regulations promulgated at the national level often become barriers to service integration for families in communities of all sizes, particularly for rural communities remote from the decision-making centers. Although rural communities are small and theoretically easier to coordinate, the reality is that services too often are fragmented and not coordinated because they are funded separately and administered and provided from an office outside the community. Rural communities suffer from a shortage of resources, a lack of service coordination, and restrictions of categorical funding streams.

One promising strategy for helping rural counties with limited resources enhance their opportunities to provide effective social services to rural residents is called "blended funding." This strategy has the goal of achieving an integrated services structure to overcome the barriers of categorical services. Blended funding is a fiscal strategy that involves the county leaders who control the funds; it can help agencies alter service delivery by combining some categorical services that fragment families and by building flexible programs to provide integrated services (Newacheck, Halfon, Brindis, & Hughes, 1998). Perhaps even more important in poor, rural counties, a blended-funding strategy can be a means of increasing the total dollars available to fund services and thereby strengthen the capacity of communities to serve their populations. Urban areas in California are using this approach to develop innovative service integration. Rural counties have even more to gain from blended-funding strategies because they are constrained by small budgets and have few resources for innovation and experimental programs (Center for Rural Pennsylvania, 1992; Chandler, Hu, Meisel, McGowen, & Madison, 1997).

Stanislaus County, in the agricultural San Joaquin Valley of California, has developed some innovative strategies for meeting social service needs. The county, which reaches from the coastal mountains to the foothills of the Sierras in the center of the state, has attracted waves of migrations of people to build farms and ranches, work the fields, or service the agribusiness economy. Numerous small towns and open spaces surround the two cities in the county. Multigenerational communities descended from Scandinavian, German Baptist, Portuguese, African, Mexican, Chinese, Japanese, East Indian, Filipino, and Assyrian ancestors maintain their ethnic identities. The descendents of some of these immigrants are now the owners and operators of the family farms and ranches and dominate the rural culture of the area. Newer immigrant groups include Southeast Asians, new immigrants from Mexico and Central America, and European Americans from other parts of the state. A major source of employment is the agricultural industry; its tedious tasks are associated with growing and harvesting crops and processing them for consumption. Agricultural work is seasonal, and many of the workers have few alternative employable skills. The unemployment rate in the county has been consistently 1 1/2 to 2 1/2 times higher than that of the state for the past 20 years (Entin, 1998).

Stanislaus County has begun to address the social needs of the county through new and innovative programs and services that apply the concepts of service integration, community-based collaboration, reinvestment, and community building. The county has used blended funding as a strategy for creating and maintaining state-of-the-art integrated service programs. The principles and strategies used in Stanislaus County provide a valuable example that might be duplicated in other rural counties. This chapter describes Stanislaus County's experience, based on interviews with administrators of three county agencies and participant observation of the author.

Like many other rural counties, Stanislaus County struggles to serve adequately many small, agriculture-based communities throughout the county. To expand resources and look for opportunities to expand services, the county agencies began to apply for grants. These efforts confronted problems, however. Although federal and state funds provide resources to cover large portions of basic services, the funds are granted with restrictions and regulations that limit the services that can be provided. They frequently require that the local community provide matching funds in order to receive the federal or state dollars. Small counties with limited local resources are not always able to receive the full benefit of the state and federal resources because they cannot provide an adequate local match. Consequently, they forego funds that could be available for vital programs and services; Stanislaus County was in that situation, with the result that the school districts in the county were not providing school-based social services for lack of funds. Categorical funding came with rigid guidelines that became entrenched in agency service delivery systems. Moreover, costs of out-of-home placements for child welfare, probation, and mental health were rising at an alarming rate. The situation called for retrenchment or creative thinking. Outside forces that encouraged the creative alternative included the national movement toward service integration, California's integrative service agency projects, state education funds for school-based services, and a growing move toward community-based collaborative projects and community-building endeavors.

SERVICE INTEGRATION

The national movement advocating integrated collaborative services is one force encouraging change in agency service delivery (Brandon, 1996; Gardner, 1992; Hooper-Briar & Lawson, 1994). Service integration means bringing together a full range of services in order to serve a whole person, family, or community. Services are provided by one social worker who functions as a direct service provider and case manager or by a team available at one location. One service integration model is "wrap-around" services, which focus on the client and family rather than categorical problems, and another is "one-stop shopping," a delivery system that provides a variety of services at one site but is operated and administered by separate agencies. Wrap-around services are typically brokered with the aid of a case manager. By combining the agency involvement, integrated services avoid situations in which the family must respond to "helpers" from several different agencies. California's mental health agencies have moved toward the wrap-around model in their systems of care for children (Chandler et al. 1997; Stroul, 1993).

Categorical funding has been identified as a barrier to service integration because it defines programs based on specific services, not individual needs. In an attempt to overcome this obstacle, the Robert Wood Johnson Foundation set out to determine whether communities would be able to integrate services effectively if the funding sources were blended. The foundation funded nine sites for a child health initiative. One component at each site called for strategies to decategorize and pool existing resources for children's services. In funding the programs, the foundation intended that with its support, the projects would gain approval for blending funds from the federal and state sources of funds; however, the foundation learned that blending funds was difficult to accomplish. Efforts to decategorize health services for children met with success in only one of the projects (Newacheck et al., 1998). Newacheck and colleagues concluded that a need existed for the following:

1. more clarity in the intent to decategorize funding
2. political support at the state and federal level as well as in the counties
3. more than three years to accomplish such arrangements.

Service integration requires large public agencies to change their modes of operation. Such dramatic changes are difficult to accomplish without a strong incentive or initiative. Blended funding used in collaborative programs can be a tool for shaking up bureaucratic rigidity and moving from patterns that follow defined regulations and service parameters toward innovation, creative thinking, and change (Gardner, 1994; Stroul, 1993).

REINVESTMENT

The reinvestment strategy encourages agencies to achieve positive outcomes. The idea of investing counters the view that services are expenditures without benefit. Framed as investments, expenditures that achieve outcomes considered desirable by the community have a pay-off. When effective programs reduce the cost of investments, a cost savings results. The reinvestment strategy applies funds that have been saved to additional preventive services.

Reinvestment and community-building approaches provide a framework for community integration (Briar-Lawson, 1998) and constitute a strategy that can be supported by the majority. The strategy rewards quality service that prevents children and youths from being removed from their families. The reinvestment strategy for meeting community needs and saving community resources is framed in terms that legislators can find acceptable and can thus persuade legislators or administrators to put money into prevention programs that tend to be difficult to sell. They can appreciate the strategy of reinvesting resources if savings can be demonstrated. It is an appealing argument that includes accountability on the part of the social service system and an opportunity to demonstrate success, not only for the service providers but also for the elected officials. Stanislaus County combined the concept of reinvestment with blended funding to gain support for innovation.

COLLABORATION

Successful integration requires continuous communication, cooperation, and collaboration among the service providers and communities; however, the three concepts are progressively more complex and difficult to operationalize in service delivery. Interagency communication and cooperation have long been understood as requirements in effective service delivery systems, but collaboration is a more complex concept and is probably essential to service integration (Gardner, 1994; Hooper-Briar & Lawson, 1994). Collaboration involves mutually developed and accepted goals and strategies as well as shared resources; in collaboration, the work of several entities is combined in such a way that their product or service cannot be identified separately. Community-based collaboration brings neighbors, clients, and service providers into an arrangement that shifts power from agencies to the community. Agency–agency and agency–community collaboration are essential structural components of service integration.

MODELS OF BLENDED FUNDING

A blended fund is a single pot of money that has been developed from several sources for a new purpose. In 1993 California enacted legislation to pilot blended funding in certain counties. That legislation authorized the transfer of funds from 15 categorical services, such as adoption services, drug and alcohol services, and housing, into a county child and family services fund. The state's Youth Pilot Program provided the opportunity for counties to apply to the state for permission to "blend funding streams to facilitate integrated services programs for children and families." This legislation, which established the authority at the state level to approve experiments with blended funding, may have been the origin of the blended-funding concept. The words from that legislation clearly indicate the purpose for experimenting with blended-funding strategies:

> The current service delivery system for children and families, based on a multitude of narrow uncoordinated, separately funded, narrowly targeted categorical programs emphasizes short-term crisis management over prevention and typically fails to address the broader needs of the child and family. . . . Integrated services efforts have identified the myriad of separate funding streams for child and family services to be a serious impediment to the provision of comprehensive child and family services. (California Welfare and Institutions Code, Section 18987, Youth Pilot Program, AB 1741, 1993)

Stanislaus County began planning to blend funds at about the same time as the legislation passed. However, rather than applying for state sanction to blend state funds at that level, the county opted to handle the administration at the county level. Theirs was a smaller undertaking, which was feasible in a county with a cooperative environment. The funds were blended in local programs but accounted for as separate funds.

Each program or project has unique characteristics, but generally the arrangements we are calling "blended funding" can be divided into four categories: blended-funds pool, leveraged funds, blended administration, and blended staffing.

A blended-funds pool is created when money from several agencies or several categorical funds is placed in a new pot of money for a new purpose to create a new integrated service. The program and budget may be managed by a newly established administration outside the existing agency administrative structure or by one of the agencies in the partnership.

In a second category, using local dollars to leverage funds increases the total dollars in the pool. The county funds provide the local match for categorical funds. Some examples of funding streams that have been used are Early and Periodic Screening, Diagnosis, and Treatment, which can pay for mental health assessments for foster children, and Medicaid dollars to help support health and mental health treatment for low-income families.

Blended administration combines several funds designated by different sources for similar purposes to be administered by one agency. This model reduces administrative costs, thus freeing more resources for services. It can be implemented when the atmosphere among agencies is collaborative rather than competitive.

Blended staffing is an approach frequently used in community-based collaboratives and school-based services. Agencies and funding sources place staff into a collaborative setting, but each staff person continues to be accountable to his or her agency as well as to the collaborative.

These models are not mutually exclusive. One program may use more than one approach to combine resources. Stanislaus County, for example, began with a pooled fund to which each of four agencies contributed noncategorized county funds. As the county developed projects, it learned how to document the services provided with categorical funds in combination with other funds in integrated programs. At that point, it moved to more complex blended-funding processes using pooled county funds to leverage more federal dollars. At this stage, the pooled local dollars provided the local match for categorical funds.

Healthy Start school-based services sites, a program of the California Department of Education, were initially funded by a state grant. As the grants ended, each school-based program was faced with finding new resources. In some programs, the school district's funds leveraged child welfare dollars to get social workers into the school setting. The blending of funds then led to blended staffing arrangements, in which various agencies sent staff to the site to provide community-based services.

Another innovation came about as a result of the regular communication and planning among the top administrators, who began to see ways of sharing administrative responsibilities for programs that were related but funded separately by the different county agencies. For example, three county agencies offering contracts for domestic violence programs placed the administration of those contracts under one agency. The administrative costs for both the granting agency and the service delivery agency were reduced by using one proposal review process for all the funds.

CONDITIONS CONDUCIVE TO THE DEVELOPMENT OF BLENDED FUNDING

Stanislaus County administrators identified specific circumstances or conditions that led them to enter into blended-funding and collaborative service programs. The six circumstances described as basic and essential for effective county-level collaborative blended-funding arrangements were as follows:

1. shared visions of service outcomes
2. a scarcity of resources in each separate agency
3. regulations and restrictions attached to categorical funding sources preventing innovation within that delivery system
4. a lack of funds in existing programs for the purpose envisioned
5. cooperative and active relationships among the agencies that allocate program funds
6. external pressures for integrative services, early intervention and successful outcomes.

A shared vision of service outcomes is the stimulating factor that motivates service providers to examine potential strategies for new approaches, and mutual objectives provide the basis for collaborative projects. The shared visions in Stanislaus County all were related to effectively assisting children and families in all of the county's communities. When agencies found they could obtain together what they could not do separately, their incentive to find ways to blend resources increased.

An existing network of relationships in which agency directors and managers talk to one another provides the environment in which the ideas are shared. Even when agencies share a set of desired outcomes, if no existing relationship and continuing communication network is operating, people are not alert to the visions and objectives they share or to their mutual needs.

Scarce resources prevent single agencies from carrying out innovative programs. Communication alone would not spur funding collaboration if individual agencies were not frustrated in their separate efforts to meet their objectives. The obstacles most frequently encountered by people trying to make changes or initiate new programs are related to inadequate resources. Small agencies, especially in rural counties, do not have large sums of money to shift between programs. A lack of resources can prevent agencies from acting alone, but when several county agencies join efforts, the obstacles are more easily overcome. The result is more money and better services.

STRUCTURING A FUNDING ARRANGEMENT

Interorganizational agreements for blended-funding arrangements occur at the executive level. Ideas may be initiated at any program level, but they must eventually reach the top, where initial agreements take place. Stanislaus County created an environment in which the executives are in regular communication. They all are members of a community coordinating council, so in addition to any personal contact they may initiate, they also come together at a monthly meeting for community planning. The top executives, using information provided by their staff or community people, identify mutual needs and objectives. They establish the larger parameters of what they want to accomplish and negotiate how much money will be spent. Administrators determine what they are able to shift from other budget items to the new project. Through this process they come to agreements about how much will be contributed by each agency.

Funds often need to be shifted from other programs, so a proposed program is not likely to happen unless the new collaborative program meets a priority need of each agency. In the initial agreements, the agencies are redirecting funds, not creating new money. For example, the county mental health agency wanted to expand its services to children, and the school-based clinics needed mental health staff. The school-based sites provided the county mental health agency with access to children in need of services. The agencies shifted mental health funds into the school program, blending mental health resources with education resources.

Once the broad outlines of a program are decided, the executives delegate implementation to the program staff. Program managers plan a structure that meets the objectives of the agencies and funding sources involved. Accounting staffs participate in planning at this level. The plans include fiscal and program accountability systems as well as staffing arrangements.

The collaborations not only blend dollars but also combine categorical requirements, regulations, eligibility, and cost accounting. To work effectively, the blended-funding arrangements require good cost accounting by competent accountants who understand and support the purpose. Additional planning is required when local sources are leveraging categorical funds. Blended funding is more work for fiscal management because the accounting procedures require more than routine adherence to county, state, and federal guidelines. The accountants create systems to provide the information needed for each funding source while allowing the services to be integrated, rather than categorical. Most of the funding agencies require unique documentation that services are being provided in accordance with the restrictions of their funding stream. Each county agency may be contributing from their county funds as well as from other funding streams. The sources vary in their flexibility and range from very restricted categorical funds, which have rigid guidelines for use and reporting, to flexible local or grant funds, which can be used for creative, flexible, and individualized integrated services. In-kind contributions of space, furniture, and equipment supplement other resources to establish new community-based operations.

Eventually, the amount an agency contributes to a program will be determined by how effective the program has been in meeting the agency's program objectives. The amount also can be affected by changes in priorities, when an agency system is under pressure to use funds elsewhere.

Once a collaboration is in place, new opportunities for collaboration arise more easily. People are talking with each other regularly at all levels, from the front-line work to top administration. When communication is regular and personal, a penned note or an e-mail message may be sufficient to begin a new collaborative effort.

What Was Accomplished with Blended Funding

Blended-funding arrangements have come about because of common goals and visions of how to accomplish those goals. The administrators of the Stanislaus County agencies involved in the blended-funding collaborations are convinced that they have been able to establish programs that are innovative. The service delivery pattern breaks the mold.

Other outcomes developed that had not been considered initially. For example, the leadership of the larger county agencies are now thinking creatively, or "out of the box," seeking new ways to accomplish their mission. Small, community-based programs believe they now have a stronger foundation with which to sustain their programs, because they are not dependent on only one funding source. When the county agencies worked in partnership with the local community, it built trust with the community. Staff developed rapport with neighbors, who in turn learned about the resources the agencies could provide. The collaboration brought customer- and family-friendly values into service delivery.

PARTNERS FOR FAMILIES AND CHILDREN, A PROJECT FROM BLENDED FUNDING

Partners for Families and Children is a project initiated with blended funds to provide intensive services for selected families with serious difficulties. The story of the use of blended funds to build innovative programs began nearly 10 years ago, when the Stanislaus County agencies who served children formed a county children's council. The council became an important vehicle for collaboration, coordination, and communication among the agencies. The council meetings were not case conferences of direct line workers, although practitioners frequently attended. The group was composed of agency directors, elected county representatives, and community leaders. The county department of mental health provided some staffing, and the health department provided other in-kind support. All the agencies and departments have contributed to one or more of the projects of the council. So, although it was not described as such, the council's beginnings were built on blended-funding arrangements. More important, this council has provided the framework for communitywide cooperation, communication, and collaboration for several initiatives, including the blended-funding initiatives described in this chapter.

The council provided a cooperative framework and networks for building the current community-based collaborative services throughout the county. Most of the services combine fiscal resources from more than one source. They use funds from local sources in one agency to leverage federal or state funds through another agency. Several school-based programs combine staff from different agencies to provide integrated services at one school site.

Partners for Families and Children was operated with a blended funds pool. It began when the directors of the Stanislaus County departments of health, mental health, social services, and probation, along with the county executive officer, initiated a project to address some specific populations of children who were being placed in very expensive foster care and group homes. They proposed that some funds from the budget of each agency be pooled into a new program to offer intensive integrated services to prevent placements. The plan included a reinvestment policy. Money saved by preventing placements would go into a reinvestment pool to pay for future prevention services and would continue to pay for the intensive prevention services. Four county agency directors, working with the county executive officer, presented a convincing proposal to the county board of supervisors. The concept of reinvestment was appealing and logical to the legislators, who approved the allocation and the reinvestment policy.

Each county agency initially contributed about $60,000, for a total pool of $250,000. Realizing that continued interagency collaboration on the project is essential, the agency directors were designated as the policy decision group. An operations team of managers from each of the agencies took on the difficult task of operationalizing and overseeing the program. A project director and multidisciplinary team provided the services.

The agency directors gave middle-management program supervisors the task of developing a program plan. An interdisciplinary team that included mental health clinicians, child welfare social workers, probation officers, and public health nurses provided the program services. The clients were either families with children in a placement out of the home or families for whom a child's placement away from the family was imminent and for whom the problems were related to substance abuse. Three specific populations that were referred to the program were children on probation as a result of their own or their parents' substance abuse, families of drug-addicted babies, and child protective service cases in which substance abuse was a contributing factor. The team served a total of 100 families at one time.

The pooled money was flexible. Some of the funds were used to match federal child welfare dollars, thus increasing the total resources for the program. The integrated staff team could determine which expenditures would help the family become able to care for its children. Direct service dollars could be expended based on treatment or service needs. Some of the services were supported by categorical service funds for mental health and health.

A committee of the children's council received funds to evaluate the project from a foundation that had an initiative to encourage reinvestment policies. Although at this writing it is still too early to report the project outcomes, preliminary reports indicate considerable cost savings from the program.

Partners for Families and Children is an example of a blended pool, developed in the environment and under the conditions described above. Some agency directors shared a vision for better outcomes for children and families. They recognized common needs and understood that each agency lacked the resources to launch a program large enough to demonstrate what needed to be done. The relationships and communication network existing in the children's council ensures continued communication. No specific funding streams would provide the integrated services that were touted as the means to get results. The four agency directors and program staff were inspired by the collaboration and gained hope for success with the children. If the program continues to be effective, the funding may continue to be available through the reinvestment process.

CONCLUSION

Blending funding streams is a process that can help social service, health, criminal justice, and mental health delivery systems in rural communities overcome the complexities that resulted from the increasing numbers of categorical funding sources. Collaboration at all levels of social service, health, mental health, and corrections agencies can actually increase the a total amount of funds available for services in a county. Blended funding is a strategy to demonstrate the value of providing intensive service at the "front end," rather than waiting until the problems are so serious that they require expensive responses; it is a logical companion to the movement for integrated and collaborative services. Stanislaus County's experience has shown some positive results and is viewed as successful by those who initiated the agreements.

Rural counties with limited resources need strategies that will increase the resources available for social services. Even though they are inadequate to meet rural needs, traditional patterns of service delivery, including categorical funding, can be difficult to change. Blended funding, along with collaborative activity, can stimulate needed changes in service delivery models and strengthen the capacities of communities to meet the needs of their residents.

REFERENCES

Bhaerman, R. D. (1994). *Integrating education, health, and social services in rural communities: Service integration through the rural prism.* Philadelphia: Research for Better Schools.

Brandon, R. (1996). The collaborative services movement: Implications for national policymakers. In K. Hooper-Briar & H. A. Lawson (Eds.), *Expanding partnerships for vulnerable children, youth, and families* (pp. 322–346). Alexandria, VA: Council on Social Work Education.

Briar-Lawson, K. (1998). Capacity building for integrated family-centered practice. *Social Work, 43,* 539–550.

California State Assembly. (1993). Assembly Bill 1741 1993–94 Regular Session: Youth Pilot Program, California Welfare and Institutions code, Section 18987.

Center for Rural Pennsylvania. (1992). *Program integration: An alternative for improving county rural human services delivery.* Harrisburg, PA: Pennsylvania General Assembly.

Chandler, D., Hu, T., Meisel, J., McGowen, M., & Madison, K. (1997). Mental health costs, other public costs, and family burden among mental health clients in capitated integrated service agencies. *Journal of Mental Health Administration, 24,* 178–188.

Davenport, J. A., & Davenport, J., III. (1995). Rural social work overview. In R. L. Edwards (Ed.-in-Chief), *Encyclopedia of social work* (19th ed., Vol. 3, pp. 2076–2085). Washington, DC: NASW Press.

Edelman, S. (1998). *Developing blended funding programs for children's mental health care systems.* Sacramento, CA: Cathie Wright Center for Technical Assistance to Children's System of Care.

Entin, K. (1998). *Critical links: Employment growth, unemployment, and welfare-to-work in Stanislaus County* (Report prepared for the Stanislaus County Board of Supervisors). Stanislaus: California State University, Center for Public Policy Studies.

Gardner, S. (1992). Key issues in developing school linked, integrative services. In R. Behman (Ed.), *The future of children: School linked services* (Vol. 2, No. 1, pp. 85–94). San Francisco: David and Lucille Packard Foundation, Center for the Future of Children.

Gardner, S. (1994). *Reform options for the intergovernmental funding system: Decategorization of policy issues.* Washington, DC: The Financing Project.

Hadley, T. R. (1996). Financing changes and their impact on the organization of the public mental health system. *Administration and Policy in Mental Health, 23,* 393–405.

Hagebak, B. R. (1980, April). *Mental health services in rural areas: The case for interagency coordination and service integration.* Paper presented at the Third Annual Georgia Primary Health Care Conference, Atlanta.

Hooper-Briar, K., & Lawson, H. (1994). *Serving children, youth and families through interprofessional collaboration and service integration: A framework for action.* Oxford, OH: Institute for Educational Renewal at Miami University and the Danforth Foundation.

Larson, L. M., Beeson, P. G., & Mohatt, D. (1993). *Taking rural into account: Report on the national public forum co-sponsored by the Center for Mental Health Services.* Washington, DC: U.S. Department of Health and Human Services, Public Health Service, Substance Abuse and Mental Health Services Administration, Center for Mental Health Services.

Newacheck, P. W., Halfon, N., Brindis, C. D., & Hughes, D. C. (1998). Evaluating community efforts to decategorize and integrate financing of children's health services. *Milbank Quarterly, 76,* 157–273.

Stroul, A. B. (1993). *Systems of care for children and adolescents with severe emotional disturbances: What are the results?* Washington, DC: Georgetown University Child Development Center.

CHAPTER THREE

A Strengths-Based Approach to Rural Sustainable Development

Craig White and Kathleen Marks

This chapter describes an approach to rural community development called "resourceful communities," which combines aspects of community organizing, economic development, and natural resource conservation to strengthen the cultures, economies, and environments of rural communities. As a strengths-based approach, the intervention is based on recognizing a community's natural and cultural assets and then using those resources in a way that celebrates and protects them for future generations. Case studies from eastern and western North Carolina suggest that the resourceful communities approach offers rural communities a path toward both human and economic capacity building. This intervention also offers social work professionals some hands-on techniques for pursuing community-based sustainable development.

A STRENGTHS-BASED INTERVENTION

The many problems that increasingly plague rural communities are easy to catalogue. They include lack of access to jobs, health care, education, and transportation; loss of culture and separation of families, as more and more people are forced to move to urban areas for employment; land loss and threats to family farming; rapid, unplanned development, as people move from urban areas into subdivisions and summer homes; and increasing rates of substance abuse, juvenile delinquency, domestic violence, and other social problems. The list goes on; all the problems are compounded by limited resources for addressing them (Coulton & Chow, 1995; Morris, 1995; World Resources Institute, 1995).

Although many social work professionals and programs work to address such issues, focusing on the problems tends to build a sense of hopelessness among both social workers and rural residents. It often seems as though no matter how much is done to address problems, they persist.

The resourceful communities approach, in contrast, seeks to preserve and strengthen rural communities by focusing on existing strengths and resources. Although it does not deny that rural areas face some serious problems, the attention to strengths promotes feelings of hope and empowerment. Both professionals and residents concentrate on their own resilience and their power to make positive changes. The positive focus gives everyone involved more energy and increases the ability to build community involvement, leading to improved success. Success builds even more energy and involvement in a positive, self-reinforcing cycle (Stout, 1996). Moreover, since the work is usually based on celebration of heritage and local economic development, the efforts successfully address the root causes of many rural communities' problems, replacing poverty and despair with economic opportunity, pride, and hope (Kretzmann & McKnight, 1993).

BACKGROUND

The resourceful communities approach was designed by Mikki Sager of the Conservation Fund, a national conservation organization that pursues land and water protection through local community partnerships. In trying to pursue conservation work in rural North Carolina, Sager recognized that protecting natural resources from exploitation could also negatively affect rural economies unless alternative economic development strategies were identified. Accordingly, Sager is pioneering a new model of conservation in which locally directed community development efforts are directly connected to land and water protection. Whereas the approach was initially designed to bridge some of the gaps between environmental organizations and rural communities, it is applicable to a wide range of organizing, planning, and development activities in rural areas.

Resourceful communities–type development efforts take a holistic approach, recognizing that in rural areas the land, the culture, the people, and the economy are all inextricably linked (Estes, 1993). Traditional music, crafts, art, and stories live today because rural residents stayed put and passed on their culture to their children and grandchildren, and most of the nation's natural areas still exist because these generations of local residents have taken good care of the land (World Resources Institute, 1995). These powerful trends are likely to continue as long as rural communities can resist the external social and economic pressures that would appropriate or destroy their cultures and their landscapes. From this perspective, protecting the land and the culture of rural America means helping local residents create economic development opportunities that celebrate and protect, rather than exploit, their natural and cultural heritage (Howe, McMahon, & Propst, 1997; Stokes, Watson, & Mastran, 1997; Stout, 1996).

From our experience, it appears that resourceful communities–type projects are successful for the following reasons:

• Community strengths and assets are emphasized.
• Broad community support is gained.

- Local ingenuity and professional expertise build creative, culturally appropriate solutions.
- Communities gain the tools to sustain their efforts, including fundraising, organizational development, connections with mentors, and networks of support.

RESOURCEFUL COMMUNITIES PROCESS

Although the process occurs differently in every town, the resourceful communities approach has demonstrated some general patterns in participatory rural development.

Getting Started

A catalyzing event—sometimes an opportunity, but often a crisis—leads to conversations about development and the direction of growth in a rural community. Local leaders, official or otherwise, then contact an external development organization or facilitator to get information or advice. If both parties are willing, this initial request for advice can evolve into a broader partnership supporting a participatory development process. At this stage, it is critical for all the partners to agree that although outside organizations may provide information and resources, the process must be "owned" and directed by members of the local community.

That catalyzing event is usually sufficient to get people talking, whether in their kitchens or local diner or on the front porch of the hardware store. With a little guidance, those conversations can develop into community meetings and planning sessions, which constitute the discussion phase of the process. As discussions continue, they should go beyond an analysis of problems or concerns and begin exploring solutions and assessing community strengths and resources.

One of the critical responsibilities of the outside partner at this point is to make sure the process is as participatory as possible. Every small town has its politics, but effective community development depends on giving everyone a voice and engaging every interest. It is critical to involve women and members of every ethnic group represented in the community; it is also important to involve both official and unofficial leaders. If people are not involved as allies at the beginning, they might wind up taking an obstructive or confrontational role later. Building this level of participation can take some time, since it often means overcoming considerable historical barriers. The strengths-based approach can be helpful in overcoming those barriers, because one can rightfully claim that every group and individual has some resources or ideas to bring to the table.

Planning

Eventually, discussions will start to crystallize around some sort of a plan. This plan is likely to be fairly general at first, along the lines of "creating more jobs" or "finding more opportunities for young people." During this phase, the outside partner can be most useful in providing information and referrals, particularly to communities in the region that have successfully handled similar problems or implemented similar plans. Relationships started during the planning and research process often develop into formal partnerships. Also, residents are inspired and encouraged when they see that similar ideas have been successful elsewhere.

As the plan begins to be more concretely defined, people begin to realize how much work will be needed to make change happen, and it is not unusual for some of them to get discouraged. During this stage, it is important to connect the plans with a detailed assessment of community strengths so that people can see not just the challenges but also the resources they have at hand. It also can be useful to help the community set some highly visible, easily achievable short-term goals to encourage people with an initial success.

Implementation

This part of the process is specific to each community's plan. In some cases, it means a large group of citizens taking political action; in others, it means establishing a community development corporation to operate local programs. It can also mean obtaining real estate to build a park or greenway, restoring historic buildings, or working on capital improvement projects to bring more visitors to the community. Regardless of the project, it is important to involve as many partners as will be productive in order to maximize the support network and public visibility of the community's work.

Most communities choose to begin with short-term projects that keep people actively involved in discussions about long-term visions and goals. As the first projects are completed, new ones are developed. Eventually, a community will work on several tasks at once, working toward both short- and long-term goals. Outside partners can help local leaders make decisions about how to work on enough projects to keep everyone busy and involved while not overextending resources by taking on too much at once.

It is also important to keep in mind what implementation means in this context. The tangible plans and projects that the community undertakes make up only half the picture. Equally valuable are the social networks, planning skills, public discussions, and new community leaders that develop because of the process. Although intangible, these are the skills and resources that will continue to shape the healthy growth of the community.

Evaluation

Evaluation of the community's work and growth is not a separate stage in the development process. It needs to be integrated fully into every part of the work. Although it is important to record quantitative effects—the number of new jobs, the income of new small businesses, the increased educational achievements of youths, and so forth—it is equally critical to record and share qualitative information. Although funders, foundations, and government partners will want to see measurable changes, they appreciate the importance of less tangible effects. Also, most people in the community will be moved and motivated by stories, not statistics. A key part of every partner's role is sharing success stories at every opportunity.

Building Capacity

During the entire process, part of the role of an outside partner is to help the community build local residents' capacity to undertake the various elements of development work. It is also critical that the outside partner help establish and strengthen a local network to provide support and technical assistance. Ultimately, the goal is to foster community independence and regional interdependence, not reliance on outside resources. Of course, this process takes years, but it is important to keep the goal of fostering self-reliance in mind, so that the partner is working *with* the community, rather than doing the work *for* it.

Long-Term Goals

The specific goals of resourceful communities interventions, of course, are particular to each community. Most communities share some general goals, however. The most important include the following:

- undertaking an economic development process that preserves and celebrates the local culture, social networks, and environment
- maximizing the community ownership of local planning and decision making
- building local residents' capacity for organizing, planning, and implementing projects
- creating a regional, mutually supporting network of organized communities and community organizations.

CASE STUDY 1

BAKERSVILLE: PARTICIPATORY REVITALIZATION IN THE NORTH CAROLINA MOUNTAINS

For generations my family has worked, played, gone to church, married, raised our children and died around this area. We made every effort to be good stewards of the land. It was not an option or an attitude, it was necessary to survive. In our nation, and all too often, the ability to exploit our resources for short-term gain has outstripped our interest in, or understanding of, the consequences for the future.

But we stand in a position today to address this imbalance, to act rather than react; to not simply plan for the future but to shape and mold it into a legacy we can
give our children without excuse or regret. . . . We welcome the opportunities that
growth offers. . . . But not at the expense of the very things that define this place and
our home.

—Ed William Wilson, III, Bakersville, NC, resident

Background

High in the Appalachian Mountains, Bakersville, North Carolina (population 339),
boasts a rich cultural heritage; families have called the area home for generations.
Located at the base of Roan Mountain, an internationally significant natural area
and the world's largest natural rhododendron garden, Bakersville has been the
home of the North Carolina Rhododendron Festival for more than 50 years, and the
town promotes itself as the "Gateway to Roan Mountain."

As growth increasingly affects North Carolina's mountain region, Bakersville
town leaders have realized the importance of maintaining local control in shaping
the future of their community. Early economic development proposals suggested
capitalizing on Roan Mountain's popularity by building a visitors' center on top of
the mountain, an idea which raised several concerns and led to the question: How
can Bakersville maintain the small town character so important to residents *and* revitalize its local economy?

Implementation

As with most resourceful communities projects, work in Bakersville began with community discussions and a motive to move forward—economic development and the
future of Roan Mountain. The discussions made it clear that building a visitors' center on Roan Mountain would both destroy the rhododendron gardens and encourage visitors to bypass the town, which would effectively eliminate many downtown
small businesses. After several meetings, which focused on the strengths that
Bakersville had to offer, community residents and leaders agreed that if they could
revitalize the downtown, the entire downtown district could serve as a visitors' center. Such a plan would increase, rather than diminish, the business income of
Bakersville while promoting and preserving the natural resources unique to this
area.

Finding Partners

During the initial discussion phase, the Bakersville community had determined its
general goal. The stage was now set to broaden the effort, solidify plans, and involve
more professional partners from outside the area.

One of the first steps was to link Bakersville's efforts with those of similar towns in the region. In 1995 HandMade in America (HIA), a regional nonprofit organization dedicated to promoting the handmade craft industry in western North Carolina, initiated its Four Small Towns Project. The project's goal was to help local leaders in Andrews, Bakersville, Chimney Rock, and Mars Hill revitalize their downtown business districts and create small-business opportunities for local residents through craft and heritage tourism development.

The Four Small Towns Project was designed to use the Main Street Program planning process developed by the National Trust for Historic Preservation and to customize it to meet the needs and the "workings" of small towns. During the first year, a "resource team," composed of downtown revitalization experts from throughout the mountain region, performed a thorough community assessment. Each town chose a similar "sister community" in the mountain region that also was working on downtown revitalization; the sister community served as a mentor and helped establish regional networks. Finally, the towns were required to attend group meetings every six weeks to report on progress, ask questions, share concerns, and swap tales about their projects. So, whereas the communities determined the direction of development, the outside partners provided access to funding, revitalization expertise, and guidance throughout the process.

Participatory Community Assessment

The resource team assessment had two goals: first, to provide an outside perspective on unrecognized resources in the town, and second, to engage the entire community in assessing the value of its culture and history. The resource team visit to Bakersville was organized by a steering committee of local residents, who tailored the agenda to meet the needs and interests of the local government, business owners, and community groups. A project coordinator worked closely with the town to help coordinate the visit and worked with the town afterward on evaluating and implementing the team's recommendations.

The resource team agendas were designed to help team members meet as many people as possible. Team visits were publicized to all members of the community through newsletters distributed with water bills, individualized letters sent to business owners, newspaper articles, and radio announcements. Homemade cinnamon buns and coffee were served in the post offices, where everyone came to get their mail, to encourage them to complete a survey. Churches and fire departments sponsored community suppers to enable resource team members to informally interview community members. To get the opinions of the elders and children of the community, the team also visited the senior center and the schools. Because the meetings and surveys used existing social networks, the assessment process was an integral part of community life, not a departure from it.

Resource team agendas also were designed to provide a historical perspective of the community, including its traditions, economy, and culture. On the first night of each visit, life-long residents, historical society members, self-taught historians, teachers, and others treated resource team members to presentations. These residents provided incomparable insights into the town's history, local characters, economy, and culture. Community leaders and project team members felt that this comprehensive communication and outreach helped generate strong local support for the community assessment process and subsequent recommendations.

Initial Plans and Projects

Reinforcing the resourceful communities strengths-based approach, the resource team visit focused on identifying the assets and resources that Bakersville could sustainably use to promote economic growth and community improvement. Several key assets were identified as potential eco- and heritage-tourism attractions, including Roan Mountain, Cane Creek, Penland School of Crafts, local craftspeople and artisans, and the historic county courthouse.

The resource team's design expert, a landscape architect, saw a great deal of potential in developing a greenway along Cane Creek, which runs through the heart of downtown. This greenway would protect the creek area and capitalize on the fact that both visitors and residents like to walk through the community. The promotions expert pointed out that very few places exist in which one can fish for trout in the middle of a downtown business district and suggested that the greenway also could showcase the fishing opportunities.

Once the initial project was chosen, local leaders identified other partners who could help with implementation. The Southern Appalachian Highlands Conservancy secured a grant to develop a walking trail along the creek. A landscape master plan was completed for the entire downtown and Creek Walk areas, and trees and rhododendrons were planted at the entrance to town. Artists from the nearby Penland School worked to create an entryway, fishing benches, and paving stones for the trail, and residents built a footbridge, gazebo, picnic area, and exercise stations.

Results

Working with local residents, outside advisors helped the community plan short-term, successful projects and identify long-term goals. The effort resulted in concrete accomplishments and boosted motivation, confidence, and pride in the community.

The Bakersville project team has recently documented the economic impact of the downtown revitalization efforts over the past 18 months. There have been three building facade restorations, two building renovations, nine new jobs, four new businesses, and a total investment of more than $446,000 in Bakersville as a result of the downtown project. Also, because of the recommendations made during the resource team visit, a heightened interest exists in environmental and land-use issues. Revitalization work in Bakersville continues, including plans for adaptive reuse of the historic 1907 courthouse and expansion of the Creek Walk. Local capacity building continues as well; volunteers in the revitalization project are being trained to serve as a team for long-term town management.

Resilience

In January 1998, Cane Creek flooded, and the crest reached almost two feet higher than any previously recorded levels, wiping out homes, roads, and most of the walking trail. Local volunteers poured out to help with clean-up and rebuilding efforts—and so did volunteers from across the region, as partners in the Small Towns Program contributed equipment, materials, and hundreds of hours of labor to the effort. The local and regional networks that were created to support new initiatives also served as a safety net in a time of crisis. Currently, town leaders and residents are working to turn the challenge into an opportunity: When a mobile home park in the middle of town was condemned because of the flood, Bakersville leaders determined to restore the site and include it in the Cane Creek Greenway plan as a new community park.

Process

Although revitalization efforts in Bakersville were unique, the project followed the resourceful communities strengths-based approach to ensure sustainable development.

- *Catalyzing event and discussions:* Town leaders and residents determined that boosting the economy by destroying Roan Mountain was too high a price. They set a general goal of revitalizing their downtown as a visitors' center to the area, capitalizing on and preserving their significant natural and cultural resources.
- *Making partnerships:* By participating in HIA's Small Towns Project, Bakersville drew on professional resources—such as funders and planners—that were otherwise difficult to obtain. The outside consultants helped them coordinate and develop external partnerships while maintaining local control of the process.
- *Community investment:* By reaching out to the entire community, the resource team built a solid base of support and understanding for revitalization efforts. Community strengths and resources were emphasized, and a spirit of cooperation was fostered.
- *Building on success:* The long-term goal—building Bakersville's economy—was paired with attainable, short-term projects, like the community assessment and the construction of the Creek Walk. Initial successes laid a positive foundation for future efforts.
- *Skills and networks:* Although outside partners assisted Bakersville with funding, organization, and implementation, residents controlled the process, so the local skills base has grown along with their ability to carry on projects effectively. In ad-

dition, regional partnerships continue, ensuring leadership development, support in times of crisis, and a strong foundation for regional planning.
- *Economic development and resource protection:* Many Appalachian towns have seen their landscapes destroyed through economic development based on logging, mining, or other forms of resource extraction. Bakersville chose a different path, rooting its successful revitalization efforts in the preservation and promotion of its cultural and natural assets.

CASE STUDY 2

TYRRELL COUNTY: LINKING THE ECONOMY TO THE ENVIRONMENT IN NORTH CAROLINA'S COASTAL PLAIN

Young people here want to work, but there aren't any jobs. You just got to give us the chance. Working with the corps lets us show people who we are and what we can do.
—Jerry Campbell, member of the Tyrrell County Youth Conservation Corps

Background

Tyrrell County, located on the coastal peninsula between the Albemarle and Pamlico Sounds, has long been one of the poorest communities in North Carolina. Both the unemployment and poverty rates tend to remain around 20 percent, and many of the residents who do have work are seasonally employed in agriculture or in service jobs at the beach, an hour's drive to the east (Howe, McMahon, & Propst, 1997).

The region is rich in natural areas and resources, however; it has almost half a million acres of land in state, federal, or private conservation ownership, including a state park and six national wildlife refuges. When the 114,000 acre Pocosin Lakes National Wildlife Refuge was created in 1990, local residents made it clear that simply adding more refuge land did not help meet their economic needs. This event sparked discussions about how natural areas might provide economic development opportunities in the region without being damaged or destroyed. In time, local leaders chose to pursue ecotourism and environmental education so that the peninsula could teach residents and visitors alike that conservation and economic development go hand-in-hand (Howe et al., 1997; Stokes, Watson, & Mastran, 1997).

Implementation

To pursue those goals, local residents established two nonprofit organizations. The Partnership for the Sounds, a five-county coalition of business, conservation, political, and community leaders, focuses on environmental education, ecotourism development, and capital improvement projects. Those projects include the restoration of historic Mattamuskeet Lodge and construction of the Estuarium, an environmental education center dedicated to North Carolina's estuaries. The partnership also operates a rest stop and visitors' center, where tourists on their way to the beach can stop and learn about local attractions, including the Scuppernong River Greenway, a 27-mile web of canoe trails, bicycle routes, and walking paths. The partnership also operates an outdoor environmental classroom and several traveling programs that educate both residents and visitors about the area's natural resources.

Even the most appealing ecological attractions, however, will not benefit the economy unless the local infrastructure can provide visitors with restaurants, hotels, shops, and ecotourism-related services, such as bicycle, canoe, and kayak rentals. The Tyrrell County Community Development Corporation (CDC) concentrates on job training and small-business development, so that local residents can reap the benefits of having an increased number of visitors in the area. One of the CDC's programs, a business incubator, helps small-business owners develop organizational and marketing plans, handle finances, learn computer and Internet skills, and create or expand their businesses.

How Community Programs Evolve: The Tyrrell County Youth Conservation Corps

The CDC also operates the Tyrrell County Youth Conservation Corps, a program that provides a good example of how resourceful communities projects develop—with broad-based community input, practical skills building, and gradual growth. Early in the discussion process, Columbia, North Carolina, residents expressed a high level of concern about the lack of training and employment opportunities for young adults. When the picture was shifted slightly to look at the situation from a strengths perspective, it became clear that between community service projects in the area and conservation projects at the surrounding parks and wildlife refuges, there was more than enough work for the young adults to do. The planning process, then, concentrated on how to provide the funding and the program structure needed to realize the potential of those employment and educational opportunities (Stokes et al.,1997).

The result was the Tyrrell County Youth Conservation Corps, a program that teaches job skills to young adults while they accomplish conservation and community-service projects. The TCYCC was initially created as a summer program for 12 local youths. On the first day, more than 50 applicants showed up ready to work, so supervisors quickly designed a plan to employ 24 of them on a part-time basis. Over the next year, the TCYCC was developed into a full-time, year-round program employing 18- to 25-year-olds from Tyrrell, Hyde, and Washington Counties.

One of the corps's first projects was the construction of a half-mile educational wetlands boardwalk next to the partnership's visitor center. To protect the swamp's sensitive ecosystem, the corps built the entire boardwalk by hand using specially designed tools. The boardwalk is popular with residents, who use it for fishing, walking, and jogging, and it is currently the most heavily used visitor attraction in the county. Such a project demonstrates that an investment in work and education for young adults can result in the creation of a tangible, valuable community resource. In addition, this success built the confidence of the corps members and helped them progress to more complex projects. Currently, the Youth Conservation Corps employs 20 young adults year-round, providing them with training and education as they undertake conservation and community-service projects across the region.

Next Step

Although the Youth Conservation Corps provided a strong foundation for employment, graduates found that they still did not have the training and expertise they needed to qualify for the more technical jobs at the parks and wildlife refuges. In 1997, the CDC decided to develop an internship program that would provide more technical training for corps graduates. The program itself was designed through a participatory process that was facilitated by a social work intern from the University of North Carolina. This facilitator worked with the Youth Conservation Corps for three months, helping corps members design the program. The facilitator also interviewed the managers of parks and wildlife refuges, letting them design a flexible internship program that would fit with their agency structures.

In the fall of 1997, the ideas of the corps members and the conservation professionals were integrated to create the Sustainable Careers Internship Program (SCIP). Currently, SCIP provides youth corps graduates with a one-year paid conservation internship at a state or federal natural resource management agency. This intensive training and employment program helps local young adults qualify for positions at these agencies or enter into higher education programs in conservation-related fields. Such connections between conservation and quality employment also strengthen the community's commitment to environmental preservation.

To build financial support for the internship program, youth corps graduates traveled to Washington, DC, where they gave slide-show presentations for officials at national conservation organizations, foundations, and the Environmental Protection Agency. The trip proved the capacity-building success of the CDC's work, because the young adults, who had been shy about speaking before a group of their peers just a year before, were now giving professional presentations to federal officials. The response was overwhelming, partly because the folks in Washington found it so refreshing to meet with successful, motivated young people and effective grassroots leaders.

Tyrrell County: Looking Ahead

Between the ecotourism development work of the Partnership for the Sounds and the business-development and job-skills training work of the Tyrrell County CDC, the regional economy is growing stronger and has increasing employment opportunities, outside investment, and locally owned small businesses. Even more important, because the CDC's programs reach all members of the community, that economic growth has benefited families at a range of income levels. Of course, poverty is still a problem in the region, and it will continue to be in the years to come. Even so, residents have learned that working together results in real progress; they can envision and create successful programs, and those successes give them the skills to tackle even bigger projects. Tyrrell County provides a model for rural areas and shows that environmental conservation, far from blocking economic development, can be a path toward creating jobs and business opportunities even in the most isolated areas.

Process

The work of the CDC and its youth programs, although only a part of Tyrrell County's regional efforts, demonstrates some of the specific steps of program implementation under the resourceful communities sustainable development process:

- *Catalyzing event and discussions:* Although the need for opportunities for youth had been clear to residents for some time, a strengths-based analysis helped them recognize the opportunity for work at parks and refuges, and public discussions generated the community investment needed to create the youth corps.
- *Making partnerships:* With the youth corps and the internship program, young adults accomplish conservation projects for the parks and refuges while the parks and refuges provide employment and training opportunities for young adults. In this case, the needs of each group provide an opportunity for the other.
- *Community investment:* As increasing numbers of young adults and business leaders are involved in conservation work, the community becomes more educated about how conservation and economic development are connected.
- *Building on success:* The part-time summer youth corps program initially created by the CDC grew along with the organization's capacity to manage programs. Now, five years after its creation, the corps is the foundation for an internship program and a model for similar programs across the state.
- *Skills and networks:* The teamwork that the youth corps developed for conservation projects translated easily into participatory program development. With increased skills and confidence, corps members were able to establish successful partnerships with local conservation agencies and national funding organizations.
- *Economic development and resource protection:* By developing ecotourism and environmental education, Tyrrell County is attracting visitors who are interested in exploring, rather than exploiting, the region's natural resources. At the same time, the work of the CDC demonstrates that conservation efforts can lead to new sources of employment and small-business development.

RESOURCEFUL COMMUNITIES: LESSONS FOR SOCIAL WORKERS

Traditional development models imply that it is difficult, if not impossible, to pursue economic development while preserving a community's cultural and natural resources (McKay, 1990). As the resourceful communities process demonstrates, however, full community involvement results in creative, sustainable solutions that have strong local support and leadership commitment to implementation. Successes in Bakersville, Tyrrell County, and other communities offer several lessons for social work practitioners pursuing sustainable development goals in rural areas.

- *Recognize rural residents' knowledge and values as exceptional resources.* Families who have lived in rural communities for generations have an understanding and appreciation of the local culture and natural systems; such insights should be recognized as valuable assets. This sense of stewardship has protected the natural and historical resources over the years, and economic need (or greed, frequently from outside sources) often is the primary factor in actions leading to cultural and environmental degradation. People live in isolated areas because they like being there and have ties to the land—their home—that are hard to replicate.
- *Understand that natural, cultural, and historic resources are inextricably linked.* In many rural areas, some of the same families have been living there for hundreds of years, so historic and cultural ties to the land are important. Meanwhile, many newcomers have moved to rural communities partly because of their natural areas, their history, and their culture. For most rural residents, local natural and cultural resources are important, and they will get involved in community-based efforts to protect these resources.
- *Find out about the local culture.* Every community has its own special characteristics that distinguish it from other communities. This "community character" is an asset and should be respected. Listening to local stories, spending time in local hangouts, and visiting important community sites can give you some appreciation for local culture.
- *Spend time with local residents, listen to their concerns, and "put yourself in their shoes."* When social workers enter a community, they tend to identify family, individual, or issue-specific problems and begin to intervene at that level. Conservationists frequently focus on natural resource issues and overlook the underlying causes of environmental degradation, which more often than not include poverty and the need for jobs. Likewise, economic developers often focus only on job development, overlooking the community's heritage and ties to the land. For local residents, social, economic, cultural, and environmental concerns all are connected, and only they will know where to start and how to make things happen. The ethic of self-determination applies to communities as well as individuals, and it is vitally important to spend time with local residents and listen to their needs, insights and concerns.
- *Help identify economic alternatives that are compatible with natural and heritage resource protection.* The key to protecting rural resources so valued by local residents is to develop new economies with jobs that are tied to protecting or restoring the community's heritage, social networks, and natural resource base. This has been the case in Tyrrell County, where fewer people are working in logging and more and more work in natural resource protection and environmental education. The new economies will build a local constituency that supports conservation and creates

the jobs they need without destroying the very resources that make that area unique.

- *Help secure funding to implement culturally appropriate and environmentally friendly actions and programs.* The surest method to encourage sustainable development is to provide technical and financial assistance for implementation. Often, outside professionals who are paid for their time expect lower-income local residents to volunteer all theirs. Helping to leverage funds to support community organizations can enable local people to get paid for their work and build the local economy. Also, whereas professional training and contacts may enable you to write grant proposals and secure government funding more easily, remember that it is equally important to pass those skills and connections on to the staff and volunteers of community organizations.

- *Work both locally and regionally.* Given the political and economic realities of community development work, one rural town working in isolation is unlikely to leverage the long-term funding resources and public awareness needed to create real change. A network of communities with shared interests provides increased political power and access to resources as well as a system of mutual support that can help each community through troubled times.

- *Help communities learn from each other.* Although Bakersville and Tyrrell County have different landscapes and different cultures and are located almost 400 miles apart, they each benefit from the experiences and successes of the other. Residents in Tyrrell County are turning a historic theater into a craft museum and, following Bakersville's example, are considering ways to make traditional craft production part of the local economy. Bakersville leaders, trying to create more opportunities for young adults, are working to develop a program similar to the Tyrrell County Youth Conservation Corps.

- *Above all, be patient.* Change does not come easily or quickly. The social and economic problems of rural areas took many years to get to this point and will take time to turn around. The positive community relationships and long-term benefits, however, will be worth the investment of time and energy.

REFERENCES

Coulton, C., & Chow, J. (1995). Poverty. In R. L. Edwards (Ed.-in-Chief), *Encyclopedia of social work* (19th ed., Vol. 3, pp. 1867–1878). Washington, DC: NASW Press.

Estes, R. (1993). Toward sustainable development: From theory to praxis. *Social Development Issues 15*(3), 1–29.

Howe, J., McMahon, E., & Propst, L. (1997). Case study: Tyrrell County, North Carolina. In J. Howe, E. McMahon, & L. Propst (Eds.), *Balancing nature and commerce in gateway communities* (pp. 40–43). Washington, DC: Island Press.

Kretzmann, J., & McKnight, J. (1993). *Building communities from the inside out: A path toward finding and mobilizing a community's assets.* Chicago: Acta Publications.

McKay, J. (1990). The development model. *Development: The Journal of the Society for International Development, 3*(4), 55–59.

Morris, L. (1995). Rural poverty. In R. L. Edwards (Ed.-in-Chief), *Encyclopedia of social work* (19th ed., Vol. 3, pp. 2068–2075). Washington, DC: NASW Press.

Stokes, S., Watson, A., & Mastran, S. (1997). Tyrrell County, North Carolina: A community takes advantage of the unexpected. In *Saving America's countryside: A guide to rural conservation* (2nd ed., pp. 80–86). Washington, DC: National Trust for Historic Preservation.

Stout, L. (1996). *Bridging the class divide and other lessons for grassroots organizing.* Boston: Beacon Press.

World Resources Institute. (1995). Women and sustainable development. In *World resources 1994–95: People and the environment* (pp. 43–60). New York: Oxford University Press.

CHAPTER FOUR

Restructuring the Delivery of Rural Human Services: The Southern Illinois Experience

Patsy Dills Tracy, Joanne Chezem, and Martin B. Tracy

One of the uncertain consequences of "welfare reform" under the Personal Responsibility and Work Opportunity Reconciliation Act (PRWOR) of 1996 is its impact on preserving and strengthening the capacity of rural communities to facilitate human services. Much of the structure of welfare reform at the state level is based on trends and patterns in urban areas, where data are more readily available and the problems are more visible. Information obtained from urban areas, however, is not always representative of rural society, and program development may not reflect careful consideration of rural conditions. This was not the case in the state of Illinois, which made special efforts to include the rural experience in its welfare reform initiative; selected aspects of the state's experience are examined in this chapter.

On July 1, 1997, Illinois collapsed most public agencies involved in human services into a single "super agency" under the Illinois Department of Human Services (IDHS). The consolidation is a result of the state's response to welfare reform, which is intended to increase family self-sufficiency by facilitating employment through an integrated system of supportive social services. Welfare reform was well underway in Illinois before the passage of the PRWOR. Although the reform initiative in Illinois incorporates many of the aspects of PRWOR, it goes far beyond simply reducing the number of recipients of Temporary Assistance to Needy Families (TANF) and related public assistance benefits. The reform in Illinois is more concerned with a comprehensive re-engineering of social services through a restructuring of the balance between public–private, state government–local government, and community–family responsibility for social welfare. In this regard it reflects a systemic response to the devolution of social welfare policies and programs, which is occurring through legislation aimed at minimizing government and maximizing community involvement. This trend has become a major feature of social policy in the United States (Cope, 1997) and, in fact, throughout the industrialized world (Chassard, 1997; Michalski, Miller, & Stevens, 1997).

The re-engineering of agency delivery of human services has been five years in the making in Illinois. It began in earnest in 1993, when Governor Edgar appointed a state task force on human service reform, which was funded by a $2.5-million grant from the Annie E. Casey Foundation. The task force was made up of public and private statewide representatives, along with personnel from the Casey Foundation. It recommended the development of two entities: (1) a state-level collaborative and (2) local community federations. These were charged with working to replace centralized decision making with a more flexible, neighborhood- and community-based process to aid in the re-engineering process. The community federations were designed to serve as learning laboratories, thereby providing valuable insight on program development and implementation at the local level (Governor's Task Force on Human Services Reform, 1998).

The impact of the welfare reform initiative on beneficiary rolls was felt throughout the period of program development that culminated in the establishment of the IDHS in July 1997. In fact, between October 1993 and December 1997, the welfare caseload of people available to work declined by 24 percent. Over the same time, the number of welfare clients who were working increased 186 percent, from 14,000 to more than 40,000. In the past four years, more than 130,000 clients worked their way off of welfare in Illinois, dropping the caseload to 155,000 recipients, its lowest level in 25 years. With 38 percent of its welfare clients now involved in work activities, Illinois has already exceeded the 1999 federal work requirement of 35 percent (Illinois Department of Human Services, 1998).

While progress was being made in helping individuals on welfare find employment, the task force was experimenting with a major overhaul of human services through five local demonstration "community collaboratives." The five demonstration projects included community groups in DuPage County, Grand Boulevard (Chicago), Springfield, Waukegan, and the Southern Seven counties. The demonstration projects were designed to provide best-practice information for the task force to use in formulating a statewide delivery system that would build human service programs that were more reliant on local capacity, resources, and involvement in partnership with the public sector.

This chapter provides a brief overview of the evolution and contributions of the community collaborative project located in the seven southernmost counties of Illinois, which are part of an area known as "Little Egypt." The demonstration project is of particular interest to those involved in providing rural human services because it was the only rural, multicounty community collaborative in the state experiment.

SOUTHERN SEVEN COUNTIES (LITTLE EGYPT)

The seven rural counties in the southernmost area of Illinois are Alexander, Hardin, Johnson, Massac, Pope, Pulaski, and Union. Located between the Ohio and Mississippi rivers, the counties cover a geographic area of approximately 2,000 square miles and have a combined population of 71,429, or about 36 persons per square mile. All the households in Hardin, Johnson, Pope, and Pulaski are considered to be in rural areas, as are at least 50 percent of the households in the remaining three counties. Poverty rates in 1995 ranged from a low of 14.2 percent in Massac County, to a high of 28.7 percent in Alexander County (Table 4-1). Unemployment rates ranged from 5.1 percent in Massac County to 13.4 percent in Johnson County.

The seven counties, along with surrounding counties in the Little Egypt area, are culturally, economically, and geographically linked to the Lower Mississippi River Delta region. Thus, they face social and economic challenges that are more characteristic of this region than of the rest of the state. At the same time, the counties benefit from being in a state that is resource rich and that has shown a clear commitment to an effective and efficient welfare delivery system through a well-designed demonstration project. Like other areas in the Lower Mississippi River Delta, it is a rural, economically depressed region that does not have the resources to support the many welfare-to-work success stories that are found in less economically stressed regions of the United States (Cope, 1997). These advantages are not necessarily the case throughout the 219 counties in the seven states (Arkansas, Illinois, Kentucky, Louisiana, Mississippi, Missouri, and Tennessee) that make up the Lower Mississippi River Delta region.

The percentage of children on AFDC in the southern seven counties before TANF became operational ranged from a low of 7.8 percent in Johnson County to a high of 32.4 percent in Alexander County (Table 4-2). The combined average for the seven counties was 15.9 percent, compared with a statewide average of 10.9 percent. In all seven counties, a significant proportion (ranging from 35.7 to 45.8 percent) of the children on AFDC were under age six. In contrast, the statewide average was 44.5 percent.

Table 4-1

Unemployment and Poverty Rates (percent) in the Seven Southernmost Counties in Illinois

County	Unemployment Rate, 1996		Poverty Rate, 1995	
	%	n	%	n
Alexander	9.4	377	28.7	2,896
Johnson	9.7	429	14.7	1,523
Hardin	13.4	255	19.7	964
Massac	5.1	391	14.2	2,160
Pope	9.2	147	16.6	746
Pulaski	9.8	291	24.9	1,838
Union	9.5	768	15.9	2,795

Sources: U.S.Census Bureau Web site (www.census.gov), February 17, 1999; Voices for Illinois Children, 1997.

Table 4-2

Percentage of Children on AFDC in the Southern Seven Counties of Illinois, June 1997

County	Percentage of All Children Enrolled in AFDC		Percentage of Children under Age 6 Enrolled in AFDC	
	%	n	%	n
Alexander	32.4	1,012	45.9	465
Hardin	11.5	147	36.1	53
Johnson	7.8	197	42.6	84
Massac	10.5	397	45.8	182
Pope	9.5	112	35.7	40
Pulaski	27.5	622	36.2	225
Union	11.9	532	44.7	238
Seven County average	15.9	431	41.0	177
State average	10.9	4,002	44.5	1,781

Source: Voices of Illinois Children, 1997.

FEDERATION OF COMMUNITY UNITED SERVICES

Under the authorization of the Governor's Task Force on Human Services Reform, a broad base of community representatives from the seven counties formed a non-profit community collaborative called the Federation of Community United Services (FoCUS). This organization committed itself to promoting the belief that empowerment of the communities is the best approach to successful community-based welfare. The intent was to improve the lives of disadvantaged children and families by creating and sustaining an environment that supported families transitioning from welfare to work as well as by facilitating the development of a viable partnership between the community and the state. The 20 to 25 members of the FoCUS board of directors was composed of farmers, bankers, educators, faith-community leaders, consumers, providers, government officials, and private business owners. In addition, a provider advisory council (PAC), composed of more than 90 social service agencies in the area, assists the FoCUS Board in identifying and addressing policy and service issues.

Processes and Outcomes

The evolution of FoCUS into a credible entity was a long process that was made possible by a combination of state government support and leadership through the Governor's Task Force for Human Services Reform, administrative leadership within FoCUS, the commitment of individuals in the seven-county community, and the assistance of human service professionals. Even with a general acceptance among all participants that reform was necessary, it has taken considerable planning, organizing, and orienting to develop a shared definition and vision of reform. That shared vision was accomplished largely through a systematic approach to communication among interested participants, between the participants and state officials, and between non–human service participants and professional human service providers. In keeping with the basic elements of discourse in building community, as promoted by the American pragmatist philosopher John Dewey, every attempt at communication in this process was intended to replace power-as-domination with power-as-problem solving; the community assumed the responsibility for solving its problems (Parsons, 1997). Although the level of agreement and communicative process that has occurred is sufficient to sustain the group through its phase as a demonstration project, a continuing challenge to maintain a shared understanding of the purpose, goals, and methods of FoCUS exists, given the wide spectrum of perceptions, attitudes, and preconceived beliefs. The most serious challenge currently facing FoCUS is to sustain itself as a viable independent organization without state financial assistance or official state affiliation.

FoCUS Goals

Following a long period of formal and informal efforts at building interpersonal relationships and information sharing, dialogue, and discussion, the FoCUS Board established the following five specific goals:

- promote self-sufficiency of the family unit
- influence system changes through negotiating revisions in human service policies, procedures, and practices
- identify and address the needs of the residents in the geographic area
- facilitate collaboration between the resources of family and community
- facilitate an efficient and effective use of resources.

From the outset, it was clear that FoCUS was not to be a new service agency. There was no intent to provide services that would compete with either existing or new social services available in the seven counties. Rather, the aim was to facilitate community involvement in identifying and using local resources as well as to develop innovative strategies to foster effective and efficient human services approaches toward economic self-sufficiency. The following sections describe a variety of interrelated mechanisms that were initiated to help achieve the goals noted above.

Negotiation Process

Perhaps one of the most essential components of the community–state partnership was the development of the negotiation process between the state and the community collaboratives. This process followed the basic tenets of organizational and group empowerment:

- Decision-making is participatory in nature and based on a team concept.
- The partners share a sense of responsibility for the mission and a belief in mutual values.
- Those involved have a high level of trust in each other.
- Human resources are valued, and time and funds are committed to education, training, benefits, and recognition.
- Authority is spread laterally, in contrast to decision-making that takes place along a more traditional, vertical line of authority.
- The group takes an innovative approach to problem-solving and thus has an improved ability to anticipate and respond to environmental influences and changes (Vogt & Murrell, 1990).

In this environment, joint state and local community negotiations were conducted for the development of FoCUS projects. The state provided staff who had the authority to make decisions as they met with community leaders. The state and the community sat at the table together, sharing information and making decisions as a team. Moreover, the empowerment of the communities through this process contributed to expanded resources at the local level (Sherman, 1997).

Identification of Barriers

The FoCUS board determined that its first task was to identify the obstacles to the delivery of human services in its rural communities; it did so through feedback from human service consumers and providers. A series of community focus group meetings revealed that the major barriers to economic self-sufficiency were reliable transportation to work sites, employment opportunities, distance to work sites, education and training locations, and lack of child care facilities. One barrier to transportation that was identified early in the process was the state regulation that counted ownership of an automobile as an asset toward income eligibility for TANF benefits. FoCUS successfully negotiated with the state to change this policy to allow vehicle ownership; this change resulted in increased opportunities for welfare recipients to move into the work force throughout the state. In addition to transportation, a number of interrelated service issues were also identified, including substance abuse, absence of preventive health care, contentious attitudes of public aid workers,[1] excessive applications for benefits, and low-paying jobs.

Among all the barriers, however, transportation clearly emerged as the single most critical impediment to self-sufficiency and human service delivery in rural areas. In response to this need, FoCUS has worked with the state to secure three federal transportation grants in southern Illinois. One grant, from the National

---

[1] The title of Public Aid Worker was discontinued on July 1, 1998.

Governor's Association, provides funds for a demonstration project that integrates human services and public transportation.

A second grant is from the Community Transportation Association of America (CTAA), which is funded by the U.S. Department of Agriculture. The grant application was submitted by the Shawnee Development Council, Inc., and FoCUS and Rides Mass Transit District (RIDES) were included as participants. The purpose of the grant is to facilitate the development of a regional, coordinated public and human service agency transportation service system in an 11-county area. The area was expanded from the seven FoCUS counties to include four other rural counties in southern Illinois served by RIDES (Gallatin, Hamilton, Scott, and White). The grant provides on-site technical assistance to initiate coordinated transit services in unserved and underserved portions of the area.

Specific tasks in the grant include

- assessing existing operators' transportation resources and capabilities
- determining existing and latent demand for transportation
- assessing operations of existing transportation providers
- developing and recommending operational alternatives for the development of regional coordinated services as well as identifying revenue sources
- identifying opportunities for job creation as a result of implementation.

The CTAA is hoping to use experiences from these grants to develop a regional rural transportation system which can be used as a model for similar rural sites in the United States.

The third grant was a state initiative that sought to establish new routes for TANF and Department of Rehabilitation consumers seeking employment, education, or training. The grant allowed transportation resources to be pooled for the disabled and for those on welfare without disabilities. Before the grant, Department of Rehabilitation–funded transportation to employment for welfare recipients was limited to daytime hours or by special contracts with employers. It had been documented that evening and weekend transportation services were not available, hours that often are the time frame for entry-level positions in rural communities. Thus, most of the newly established routes under the grant occurred during evening and weekend shifts to help address this problem.

Family Self-Sufficiency Program

Building on the need for transportation, FoCUS developed a model demonstration program using temporarily reassigned personnel from state human service agencies. The program was designed to assist TANF or other public assistance recipients who were seeking employment and who were disadvantaged by the absence of reliable transportation. The demonstration program led to the development of the Family Self-Sufficiency Program (FSSP) for self-selected people in the seven-county region who meet two basic criteria: (1) They are a current recipient of any form of public assistance, and (2) their opportunities for full-time employment are impeded by transportation problems. An important aspect of the model was the use of a "wrap-around" model of social services, which deployed the state service workers as "family advocates"; they helped FSSP participants access local resources ranging from relatives and neighbors to businesses and social services in addition to assisting with their transportation needs. The family advocate and the members of the wrap-around service system use a comprehensive, systemic, team-oriented approach involving employment, transportation, family functioning, and family support services (including referrals to state agencies). The family advocate also works with the family to identify and engage informal support from neighbors, family, extended family members, and volunteers.

Isolated Impediments to Work

Once the family advocates began working with families, a number of additional impediments were identified that had not been included in the original needs assessment. They included isolated needs that were generally restricted to a small proportion of the families, such as health problems (for example, obesity, multiple sclerosis, and dental needs), legal problems (for example, felony convictions or suspended driver's licenses), and housing (for example, poor housing conditions).

Streamlined Services

A more widespread obstacle to self-sufficiency involved the complexity of using multiple case managers for individuals and families who came into the welfare system at different times for seemingly unrelated needs. This problem was particularly acute in a regional health agency. Through its connections with the state as a FoCUS participant, the agency was able to collaborate with state officials to develop a streamlined intake, assessment, and case management system for families based on a team approach to service delivery.

Approved State Waivers

A fundamental part of the relationship between FoCUS and the task force was the agreement to identify barriers that impeded effective and efficient responses to diverse situations regarding employment of participants in the FSSP project. As noted above, the issue over vehicle ownership was a major barrier that was resolved in negotiations with the state. Over the course of two years, several administrative impediments that prevented or delayed implementation of strategies for helping participants become self-sufficient were brought to the attention of the task force. To overcome those administrative problems, the task force worked with state officials to issue waivers for the FSSP project. Six waivers relative to standard public assistance eligibility criteria in Illinois were issues for FSSP participants (see Table 4-3).

Table 4-3

Waivers Approved by the State

- One motor vehicle is exempt regardless of value if it is necessary for employment or for adequate training for employment (May 29, 1996).
- There is a $1,000 liquid asset limit for participating families (May 29, 1996).
- Initial Employment Expenses can be extended one year with a limit of $1,000 annually (October 23, 1996).
- Clients who obtain employment or increased earnings that would result in a spend-down obligation may be continued as medical assistance case with no spend-down for one year (October 23, 1997).
- Flex-Funding Proposal is accepted with the understanding that specificity on tracking, evaluating, and reporting outcomes on the use of flex-funding (January 14, 1997).

Source: Federation of Community United Services, July 1998.

The waiver for Initial Employment Expenses changed the state $400 limit on incidental expenses related to maintaining a job, a benefit that could be used only within the first 30 days of employment or before employment. The waiver negotiated by FoCUS allowed up to $1,000 in expenses that could be used during the first year of employment. This change was important for workers to retain employment. If his or her car broke down after the worker had been on the job for only two months, for example, he or she could access the funds for the necessary repairs. When the new Department of Human Services was established on July 1, 1998, the annual allowance was increased to $1,200 for the FSSP participants.

A Flex-Funding proposal for the FSSP project was made to the state to give the Family Advocates more latitude in quickly accessing funds for minor expenditures related to work. This might include, for example, purchasing a car battery or tires. The state agreed to provide a restricted pool of dollars that could be used in this manner to assist families to become self sufficient. However, these funds were to be used only after all private and public resources had been exhausted and the needs of the family were still unmet. In the demonstration project, there were few requests for these funds, as it was found that most family needs could be met through traditional services.

Professional Advisory Council

Previous experiences of the Annie E. Casey Foundation's "New Future" community-building initiatives have shown that using a top-down, institutional approach that primarily relied on collaboration among professional social service providers was ineffective (White & Wehlage, 1995). To prevent this problem from occurring with FoCUS, a group of professional human service providers met with FoCUS staff to establish an ancillary advisory body known as the Provider Advisory Council (PAC) that would be open to all social service agencies in the seven counties. The PAC's membership now comprises more than 90 public and private social service agencies, which have created an important forum for discussion and dialogue among agencies that was not in place before FoCUS. Rather than selecting a few providers to serve on the FoCUS board (and thereby isolating providers who were not selected), it was decided to let PAC members elect their own representatives to serve on the FoCUS Board. Recently, the PAC was renamed the Provider Action Coalition.

As the PAC providers in southern Illinois communicated their frustrations about the delivery system to the FoCUS board at numerous orientation meetings, community participants became more appreciative of the systemic difficulties in service delivery and of what providers needed to help consumers toward self-sufficiency. In turn, the providers began to appreciate the community's newfound interest and willingness to assist the providers with problem solving. As relationships began to develop between the PAC and the FoCUS board, the Board of Directors had to assuage concerns among the providers that FoCUS would be a competitive agency that would provide direct services and vie for grants and government contracts.

SELECTED OUTCOMES

FoCUS led to the creation of the PAC and improved communication and networking among disparate individuals in the seven-county area. In addition, the FSSP project under FoCUS accomplished a variety of beneficial outcomes for both the family participants and the Family Advocates. Those outcomes include job placement, job promotions, home purchases, vehicle purchases and repairs, obtaining driver's licenses, completion of associate's degrees, use of the Earned Income Tax Credit, acquisition of telephones, child care, and reduced dependence on public assistance and food stamps.

The family advocates who were reassigned from state agencies to be the front-line workers in the FSSP program also were affected by their experiences. They noted that getting to know the participants and going to their homes greatly enhances the assessment process and results in more appropriate service referral. They also felt that participants were in a better situation to make informed decisions, in part a result of providing information under conditions that are more conducive to effective communication and personal interaction.

IDHS

At the state level, the process of welfare reform involving the community collaboratives eventually led to the strengthening of efforts for a consolidation of public human service agencies. The subsequent reorganization combined the programs of three Illinois state departments: the Department of Mental Health and Developmental Disabilities, the Department of Alcoholism and Substance Abuse, and the Department of Rehabilitation Services. In addition, parts of three other state agencies were merged into the IDHS, including the Department of Public Aid

(cash assistance, food stamps, Medicaid eligibility determination, employment programs, child care, and social service programs), the Department of Public Health
(the WIC program, family case management, and other health-related direct service
and prevention programs), and the Department of Children and Family Services
(employment-related child care and youth services).

The mission of IDHS is "to assist Illinois residents to achieve self-sufficiency, independence, and health to the maximum extent possible by providing integrated
family-oriented services, promoting prevention, and establishing measurable outcomes, in partnership with communities." The new agency is implementing a number of innovative procedures in its 131 full-service local IDHS offices, including the
following:

- *One-stop shopping.* IDHS clients can be connected to a wide range of human services at one location. Using a family-centered approach, intake and service-
  coordination personnel in each local office will be able to identify needs; determine eligibility for benefits; link clients to training programs, employers, and
  child care; and make referrals to other community services.
- *Identifying a family's need.* In the initial interview, IDHS focuses on identifying the
  kind of help and assesses the clients' and families need to move from welfare to
  work and to reach self-sufficiency or maximum independence. This objective
  guides all service planning.
- *Service coordination.* After their case is processed, clients see a IDHS service coordinator, who will ensure that services to meet their family's needs and goals are coordinated.
- *Working toward one goal.* Clients and their service coordinator are always working
  toward the same goal: self-sufficiency or maximum independence. Clients are
  fully involved in service planning and share responsibility for reaching their goals.
- *Community partnership.* Each local IDHS full-service office will collaborate with local government; key community leaders; employers; social service providers;
  health and disability providers; advocacy groups; and social, religious, and other
  institutions to help families achieve self-sufficiency or maximum independence
  goals (IDHS, 1997).

SUMMARY

The state human services reform demonstration project in the seven rural counties
of southern Illinois, FoCUS, has played an instrumental role in the statewide initiative to re-engineer the human services delivery system. The immediate objective of
local and state reform has been to reduce the TANF rolls, but a much more comprehensive goal exists, that of building community capacity through a reformulated
mix of public–private, state–local, and community–family provision and coordination of services at all levels. The clear intent is to shift much of the responsibility for
addressing human service needs to the local community, working in tandem with
state agencies.

Within the rural context, as experienced by the FoCUS demonstration project, initial outcomes indicate that the process of bringing diverse organizations in the area together for dialogue on welfare services and benefits has indeed had a positive impact on community commitment and capacity building. The process has strengthened formal and informal interaction between community and human service agencies, public and private service providers, diverse community organizations, community and educational institutions (K–16), service providers and educational institutions, and service providers and informal support systems.

As is characteristic of many rural areas, there were strong pre-FoCUS linkages among social service providers, county officials, and educators. However, FoCUS facilitated improved interaction between these community entities, especially with regard to developing a better common understanding of welfare programs and appreciation for the barriers to the development of viable approaches to reducing local welfare roles. The lessons from the process for bringing diverse community elements together to address welfare issues are similar to the experiences from the community collaboration that is required for rural communities to effectively compete for federal rural Empowerment Zones and Economic Community (EZ/EC) funds. In brief, processes that induce community groups to work together for a common purpose are more likely to develop an environment of cooperation and a recognition of shared responsibility and resource commitment to achieve shared goals.

In the initial interview, IDHS focuses on identifying the kind of help that an individual needs to find and to keep a job, including identifying potential workplaces, job coaching, interviewing techniques, and the like. It also assesses the needs of the clients and families in terms of the types of social supports (such as transportation, child care, and addiction treatment) that will be required to move from welfare to work and to reach self-sufficiency or maximum independence. This objective guides all service planning.

As a major feature of the process of community building initiated by welfare reform in Illinois, FoCUS also has been instrumental in identifying the primary barriers to service delivery in a rural area, including reliable transportation to work sites, employment opportunities, distance to work sites, education and training locations, and child care facilities. These barriers are not necessarily unique to the rural experience. Within the FoCUS experience, however, effective resolutions to the barriers in rural areas clearly support the view that policies and programs need to be attentive to the unique cultural, geographic, demographic, and economic features that influence social service delivery systems in rural communities. In many instances a difference seems to be simply a matter of scale. For example, transportation barriers in a large, sparsely populated geographic area take on a different dimension from those in a geographically small, densely populated urban area. One obvious difference is that the geographic scale in rural areas limits the feasibility for public (or for-profit) transportation.

Cultural differences exist as well. The issue of increased discretionary spending of flexible funds requested by the family advocates in FoCUS brought out the question of the state's trust in the family advocate to make an informed and quick decision without an unnecessarily restrictive safeguard system. To question the integrity of the family advocate, who had close personal knowledge of the family and its needs, was culturally offensive. The economic scale in rural areas is also different. A relatively small allowance for flexible spending, which might have minimal impact in urban Chicago, can make a tremendous difference in southern Illinois. Thus, decisions at the state level need flexibility that allows for local conditions and situations.

The hope in southern Illinois is that the community networks developed through FoCUS will continue to work toward ever increasing communication and collaboration. Clearly, efforts at re-engineering human services will be effective only if the state, communities, professional service providers, and consumers can cooperate in setting common goals and agreeing on strategies that are appropriate for a given region in a state as large and diverse as Illinois. It is equally important to the success of reform measures that all who are involved approach the process in the spirit of pragmatism—the notion that we learn what works by experimenting and by recognizing the importance of constantly revising and adapting programs and policies to new social and economic realities. The experience of FoCUS would strongly suggest that flexibility in program features and adaptability to individual and family situations is a central feature of community–state partnerships that succeed in delivering human services in rural areas.

REFERENCES

Chassard, Y. (1997). Social protection in the European Union: Recent trends and prospects. In *Adapting to new economic and social realities: What challenges, opportunities and new tasks for social security?* (pp. 161–167). Geneva: International Social Security Association.

Cope, M. (1997). Responsibility, regulation, and retrenchment: The end of welfare? In L. A. Staehelin, J. E. Kodras, & C. Flint (Eds.), *Urban affairs annual reviews: Vol. 48. State devolution in America: Implications for a diverse society* (pp. 181–205). Thousand Oaks, CA: Sage Publications.

Governor's Task Force on Human Services Reform. (1998). Illinois: Reforming human services, building a better future for children, families & communities. Springfield, IL: Author.

Illinois Department of Human Services. (1998). *Illinois on target with welfare reform* [On-line]. Available: http://www.state.il.us/agency/dhs/comm2-12.htm

Illinois Department of Human Services. (1997). *Service delivery approach* [On-line]. Available: http://www.state.il.us/agency/dhs/approach.htm

Michalski, W., Miller, R., & Stevens, B. (1997). Economic flexibility and social cohesion in the twenty-first century: An overview of the issues and key points of discussion. In *Societal cohesion and the globalising economy: What does the future hold?* (pp. 7–25). Paris: Organisation for Economic Cooperation and Development.

Parsons, M. D. (1997). *Power and politics: Federal higher education policymaking in the 1990s.* Albany: State University of New York Press.

Sherman, R. (1997). *Evaluation of community federations short-term projects: Interim evaluation report executive summary.* Chicago: Illinois Department of Human Services, Division of Community Operations.

Vogt, J., & Murrell, K. (1990). Empowerment in organizations: How to spark exceptional performance. San Diego: Pfeiffer & Co.

Voices for Illinois Children (1997). *Illinois Kids Count: Learning begins at birth 1997–1998.* Chicago: Author.

White, J. A., & Wehlage, G. (1995). Community collaboration: If it is such a good idea, why is it so hard to do? *Educational Evaluation and Policy Analysis, 17,* 23–38.

CHAPTER FIVE

Squeals and Deals:
The Impact of Corporate Hog Farming
on Rural Communities

Judith A. Davenport and Joseph Davenport, III

Social workers long have focused on how changing agricultural practices affect small towns and rural communities (Davenport & Davenport, in press). Technological changes in agricultural production continually roll through the hinterlands with results that often are a mixed blessing. Fewer and fewer people are required to produce an increasing number of products. American consumers enjoy the cheapest food products in the world (relative to income), while former farm personnel are freed to do other things. The displacement of agricultural workers, however, has resulted in declining populations in many rural areas, leading to such effects as secondary businesses failing, churches closing, schools consolidating, and rural institutions and cultures generally withering away (Davenport & Davenport, 1995; Jacobsen & Sanderson-Alberson, 1987).

Corporate hog farming, which is variously called "factory farming," "industrialization of agriculture," or "corporatization of agriculture," is a relatively recent phenomenon that promises to be still another force for change (Thu, 1995). This force has picked up considerable speed in the mid-1990s, and its effect is being felt across the Midwest, the Southeast, and now the Rocky Mountain West. Proponents of the approach tout it as inevitable and argue that it will strengthen rural communities through its promise of new employment possibilities, increased tax bases, greater efficiencies associated with size of operations, and revitalization of parts of rural America. Opponents, of course, see the opposite and warn against fewer overall jobs, reduced tax bases, illusionary gains in efficiencies, and a devitalization of rural areas. They also point to increased air, ground, and water pollution, which further degrade the quality of life and economic viability of rural living.

Large-scale corporate hog production is a relative concept with no single defining feature or qualitative measure. Agricultural specialists, however, characterize it according to a range of interrelated measures, including separate management, labor, and ownership; a limited role of family labor, if any, in the operation; absentee owners, management, and labor, in many cases; a nonfamily corporate or company organizational structure; and capital-intensive production technology.

In corporate farming operations, hogs are raised in huge numbers and processed through assembly-line technologies. Wastes from so many animals in a confined factory are typically stored in large lagoons, sprayed onto adjacent fields, or both. Rural residents complain about overwhelming odors, contamination of water supplies, and the loss of a sense of community and of local control (Thu, 1995).

To date, rural social workers have been relatively quiet about the effects of corporate hog farming on rural communities. Based on discussions at meetings of the National Rural Social Work Caucus and dialogues at previous rural social work conferences, however, the authors have found that large numbers of rural social workers appear to support the concept of family farms and sustainable agriculture and that most have problems with the growing concentrations of economic power attendant to corporate hog farming. Social work's allies from the earlier farm crisis (for example, family farm groups, rural crisis centers, small town merchants, and academicians) have tended to join forces with environmentalists and populists to wage war on the perceived threat (Uhlenbrock, 1998). Public figures, such as Willie Nelson, Jesse Jackson, and others have appeared at rallies to speak out against the trend toward corporate farming (Glover, 1998; Knight, 1997). State and local politicians also have become increasingly involved (personal communication with C. Graham, member of the Missouri House of Representatives, March 25, 1998). Although the problems and issues may be clear to some parties, the situation is really quite complex. Each side is able to marshal rationales, statistical data, and arguments that are difficult to sort through. Consequently, it is incumbent on rural social workers to study the perceived problem in some depth before committing themselves to policy and action recommendations.

To aid in this process, the authors undertook an exploratory effort to gather as much information as possible from diverse perspectives, including personal interviews with farm advocates, environmentalists, social scientists, and politicians in two states. A variety of books, journals, monographs, letters, reports, and pieces of legislation were reviewed. Case examples of controversial measures, as portrayed in daily and state newspapers, were collected from Missouri, a state with considerable corporate hog farming (Bishop,1998; Midkiff, 1998; Stroud, 1997), and Mississippi, a state that has just begun dealing with these issues (Ammerman, 1998a, 1998b; "Hog farms," 1998; Mord, 1998).

CHANGING STRUCTURE OF THE HOG INDUSTRY

Plain (1997) provided an excellent overview of the changing structure of the hog industry, which noted that the number of U.S. farms raising hogs peaked in 1920 at 4.85 million farms, declined to 3.3 million by the end of World War II, dropped to 1.85 million in 1959, and fell from around 1 million in 1967 to 157,450 in the last USDA survey. Plain predicted that only 120,000 hog farms will be left by the year

2000; in other words, hog farming has declined from 4.85 million farms to 120,000 in 80 years! The number of hogs over the same time period, however, which fluctuates in cycles, ranges from 50 to 62 million. Commercial pork production has increased 1.5 percent per year since 1930, and it is projected that the U.S. pork industry will probably slaughter an estimated 100 million hogs in a calendar year within the next several years. Furthermore, in 1996 the U.S. pork industry went from being a net importer of pork to a net exporter.

Technological change in the hog industry stems from factors that directly affect hogs. The factors include moving animals indoors, adoption of all-in or all-out production, segregated early weaning, split-sex feeding, and terminal breeding programs. Such changes have resulted in steadily improving statistics in pigs per litter, farrowings per animal, and hog slaughter per sow. Plain (1997) suggested that this technological change puts pressure on hog operations to get larger. The cost of space per hog is lower in large buildings; hog operations of more than 2,000 head averaged 8.775 pigs per litter, whereas farms with fewer than 100 head averaged only 7.35 pigs per litter.

Another factor of increasing importance is the change in ownership of hog production resulting from separation of the functions of ownership, management, and labor. Traditionally, small farmers owned, managed, and labored on their own farms. Today, large investors may provide capital while a management team secures necessary labor. In other words, hog production is becoming like the rest of the U.S. economy—industrialized.

The location of U.S. hog farms is another factor undergoing significant change. Historically, it was believed that hog farms needed to be located in close proximity to where the food for the hogs was grown. Since hogs were typically fed corn, hogs were most often grown in areas that were large producers of corn. Midwestern states are known both for their corn production and their hogs; Iowa has led the pack for almost 100 years. The number of hogs in Iowa, however, has dropped, from 24.5 million in 1974 to 21.72 million in 1996. Over the same period, the number of hogs in North Carolina increased dramatically, from only 3.45 million in 1974 to 11.7 million in 1994, 16.56 million in 1996, and an expected 20 million by 2000.

Because the number of hogs in Iowa is expected to fall to 19 million in 2000, it is projected that North Carolina will become the hog king as we enter the next century. The North Carolina success story has apparently refuted the belief that proximity to corn supplies was crucial. Producers now believe that hogs can be grown almost anywhere that local regulations are not an obstacle.

Executives of hog-producing corporations are increasingly sensitive to the criticisms that are being leveled against corporate hog farming. Those executives sometimes can be influenced by "anti-big, anti-hog" sentiment. Consequently, we are beginning to see a slow shift in corporate hog operations away from the Corn Belt to the West (Mo & Abdalla, 1998). States such as Oklahoma and Utah already are beginning to experience significant growth in their hog operations. This appears to be a result of the fact that in less densely populated regions, there are fewer people to complain about such matters as odors and waste spills. In addition, the arid conditions found in many western states tend to reduce odors while facilitating the spreading of hog waste on the land without a major risk of contaminating waterways. Interestingly, while North Carolina has experienced tremendous growth in hog farming, other states such as South Carolina and Virginia, which border North Carolina, are not even among the top 20 hog-producing states. This situation is generally felt to be a result of the fact that there has tended to be significantly more public resistance in those states to large-scale corporate hog farming. More recently, however, public resistance has been increasing in North Carolina as well.

The average size of hog farms has increased from only 88 head in 1977 to 357 in 1996. Three hundred and fifty-seven hogs in inventory will annually produce about 650 head for market. Because this production level requires only 1,100 to 1,200 hours of labor per year, the average U.S. hog operation is still a part-time job. At the same time, quadrupling the average size of a hog operation has been necessary to maintain income, because average profitability per hog has declined by two-thirds over the past 30 years.

Despite the decline in profit per pig, larger farms have used numbers to gain investment returns of 15 percent to 20 percent. Consequently, more large firms and investors have been attracted to the industry. The top U.S. hog operators in 1996 included the giant North Carolina Murphy Family Farms (260,000 sows), Smithfield Foods (112,000), Carroll's Foods (111,400), Tyson Foods (110,000), Premium Standard Farms (105,000), and Prestage Farms (102,200).

Notwithstanding the huge numbers of hogs controlled by the corporations listed above, the market is not yet completely controlled by only a handful of operators, although the trend is clearly in that direction. The largest 4,760 operators account for 50 percent of U.S. marketing. By the year 2000, it is estimated that 2,500 hog operators will constitute 50 percent of production. Significantly, firms marketing more than 50,000 head per year should account for less than 0.2 percent of the hog farms and produce more than 30 percent of the hogs. In fact, Miller (1998) reported that just 94 of those large producers accounted for 34 percent of the 1997 U.S. slaughter. The trend is clear. According to Plain (1997):

> The U.S. hog industry can be divided into two groups. The larger firms represent a growing industry. Each year there are more firms and hogs in this group than the year before. States which make these larger hog firms feel welcome are likely to be major hog producers in the future. Small firms constitute a dying industry. Each year there are fewer firms and fewer hogs in this group. . . . It now appears that only those firms marketing more than 3,000 hogs per year are increasing in number. (p. 10)

ARGUMENTS FOR AND AGAINST CORPORATE HOG PRODUCTION

Although Plain's (1997) overview of the changing hog industry provided much valuable statistical data on numbers and trends, his work assumed a certain inexorable, inevitable force that cannot be stopped. He barely mentioned environmental concerns and gave no consideration to possible social costs, let alone the social value of small, diversified family farms and farm communities. Voogt (1996) provided an excellent analysis of these concerns.

Supporters of corporate hog operations laud the creation of jobs in rural communities. For example, National Hog Farms' 320,000 hog per year facility in Colorado employs 165 people at an average of $15,000 per year (Obmascik, 1994), and Circle Four Farms in Utah plans to hire 600 employees in three counties to produce a stunning 2.08 million swine per year. Premium Standard Farms claimed 650 jobs in the economically hard-pressed Missouri counties of Mercer, Sullivan, and Putnum (Freese, 1994). It claimed an average payroll of $22,000 per person; $13,000 was its lowest annual wage (Keahey, 1995). Slaughter and processing plants, which tend to be located near large hog concentrations, are another source of jobs. Circle Four Farms plans a Utah facility that will hire 550 to 1,200 people. Additionally, some communities lure such plants from other areas. For example, Guymon, Oklahoma, was successful in recruiting from Liberal, Kansas, a slaughter–processing plant which held the promise of 1,400 jobs and a $25,000,000 payroll (Stull, 1994).

Proponents also point to increased wages, salaries, and profits of secondary businesses that deal with the corporate hog industry (Kansas Pork Producers Council, 1995). Such businesses include feed processors, feed suppliers, feed transporters, construction contractors, construction equipment suppliers, veterinarians, consultants, and suppliers of animal health products. Proponents argue that these businesses should produce financial opportunities for local banks and investors.

Proponents of corporate hog farming generally point to the "ripple" effect of such spending throughout a community's retail establishments. Wages and salaries from the hog industry and secondary businesses flow to providers of health care, apartments, clothing, appliances, automobiles, food, and homes, among other goods and services. Large hog facilities and processing plants are purported to stimulate home construction and personal lending.

Some supporters also argue that there are social benefits that accompany corporate hog-production operations, including increased community visibility, variety, and quality of life. Supporters also suggest that the community will benefit from more and different religious denominations, larger schools with more opportunities for students, and additional funding for recreational facilities and services as a result of corporate hog operations' coming to the community.

A boon for economically hard-pressed small towns and rural communities is an increase in total tax revenues. Theoretically, the introduction of corporate hog farming should increase jobs, which should attract more people, which should lead to expansion of the property tax base, which should result in increased funding for schools and town and county services. Furthermore, it is suggested that the "ripple" effect should result in increased sales taxes as money flows into the local economy.

Corporate hog-farm enthusiasts maintain that laws protecting family farms are a form of economic protectionism. They argue that the laws hurt the economy and consumers by protecting an industry from the free market. States with such laws have lost hog production to other states free of such onerous regulations.

Furthermore, supporters frequently cite the greater efficiencies of corporate hog production that stem from scale and size. Such factors include limited liability, pooling of capital, favorable tax treatment, ease of transfer of fractional interests, facilitation of intergenerational transfers, better fringe benefits for employers and employees, ability to raise and transfer funds from outside agriculture, and economies of scale. These efficiencies are presumed to provide a lower-priced and higher-quality product.

Supporters claim that corporate hog production enables new farmers to begin farming through production contracts. Otherwise, many young farmers would be locked out of business because of high front-end costs. Corporate producers assist young farmers in securing capital to begin hog production.

Finally, proponents maintain that the economic development possibilities of large facilities actually can save and revitalize rural communities (Warrick & Stith, 1995). Examples include North Carolina corporate hog farms rescuing stumbling tobacco communities, Utah hog farms replacing declining railroad centers, and eastern Colorado operations uplifting the area after massive farm failures.

Proponents of family farms who claim they will be driven out of business by the efficiencies and standardization of corporate entities counter these arguments. Ironically, governmental bodies and universities supported by tax revenues generated in part from small farmers have often conducted research for the corporate firms, which then compete against the small farmers. Additionally, some communities and states provide tax abatements and incentives to corporate firms, which are then even better able to undercut the small farmers.

Supporters of family farming fervently believe that the rural way of life is a value worth protecting, even if a free market does not protect this value. Residents of Great Bend, Kansas, alarmed at the specter of a $100 million pork processing plant, threw out of office the city council officials who supported the proposal (Dvorak, 1998). Many people view family farmers as an American tradition that has contributed to and shaped this country. Furthermore, they declare that Jefferson's view that agriculture producers should be morally sound, politically free, and not subject to the demands of the marketplace (Voogt, 1996) is best demonstrated by family farms, not corporations.

Supporters of family farms also point out that corporate hog operations can create communities that expand too rapidly, leading to boom-town phenomenon (Davenport & Davenport, 1979). Veterans of the many energy boom towns of the 1980s can attest to the dramatic increase in social problems (for example, child abuse, domestic violence, and alcoholism) in those frenetic environs. Critics cite the example of Garden City, Kansas, where Iowa Beef Producers began a large operation in 1980 (Voogt, 1996). The public schools experienced a 46 percent jump in enrollment and a 36 percent dropout rate, which was the highest in the state. Rates for violent and property crime rose sharply, even though the rates for the state dropped. Poverty rose, and food-pantry distributions more than doubled. Affordable housing and adequate medical care became scarce, and the local government's ability to provide social services was reduced as a result of tax concessions used to attract corporate agricultural entities.

Family farm proponents argue that a more stable economic environment is likely to exist when there are many small producers rather than one or a few large facilities in a particular area. When a large corporate hog operation locates in a rural community, it may drive small hog farmers out of business. After small operators are gone, the closure or relocation of the large corporate entity can be devastating. Jobs related directly and indirectly to hog production vanish, while unemployment and related social problems often skyrocket. If local and state governments attempt to keep the corporate operation from moving by offering greater tax concessions and incentives, the long-range effect may be to further reduce the tax base, decreasing the money available for pressing social problems.

Supporters of family farms decry the possibility of out-of-state or even international firms forcing family hog producers out of business in some states. For instance, a Japanese firm, Nippon Meat Packing, has opened a 540,000 swine per year plant in Texas that is expected to drive many of that state's small producers out of business (Lee, 1995).

Opponents of corporate farms caution that their touted benefits for local economies are not as great as claimed. Corporations often manage their own feed-producing and feed-transporting operations in a vertically integrated corporate structure. This saves them money, but it is at the expense of local businesses that have lost local customers as small farms go out of business. Furthermore, because corporate farms tend to buy their equipment and supplies from national, out-of-state suppliers, additional economic pressures are placed on small local businesses that have depended on traditional family farms. Even local banks, which eagerly anticipate an economic boom, can be shut out if corporations use large, national banks for loans and other services.

Opponents also argue that contract hog production is not the boon for young farmers hoping to enter the field that the corporations claim it is. They point out that the contractee has little bargaining power with the large contractor, who uses skilled lawyers to complete the arrangements in favor of the corporation. The small producer may have only one contractor in the region; consequently, he or she has limited choices. The contractor, in contrast, can pick and choose from among many small producers. Furthermore, because of economies of scale, the contractor often can produce hogs at a lower cost than the small contractee can. Consequently, small producers primarily are used when prices are depressed. Some analysts argue that the small contractees become economic serfs or low-wage slaves (Freese, 1994).

When large numbers of migrant workers are required for slaughter and processing plants in rural areas, a variety of social problems may arise. The term "boomtown bifurcation" was used in western energy boom communities as southern oilfield and construction personnel poured into quiet western cattle towns (Davenport & Davenport, 1980). Their accents, cultural backgrounds, religious preferences, lack of community attachment, and other differences often created divisiveness and conflict. Similarly, many corporate hog firms are employing large numbers of immigrant workers directly from Mexico or southwestern states. The immigrants may not be assimilated easily into the town's social fabric (Lambrecht, 1997); many of them are poor, speak little English, send large portions of their pay outside the local community (to their families in Mexico or elsewhere), prefer Catholic churches in towns where Catholics are few, and make little effort (or are not encouraged) to participate in community affairs. Despite industry claims, many immigrant workers are poorly paid and find it difficult to secure adequate housing, health care, and social services. Claims on public and private sources of aid tend to rise.

ENVIRONMENTAL PROBLEMS

Raising hogs either on corporate or family farms tends to be a messy business with serious environmental implications, according to Mississippi State University social scientist F. Howell (personal communication, June 2, 1998). Odors can decrease the quality of life and depress property values (Associated Press, *St. Louis Post-Dispatch,* May 16, 1998). In fact, Thu and Durrenberger (n.d.) found North Carolinians especially concerned about odors:

> The awful smell from hog facilities disrupt[ed] the lives of neighbors and communities. People stopped grilling outside and having picnics, friends stopped coming over to play cards, relatives refused to visit, children couldn't play in the yard, plans to build porches and patios were forestalled, laundry couldn't be hung out to dry, and children were taunted on school buses because they had absorbed the smell while standing at bus stops. (pp. 3–4)

Ground and surface water may be contaminated. Although family farms certainly do not always engage in sustainable agriculture practices, many environmentalists believe that corporate facilities are much greater offenders because of their large numbers and sheer concentrations of animals (Midkiff, 1998). To gain an understanding of the sheer quantity of waste produced by corporate hog farms, consider that each year, a single Missouri corporate hog facility produces an amount of sewage equivalent to the combined amounts generated by the cities of Columbia, Springfield, and St. Joseph, Missouri, cities totaling more than 250,000 residents (Wenzel, 1998).

Environmentalists claim that family farms are much more likely than their corporate counterparts to practice sustainable agriculture (Midkiff, 1998), where animals eat crops grown in the fields and replenish the soil with their wastes. Corporate hog producers, environmentalists suggest, will use their efficiencies of scale in purchasing and pricing to force small farms to specialize in animals or crops, thereby losing sustainability. For example, small farmers unable to compete with corporate hog prices may cease growing hogs and grow only grain to sell. They may remain in business, but they must purchase fertilizer rather than use hog waste. In short, their farms have lost the ability to sustain themselves, and they are more dependent on outside forces for survival. Additionally, large corporate hog facilities frequently lack adequate acreage to safely absorb their huge amounts of waste.

Environmentalists note that spills from waste storage lagoons affect ground and surface water. A single North Carolina spill contained 25 million gallons that polluted waterways, and a single Missouri spill killed at least 173,000 fish (personal communication with K. Midkiff, program director, Ozark Chapter, Sierra Club, April 9, 1998). These spills have the potential to virtually kill a river. Leaks in lagoons also can pollute ground water. One study showed that one-half of the existing lagoons in North Carolina leak badly enough to contaminate ground water (Warrick & Stith, 1995). Lagoons also create ammonia gas, which when mixed with rain negatively affects rivers and lakes.

People concerned about the environment also have expressed concerns that too much hog waste has been sprayed onto land. Tests in North Carolina showed nitrate contaminants threatening ground water. Concern is also expressed over disposal of hogs that die in the production process. Burial pits can pollute surface and ground water through nitrates, ammonia, and disease organisms.

Although serious, these environmental concerns are not accepted as gospel by corporate pork producers and agricultural scientists. Avery (1997) maintained that North Carolina's Albemarle and Pamlico Sounds are not being harmed by "nutrient soup" from hog wastes because the industry is not allowed to discharge any into ground or surface waters under the state's zero-discharge standard. He also notes that in spite of alarmists' cries, the recent hurricanes invaded only 0.5 percent of hog lagoons, whereas 40 percent of the state's municipal waste-treatment systems were victims.

Additional information is available through the National Pork Producers Council in cooperation with the National Pork Board (1998). Their flyer *Manure Resource Facts* includes the following information:

> The protection of our water resources from contamination is a high priority of the pork industry. While much has been written and said in recent months about water quality concerns related to the pork industry, many of the reports on which this discussion is based have lacked the perspective needed to make fact-based decisions about important industry issues. Many of these reports have been one-sided, inflammatory and driven by concerns unrelated to the environment.
>
> The effect of these reports has been to mischaracterize the pork industry as unregulated, unsustainable and uninterested in the proper utilization of manure as a fertilizer. This could not be further from reality.
>
> The United States is not staggering under a mountain of hog manure as some reports would lead a reader to believe. Swine manure is a natural, sustainable fertilizer, which saves billions of cubic feet of natural gas which would be otherwise used to manufacture fertilizer. Swine production, in fact, all livestock production combined, produces nowhere near enough manure to meet the needs of crops and forages grown in the United States right now. At present, crop farmers apply significantly more nitrogen from manufactured fertilizer compared to nitrogen from all livestock manure sources combined.
>
> Concentrated hog feeding operations are held to a zero discharge standard in their management of manure. All manure from a concentrated hog operation is required to be totally contained at the farm. When it is later applied to land as a fertilizer, it must be applied in such a way that it does not result in pollution of surface or groundwater. (p. 1)

Obviously, environmental issues can and do affect the quality of life in small towns and rural communities; the issues are both controversial and complex. They require objective, scientific examination because each side is probably prone to exaggerate its claims. It must be recognized that these issues have split not only rural communities but also churches and families. New research promises to develop strategies and technologies that will greatly reduce many of the problems, particularly odor. In fact, some activists fear that improvements in odor control may take away a potent organizing issue.

IMPLICATIONS FOR RURAL SOCIAL WORKERS

Rural social workers must first decide whether they are going to play a meaningful role in the debates and struggles over the future of corporate hog farming in rural communities. This particular issue, of course, must be examined in the context of the economic restructuring occurring across agriculture in general. As this chapter suggests, even a cursory overview of the hog industry reveals an extremely complex and emotional subject.

Engaging in the debate over corporate hog farming and other types of corporate agribusinesses requires considerable knowledge of the particular type of farming, agricultural economics, rural economic and social development, and environmental concerns. Failure to become actively involved in the debate will not insulate rural social workers from the need to respond in some form or fashion. There will be no safe sidelines from which to view the fray. Rural communities experiencing boom growth from corporate expansion will require the services of rural social workers. Conversely, rural communities experiencing decline from the loss of a corporate facility or the disappearance of small farms will also require assistance. Social work experiences with energy boom towns of the 1970s and 1980s and the farm crisis communities in the 1980s have taught us that a variety of responses can be helpful, including the establishment of crisis lines, interdisciplinary teams, support groups, and information and referral services (Davenport & Davenport, 1998).

Rural social workers interested in being more proactive have many options, depending on their assessment of the costs and benefits of corporate hog production. Some may believe that the economic benefits outweigh the costs, especially if environmental concerns are addressed and if plans are in place to hire and buy locally whenever possible. Such social workers might initiate or join committees or task forces that study the situation, consider alternatives, educate the public, and ensure that the corporations fulfill their agreements. Their roles may be part of an overall economic development strategy.

Other rural social workers may conclude that the social and economic costs to particular communities and to rural America in general are too high and that they represent yet further assaults on a rural culture and lifestyle they cherish. As a result, they may choose to fight "big pig."

Academicians can help by conducting research that documents the social costs, developing training materials for rural practitioners, consulting on group-organizing and policy matters, and placing practicum students in relevant settings (for example, rural crisis centers and state policy offices). The need for truly objective social research is imperative. Thompson and Haskins (1998) critiqued three university studies on the economic effects of large-scale hog operations and found them fatally flawed because of their procorporate farm bias.

Rural social workers on the scene, such as V. Keller, a former hog farmer, state employee, and University of Missouri–Columbia social work graduate student, may be employed full-time by public or nonprofit organizations. Consequently, they may have to volunteer their time to the struggle (personal communication with V. Keller, Missouri Division on Aging, February 12, 1998). Their skills, however, are invaluable: DeLind (1995) described one Michigan community's effort against a corporate farm that included numerous strategies and tactics basic to social work's armamentarium. Social workers know how to gather and assess data; link communities with outside experts; organize and lead groups; network among groups, communities, and organizations; form alliances and coalitions; educate the public via editorials, letters to the editor, forums, and media presentations; gather petitions; use ordinances and lawsuits; develop legislation; and cultivate political support. Social workers may have occasion to use disruptive tactics, in the tradition of Alinsky (1971), but should refrain from illegal acts, such as those that occurred in Mississippi where overzealous activists burned corporate trucks and freed hundreds of hogs, many of which subsequently died from the sweltering heat (Ammerman, 1998b).

Because the large corporate producers are national in scope, employing cadres of attorneys and lobbyists, it is imperative that local groups join with others and maintain contact with the diverse coalition battling the large producers. Traditional farm advocacy groups may find labor a receptive ally on this issue, and environmental groups, such as the Audubon Society (Williams, 1998) and the Sierra Club, can bring added numbers, clout, and resources (personal communication with K. Midkiff, program director, Ozark Chapter, Sierra Club, April 9, 1998). Other groups, which ostensibly are supportive of rural communities, are now seen in some states as the enemy. Those groups include some Farm Bureaus, state pork councils, and some universities' colleges of agriculture, extension services, and even the USDA. Although those organizations are seen as tilting toward "big pig," "friendlies" in those settings, who can provide valuable contacts and information, should not be overlooked.

Rural social workers must think carefully about where, when, and how they should intervene and how to calculate success. For example, blocking a corporate hog facility in one county may simply send it to an adjacent county that is less organized to fight or even more receptive to promised economic development. The facility may undercut prices and reduce sales opportunities in a multicounty region. To counter the influence and power of the corporate producers, alliances, networks, and coalitions may be necessary across the entire state. Even then, large firms can move across state lines and threaten family farms in nearby states. National efforts to affect policy appear warranted but are difficult to implement. Corporate producers have deep pockets, legions of lawyers, and scores of lobbyists to influence a Congress that is seemingly content to allow greater and greater concentrations of economic power (for example, the banking, telecommunications, and defense industries). Finally, it must be recognized that continuing protests have already led some firms to move operations to Mexico, Brazil, and Argentina, and other producers are considering Canadian locations (Bernick, 1998).

Even if communities successfully thwart corporate farm operations, ill feelings may threaten community cohesion for years. Rural social workers who are trained in conflict resolution and mediation will find their skills sorely needed in community healing processes. Rural practice wisdom includes the observation that if not resolved early, small town disputes may last for generations.

Rural social workers and their allies may believe that the best course of action is not all-out acceptance of corporate farming or a scorched-earth attack on such enterprises. They may believe that some type of balance may be possible. According to Voogt (1996), who made a comprehensive analysis of corporate hog production in Kansas:

> A reenactment of the prohibition of corporate ownership of hog production facilities would not adequately protect the small family hog producer. In addition, a prohibition would prevent Kansans from realizing the economic benefits of corporate hog production. Kansas communities, however, must be careful not to offer too significant a tax break to corporate producers because tax revenue is needed to cope with the social and environmental costs associated with these large producers. (p. 234)

Voogt also points out that

> . . . a Kansas production contract law which levels the parties' bargaining power can be used to enable the small family hog producer to be competitive with the corporate producer. Large corporate producers should also be more strictly regulated by Kansas environmental law than small producers because large hog producers have a potentially greater impact on the environment, and strict regulation of large producers will make the small producer more competitive. (p. 234)

CONCLUSIONS

Corporate hog production is increasing rapidly in the United States with a corresponding decline in family farms. Although some see the trend as positive in its overall economic benefits, others fear a further diminishment of rural life and culture. In this chapter, we explored the changing structure of the hog industry, examined the arguments for and against corporate swine production, addressed prominent environmental concerns, and provided examples of possible strategies and tactics that may be used by rural social workers. Because the growth in corporate agriculture seems likely to continue, the social work profession should devote more attention and resources to this subject. A policy plank might be included in a NASW national policy statement on economic and social development or rural social work. Collaboration with other professions (for example, environmental sciences and agricultural economics) and interest groups (for example, the Sierra Club and the Audubon Society) is imperative. This article contains many suggestions that can be adopted by practitioners, educators, researchers, and policymakers. The social work profession, with its ecosystem perspective on social problems, is ideally suited to coordinate a multigroup coalition. Time is of the essence, however, and immediate action is needed.

REFERENCES

Alinsky, S. (1971). *Rules for radicals.* New York: Random House.

Ammerman, J. (1998a, January 28). Group raises stink over hog-farm bill. Jackson, Mississippi, *Clarion-Ledger,* p. 1.

Ammerman, J. (1998b, May 6). Dozens of hogs dead after vandals hit farm. Jackson, Mississippi, *Clarion-Ledger,* pp. 1A, 6A.

Associated Press. (1998, May 16). Illinois county lowers land value near hog farm. *St. Louis Post-Dispatch,* p. B4.

Avery, D. T. (1997, December 2). Hogwash: North Carolina buys into environmentalist propaganda. *Columbia Daily Tribune,* p. A1.

Bernick, J. (1998, May/June). Southern hospitality: While the U.S. debates hog production, South America welcomes a market. *Farm Journal,* p. 30.

Bishop, B. (1998, March 22). Hogging the spotlight: National clamor over pig operations overlooks the struggles of family farms. *Columbia Daily Tribune,* p. A7.

Davenport, J., & Davenport, J. A. (1980). Boom town bifurcation. In J. Davenport & J. A. Davenport (Eds.), *The boom town: Problems and promises in the energy vortex* (pp. 43–53). Laramie: University of Wyoming Press.

Davenport, J., & Davenport, J. A. (1998). Rural communities in transition. In L. H. Ginsberg (Ed.), *Social work in rural communities* (3rd ed., pp. 39–54). Alexandria, VA: Council on Social Work Education.

Davenport, J. A., & Davenport, J. (1995). Rural social work overview. In R. L. Edwards (Ed.-in-Chief), *Encyclopedia of social work* (19th ed., Vol. 3, pp. 2076–2085). Washington, DC: NASW Press.

Davenport, J. A., & Davenport, J. (in press). Eduard C. Lindeman's *The Community:* A diamond anniversary retrospective on its contributions to rural social work. *Human Services in the Rural Environment.*

Davenport, J. A., & Davenport, J. (Eds.). (1979). *Boom towns and human services.* Laramie: University of Wyoming Press.

DeLind, L. G. (1995). The state, hog hotels and the "right-to-farm:" A curious relationship. *Agriculture and Human Values, 12*(3), 34–44.

Dvorak, J. A. (1998, May 6). Hog farms throw fat into hot political fires: Voter reaction to corporate plan shakes up Great Bend. *Kansas City Star,* pp. A1, A10.

Freese, B. (1994, April). Fed up with the big boys: Missouri farmers protest Continental Grain and other corporate hog farms moving into their state. *Successful Farming,* pp. 18–20.

Glover, M. (1998, June 29). Jesse Jackson says he may run for president: He pays a visit to Iowa, seeking support for views. *St. Louis Post-Dispatch,* p. A4.

Hog farms: Don't let N.C. fiasco happen here [Editorial]. (1998, March 2). Jackson, Mississippi, *Clarion-Ledger,* p. 6A.

Jacobsen, G. M., & Sanderson-Alberson, B. (1987). Social and economic change in rural Iowa: The development of rural ghettos. *Human Services in the Rural Environment, 11,* 58–65.

Kansas Pork Producers Council. (1995). *Hog industry's contribution to local and state economies.* Topeka, KS: Author.

Keahey, J. (1995, April 9). Pig farm to bring home big bacon, but Utahans not whole hog in support. *Salt Lake Tribune,* p. F1.

Knight, L. D. (1997, October 19). Farm Aid keeps fighting for Missouri family farms. *Columbia Daily Tribune,* p. E6.

Lambrecht, B. (1997, December 28). Influx of Hispanic workers alters culture of small southwestern Missouri towns. *St. Louis Post-Dispatch,* pp. A1, A 12.

Lee, S. H. (1995, July 30). Giant, corporate hog farms are gaining a foothold in the panhandle, but small operators are raising a stink. *Dallas Morning News,* p. 1H.

Midkiff, K. (1998, February 20). Graham's bill against big pig helps propel the good fight. *Columbia Daily Tribune,* p. 6.

Miller, M. (1998, June). Moving into the 21st century: The "big guys" may not be as big as you think. But they plan to get bigger. *Pork,* pp. 66, 68.

Mo, Y., & Abdalla, C. W. (1998, June 1). Analysis finds swine expansion driven most by economic factors, local decisions. *Feedstuffs: The Weekly Newspaper of Agribusiness,* pp. 20, 29–35.

Mord, R. (1998, June 2). Hog farm foes suing officials over strategies. *Starkville Daily News,* p. 1.

National Pork Board. (1998, March 19). Pork industry environmental impact facts. *Manure Resource Facts* [On-line]. Available: http://www.nppc.org/PROD, Environmental Section/ manurefacts.html

Obmascik, M. (1994, July 31). Welcome to hog heaven: Midwest tilt toward family farms turns Colorado into a park paradise. *Denver Post,* p. B1.

Plain, R. L. (February 6, 1997). *Changing structure of the hog industry—U.S. and abroad.* Paper presented at the Professional Swine Producers Symposium, Lansing, Michigan.

Stroud, J. (1997, January 1). Hog-producing giant created in Missouri. *St. Louis Post-Dispatch,* pp. C1, C8.

Stull, D. D. (1994). Of meat and (wo)men: Meatpacking's consequences for communities. *Kansas Journal of Law and Public Policy, 3,* 112–113.

Thompson, N. L., & Haskins, L. (1998). *Searching for sound science: A critique of three university studies on the economic impacts of large-scale hog operations.* Walthill, NE: Center for Rural Affairs.

Thu, K. (Ed.). (1995). *Understanding the impacts of large-scale swine production: Proceedings from an interdisciplinary scientific workshop.* Des Moines, IA: North Central Regional Center for Rural Development.

Thu, K., and Durrenberger, E. P. (n.d.). *North Carolina's hog industry: The "rest of the story."* Unpublished manuscript.

Uhlenbrock, T. (1998, February 1). Neighbors say hog farms threaten the quality of rural life. *St. Louis Post-Dispatch,* pp. A1, A8.

Voogt, E. (1996). Pork, pollution, and pig farming: The truth about corporate hog production in Kansas. *Kansas Journal of Law and Public Policy, 5,* 219–238.

Warrick, J., & Stith, P. (1995, February 25). The smell of money. Raleigh, NC, *News and Observer,* p. 1A.

Wenzel, B. (1998, April 15). National campaign for family farms and the environment: Environmental and human health impacts of family farms. *Rural America/In Motion Magazine* [On-line]. Available: http://www.inmotionmagazine.com/hogenv.html

Williams, T. (1998, March/April). Assembly line swine. *Audubon,* 26–33.

SECTION III

THE IMPORTANCE OF FAMILES

The family continues to be the primary social institution and is the first source of social support and problem solving, whether in rural or urban areas. Essential to the definition of family are kinship and neighborhood ties such as fictive kin. In this section, the authors present content that supports the importance of family in rural communities and identify mechanisms to strengthen and empower rural families that will ultimately result in a more powerful community.

Sharon B. Templeman, in chapter 6, discusses the significance of family preservation in rural communities. Using the Virginia Comprehensive Services Act for At Risk Youth and Families (CSA), this author examines the relationship between child risk factors and indicators of community well-being in 23 rural Virginia counties. She also measures the extent to which the relationships changed over a six-year period before and after the implementation of the CSA. Based on her findings, Templeman indicates that the community is an appropriate unit of analysis but that evaluation of individual success must also be considered. Based on her research, she cautions social workers to be vigilant and to avoid exchanging gains for some families at the expense of others.

In chapter 7, Ellen L. Csikai and Kathleen Belanger examine the training needs and interests of foster parents in a 15-county rural region of East Texas. Based on the results of the authors' survey, the foster parents have a fairly strong interest in all the subject areas presented to them. They are particularly concerned about developing behavior management skills and enhancing their abilities to teach ethics and values to the children in their care.

Police and social workers often must work together to address the problem of family violence, which is difficult to do in rural communities and small towns because of rigid family roles, geographic barriers, and lack of services. In chapter 8, T. Laine Scales and H. Stephen Cooper describe research in Nacogdoches, Texas, designed to better understand law enforcement officers' and social workers' attitudes toward each other and toward different aspects of family violence. Based on their research, the authors conclude that rural law enforcement officers are more resistant than rural social workers to working cooperatively in addressing family violence.

CHAPTER SIX

Family Preservation in Rural Communities: Is It Working?

Sharon B. Templeman

To preserve and strengthen rural communities, we need to find effective ways to preserve and strengthen rural families. Measuring family preservation outcomes in all types of communities has challenged child welfare professionals, policymakers, and researchers for more than a decade (American Humane Association [AHA], 1995, 1996, 1997; Blythe, Salley, & Jayaratne, 1994; Heneghan, Horwitz, & Leventhal, 1996). Defining family preservation services, determining what outcome measures to use other than out-of-home placement prevention and deciding how to measure effectiveness are at the center of the debate.

Additionally, although an abundance of research on family preservation outcomes now exists (Blythe, Salley, & Jayaratne, 1994; Templeman, 1998), a paucity of family preservation outcome research has been conducted on rural communities. Yet it is widely accepted that the organization and delivery of services to rural families presents challenges and frustrations that are unique as a result of limited resources, diversity of need, and difficulty in access (Knitzer & Olson, 1982; Takeuchi, Bui, & Kim, 1993; Tolan, Ryan, & Jaffe, 1988). A recent search of three comprehensive databases yielded only one study concerning family preservation services in rural areas, and it was descriptive rather than empirical (Sheldon-Keller, Koch, Watts, & Leaf, 1996).

This chapter reports on a study of the impact of family preservation services on 23 rural Virginia communities. For purposes of this study, the rural community was the unit of analysis, and family preservation services were defined using the flexible, community-specific, wrap-around definition espoused by Virginia's Comprehensive Services Act for At Risk Youth and Families (CSA) (Comprehensive Services Act, Code of Virginia, 1950, as amended).

Through the use of a hierarchical linear model analysis, four predictors of community well-being (low birthweight, school dropout, births to girls, and poverty) were compared with five factors traditionally considered to be risks for children (early school failure, juvenile arrests, child maltreatment, violent teen deaths, and foster care placement). The comparisons were made over a six-year period using a time-series design.

The findings suggest that the community is an appropriate unit of analysis to study but that evaluation of individual success must also be considered. Measuring change through the use of the two-level hierarchical linear model appears to be a promising model compared with analyses more commonly used in time-series designs.

STUDY

In July 1993, the Commonwealth of Virginia took the nationwide lead regarding the universal implementation of family preservation services for children with serious emotional disorders and their families by implementing the Comprehensive Services Act For At Risk Youth and Families. Because Virginia was the first state to use the family preservation model uniformly statewide and simultaneously implement the model in all counties in the state, Virginia was a good population for study. It offered the history and experience necessary for an investigation of whether, practically speaking, Virginia's children, families, and communities are better off since family preservation services were implemented. It was hypothesized that family life in communities was improving as a result of the new service delivery paradigm. Furthermore, considering the methodological criticisms of current family preservation outcome studies, a model for measuring effectiveness was developed. Through the use of a time-series design, indicators traditionally considered as risks to children were compared with indicators of community well-being for a group of 23 rural communities in Virginia at six points in time: yearly intervals in the two years before the implementation of the CSA, the year the CSA was implemented, and at yearly intervals during the three years following implementation of the act.

FAMILY PRESERVATION SERVICES

Family preservation is child welfare's most recent attempt to address the needs of children at risk and their families. Family preservation services originally were initiated through the Omnibus Budget Reconciliation Act of 1993 (U.S. Congress, 1935, as amended). Later renewed through the Promoting Safe and Stable Families program, family preservation services aim toward a number of goals, including early identification and intervention, individualized services for the child and family, services that are within the most normative environment, partnership with families, strengths-based service delivery, cultural competence, unconditional care, and flexible and "seamless" funding (Stroul, Lourie, Goldman, & Katz-Levy, 1994). Proponents of family preservation (Bath & Haapala, 1994; Berry, 1993, 1995; Henggler, Melton, Smith, Schoenwald, & Hanley, 1993; Morris, Suarez, & Reid, 1997; Scannapieco, 1994; Templeman, 1998; Unrau, 1995) view family preservation neither as a panacea for family dysfunction nor as a substitute for adoption. Rather, it is an opportunity to allow families and children the maximum opportunity to succeed in their original structure.

THEORETICAL FRAMEWORK

Risk and resiliency theory presents a model that focuses on variations in response to risk and works to prevent harm through protection. According to Hawkins, Catalano, and Associates (1992), it is based on the premise that to prevent a problem, one must first know what factors increase the chance of the problem's occurrence. One must then find ways to reduce these risk factors.

Catalano, Chappell, and Hawkins (1994), Hawkins, Catalano, and Associates (1992), and Rutter (1987, 1990) all made a strong case for interventions that use a risk-focused approach to reducing problem behaviors such as neglect or violence. Their research has shown that a number of risk factors increase the likelihood of harm. Identifying and understanding the risk factors are the first steps toward identifying effective means of prevention. The more risk factors to which a person is exposed, the greater is the likelihood that he or she will encounter harm. Similarly, there are certain protective factors that can help shield vulnerable people from harm. Protective factors are the aspects of people's lives that counter or provide buffers against risk factors. Protective factors protect by either reducing the effects of risks or by changing the way that people respond to risks.

Furthermore, Catalano and colleagues (1994) delineated different categories of risk and protective factors according to the life domain within which they are likely to occur. For example, some factors are likely to exist in the broader community, others in the family, and still others in the individual or peer realm. The model assumes that if risk factors can be reduced while protective factors are increased, harm can be prevented. Taking into account the risk factors, for this study the CSA represented a comprehensive, collaborative model of protection for communities in Virginia.

CSA

Formally enacted on July 1, 1993, the CSA is based on the family preservation model of service delivery to families. The intent of the CSA is to "create a collaborative system of services and funding that is child-centered, family-focused, and community based when addressing the strengths and needs of troubled and at-risk youths and their families in the Commonwealth" (Comprehensive Services Act, Code of Virginia, 1950, as amended). The law has several purposes and establishes expectations for multiple effects.

Among the purposes and effects of the CSA is to ensure that services and funding are consistent with the Commonwealth's policies of preserving families and providing appropriate services in the least restrictive environment while protecting the welfare of children and maintaining the safety of the public. Another purpose is to identify and intervene early with young children and their families who are at risk of developing emotional or behavioral problems or both, as a result of environmental, physical, or psychological stresses. Designing and providing services that are responsive to the unique and diverse strengths and needs of troubled youths and families is equally important. Other purposes include increasing interagency collaboration and family involvement in service delivery and management, encouraging public and private partnerships in the delivery of services to troubled and at-risk youths and their families, and providing communities with flexibility in the use of funds. Communities are authorized to make decisions and be accountable for providing services and are held accountable for their decisions (Comprehensive Services Act, Code of Virginia, 1950, as amended).

Specifically, the CSA uses a tiered structure of planning and management teams composed of representatives of the various public agencies, parents, representatives from the private sector, and other officials, such as law enforcement officials, judges, and local government officials. The team members work collaboratively to develop local policy; design, approve, and review child-specific treatment plans; authorize funding; develop new resources; and provide fiscal oversight. Thus, each community's array of services and approach to service delivery varies according to the diversity and uniqueness of its families. In other words, service planning is individualized both at the family and community levels. Under the CSA, families now experience earlier intervention, flexible funding, a more user-friendly process that involves them in service planning, and increased options through a broader array of services than was received by families before the legislation (Council on Community Services for Youth and Families, 1991).

DEFINING THE CONCEPTS

The definition of family preservation services specified by the CSA and used in Virginia is similar to the wrap-around definition offered by Thieman and Dail (1992). They suggested that family preservation services should offer a broad, creative range of services, including those most immediately needed by the family, such as food, money, shelter, and medical attention. Services should also respond to severe but less visible needs of families and be easy to use. In their view, direct, plentiful, individualized, labor-intensive services must be offered in ways that respond to the self-articulated needs of the families. A similar definition was used for this study. Rather than a discrete, time-limited program design such as Homebuilders, the CSA sets forth a functional model of a system of care in which local service systems collaboratively plan, fund, manage, and operate on behalf of troubled children and their families. Authority for making program and funding decisions is at the community level, but services are individualized to and are developed jointly with families (Macbeth, 1993).

The definition of "at risk" used for the purposes of allocating funds for family preservation services through the CSA includes children who meet one or more of the following criteria:

1. Eligible children have emotional or behavioral problems that have persisted over a significant period of time or, though only in evidence for a short period of time, are of such a critical nature that intervention is warranted;
2. these problems are significantly disabling and are present in several community settings such as at home, in school, or with peers;
3. these conditions require services or resources that are unavailable, inaccessible, or that are beyond normal agency services; and
4. ... these problems demand routine, collaborative processes across agencies or require coordinated services by at least two agencies. (Commonwealth of Virginia, Office of Comprehensive Services, 1993)

MEASURING FAMILY PRESERVATION OUTCOMES

Since the enactment of the CSA, the U.S. Congress has enacted the Family Preservation and Family Support Services Program (FPFSSP)[1] (DHHS, 1994), legislation that encouraged states to establish community-specific systems of care based on family preservation ideology. Thus, the array of services varies significantly from state to state, region to region, and community to community. The FPFSSP received wide support from child and family advocates because of general agreement with the emphasis placed on providing quality services to children at risk or to families on the brink of disintegration.

Important questions, however, arise about how the effectiveness of services is to be measured. Many observers were concerned that we had nationally embraced an amorphous paradigm shift without a priori scientific evaluation of its effects (Young, Gardner, Coley, Schorr, & Bruner, 1994). Research studies of family preservation services are fraught with inconsistent results and stimulate questions in need of further research (Bath & Haapala, 1994; Blythe, Salley, & Jayaratne, 1994; Ronnau, 1993; Tracy, Whittaker, Pugh, Kapp, & Overstreet, 1994; Wells & Freer, 1994). The outcome studies that do exist are frequently criticized as methodologically flawed (Blythe, Salley, & Jayaratne, 1994; Dore, 1993; Eamon, 1994; Gelles, 1993; Heneghan, Horwitz, & Leventhal,1996; Pence, 1993; Rossi, 1991, 1992; Thieman & Dail, 1992; Wells & Biegel, 1992). Among the flaws cited are the lack of randomized control-group comparisons with traditional treatment; the selection of individual families as the unit of study, which creates difficulties as a result of attrition or refusal to participate; and inability to detect an effect because of small sample sizes. Problems also cited as troublesome included defining the at-risk population, sample selection, and interventions; variations in treatment modalities; nonblinded determination of outcomes; and disagreement on which measures to use.

---

[1] Title IV-B of the Social Security Act, Subpart 2, Family Preservation and Support Services; Omnibus Budget Reconciliation Act of 1993.

NEED FOR FURTHER RESEARCH

The models of outcome evaluation in the literature leave gaps in the information necessary to answer important questions about the effectiveness of the family preservation paradigm. First, conflict exists about what the outcome studies should measure (Blythe, Salley, & Jayaratne, 1994; Schorr, 1994; Wells & Beigel, 1990; Young, Gardner, Coley, Schorr, & Bruner, 1994). Is an individual, family, community, system, or some combination outcome the "best" unit of measurement? Second, the most representative predictors of progress were still to be determined. Early in the history of family preservation research, Rossi (1992) questioned the use of out-of-home placements as the dependent variable and made a case for randomized, controlled experiments that measure changes in the well-being of children and families as the criteria of success. Yet, most studies have used the number of out-of-home placements or preventions as the sole measure of effectiveness and ultimate outcome, despite recommendations for different criteria of success. Even studies that set out to evaluate the success or failure of family preservation services by measuring improvement in parenting skills or child and family functioning finally settled on the number of placements as the standard (Templeman, 1998). Third, to reconcile cost with measurable outcomes, we must be able to quantify improvement. In the long range, services must be written into budgets. None of the studies in the literature review conducted for this study answered all of these questions.

STUDY DESIGN

The questions identified in the literature were addressed in our study in the following ways. The unit of analysis selected for the study was the community. To measure change in community well-being, a set of risk factors and predictors of risk to measure change were identified. The selection of indicators of community well-being was guided by recommendations made, but not yet implemented, by current research (AHA, 1995; Center for the Study of Social Policy, 1994; Galano, Nezlek, & Wood, 1997; Missouri Family Investment Trust, 1994; Nezlek, Galano, & Gholston, 1996; Young, Gardner, Coley, Schorr, & Bruner, 1994). Through an iterative process, a set of five factors traditionally considered to be risks to children and a set of four predictors of community well-being were selected (see Table 6-1). Analyses were developed to answer the following questions:

1. Did low birthweight, school dropout, births to girls, or poverty significantly predict *early school failure*? If so, did this relationship differ by year before and following implementation of the CSA?
2. Did low birthweight, school dropout, births to girls, or poverty significantly predict *juvenile arrests*? If so, did this relationship differ by year before and following implementation of the CSA?
3. Did low birthweight, school dropout, births to girls, or poverty significantly predict *child maltreatment*? If so, did this relationship differ by year before and following implementation of the CSA?

Table 6-1

Variables

Dependent Variables: Factors traditionally and in the literature associated with risk to children.
- Early school failure (percentage of fourth graders scoring below the 25th percentile on standardized tests)
- Juvenile arrests (per 100,000)
- Child maltreatment (per 1,000)
- Violent teen deaths (per 100,000)
- Children placed in foster care (actual number placed in alternative family and institutional settings

Independent Variables (Predictors of community well-being:; factors that measure the impact of family preservation on the broader community)
- Number of low birthweight babies (out of the total number of live births in the year)
- Percentage of ninth through 12th graders dropping out of school
- Number of births to girls ages 15to 17 (per 1,000)
- Poverty rate (based on parental eligibility for Aid to Families with Dependent Children [AFDC]) per 1000

4. Did low birthweight, school dropout, births to girls, or poverty significantly predict *violent teen deaths?* If so, did this relationship differ by year before and following implementation of the CSA?
5. Did low birthweight, school drop out, births to girls, or poverty significantly predict *foster care?* If so, did this relationship differ by year before and following implementation of the CSA?

Method

The study was carried out as a time-series analysis. A time-series analysis is an extension of the pretest–posttest design in which the assessment of a causal claim can be made more reliably than in a single pretest–posttest design. The time-series design has often served as an unplanned, post hoc evaluation of governmental or institutional reform (Glass, Willson, & Gottman, 1975).

Campbell (1969) has argued compellingly that, as in this study, the post hoc time-series analysis of archival data is an important tool for use by social scientists. Frankfort-Nachmias & Nachmias (1992) supported the use of nonintrusive, secondary data for conceptual–substantive, methodological, and economical reasons and referred to the time-series analysis as effective in situations in which no comparison group is available for assessing cause-and-effects relationships.

Sample

For implementation of the CSA, Virginia was divided into 137 localities. Some localities were counties, some were cities, and others were combined jurisdictions that had elected to work cooperatively as one locality. In the CSA design, funds were allocated to localities based on a state funding formula. This formula gave equal weight to the total locality youth population; households receiving food stamps with children under age 18; and risk factors, including child protective services complaints, juvenile court complaints, and children diagnosed by schools as seriously emotionally disturbed or seriously learning disabled. The 137 localities were divided into three categories: the "least-funded" (those initially targeted to receive up to $100,000), the "average-funded" (those targeted to receive between $100,001 and $300,000), and the "highest-funded" (those who could initially expect state funding in excess of $300,000) (Commonwealth of Virginia, Office of Comprehensive Services, 1993). Each category accounted for approximately one-third of the total population of localities in the state.

For this study a purposive sample of 23 localities was drawn from the 46 in the "average-funded" category. To minimize random heterogeneity of subjects, a threat to statistical validity, the sample included only rural localities with a population density of fewer than 100 people per square mile. To minimize diffusion, none of the five localities that had participated in the initial "demonstration" project and none of the localities contiguous to them were selected. In addition, four localities that were considered as two localities for funding purposes but as separate localities statistically were excluded. Following an iterative process of inclusion based on these factors, a sample of 23 rural localities, situated throughout the state, was studied. Temporal order of selection was not a factor because the CSA was implemented at a specific time point.

Data Collection

Because the CSA was officially implemented statewide on July 1, 1993, the posttest period covered the three years following implementation (that is, 1994, 1995, and 1996) to allow for the "start-up" phase of implementation of the legislation. The pretests were conducted two years before implementation of the CSA (that is, in 1991 and 1992). Data also were collected at the time of implementation of the CSA (that is, 1993), for a total of six data collection time points.

Data Sources

The most complete and reliable sources of data were those compiled by Galano, Nezlek, and Wood (1997) and Nezlek, Galano, and Gholston (1996) in the KIDS COUNT in Virginia, which included the years 1991 through 1997. Original sources of this data included the Virginia Department of Education; Virginia Department of Commerce, Economic, and Statistics Administration; U.S. Bureau of the Census; Virginia Commonwealth University Research Laboratory; Virginia Department of Youth and Family Services; University of Virginia Center for Public Service; and Virginia Department of Health, Center for Health Statistics. KIDS COUNT data is available in most states.

Data Analysis

Byrk and Raudenbush (1987) asserted that finding adequate measures of change and valid research techniques for change has long perplexed behavioral researchers, causing many analysts to question whether measuring change is a worthwhile endeavor. Research on change has been plagued with conceptual, measurement, and design concerns. Conceptually, the authors suggest that researchers rarely have addressed a model of individual growth of the phenomenon under study. Methodologically, researchers have failed to measure rate of change, instead relying on tests that measure at a fixed point in time. More relevant to this study, Byrk and Raudenbush reported that researchers have made compromises in design by measuring at only two time points. In instances in which data have been measured on multiple occasions, the data have typically been analyzed as a series of separate designs with two time points. The methodological problems have "led to a bewildering array of well-intentioned but misdirected suggestions about the design and analysis of research on human change" (p. 147).

The use of hierarchical linear model (HLM) analysis to measure change has been recommended (Byrk & Raudenbush, 1992; Raudenbush, Brennan, & Barnett, 1995). Gibbons and colleagues (1993) agreed that the use of the HLM, also referred to as "random regression analysis," minimizes risks posed by missing data, time-varying covariates, and irregular measurement occasions. Because these risks were minimized in this study's data set, the major advantages of HLM for this study were the ability to address serial correlation and to examine change in community well-being over time.

CONSTRUCTING THE MODELS

A series of five HLM analyses was performed to analyze the data collected in this study. Each analyzed the relationship between a child risk factor (that is, dependent variable) and a set of predictors of community well-being (that is, independent variables). A Pearson correlation matrix was calculated to determine if multicollinearity was a factor. All correlations were to less than .5.

As noted by Byrk, Raudenbush, and Congdon (1996), behavioral and social science data often have a nested structure, in which repeated observations are collected on a set of individuals who are nested within an organizational unit, such as a school or workplace. These organizational units are then nested within a broader location in a community, state, or country. In this study counties were nested within six points in time: two years before implementation of the CSA, the point at which the CSA was implemented, and three years thereafter. Thus, each analysis in this study included a second-level analysis to examine the nesting of the 23 communities within the six points in time. This approach allowed an examination of whether relationships between risk factors and indicators of community well-being changed over time and thereby attempted to answer the question of whether the CSA has had an impact as a protective factor on community well-being.

Only two items of data were missing within the parts of the *KIDS COUNT in Virginia* data sets (Galano, Nezlek, & Wood, 1997; Nezlek, Galano, & Gholston, 1996): the number of juvenile arrests in 1996 in one community and the number of fourth graders performing below the 25th percentile in 1995 in another community. For both items, the mean score was imputed. The low incidence ($< .08$ percent) of missing data and the apparent randomness of occurrence suggest that assigning values for missing data did not influence the results (Cohen & Cohen, 1983).

RESULTS

Of the five models on which HLM analyses were performed, significant relationships were detected between a child risk factor and an indicator of community well-being within two separate models.

Early School Failure

In the model that tested the significance of relationships between early school failure as the risk factor (dependent variable) and low birthweight, school dropout, births to girls, and poverty as the independent variables (see Table 6-2), school dropout was significant at $p = .027$. The relationship between school dropout and early school failure changed erratically over time, demonstrating no stable rise or decline in the relationship (see Table 6-3). The final effect was a slight rise in the relationship. The test for homogeneity of variance was not statistically significant ($p > .500$), indicating that this assumption was met.

Foster Care

In the model that tested the significance between foster care as the risk factor with low birthweight, school dropout, births to girls, and poverty as the set of predictors

Table 6-2

Level 1 Results from Intercept- and Slopes-as-Outcomes Model for Early School Failure

Variable	Fixed Effects			
	Coefficient	SE	T Ratio	p Value
Intercept	4.725	3.133	1.508	0.192
Low birthweight	0.268	0.320	0.836	0.441
School dropout	1.283	0.392	3.271	0.027
Births to girls	0.174	0.101	1.713	0.147
Poverty (AFDC)	0.044	0.025	1.741	0.141
Legislation	−0.002	0.024	−0.122	0.908
	Level 1		58.94417	

Table 6-3

Level 2 Results from Model for Early School Failure

		Slope			
	Intercept	Low Birthweight	School Dropout	Births to Girls	Poverty
1991	−8.620	2.327	1.738	0.116	0.019
1992	9.586	−0.119	2.026	−8.080	0.095
1993	9.518	−0.049	0.769	0.212	0.017
1994	0.031	0.202	1.507	0.456	−0.008
1995	2.470	0.117	0.881	0.369	0.033
1996	7.009	0.364	1.872	−0.104	0.069

of community well-being, two relationships were statistically significant. First, low birthweight was a statistically significant ($p = .006$) predictor of foster care. Second, poverty was found to be a statistically significant ($p < .0005$) predictor of foster care (see Table 6-4). (See Table 6-5 for slopes by year for each predictor.) The test for homogeneity of variance was not statistically significant ($p > .500$), indicating that this assumption was met.

The relationship between foster care and low birthweight fell dramatically between 1991 and 1994, but it rose sharply again between 1994 and 1996 (see Table 6-5). The overall effect of the relationship increased from 1991 to 1996. The relationship between foster care and poverty declined in 1992, rose in 1993, and then declined steadily from 1994 to 1996. The overall effect of the relationship decreased between 1991 and 1996.

Juvenile Arrests, Child Maltreatment, and Violent Teen Deaths

In the models that had juvenile arrests, child maltreatment, and violent teen deaths as the risk factors (dependent variables) with low birthweight, school drop-

Table 6-4

Results from Intercept- and Slopes-as-Outcomes Model for Foster Care Fixed Effects

	Coefficient	SE	t Ratio	p Value
Intercept	29.075	4.416	6.583	< 0.0005
Low birthweight	−2.198	0.484	−4.535	0.006
School dropout	−1.260	0.773	−1.631	0.163
Births to girls	−0.201	0.103	−1.937	0.109
For poverty (AFDC)	0.288	0.035	8.055	< 0.0005
Legislation	0.280	0.278	1.008	0.360
	Level 1 163.155			

Table 6-5					

Level 2 Results from Model for Foster Care

		Slope			
	Intercept	**Low Birthweight**	**School Dropout**	**Births to Girls**	**Poverty**
1991	24.415	−2.792	0.292	−0.257	0.380
1992	23.146	−1.569	−1.501	−0.152	0.269
1993	22.198	−2.446	0.901	−0.401	0.340
1994	46.818	−3.399	−0.999	−0.565	0.337
1995	39.963	2.499	−2.465	−0.115	0.271
1996	24.211	−1.386	−1.630	0.061	0.259

out, births to girls, and poverty as predictors, there were no statistically significant findings.

DISCUSSION

The study reported in this chapter investigated the relationships between child risk factors and indicators of community well-being in 23 rural counties and the extent to which those relationships varied over a six-year period before and after the implementation of the CSA. When addressing the relationships between the risk factors and the indicators of community well-being in this study, it is important to acknowledge that this study was based on concurrent data. Therefore, the findings of relationship between any specific risk factor and any specific indicator of community well-being are not directly related but are measured at the same time regarding different children. For example, juveniles arrested between 1991 and 1996 are not the same babies born during this period. Likewise, the fourth graders who fell below the 25th percentile on achievement tests were not the same children born to teen mothers between 1991 and 1996.

Because the hierarchical linear model analyzes data on two levels, (counties are nested in six time points) it was necessary to evaluate the findings and implications for both levels. First, to respond to the question of whether the indicators of community well-being were significant predictors of child risk, the relationships between variables had to be examined. Second, it was necessary to examine the significant relationships to determine whether the relationships changed over time. Observation over only a brief, three-year period would hint at whether the CSA had served as a protective factor for the communities. Additionally, it was important to probe the new model of outcome evaluation to assess its appropriateness and viability as an alternative to the common models questioned by researchers. In other words, the study set out to determine whether the measurement of change in indicators of community well-being over time is a more accurate evaluation of the effectiveness of family preservation services than simply measuring the numbers of out-of-home placements into foster care.

FINDINGS RELATED TO THE RELATIONSHIPS BETWEEN RISK FACTORS, COMMUNITY WELL-BEING, AND THE CSA AS A PROTECTIVE FACTOR

Early School Failure

A statistically significant relationship between early school failure (dependent variable) and school dropout rates (independent variable) was found. This finding was consistent with previous research studies that point to the vulnerability of children who are born to parents who did not complete high school (Federal Interagency Forum on Child and Family Statistics, 1997; Knitzer & Page, 1996). The level of maternal education is closely related to outcomes for children. Children born to mothers with less than a high school education generally are less successful than children whose mothers completed high school. For example, young children whose parents read to them are more proficient in language acquisition, literacy development, achievement in reading comprehension, and overall success in school than children who are not read to. As a mother's education increases, so does the likelihood that the child is read to regularly.

Teens who drop out of high school are at increased risk of criminal behavior, dependence on social services, unemployment, loss of school-based role models, and poor health (Galano, Nezlek, & Wood, 1997). The risks are passed on to their own children, who in turn are more likely to drop out of school and to later become teen parents themselves (Galano, Nezlek, & Wood, 1997; National Commission on Children, 1991; National Commission on the Role of School and the Community in Improving Adolescent Health, 1990; Nezlek, Galano, & Gholston, 1996).

This finding would cause one to speculate that births to girls would also be a significant predictor of early school failure. It is likely that low power or too little time for observation concealed this effect.

The observed relationship between early school failure and school dropout was volatile throughout the six-year period and was much greater in 1996 than in 1991. It was not possible from the results of this study to determine whether school dropout rates were as strong a predictor of eventual fourth grade failure following the implementation of the CSA as before the legislation. A longer period of observation is necessary.

No significant relationships between early school failure and low birthweight, births to girls, or poverty were found, suggesting either that the implementation of the CSA has had little, if any, impact on these indicators of community well-being or that existing impact was not detected in this analysis. Except for poverty, this result was expected. In this concurrent data set, all fourth graders in this study were already in school when the CSA was implemented. Therefore, early intervention efforts provided through the CSA could not have affected these children.

The absence of a significant relationship between early school failure and family poverty was somewhat surprising, however. Families of the fourth graders could have been among those receiving AFDC. It is possible that the lack of a demonstrated effect is related to the complexity of the problem of poverty (that is, many correlates affect this relationship) or to factors within the study, such as low power or the use of a measure that was not sensitive enough to detect an effect.

Juvenile Arrests

Low birthweight, school dropout, teen pregnancy, and poverty were not found to be significant predictors of juvenile arrests. This finding contrasts with those of other studies (Baron & Hartnagel, 1997; Dawkins, 1997; Galano, Nezlek, & Wood, 1997; Winters, 1997), which link juvenile delinquency and criminal behavior to school problems; antisocial peer and neighborhood influences; family dysfunction; and individual characteristics, such as learning disabilities.

The lack of statistically significant findings relative to these risk factors may signal the need for interventions specifically related to this area of risk. Successful family preservation intervention models must provide multiple prevention and intervention strategies that target many levels, including high-risk youth, high-risk families, and high-risk areas of the community (Developmental Research Programs [DRP], 1994). The findings may also indicate that the CSA did not offer enough services at multiple levels in the selected communities to offset the multiple risk factors faced by families. It is also highly likely that three years may be too soon to expect measurable results.

Child Maltreatment

Similarly, low birthweight, school dropout, teen pregnancy, and poverty were not statistically significant predictors of child maltreatment. As with juvenile arrests, it was no surprise that within three years the CSA could not affect the risk of child maltreatment. As Wells and Tracy (1996) maintained, child maltreatment is believed to occur when multiple risk factors outweigh multiple protective factors. Thus far it appears that the CSA has not provided enough protection to have a significant effect on the risks of child maltreatment. This lack of significant findings is in keeping with the meta-analysis by Schuerman and Littell (1995), who found little evidence that family preservation intervention has yet made a significant impact on child abuse and neglect. This finding is consistent with the findings of the National Academy of Sciences Panel on Research on Child Abuse and Neglect (as cited in Schuerman & Littell, 1995), which reported that those who are most at risk for child maltreatment may be less likely to participate in interventions or may have difficulty implementing changes in their social context.

Violent Teen Deaths

The lack of significant findings regarding violent adolescent deaths from unintentional injuries, homicide, and suicide is consistent with the literature (Fingerhut, Annest, Baker, Kochanek, & McLaughlin, 1996; Public Health Service, 1993; Singh & Yu, 1996), which demonstrates no appreciable reduction in youth mortality, especially among males, in the past four decades. This sample of Virginia communities is exceptional in that the aggregated violent teen death rate fell from 87.69 per 100,000 population to 72.14 from 1991 to 1996, unlike the national trend, which has remained stable at approximately 89.0 per 100,000 since 1990. The Federal Interagency Forum on Child and Family Statistics (1997) found that the adolescent violent death rate rose from 80.4 per 100,000 in 1985 to 89.0 in 1990 and has been relatively stable since. The death rate for black male adolescents rose dramatically between 1985 and 1994, from 125.3 per 100,000 population to 231.6. These statistics point out the difficulty of affecting factors that influence this variable.

Foster Care

Two findings regarding foster care in this study were statistically significant: the relationships between foster care and low birthweight and foster care and poverty.

The finding that low birthweight is a predictor of foster care supports those of other researchers, including Galano and colleagues (1997) and others (Kiely, Brett, Yu, & Rowley 1994; National Commission on Children, 1991; Nezlek, Galano, & Gholston, 1996; Werner, 1987) who have described the risks of low birthweight. Consequences of low weight at birth that follow children into adolescence and make success more difficult include sensory impairment, developmental and learning disabilities, mental retardation, and sight and hearing deficiencies, all of which have been linked to difficult behavior, conduct disorders and, eventually, to antisocial personality disorders. For example, low birthweight can lead to disabilities, which mar one's self esteem, thus impairing one's learning and social relationships. According to a study of 14 Virginia communities (Virginia Department of Mental Health, Mental Retardation and Substance Abuse Services [VDMHMRSAS], 1996), the most frequently cited presenting problem for children considered at risk of foster care placement during a two-year period were related to delinquency, acting-out behavior, and poor academics as opposed to maltreatment.

When observing the change in the relationship between foster care and low birthweight over time, the results demonstrated that the strength of this relationship decreased steadily from 1991 until 1994, at which time the relationship rose steadily until 1996. This finding could indicate that progress has been made in the Virginia communities under study. Juveniles who were underweight at birth may now have a better chance of avoiding foster care placement than they did before implementation of the CSA. In other words, family preservation intervention through the CSA may have served to protect low birthweight infants from the danger of eventual family disintegration. Certainly, this connection is made with caution because the decreased relationship between foster care and low birthweight could be attributed to other factors, such as special initiatives unrelated to the CSA, a change in attitude toward foster care, or other spurious factors. Given the collaborative nature of family preservation services under the CSA, however, and the strong emphasis on placement prevention, it is also possible that CSA planning and intervention may have affected this relationship.

The additional finding that poverty is a statistically significant predictor of foster care was not surprising, in light of the pervasive negative effects that poverty has on the physical, emotional, educational, and social success of children, resulting in disproportionate representation of poor children in child-related systems. As Eamon (1994) proclaimed, until family poverty is significantly reduced through social policy legislation, family preservation intervention will have disappointing outcomes for a large number of clients.

Although somewhat erratic, the declining relationship between foster care and poverty over this six-year study may point to progress in efforts through CSA interventions. This may be particularly true if, as is pervasive throughout family preservation outcome studies, efforts are directed more toward foster care prevention than toward other community indicators of well-being. Significant relationships between foster care and school dropout rates and births to teens were not found.

FINDINGS RELATED TO THE SUITABILITY
OF THE COMMUNITY-LEVEL MODEL

The model developed in this study for evaluating family preservation outcomes successfully addressed various methodological concerns voiced by researchers. In response to ongoing questions about what outcome studies should measure and recommendations that measures should include factors other than out-of-home placements, this model measured factors traditionally identified as risks to children against indicators of community well-being. In response to the debate about whether the individual, family, community, systems, or some combination outcome is the "best" unit of measurement (Blythe, Salley, & Jayaratne, 1994; Schorr, 1994; Young, Gardner, Coley, Schorr, & Bruner, 1994), this study diverged from the individual and family units most commonly used in family preservation research by focusing on the community. As an alternative unit of analysis, the community appeared most prevalently in the literature (Bruner, 1994; DRP, 1994; Hazel, Barber, Roberts, Behr, Helmsletter, & Guess, 1988; Heneghan, Horwitz, & Leventhal, 1996; Melaville, Blank, & Asayesh, 1993; Wells & Biegel, 1990).

Furthermore, in answer to the criticism that finding adequate measures of change and valid research techniques has caused many researchers to question whether measuring change is a worthwhile endeavor, a prototype was developed that responds to these concerns. In a traditional comparison of child risk factors over time through an ANOVA on the difference scores or a repeated measures ANOVA, the researcher would obtain only the mean scores of the sample in a simple pretest–posttest design. However, by using the HLM, the researcher has the advantage of an added dimension: viewing changes in the relationships between indicators of child risk and the potential predictors of community well-being over time (that is, counties nested within time), compared before and after implementation of the CSA.

CONCLUSIONS AND RECOMMENDATIONS

The findings in this study provide both hope and caution for Virginia's rural communities where the CSA is concerned. The progress toward reducing risks of poor children to enter foster care indicates that this population is benefiting. This trend toward improved outcomes for poor children signals hope that interventions designed according to the family preservation principles of child-centered, family-focused, community-based, and culturally sensitive service delivery are headed in the right direction. At the same time, an increase in the number of children placed outside their own homes in the sample during this time might suggest that the risks for nonpoor children increased. Social workers must be vigilant to not exchange gains for some families at the expense of others.

This study points only to a change in direction of a trend, not to the dissolution of the problems. If low weight at birth predicts subsequent placement in foster care, it is essential that social workers advocate for adolescent prenatal care while intervening early, along with medical professionals, to assist families in the care of infants who were low weight at birth. This finding particularly points to the need for the continued and expanded collaborative process—already an integral part of the CSA—through public–private partnerships with medical professionals, hospitals, clinics, and public health services.

Likewise, if school dropout predicts early school failure for future children, it is crucial that communities provide long-term early intervention programs that strengthen school participation, commitment, and success. The cooperative assessment and planning processes among schools, mental health, social services, and other community service providers that are so integral to the CSA must provide the environment for children to succeed educationally, thus breaking the cycle of generational school failure.

These shifts in trends are extremely fragile, however. They compete against powerful national trends that endanger the well-being of communities and families with children, and they threaten to reverse the impact of family preservation interventions. For example, the national trend toward managed care, which purports to cut costs but is culturally blind and is the antithesis of family preservation principles, is a strong force. Families with children need medical care that is not intimidating, is accessible under the most difficult circumstances, and respects cultural diversity. In the practice experience of this author, managed care is typically centrally located, which makes access difficult for those who lack transportation. Further, managed care services are usually delivered uniformly, without regard for cultural beliefs and traditions.

This study has provide a model for its replication in other communities and states. We strongly recommend research to examine the impact of family preservation interventions over a longer period of time and with larger samples using this model. Replicating the study for other types of communities, such as urban and suburban, is also warranted. In keeping with the flexible, community-specific philosophy of family preservation ideology, as communities prioritize needs and develop systems of care that reflect those needs, evaluation should measure outcomes specific to the communities' priorities. This model should be adapted to measure the indicators of child well-being most important to the community in question. In addition, we encourage a future qualitative study, similar to that conducted by Cheung, Leung, and Alpert (1997) and particularly recommended for rural communities by Jacobsen (1988), to seek out the differences in implementation among communities. This study would assess and shed light on the degree to which rural communities in Virginia have taken a stake in the family preservation paradigm through the CSA and have trained professionals to assist families in new ways.

The reader is cautioned against the distortions of ecological fallacy. With the community as the level of analysis, relationships that are significant at the community level cannot be extrapolated to the individual, family, or other levels. A community-level model cannot replace the need to measure change in individual or family well-being. Family risk factors must be addressed with family protective factors, and individual risks must be countered at the individual level. A community-level model is just one performance measure among several that will measure the effectiveness of agency or program service delivery. To measure outcomes, we must still know whether services are working for individual children and for individual families. Outcomes-based decision making is a basic approach that sets out the conditions of well-being we wish to achieve and steers our use of resources to achieve those conditions. If done well, it must go beyond solely government-based solutions to address interagency, cross-community responsibilities for the well-being of children, families, and the communities in which we live.

STUDY LIMITATIONS

A critical limitation in this study may have been low power, which could account for the lack of statistically significant findings regarding some variables. Although a sample of 23 counties with 54 observations each (that is, nine variables at six points in time) was sufficient to build a two-level hierarchical linear model that detected some statistically significant effects, it is likely that observations over a longer period of time or with more counties would provide greater power to detect an effect in more of the models.

If the CSA is providing protection from risks, it is not known what particular aspects of CSA implementation through family preservation intervention are responsible for this protection. Further research is warranted to make this known. Similarly, in models in which no significant relationship exists between the risk factors and the predictors of community well-being, it is not known what happened to the relationships over time. It is important to probe further to determine why the relationships between the remaining risk factors (that is, juvenile arrests, child abuse and neglect, and violent teen deaths) were not significantly related to the indicators of community well-being and were not affected by family preservation intervention.

Another limitation of this study is generalizability. Although a model for evaluating the effectiveness of family preservation interventions was developed in this study for use by other communities or states, the results of this evaluation are not necessarily relevant to localities in Virginia of different sizes or economic levels, to localities that had the benefit of participating in demonstration projects, or to other states.

Finally, the intent of this study to evaluate systems reform for observable change in community indicators within three years after implementation was an ambitious goal. The CSA is a far-reaching piece of legislation that has required start-up costs, new operating procedures, training, and community education. It is commonly acknowledged that some situations get worse before getting better. Some program elements may be designed so that effects are seen a generation or more after intervention. Thus, at best it is likely still too soon to detect an effect of the CSA in areas in which no effect was found.

REFERENCES

Action Alliance for Virginia's Children and Youth. (1995). *KIDS COUNT in Virginia: Preparing for the 21st century.* Richmond, VA: Author.

Administration on Children, Youth, and Families, Children's Bureau. (1994). *Program instruction—Implementation of new legislation: Family Preservation and Support Services, Title IV-B, Subpart 2.* Washington, DC: Author.

American Humane Association. (1995). *Second national roundtable on outcome measures in child welfare services: Summary of proceedings.* Englewood, CO: Author.

American Humane Association. (1996). *Third national roundtable on outcome measures in child welfare services: Summary of proceedings.* Englewood, CO: Author.

American Humane Association. (1997). *Fourth national roundtable on outcome measures in child welfare services: Summary of proceedings.* Englewood, CO: Author.

Baron, S., & Hartnagel, T. (1997). Attributions, affect, and crime: Street youths' reactions to unemployment. *Criminology, 35,* 409–434.

Bath, H. & Haapala, D. (1994). Family preservation services: What does the outcome research really tell us? *Social Services Review, 68,* 386–404.

Berry, M. (1993). The relative effectiveness of family preservation services with neglectful families. In E. S. Morton & B. K. Grigsby (Eds.), *Advancing family preservation practice* (pp. 70–98). Newbury Park, CA: Sage Publications.

Berry, M. (1995, Summer). An examination of treatment fidelity in an intensive family preservation program. *Family Preservation Journal,* 25–50.

Blythe, B., Salley, M., & Jayaratne, S. (1994). A review of intensive family preservation services research. *Social Work Research, 18,* 213–224.

Bruner, C. (1994). *Toward improved outcomes for children and families: A framework for measuring the potential of comprehensive services strategies.* Des Moines, IA: Child and Family Policy Center.

Byrk, A., & Raudenbush, S. (1987). Application of hierarchical linear models to assessing change. *Psychological Bulletin, 101,* 147–158.

Byrk, A., & Raudenbush, S. (1992). *Hierarchical linear models.* Newbury Park: Sage Publications.

Byrk, A., Raudenbush, S., & Congdon, R. (1996). *HLM: hierarchical linear and nonlinear modeling with the HLM/2L and HLM/3L programs.* Chicago: Scientific Software International.

Campbell, D. (1969). Reforms as experiments. *American Psychologist, 24,* 409–429.

Catalano, R., Chappell, P., & Hawkins, J. (1994). *Communities that care: Orientation to risk-focused prevention.* Seattle: Developmental Research and Programs.

Center for the Study of Social Policy. (1994). *Financing reform: As in how to pay for reform of family and children's services.* Washington, DC: Author.

Cheung, M., Leung, P., & Alpert, S. (1997). A model for family preservation case assessment. *Family Preservation Journal, 2,* 1–20.

Cohen, J., & Cohen, P. (1983). *Applied multiple regression/correlation analysis for the behavioral sciences* (2nd ed.). Hillsdale, NJ: Lawrence Erlbaum Associates.

Commonwealth of Virginia, Office of Comprehensive Services. (1993). *Implementation manual.* Richmond, VA: Author.

Comprehensive Services Act, Code of Virginia (1950). As amended, Chapter 46-2.1-744 through 2.1-754.

Council on Community Services for Youth and Families. (1991). *Improving care for troubled and "at risk" youth and their families: Restructuring service delivery and funding. A report to the Governor and General Assembly.* Richmond, VA: Author.

Dawkins, M. (1997). Drug use and violent crime among adolescents. *Adolescence, 32,* 395–405.

Developmental Research Programs. (1994). *Communities that care.* Seattle: Author.

Dore, M. (1993). Family preservation and poor families: When "homebuilding" is not enough [Special issue]. *Families in Society, 74,* 545–556.

Eamon, M. (1994). Poverty and placement outcomes of intensive family preservation services. *Child and Adolescent Social Work Journal, 11,* 349–361.

Evaluation of the Comprehensive Services Act. (1994). Virginia Assembly Joint House Resolution No. 56.

Federal Interagency Forum on Child and Family Statistics. (1997). *America's children: Key national indicators of well-being.* Washington, DC: Author.

Fingerhut, L., Annest, J., Baker, S., Kochanek, K., & McLaughlin, E. (1996). Injury mortality among children and teenagers in the United States. *Injury Prevention, 2,* 93–94.

Frankfort-Nachmias, C., & Nachmias, D. (1992). *Research methods in the social sciences.* New York: St. Martin's.

Galano, J., Nezlek, J., & Wood, L. (1997). *KIDS COUNT in Virginia: 1997 data book.* Richmond, VA: Action Alliance for Virginia's Children and Youth.

Gelles, R. (1993). Family reunification/family preservation: Are children really being protected? *Journal of Interpersonal Violence, 8,* 557–562.

Gibbons, R., Hedeker, D., Elkin, I., Waternaux, C., Kraemer, H., Greenhouse, J., Shea, T., Imber, S., Sotsky, S., & Watkins, J. (1993). Some conceptual and statistical issues in analysis of longitudinal psychiatric data. *Archives of General Psychiatry, 50,* 739–750.

Glass, G., Willson, V., & Gottman, J. (1975). *Design and analysis of time-series experiments.* Boulder, CO: Colorado Associated University Press.

Hawkins, J., Catalano, R., & Associates. (1992). *Communities that care: Action for drug abuse prevention.* San Francisco: Jossey-Bass.

Hazel, R., Barber, P., Roberts, S., Behr, S., Helmsletter, E., & Guess, D. (1988). *A community approach to an integrated system for children with special needs.* Baltimore: Paul H. Brookes.

Heneghan, A., Horwitz, S., & Leventhal, J. (1996). Evaluating intensive family preservation programs: A methodological review. *Pediatrics, 97,* 535–542.

Henggler, S., Melton, G., Smith, L., Schoenwald, S., & Hanley, J. (1993). Family preservation using multisystemic treatment: Long-term follow-up to a clinical trial with serious juvenile offenders. *Journal of Child and Family Studies, 2,* 283–293.

Jacobsen, G. (1988). Rural social work research: A case for qualitative methods. *Human Services in the Rural Environment, 11,* 22–28.

Kiely, J., Brett, K., Yu, S., & Rowley, D. (1994). Low birth weight and intrauterine growth retardation. In L. S. Wilcox & J. S. Marks (Eds.), *From data to action: Centers for Disease Control public health surveillance for women, infants, and children.* Atlanta: Centers for Disease Control and Prevention.

Knitzer, J., & Olson, L. (1982). *Unclaimed children: the failure of public responsibility to children and adolescents in need of mental health services.* Washington, DC: Children's Defense Fund.

Knitzer, J., & Page, S. (1996). *Map and track: State initiatives for young children and families.* New York: National Center for Children in Poverty.

Macbeth, G. (1993). Collaboration can be elusive: Virginia's experience in developing an interagency system of care. *Administration and Policy in Mental Health, 20,* 259–281.

Melaville, A., Blank, M., & Asayesh, G. (1993). *Together we can: A guide for crafting a profamily system of education and human services.* Washington, DC: U.S. Government Printing Office.

Missouri Family Investment Trust. (1994). *Guidelines for becoming a community partnership for families and children.* Unpublished manuscript.

Morris, E., Suarez, L., & Reid, J. (1997). Behavioral outcomes of home-based services for children and adolescents with serious emotional disorders. *Family Preservation Journal, 2,* 21–32.

National Commission on Children. (1991). *Beyond rhetoric: A new American agenda for children and families.* Washington, DC: U.S. Government Printing Office.

National Commission on the Role of the School and the Community in Improving Adolescent Health. (1990). *Code blue: Uniting for healthier youth.* Alexandria, VA: National Association of State Boards of Education.

Nezlek, J., Galano, J., & Gholston, S. (1996). *1996 KIDS COUNT in Virginia: Kids and communities.* Richmond, VA: Action Alliance for Virginia's Children and Youth.

Pence, D. (1993). Family preservation and reunification in intrafamilial sexual abuse cases: A law enforcement perspective. *Journal of Child Sexual Abuse, 2,* 103–108.

Public Health Service. (1993). Measuring the health behavior of adolescents: The youth risk behavior surveillance system and recent reports on high-risk adolescents. *Public Health Reports, 108*(Suppl. 1).

Raudenbush, S., Brennan, R., & Barnett, R. (1995). A multivariate hierarchical model for studying psychological change within married couples. *Journal of Family Psychology, 9,* 161–174.

Ronnau, J., & Marlow, C. (1993, November). Family preservation, poverty, and the value of diversity. *Families in Society,* 538–544.

Rossi, P. (1991). *Evaluating family preservation programs: A report to the Edna McConnell Clark Foundation.* New York: Edna McConnell Clark Foundation.

Rossi, P. (1992). Strategies for evaluation [Special issue]. *Children and Youth Services Review, 14,* 167–191.

Rutter, M. (1987). Psychosocial resilience and protective mechanisms: Special report. *American Journal of Orthopsychiatry, 57,* 316–331.

Rutter, M. (1990). Psychosocial resilience and protective mechanisms. In J. Rolf, A. S. Masten, D. Cicchetti, K. H. Neuchterlein, & S. Weintraub (Eds.), *Risk and protective factors in the development of psychopathology* (pp. 181–214). New York: Cambridge University Press.

Scannapieco, M. (1994). Home-based services programs: Effectiveness with at risk families. *Children and Youth Services Review, 16,* 363–377.

Schorr, L. (1994). The case for shifting to results-based accountability. In N. Young, S. Gardner, S. Coley, L. Schorr, & C. Bruner (Eds.), *Making a difference: Moving to outcome-based accountability for comprehensive service reforms* (pp. 13–29). Falls Church, VA: National Center for Service Integration.

Schuerman, J., & Littell, J. (1995). *Problems and prospects in society's response to abuse and neglect.* Chicago: University of Chicago, Chapin Hall Center for Children.

Sheldon-Keller, A., Koch, J., Watts, A., & Leaf, P. (1996). The provision of services for youth with serious emotional behavioral problems: Virginia's Comprehensive Services Act. *Community Mental Health Journal, 32,* 481–495.

Singh, G., & Yu, S. (1996). Trends and differentials in adolescent and young adult mortality in the United States, 1950 through 1993. *American Journal of Public Health, 86,* 560–564.

Stroul, B., Lourie, I., Goldman, S., & Katz-Levy, J. (1994). *Profiles of local systems of care for children and adolescents with severe emotional disturbances.* Washington, DC: Georgetown University Child Development Center, CASSP Technical Assistance Center.

Takeuchi, D., Bui, K., & Kim, L. (1993). The referral of minority adolescents to mental health centers. *Journal of Health and Social Behavior, 34,* 153–164.

Templeman, S. (1998). *Evaluating family preservation services from a community well-being perspective: A time series analysis of Virginia's Comprehensive Services Act for At Risk Youth and Families.* Unpublished doctoral dissertation, University of Maryland, Baltimore.

Thieman, A., & Dail, P. (1992, January). Family preservation services: Problems of measurement and assessment of risk. *Family Relations,* 1–6.

Tolan, P., Ryan, K., & Jaffe, C. (1988). Adolescents' mental health service use and provider process, and recipient characteristics. *Journal of Clinical Child Psychology, 17,* 229–236.

Tracy, E., Whittaker, J., Pugh, A., Kapp, S., & Overstreet, E. (1994). Support networks of primary caregivers receiving family preservation services: An exploratory study. *Families in Society, 75,* 481–491.

Unrau, Y. (1995). *Predicting child abuse and service outcomes in an intensive family preservation services program.* Unpublished doctoral dissertation, University of Utah, Salt Lake City.

U.S. Congress (1935). Social Security Act, as amended, Omnibus Budget Reconciliation Act of 1993 (PL 103-66, Section 13711), codified as Subpart 2 of Title IV (42 USC, Sections 430, et seq.).

Virginia Department of Mental Health, Mental Retardation, and Substance Abuse Services (1996). *Comprehensive Services Act Trust Fund Projects Evaluation Report, FY93–FY95.* Richmond, VA: Author.

Wells, K., & Biegel, D. (1990, February). *Intensive family preservation services: A research agenda for the 1990's.* Final report presented at the Intensive Family Preservation Services Research Conference, Cleveland, Ohio.

Wells, K., & Biegel, D. (1992). Intensive family preservation services research: Current status and future agenda [Special issue]. *Social Work Research and Abstracts, 28,* 21–27.

Wells, K., & Freer, R. (1994). Reading between the lines: The case for qualitative research in intensive family preservation services. *Children and Youth Services Review, 16,* 399–415.

Wells, K., & Tracy, E. (1996). Reorienting intensive family preservation services in relation to public child welfare practice. *Child Welfare, 45,* 667–675.

Werner, E. (1987). Vulnerability and resilience in children at risk for delinquency: A longitudinal study from birth to young adulthood. In J. D. Burchare & S. N. Burchard (Eds.), *Prevention of delinquent behavior.* Newbury Park, CA: Sage Publications.

Winters, C. (1997). Learning disabilities, crime, delinquency, and special education placement. *Adolescence, 32,* 451–462.

Young, N., Gardner, S., Coley, D., Schorr, L., & Bruner, C. (1994). *Making a difference: Outcome-based accountability for comprehensive service reforms.* Falls Church, VA: National Center for Service Integration.

CHAPTER SEVEN

Assessing the Training Needs and Interests of Rural Foster Parents

Ellen L. Csikai and Kathleen Belanger

From a child welfare and social work perspective, preserving and strengthening communities includes support for everyone involved in the care of children. Training and support is especially important for foster parents caring for children with complex social, psychological, and medical needs. Access to such training and support is often lacking in rural communities, possibly resulting in increased risks for children, such as further neglect or abuse and multiple placements. More broadly, a lack of support may engender a lack of confidence in the "system" in the eyes of the community. This chapter presents the results of a study conducted in East Texas that identified training needs of rural foster parents and their preferred methods of delivery and support.

The number of children living in foster care in the United States has increased tremendously in the past 20 years. In 1993, 464,000 children were living in out-of-home care; it is predicted that by the year 2000, the number will increase to 850,000 (Altshuler, 1997; Children's Defense Fund, 1995; Gleeson, 1995; Gleeson & Craig, 1994). Protection from abuse or neglect is the primary reason that children enter foster care. Other reasons include absence of a parent or other parental problems, truancy, and delinquency. Children entering foster care often have complex needs and have been found to have a higher risk for medical and psychosocial problems than children in their natural homes (Hochstadt, Jaudes, Zimo, & Schachter, 1987).

The goals of out-of-home care include providing a temporary, safe, and nurturing environment for children; achieving a permanent home with natural families, if possible; and minimizing the adverse effects of the experiences that led to placement (Everett, 1995; George, Wulczyn, & Fanshel, 1994). An emphasis in recent years on the reunification of children with their families has reinforced the role of the foster parent as a part of a team. Foster parents must be properly trained in order to fulfill their roles as parents to children with multiple difficulties and as members of professional, multidisciplinary teams working toward family preservation and permanency planning (Everett, 1995; Pasztor, 1985). "Recruiting, training, and supporting foster parents are key issues in child welfare services that will be necessary in the next 10 years" (Everett, 1995, p. 387).

Requirements for training of foster parents typically vary by state. Although the number of children living in foster care and the severity of their problems have grown in recent years, rural foster parents, like their urban counterparts are expected and required to maintain licenses through continued training. Many rural counties, however, do not offer within a reasonable distance the kinds of training most helpful to foster parents. Consequently, many rural foster parents must travel for several hours to a training location and find or construct their own training opportunities while they manage the care of the children.

Training methods and delivery modalities also differ widely; they include sessions offered by local child protection agencies, foster care agencies, foster parent associations, local community agencies, and universities. Many agencies use a team approach to training, using caseworkers, foster parents, and community professionals to conduct sessions (Pasztor, 1985). In rural areas, however, access to those resources is limited despite the need for training. Along with relating valuable knowledge, ongoing training also provides an important source of support for foster parents (Molin, 1994).

Content areas of foster parent training should include child developmental and medical needs; behavior management; effects of separation of children from their families; and the needs and therapeutic treatment of children who have experienced neglect or physical, sexual, or emotional abuse and other forms of family violence (Everett, 1995; Pasztor, 1985). To design an effective foster parent training curriculum, many factors must be considered, such as the professional resources available in the community, access of foster parents to learning resources and, particularly in rural communities, the physical proximity of foster parents to each other and to potential training sites. Perhaps the most important consideration, however, may be the input of foster parents as to their training needs and interests (Noble & Euster, 1981). Inclusion of foster parents in the development of a training program allows foster parents to feel connected with the local agencies and with each other, a bond which is especially important in rural areas.

To provide foster parents with continuing and responsive educational experiences that enable them to meet licensing needs as well as ongoing needs for information and support, a university in East Texas and the regional child protection agency entered into a collaborative relationship. The first step in their process was to determine the foster parents' perceived training needs. Thus, foster parents in rural East Texas were surveyed regarding past training, future training needs and interests, and past and preferred methods of delivery of foster parent training.

METHOD

Sample and Procedures

Current foster parents within a 15-county area in East Texas, based on the lists of the regional child protection services, were included as potential participants in the study. A four-page survey was administered in two ways. First, all foster parents attending a Foster Parent Association training session on various topics, including HIV/AIDS, were given an opportunity to respond to the survey during the session. Also, the survey was mailed to all 291 foster parents in the region with instructions that if they had previously responded, they should not do so again. A return stamped envelope was included with the survey. A total of 84 completed survey instruments (one unusable) were obtained through the two methods, for a response rate of 29 percent.

The average age of the foster parents was 48 years. Most of the foster parents were married (69 percent); 20 percent were single, 5 percent were divorced, 4 percent had "other" marital status, and 1 percent was separated. Sixty-three percent of the respondents were white, 30 percent were African American, 6 percent were of "other" ethnicity, and 1 percent were Native American. The respondents had an average of eight years experience as a foster parent; the range was from zero (new foster parents) to 58 years of experience. The experience with their current agency affiliation ranged from 0 to 36 years; the average was 6 years. The respondent foster parents were currently caring for an average of two foster children and had cared for an average total of 27 foster children during their foster parenting experience.

Instrument and Measures

The study used a four-page survey instrument to obtain information on the content of foster parents' past training, their training interests, the methods of delivery of their previous training, and the parents' preferred training methods as well as their level of access to the Internet. The demographic information described above also was obtained.

Training issues were addressed in the first section of the instrument. Foster parents were asked about the amount of formal or informal training they had received in 10 subject areas, including behavior management, learning disabilities, stress management, and teaching values and ethics to children. The foster parents responded according to a five-point Likert-type scale ranging from 1 (no training) to 5 (extensive training). The subject areas were then listed along with additional subject areas relating to various social issues and treatment, such as teen pregnancy, child neglect, physical abuse, and sexual abuse. Foster parents were asked to indicate areas in which they would like to receive training using a Likert-type scale ranging from 1 (strongly disagree) to 5 (strongly agree).The subject area list included health care issues, such as prevention, failure to thrive, medical management of childhood diseases, and mental illness in children were included.

Methods of delivery of foster parent training were measured by asking foster parents how they had received training in the past and how they would like to receive training in the future. A list of methods was provided that included agency-sponsored training sessions, community seminars, written materials, and speakers at foster parent association meetings. Respondents were asked to check all areas in which they had received training. The list was then repeated, and foster parents were asked to indicate all the methods through which they would like to receive training.

Table 7-1

Past Training Reported by Foster Parents (N = 83)

Subject	Mean	SD
Behavior management	3.32	1.05
Normal childhood developmental stages	3.30	1.07
Family decision making	3.27	1.05
Teaching values and ethics to children	3.27	1.07
Socialization skills for children	3.05	1.07
Learning disabilities	2.98	1.08
Stress management	2.98	1.20
Managing relationships with community providers	2.93	1.25
Cultural diversity	2.41	1.15
Changes in welfare system	2.23	1.14

NOTE: Responses were based on a 5-point Likert-type scale: 1 = none; 2 = a small amount; 3 = a moderate amount; 4 = a large amount; 5 = extensive.

FINDINGS

Past Training and Future Interests

As shown in Table 7-1, the subject areas in which the foster parents had received the most training were behavior management and normal childhood developmental stages. They also reported a moderate amount of exposure to family decision making and teaching values and ethics to children.

Table 7-2 shows the areas of training needs reported by the foster parents respondents in our study. As indicated in the table, respondents were most interested

Table 7-2

Training Needs Reported by Foster Parents (N = 83)

Subject	Mean	SD	% FPs Agreed*
Teaching values and ethics to children	4.16	.83	84
Behavior management	4.12	.75	89
Learning disabilities	4.12	.79	86
Stress management	4.01	.74	82
Socialization skills for children	3.96	.71	82
Changes in welfare system	3.90	.87	68
Normal childhood developmental stages	3.86	.80	75
Managing relationships with community providers	3.86	.82	74
Family decision making	3.84	.83	69
Cultural diversity	3.82	.96	71

*Includes those who agreed or strongly agreed

NOTE: Responses were based on a 5-point Likert-type scale: 1= strongly disagree; 2 = disagree; 3 = uncertain or neutral; 4 = agree; 5 = strongly agree.

Table 7-3

Training Areas in Which Foster Parents Expressed Interest ($N = 83$)

	Mean	SD	% FPs Agreed*
Social Issues:			
Child neglect	4.28	.82	89
Physical abuse	4.17	.82	83
Sexual abuse	4.16	.86	84
Domestic violence	3.99	1.02	79
Substance abuse/alcoholism	3.96	1.03	80
HIV/AIDS	3.87	1.00	72
Teen pregnancy	3.56	1.19	64
Health Care Issues:			
Mental illness in children	4.21	.88	86
Failure to thrive	4.21	.92	87
Prevention (variety of problems)	4.12	.94	83
Fetal Alcohol Syndrome	4.12	.97	87
Accessing health care	3.99	.88	79
Medical management of childhood diseases	3.99	.88	81
Mental illness in adults	3.95	.97	79
Normal medical management in childhood	3.89	.97	77

*Includes those who agreed or strongly agreed
NOTE: Responses were based on a 5-point Likert-type scale: 1 = strongly disagree; 2 = disagree; 3 = uncertain or neutral; 4 = agree; 5 = strongly agree.

in receiving training in teaching values and ethics to children, behavior management, and learning disabilities. However, the foster parents who responded to our survey indicated a fairly strong interest in all subject areas.

Table 7-3 shows the areas of training needs identified by the respondents. Foster parents indicated an interest in a number of social and health care issues, although they again expressed fairly high levels of interest in all topics listed. Child neglect and physical abuse were social issues in which the foster parents indicated they would like to receive further training. Mental illness in children and failure to thrive were found to be the health care areas of greatest interest to the respondents.

Methods of Delivery

As shown in Table 7-4, most of the respondents reported that they had received training in the past through agency-sponsored sessions and written materials. The respondents also indicated that they frequently obtained training from speakers at foster parent association meetings. At least two-thirds of the respondents indicated that they preferred receiving training through each of the following methods: agency-sponsored sessions, written materials, speakers at meetings, and individual contacts with their caseworkers. Interestingly, 30 percent of the parents indicated a

Table 7-4

Past and Preferred Training Methods Reported by Foster Parents ($N = 83$)

Method	Past (%)	Preferred (%)
Agency-sponsored training	91	87
Written materials	90	75
Speakers at foster parent association meetings	84	82
One-to-one contact with caseworker	84	66
Informal discussion with community members	43	43
University seminars/courses	61	56
Previous foster care agency	36	25
Local library/bookmobile	35	37
Information on Internet	13	30

NOTE: Respondents could indicate all methods that applied to their circumstance.

preference for receiving information on the Internet. In response to a separate item, 25 percent of the respondents reported that they had access to the Internet. Of note is that 5 percent of respondents wanted to receive information over the Internet but did not have access, which may represent the increasing interest in having Internet access or that some foster parents may have access in their workplaces.

DISCUSSION AND IMPLICATIONS

Perhaps the most striking but not surprising finding of this study is that foster parents have a desire for increased training that will assist in the care of the difficult and vulnerable children entrusted to them. Foster parents expressed a strong interest in all subject areas presented to them in the survey. The great interest in all types of training may be an indication of the difficulty rural foster parents have in obtaining training at all and their enthusiasm for the possibility of receiving training, especially training that responds to their perceived needs. Particularly notable is the continued interest in behavior management and in teaching ethics and values to children, even though they had received a moderate of amount of training in these areas in the past. Foster parents confront these areas on a daily basis and thus need continual reinforcement of how to handle situations that arise.

The high level of interest in the topic of teaching values and ethics to children was not anticipated. This response may reflect the rural nature of the population in light of the fact that rural communities tend to reflect traditional moral values and sanctions (Ginsberg, 1993). Foster parents may increasingly find it difficult to relate these values to children who may not have had a strong foundation in moral values.

Other areas in which foster parents expressed an interest also point to the complex problems that they face when a child is placed in their care. The interest in knowledge about learning disabilities and how to teach socialization skills to children shows recognition of the multiple psychosocial difficulties that abused and neglected children bring into foster care. It comes as no surprise, then, that the foster parents indicated an interest in stress management training. One can imagine that the challenging situations confronted by foster parents would naturally contribute to an elevation of their day-to-day stress levels. Because foster parents are partners in reaching the goals of child protection, training similar to that offered to caseworkers as they negotiate their extremely stressful jobs needs to be offered to foster parents, to assist them in dealing with their stressful situations.

The subject areas of child neglect, physical abuse, and sexual abuse were also areas of great interest to the respondents. Since most children enter out-of-home placement as a result of issues of abuse or neglect, it seems that how to reinforce appropriate treatment related to such issues would be a part of all foster parent training. Although foster parents do receive extensive training on these topics before receiving the first child in their home, results suggest that foster parents need continual training with respect to abuse and neglect and that they may not perceive that saturation in this topic area is possible. The respondents also indicated that they need updates and information regarding current trends in incidence, prevalence, and treatment of abused and neglected children and their families. Issues that are increasingly evident in society, such as domestic violence and substance abuse, the effects of which foster parents may directly observe by foster parents, also were areas of great interest.

The respondents also were interested in learning about various health care issues as they may affect foster care. Often children entering foster care have a history of inconsistent health treatment which foster parents must rectify. Interest areas noted in this study may reflect the situations that foster parents are increasingly seeing, such as mental illness in children, failure to thrive, and fetal alcohol syndrome.

Past methods of delivery of foster parent training fairly closely parallel how foster parents would like to continue receiving training. Foster parents indicated a preference for attending seminars sponsored by the agencies or foster parent associations over written materials or one-to-one contact with caseworker. The respondents seem willing to travel to central sites for training, such as foster parent association meetings. The meetings provide a good forum for training because they may be relatively close to the foster parents' homes as well as because the parents will likely be able to receive a concentrated number of training hours (possibly 3 to 6 hours). Agency-sponsored training also relieves foster parents from the responsibility of seeking out training sources. Additionally, training in group settings offers parents the opportunity to alleviate some of their isolation as rural foster parents and gain support from other foster parents. It is uncertain whether the Internet is a viable avenue for foster parent training. Interestingly, whereas 13 percent of the survey respondents have used the Internet in the past for training, 30 percent indicated an interest in using it as a resource in the future. As more people gain access to the Internet, Web-based instruction may assume greater importance as a method of delivery of training to rural foster parents. What is clear is that all methods of training delivery offer an outlet whereby foster parents can increase their knowledge.

Because more than one-half of the respondents indicated an interest in university seminars and courses, it may be useful for schools of social work at colleges and universities to form partnerships with local child protection agencies to offer such courses. Universities have a wealth of knowledge about child abuse and neglect and about specific issues, trends, and interventions that would be important to share with foster parents. Those in the academic arena also possess the expertise to provide this information in a usable format. Universities in rural areas are an invaluable resource to be tapped.

One of the major limitations of this study was its fairly low response rate. Since the survey was conducted, new information indicates that some people should not have been included because they were no longer serving as foster parents. Consequently, the response rate may have been higher than reported. Also, the foster parents who returned the survey may be those who in fact are most interested in receiving training. The low response rate and the targeted nature of this study, however, make it impossible to generalize from the findings. Results should therefore be interpreted with caution and be used only as indications of areas for continued research, one area of which would be to compare the responses of rural foster parents with their urban counterparts to determine whether perceived training needs differ.

CONCLUSIONS

Foster parents face increasing challenges in their day-to-day care of foster children. As a result, they are perhaps the best source for information on what the current problems are with children in out-of-home placements. Professionals need to solicit the input of foster parents to effectively address current issues in training curricula. Access to training, especially that based on the needs and interests of foster parents, must be provided through professional collaborative efforts in the child protection community. In rural areas, the particular barriers of isolation and distance mean that a variety of methods must be offered for foster parent training.

REFERENCES

Altshuler, S. J. (1997). A reveille for school social workers: Children in foster care need our help! *Social Work in Education, 19,* 121–127.

Children's Defense Fund. (1995). *The state of America's children yearbook 1995.* Washington, DC: Author.

Everett, J. E. (1995). Child foster care. In R. L. Edwards (Ed.-in-Chief), *Encyclopedia of social work* (19th ed., Vol. 3, pp. 375–379). Washington, DC: NASW Press.

George, R., Wulczyn, F., & Fanshel, D. (1994). A foster care research agenda for the '90s. *Child Welfare, 73,* 525–549.

Ginsberg, L. (1993). *Social work in rural communities* (2nd ed.). Alexandria, VA: Council on Social Work Education.

Gleeson, J. P. (1995). Kinship care and public child welfare: Challenges and opportunities for social work education. *Journal of Social Work Education, 31,* 182–193.

Gleeson, J. P., & Craig, L. C. (1994). Kinship care in child welfare: An analysis of states' policies. *Children and Youth Services Review, 16*(1/2), 7–31.

Hochstadt, N. J., Jaudes, P. K., Zimo, D. A., & Schachter, J. (1987). The medical and psychosocial needs of children entering foster care. *Child Abuse & Neglect, 11,* 53–62.

Molin, R. (1994). Foster families and larger systems: Image and identity. *Community Alternatives: International Journal of Family Care, 6,* 19–25.

Noble, L. S., & Euster, S. D. (1981). Foster parent input: A crucial element in training. *Child Welfare, 60,* 35–42.

Pasztor, E. M. (1985). Permanency planning and foster parenting: Implications for recruitment, selection, training, and retention. *Children and Youth Services Review, 7,* 191–205.

CHAPTER EIGHT

Family Violence in Rural Areas: Law Enforcement and Social Workers Working Together for Change

T. Laine Scales and H. Stephen Cooper

This chapter reports on an exploratory survey of law enforcement officers and social workers in a nonmetropolitan/rural area that set out to compare views and attitudes toward family violence interventions. The survey also explored views of each professional group toward the other. Results revealed that many stereotypes about each professional group prevail. Those stereotypes must be addressed in order for the two professional groups to cooperate in efforts to reduce rural family violence.

INTRODUCTION

In recent years, the issue of family violence has gained increasing attention from the media, law enforcement personnel, social workers, and both the U.S. Congress and state legislatures. Numerous studies have investigated aspects of family violence, such as the effects on the family and community, and common characteristics of the parties involved (Abel & Suth, 1987; Arthur, Sisson, & McClung, 1997; Burris & Jaffe, 1983; Buzwa & Buzwa, 1990; Davis, Hagen, & Early, 1994; Fein & Knaut, 1986; Holmes, 1982; Home, 1994; Parkinson, 1980; Powell, 1994; Schmidt & Sherman, 1993; Treger, 1980).

Four million women are victims of family violence each year, and one in every four women is likely to be abused by a partner within her lifetime (Dwyer, Smokowski, Bricout, & Wodarski, 1995). Also, more than 50 percent of married couples in the United States experience one or more episodes of family violence during their marriage (Dwyer et al., 1995). From these statistics, one may quickly conclude

This research project was partially funded by the Office of Research and Sponsored Programs, Stephen F. Austin State University, Nacogdoches, Texas.

that family violence is a major problem in our nation. Family violence in small towns and rural areas, however, has received little attention from researchers.

Cooperative programs involving law enforcement personnel and social workers have been successfully used in urban areas to combat the problem of family violence and to increase interaction between these two professional groups (Arthur, Sisson, & McClung, 1977; Fein & Knaut, 1986; Holmes, 1982; Powell, 1994). One notable educational effort, implemented in Greenville, North Carolina, attempted to increase social workers' and police officers' awareness and understanding of each other's values and methods of intervention (Powell, 1994). The program achieved this by conducting a three-day seminar for law enforcement officers and social workers, which was intended to help them learn to work together. The Hartford, Connecticut, Police Department (Fein & Knaut, 1986) implemented another successful program with an educational base. This program used cross-training of the two professional groups to increase their ability to work together to combat family violence.

These programs have not addressed the specific problems that are common in rural areas and small towns, such as decreased confidentiality; increased likelihood that the professional may hold long-time acquaintance or kinship with the parties involved in the violence; and the wide acceptance of paternal and traditional values, which often condone violence toward women. Along with those problems, members of families residing in small towns and rural communities who are experiencing violence often have to deal with chronic suffering, powerlessness, lack of alternatives, and society-induced distortions about roles and obligations. In addition, the trauma of family violence in small towns and rural areas is magnified by a lack of opportunities, a lack of community support and services, and geographic isolation (Olson, 1988).

As a result of a lack of adequate services for the people affected by rural family violence, social workers and law enforcement officers must engage in a cooperative response effort to decrease the rate of occurrence. For such an effort to be successful, social workers and law enforcement officers must understand the similarities and differences in their views and attitudes toward all aspects of family violence. They also must teach, recognize, and respect the views and values of the other profession.

As a beginning step in this process, an exploratory study was conducted to identify social workers' and law enforcement officers' differences in points of view. Part of the study involved comparing the responses of rural social workers and law enforcement officers to a family violence case scenario. In addition, the attitudes of each group of professionals toward one another were examined. The findings are being used to design a model educational program to prepare rural police officers and social workers to work together in addressing the rural family violence problem in the United States.

METHOD

Design

The study reported in this chapter used a two-group single-factor design to examine the attitudes of law enforcement officers and social workers toward one another and their attitudes toward different aspects of family violence. Specifically, the survey instrument examined opinions regarding the following seven topics:

1. the locus of responsibility for filing charges
2. the use of interventions other than arrest
3. the effects of the aggressor's gender upon the decision to intervene
4. the use of social workers in cases of family violence
5. professional characteristics
6. differences in values
7. judgments regarding willingness to work together.

The seven items listed above were the dependent variables in the study. They were measured both by quantitative analysis and a series of open-ended questions to provide further qualitative information.

Location of the Study

The study took place in Nacogdoches, Texas, which has an population of approximately 30,000. Nacogdoches is a small town in Northeast Texas, which is a predominately rural region. In contrast to the rest of the state, population density is low (50.2 residents per square mile compared with the state average of 65.6 residents per square mile). The nearest major metropolitan area (Houston) is approximately 130 miles away. The economic system of Nacogdoches relies heavily on agriculture, timber, and related industries. The above characteristics, when examined in the context of rurality as defined by Ginsberg (1993) and Coward (1992, as cited in Ginsberg, 1993) support the authors' decision to label Nacogdoches as a rural/nonmetropolitan town.

Participants and Procedures

Thirty-five officers of the City of Nacogdoches Police Department were given a copy of the survey instrument and were assured of confidentiality if they chose to participate. The officers were instructed that if they wished to participate, they should complete the survey and return it to the Patrol Captain. Fifteen of the law enforcement officers returned a completed survey. The group of responding officers included 14 men, one woman, nine patrol officers, and six patrol supervisors (including lieutenants, sergeants, and corporals). The officers were not required to participate, and they were not compensated.

The social work sample consisted of 70 social workers who were identified from the mailing list for all the licensed social workers residing in Nacogdoches County. The 70 social workers were each mailed a survey along with instructions asking them to complete it and return it using the included self-addressed stamped envelope. Sixteen of the social workers completed and returned the survey. The group of responding social workers consisted of five men, 10 women, eight Licensed Social Workers (LSW) holding a BSW, and eight licensed master social workers (LMSWs), each holding an MSW. As with the law enforcement officers, the social workers were not required to participate and were not compensated for their participation.

Research Questions

The study set out to answer the following five questions:

1. Do nonmetropolitan/rural social workers and law enforcement officers have different views regarding arrest, alternative interventions, gender of the aggressor, and the use of social workers for intervention in cases of family violence?
2. Do nonmetropolitan/rural social workers hold common stereotypes of law enforcement officers as punitive, pessimistic, and lacking in empathy?
3. Do nonmetropolitan/rural law enforcement officers hold common stereotypes of social workers as unable to separate their personal feelings from their job, as too empathetic, and as too idealistic?
4. Do nonmetropolitan/rural social workers and law enforcement officers believe that their values vary significantly from one another?
5. Do nonmetropolitan/rural social workers and law enforcement officers believe that they could work together to achieve a common goal?

Instrument

The survey instrument consisted of a scenario in which a law enforcement officer is dispatched to a family violence call. The officer arrives on the scene and gathers information that details the situation. The scenario included bodily injury occurring between married parties. After reading the scenario, both the social worker and the law enforcement officer respondents were asked to answer a series of questions regarding possible responses of the police officer. This was followed by five statements to which participants responded using a seven-point Likert-type scale, which ranged from "strongly agree" (a score of 1) to "strongly disagree" (a score of 7). The statements were as follows:

Social Workers

1. Police officers are not open to methods of intervention other than punishment.
2. Police officers lack the ability to utilize empathy in their interventions.
3. Police officers are too pessimistic.
4. The values of police officers vary significantly from those of social workers.
5. Police officers and social workers could never effectively work together to achieve a common goal.

Police Officers

1. Social workers are unable to do their job effectively without allowing their personal feelings to influence their decisions.
2. Social workers are too empathetic in their approach to intervention.
3. Social workers are too idealistic.
4. The values of social workers vary significantly from those of police officers.
5. Social workers and police officers could never effectively work together to achieve a common goal.

The above statements were designed to measure the views each group of respondents held toward the other profession, their perceived differences in professional values, and their views toward working with the other profession in achieving a common goal. The final portion of the instrument was open ended, and it asked respondents to describe, in three sentences or less, their views of the other profession.

RESULTS

The study used qualitative analysis to examine answers to the open-ended questions and statements that targeted the participants' attitudes toward family violence and the other profession. The themes identified were used to supplement the results of the quantitative analysis, which focused on the five statements that the participants were asked to rate using the seven-point scale. Results for the statements were obtained by calculating a mean score, by profession, for each question. Since the fourth and fifth statements were the same for both professions, responses were also subjected to a single-factor analysis of variance (ANOVA). Because of the small sample size, the data were analyzed using nonparametric tests, which indicated that the data pattern was consistent with those of a parametric test. Table 8-1 shows the results of the quantitative analysis of responses from social workers and law enforcement officers to the questions posed in the study.

Responses of Rural Law Enforcement Officers

The analysis of the law enforcement responses yielded some interesting results. As shown in Table 8-1, the mean for the first statement (4.50) indicates that law enforcement respondents somewhat agree that social workers are unable to perform their job without allowing their personal feelings to influence their decisions. The responses to the second statement ($\xi = 3.50$) suggest that law enforcement respondents believe that social workers are too empathetic in their interventions. The mean for statement three (3.27) conveyed the belief that law enforcement respondents view social workers as too idealistic. The responses to statement four ($\xi = 4.00$) indicated that law enforcement respondents agree there is a significant difference in the values of each profession. Finally, the mean for statement five (5.33) suggests that law enforcement officers may have some difficulty working with social workers toward the achievement of a common goal.

The law enforcement officers' responses to open-ended questions may explain some of the views expressed in the Likert scale ratings. The next sections provide a thematic summary of responses to two of the relevant questions.

Question 1

If you had immediate access to a social worker that could provide intervention, would you consider it as an alternative to arrest. Why or why not?

About one-half of the respondent police officers indicated that they would consider using a social worker and indicated that the worker might have some specialized skills such as counseling. Many respondents, however, including those who answered "yes" to the question, expressed doubts that they could reach a social worker immediately. A few respondents indicated a belief that social workers were idealistic in their views of how the situation should be handled and were uneducated about the law. One officer wrote:

No. Because what rare occasions you can possibly get a social worker to answer the phone, much less respond to a scene, they are only concerned with maintaining the family unit and are oblivious to Texas Penal Code . . . when is the last time ANY of them read the Penal Code?

Another respondent echoed this view of the idealistic social worker: "Most social workers I've dealt with lack a grasp of how real life has to be handled at times." Other respondents indicated that social workers may be useful, but their counseling should be used as a prevention of further violence rather than as an alternative to arrest.

Question 2

In your own words and in three sentences or less, please describe how you view social workers.

Responses to the final open-ended question supported the Likert scale responses concerning officers' views toward social workers, although four respondents did not answer the question. Several respondents used the words "idealistic" or "naive" in their descriptions; one said social workers "need to wake up to the real world." Several respondents again indicated frustrations that social workers do not respond immediately to crisis situations: "They [social workers] would be more effective if they would respond when need[ed]. As it stands, they tend to have an officer refer the situation to their hours, not the hours they are need[ed]." One officer indicated that because social workers are primarily women, "sometimes this may cloud their view toward the female side." Several suggested that social workers might ride with officers as part of their training. One officer noted, "I think many [social workers] need to experience life in the neighborhood with the people they service to see the root of the problem."

One officer expressed an opinion that the two professions could work together, noting that "social workers are a great asset and a great need for the police department. . . . A social worker and law enforcement official would make a great team." This response, however, was clearly a minority opinion among the law enforcement officers who responded to the survey.

RESPONSES OF RURAL SOCIAL WORKERS

The social workers' responses tended to be more optimistic than those of the law enforcement officers (see Table 8-1). The mean for statement one (5.44) showed some disagreement regarding the statement that law enforcement officers are not open to using interventions other than punishment. The second statement ($\xi = 5.63$) conveyed some disagreement with the statement that police officers lack the ability to be empathetic. Responses to statement three ($\xi = 5.13$) reflected social workers' tendency to disagree with the statement that law enforcement officers are too pessimistic. The mean for statement four (4.44) indicated that social worker respondents believe that a difference exists between the values of the two professions. Responses to the final statement ($\xi = 6.56$) reflected the social worker respondents' strong belief that the two professions could work together to achieve a common goal.

The open-ended questions reinforced the quantitative results: The social workers who responded to the survey were very positive about cooperating with police officers. Social workers were asked the following question:

Do you think the outcome of the situation could have been improved if the police officer had immediate access to a social worker? Why or why not?

Table 8-1

Results of Quantitative Analysis

Statement #	Social Workers		Law Enforcement Officers	
	Mean Score	SD	Mean Score	SD
1	5.44	.96	4.50	1.87
2	5.63	.81	3.50	1.65
3	5.13	1.20	3.27	1.87
4	4.44	1.50	4.00	1.93
5	6.56	.51	5.33	1.45

NOTE: The subjects responded to each question using a 7-point Likert-type scale; the higher the number, the greater the disagreement with the statement.

All the social workers who responded answered "yes" or "maybe," indicating that the skills of law enforcement officers and social workers could complement one another. Many respondents indicated that social workers would be more familiar with community resources and could make referrals. Social worker respondents also mentioned counseling and crisis intervention skills as being helpful.

One respondent noted how the roles of a police officer–social worker team might be divided: "The officer could concentrate on the protection and law enforcement while the social worker can focus on support and linking to resources." Another social worker respondent indicated that the roles depended on the officer's interpersonal skills, implying that if the officer had some counseling skills, he or she might be able to provide the same services as a social worker.

Although the social workers were optimistic about working with police officers, some of their comments, by portraying law enforcement officers as unfeeling and concerned mainly with punishment, indicated that the stereotypes prevail. For example, one police officer noted that "the social worker could have possibly talked to the [wife in the scenario]; the police officer may not have as much compassion or patience to deal with her." Another social worker stated, "The social worker could look at [the] whole picture and advise them on treatment to work through problems rather than just punishing them."

When asked to describe their views of police officers, social worker respondents provided overwhelmingly positive descriptions, using adjectives such as "brave," "supportive," "helpful," "caring," "empathetic," "role models," "heroes," "dedicated," "hardworking," "underpaid," "ethical," "polite," "tolerant," and "fair." Some social worker respondents reported positive experiences working with police officers. A few social workers, however, noted that a certain type of police officer may be "a bad apple" who may be apathetic and punitive. One social worker respondent who held a minority opinion said, "Police have a very limited view of domestic violence and lack training that would make them effective in these situations."

SUBSEQUENT ANALYSIS

Since statements four and five were the same for each profession, further tests were performed to analyze the data. A single-factor ANOVA for statement four found no significant difference between the two groups; $F(1, 29) = .50$, $p = .485$, $MS_E = 2.96$, meaning that both professions agree that a difference exists in their professional values. A second single-factor ANOVA found a significant difference in ratings for statement five; $F(1, 29) = 10.20$, $p < .05$, $MS_E = 1.15$, meaning that social workers disagreed with the statement more strongly than law enforcement officers did. A follow-up t test, which was adjusted for a lack of homogeneity in variance, indicated a significant difference: $t(1, 17.26) = 3.11$, $p < .05$.

INTERRELATIONSHIPS AMONG MEASURES

Although the sample size was not large enough to make inferences from observed correlations, bivariate correlations were examined among dependent measures.

Correlation data for social workers indicated that the law enforcement officer's empathy is important to cooperation: The stronger their belief that law enforcement officers lacked the ability to use empathy, the more likely social workers were to believe they could not work cooperatively with law enforcement officers. Results also suggest that responses to the first four statements were consistent with one another as well as with the fifth statement. The correlation analysis for the law enforcement officers indicated that the social workers' ability to separate personal feelings from duty is essential to cooperation. The stronger the belief that social workers could not separate their personal feelings from their job, the more likely the law enforcement officer was to agree that they could not work together in a cooperative effort. However, no significant correlation existed between statement five and the other statements, indicating hat the attitudes measured by statements two, three, and four may not have been the ones responsible for officers' pessimism toward working cooperatively with social workers.

DISCUSSION

Rural Law Enforcement Officers

The results of this study indicate that rural law enforcement officers who responded to the survey tend to believe that social workers are unable to separate their personal feelings from their work, that social workers are too empathetic and idealistic, and that social workers have different values from law enforcement officers. Law enforcement officers displayed a tendency to agree with the statement that the two professions could never work cooperatively to achieve a common goal.

It is worth noting that according to the correlation analysis, the research instrument may not have adequately addressed the source of the pessimism regarding cooperative efforts. Also, the standard deviations for each statement indicate that the officers are not all of one mind on these issues; rather, a wide variety of opinions exist. Written responses to the open-ended questions indicated that the attitudes may be a result of the officers' perceptions that social workers were naive, idealistic, inaccessible, unfamiliar with the Texas Penal Code, only concerned with family preservation, and unfamiliar with the environment in which their clients live.

What could be the source of the law enforcement officers' attitudes toward social workers, if they are not related to the topics addressed by this instrument? It appears that the officers were referring to the employees of Child Protective Service (CPS), which employs many workers who are not social work professionals, rather than considering only professional social workers. Child Protective Services (CPS) is probably the social service agency with which the rural law enforcement officers most often deal. Thus, the perception of inaccessibility of social workers could be related to the fact that CPS workers hold normal office hours and are on call through an 800 line when the office is closed. This topic warrants further investigation to clarify whom police officers see as social workers, the context of their contacts with CPS, and the systematic changes they think would be beneficial.

Rural Social Workers

The rural social workers who participated in this study tended to respond more positively to the idea of working cooperatively than did the rural law enforcement officers. The rural social workers' responses indicate that they tend to view law enforcement officers as being somewhat open to alternatives to arrest and able to use empathy in their interventions. However, the quantitative data point to a continuation of the stereotypes that law enforcement officers are too pessimistic and that there is a difference in the values of each profession. Although social workers perceived a difference in values, they felt strongly that the two professions could work together toward a common goal. Unlike law enforcement officers, the standard deviations for their responses indicated more uniformity in their attitudes. Why would the answers of the social workers be more positive than those of the law enforcement officers?

The social workers' responses to the open-ended questions indicated respect for law enforcement officers and of their obligation to protect the public. Some answers indicated an understanding of the stress of the law enforcement job and the unpleasant aspects that officers must experience. Several of the social workers commented that they could not do the job of a law enforcement officer. These statements indicate an understanding that law enforcement is a necessary component of our society and an empathetic understanding of why police officers may seem pessimistic and punitive.

IMPLICATIONS FOR AN EDUCATIONAL PROGRAM

Because family violence is widespread in small towns and rural communities and resources to deal with the problem are scarce, it important that professionals who are called upon to address the problem find ways to effectively work together. In many small towns and rural communities, the law enforcement personnel and social workers could be of significant help to each other if they could develop mutual respect and trust and find ways to collaborate. The purpose of this study was to gain information to aid in designing a cooperative program between rural social workers and law enforcement officers. To be effective, such a program must address the attitudes that law enforcement officers hold toward social workers, and vice versa.

The study's findings suggest that further investigation of rural law enforcement officers' attitudes toward social workers and toward a cooperative program is warranted. Future research should examine how law enforcement officers define "social worker," the context of their professional contacts, and the specific differences in attitudes among the rural officers. Those findings will help clarify the source of their attitudes toward social workers and target the areas of possible resistance to a cooperative program. Clarifying those issues is important: For the program to be effective, the professionals involved must believe that their individual concerns are addressed.

Rural social workers must understand that rural law enforcement officers often seem pessimistic and "jaded" because they deal with devastating social problems,

often without resources to alleviate them, which leads to frustration and low tolerance. For example, police officers frequently are expected to wear "hats" including
those of social worker, minister, psychologist, parent, athletic coach, employment
counselor, substance abuse prevention educator, and crime prevention counselor
(Rachlin, 1997). Yet, they are often not adequately trained to fulfill these roles.
Rural social workers also should be aware that rural police officers have a legal responsibility to quell the immediate problem and make sure that the parties involved
will be safe after they leave, which means that they must deal with family violence
right away. Social workers could assist by providing police with training in crisis intervention and making referrals as well as by setting up an assistance program for officers that would be accessible on a 24-hour basis.

Another important area to be addressed in designing a cooperative program is
the difference in values both groups of professionals perceive. The training curriculum must include a review of the specific differences in job responsibilities, policies, and laws for the two professions. The program should address similarities in values and goals in order to enhance the cooperative spirit. For example, police
officers are charged with protecting the public by enforcing the laws that are created
by society through its elected government. Police are thus both agents of the government and servants of the public. This dual role also is held by social workers, who
are often employed in government agencies and other public organizations. Social
workers in these agencies protect the public not by arrest but through empowerment, education, and advocacy. Both professions have the same obligation to protect the public; they just use different methods.

The above example indicates that the two professions have common goals and
interests that could be used to overcome the barriers that separate them. According
to Treger (1981), the barriers are differences in philosophy, preconceptions, dis-
trust, and uncertainty. It seems likely that those barriers could be overcome by education, which is exactly what was done in a model education program for police officers and social workers in Greenville, North Carolina. Realizing that most crisis
intervention training for law enforcement officers has been traditionally taught by
officers, the Greenville group used an interdisciplinary team composed of social
work faculty, criminal justice faculty, and others to teach a group of law enforcement
officers and social workers. Powell (1994) reported that during the session called
"Child Abuse and Domestic Violence" the police officers focused on punishment of
perpetrators, whereas social workers focused on rehabilitation of the parties involved. Powell states, "No resolution was found, but each side listened to the views
of others" (p. 30). The success of the Greenville program was apparent when one
social worker said, "I will never work with a police officer again with my old stereotypes; I know that he or she has feelings and frustrations just like me" (p. 32).

Although the Greenville educational program addressed barriers created by a
difference in professional views and philosophies (Powell, 1994), it does not appear
that barriers specific to rural areas were considered. The rural aspect of the problem is important because it has implications both for the educational and the intervention components of a cooperative program. Many rural families still adhere to
patriarchal values, which foster role expectations such as "stand by your man" and

"a woman's place is in the home" and beliefs that a woman cannot survive on her own (Olson, 1988). Failure to adhere to these expectations may lead to stigmatization and possible isolation of rural women from their natural support groups. The presence of "traditional family values" and stereotypes are thought to increase the likelihood of abuse and lower the chance that the victim will leave the relationship (Davis, Hagen, & Early, 1994). The tendency to remain in an abusive relationship also is increased by the lack of accessibility to shelters and services for family violence (Davis et al., 1994). Thus, an educational program must teach participants about the aspects of family violence that are unique to rural areas.

Once the educational component is implemented, plans for a joint intervention program may be developed. As noted above, this type of program has proven successful in urban environments. A program for rural professionals, however, must address areas of concern specific to rural and nonmetropolitan areas. For example, each of the following areas of concern may affect the problem of family violence: public transportation, employment and housing assistance, healthcare for women, family violence shelters, child care, community-based education and support, and counseling services. The program would also need to address rural family values, and role expectations, decreased confidentiality in dealing with cases, and the likelihood that the professional may be acquainted with or kin to the parties involved. If those areas were adequately addressed, a joint effort would help the two professions ensure the citizens' rights to equal protection, autonomy, empowerment, and self-determination. The program could be enhanced through including existing community programs, churches, civic groups, social clubs, and schools. The synthesis of those elements into a comprehensive program would strengthen the relationship between the two professions and ultimately enhance their ability to respond effectively to family violence in rural and nonmetropolitan communities.

CONCLUSION

Family violence is destroying U.S. families. The rural community, which prides itself on the preservation of family, is not immune to this blight. Rigid family roles, geographical barriers, and a lack of services exacerbate the problem in rural areas. To combat this problem, a multidisciplinary approach involving law enforcement personnel and social workers must be used. The success of such a program will depend on the identification and resolution of each professions' attitudes and concerns. Once they have been recognized, they can be addressed by education, which will foster a cooperative effort.

Although the small number of respondents in this exploratory study limits the extent to which results may be generalized, the initial data suggest that rural law enforcement officers are more resistant than rural social workers to working cooperatively to address family violence. It appears that this attitude stems from law enforcement officers' perceptions that social workers are inaccessible and that the two groups' values differ. Despite some genuine differences in values and approaches, the two professions share a common goal: to protect and serve society. This common goal is the key to developing a unified effort to alleviate the problem of family violence. As police departments become more community oriented and as rural areas continue to be confronted with shrinking resources and fewer services, an educational program to foster cooperation between rural social workers and law enforcement officers can benefit rural communities.

REFERENCES

Abel, E. M., & Suth, E. K. (1987). Use of police services by battered women. *Social Work, 32*, 526–528.

Arthur, G. L., Sisson, P. J., & McClung, C. E. (1997). Domestic disturbances—A major dilemma and how one major city is handling the problem. *Journal of Police Science and Administration, 5*, 421–429.

Burris, C. A., & Jaffe, P. (1983). Wife abuse as a crime: The impact of police laying charges. *Canadian Journal of Criminology, 25*, 309–318.

Buzwa, E. S., & Buzwa, C. G. (1990). *Domestic violence: The criminal justice response.* Newbury Park: Sage.

Davis, L. V., Hagen, J. L., and Early, T. J. (1994). Social services for battered women: Are they adequate, accessible, and appropriate? *Social Work, 39*, 695–704.

Dwyer, D. C., Smokowski, P. R., Bricout, J. C., & Wodarski, J. S. (1995). Domestic violence research: Theoretical and practice implications for social work. *Clinical Social Work Journal, 23*, 185–196.

Fein, E., & Knaut, S. A. (1986). Crisis intervention and support: Working with the police. *Social Casework: The Journal of Contemporary Social Work, 67*, 276–282.

Ginsberg, L. H. (1993). *Social work in rural communities* (2nd ed.). Alexandria, Virginia: Council on Social Work Education.

Holmes, S. A. (1982). A Detroit model to police–social work cooperation. *Social Casework: The Journal of Contemporary Social Work, 63*, 220–226.

Home, A. M. (1994). Attributing responsibility and assessing gravity in wife abuse situations: A comparative study of police and social workers. *Journal of Social Service Research, 19*, 67–84.

Olson, C. S. (1988). Blue Ridge blues: The problems and strengths of rural women. *Affilia, 3*, 5–17.

Parkinson, G. C. (1980). Cooperation between police and social workers: A neglected area of social work education. *Journal of Education for Social Work, 14*, 98–103.

Powell, J. Y. (1994). Mobilizing a school of social work faculty to provide interdisciplinary crisis intervention training for police officers and social workers. *Journal of Continuing Social Work Education, 6*(1), 28–32.

Rachlin, H. (1997). Creative community policing programs. *Law and Order: The Magazine for Police Management, 45*, 24–34.

Schmidt, J. D., & Sherman, L. W. (1993). Does arrest deter domestic family violence? *American Behavioral Scientist, 36*, 601–609.

Treger, H. (1980). Guideposts for community work in police–social work diversion. *Federal Probation, 44*, 3–8.

Treger, H. (1981). Police–social work cooperation: Problems and issues. *Social Casework: The Journal of Contemporary Social Work, 62*, 426–433.

SECTION IV

EXEMPLARY SERVICES AND PROGRAMS

The exemplary services and programs that the authors present in this section provide an overview of the innovative ways in which social workers and other human service practitioners are attempting to address social problems in rural communities and small towns. The authors have identified unique programs that target specific social problems; the programs can serve as models for social workers seeking resourceful and creative ways to help their communities

In chapter 9, Anna Scheyett and Thomas Fuhrman examined Carolina Alternatives (CA), a Medicaid 1914(b) public-sector capitated managed behavioral health care program for children in North Carolina. CA is a pilot program with 10 area program (single or multicounty catchment areas) participants. Scheyett and Fuhrman sorted the 10 participants into three groups: rural, urban, and mixed. The authors wanted to know whether (1) differences existed in how managed care provider networks developed in the three sites, (2) managed care had an impact on access to service, (3) actual services available to incorporate into a provider network in each area differed, and (4) differences existed in the total cost of care per client in the three sites. They concluded that a public-sector managed behavioral health care capitated model can be successful in rural areas.

Deborah Zuver, in chapter 10, describes the implementation of Project HOPE—a Federal Emergency Management Agency (FEMA)-funded crisis-counseling program in North Carolina. Project HOPE provided outreach services to residents of 18 diverse communities in the state during the nine-month recovery phase following a major hurricane in 1996. Project HOPE met the needs of a diverse population through the cooperation of many social service agencies and organizations. Furthermore, the author concludes, linkages were created and strengthened that opened new lines of communication and enhanced collaboration, which is ongoing.

In chapter 11, Ameda A. Manetta presents research conducted with a self-identified group of 44 rural suicide survivors. Responding to advertisements placed in two newspapers, people who knew a person who had completed suicide and were willing to complete a questionnaire were invited to telephone the researcher. Questionnaires were mailed to those respondents. Manetta's findings indicate that among the rural residents, no significant difference existed in their use of professional helpers compared with their use of a network of natural helpers.

Amelia C. Roberts, Smith Worth, and Raymond Kirk discuss in chapter 12 the use of an Enhanced Employee Assistance Program (EEAP) as a valuable resource and an innovative model to support welfare recipients who are entering the labor market and who are identified as having alcohol and drug problems that might interfere with their job performance. The authors provide an overview of the new welfare law, barriers facing recipients, special issues in rural communities, and the use of EEAPs to address alcohol and drug issues. They conclude by presenting a case example of an EEAP model in a rural community in North Carolina.

In chapter 13, Kenneth R. Wedel and Fran C. Butler present a detailed discussion of the Personal Responsibility and Work Opportunity Reconciliation Act of 1996 (PRWORA) and the resulting Temporary Assistance to Needy Families (TANF) program. The issue of transportation is critical to the success of this welfare reform effort because the lack of transportation is an obstacle to successful employment in rural areas. Because rural mass transit programs and funding sources are limited, the authors predict a heightened nationwide interest in addressing the transportation needs of welfare recipients.

In chapter 14, Judson H. Morris, Jr., and Lynne Clemmons Morris focus on the use of outdoor murals as community projects to create "walls of pride" for residents of four small eastern Washington state towns. The murals helped the residents of the towns to remember their roots, traditions, and connections. The authors analyzed the mural projects using a series of group interviews with town residents. The four group interviews focused on planning, designs, financing, painting, community involvement, decision making, time frames, and economic development.

In chapter 15, Anne-Linda Furstenberg and Denise Gammonley describe a program designed to supplement scarce mental health resources to meet the needs of older people with mental illness in rural areas. The program model emphasizes the natural abilities of competent and caring community members to help adult mental health consumers build the skills and motivation necessary for effective community functioning. Supportive supervision, directed at helping the companions solve problems that arise in work with their consumers, is critical for preventing burnout and ensuring long-term commitment of the companions to the program.

CHAPTER NINE

Managed Behavioral Health Care in a Rural Environment: Carolina Alternatives

Anna Scheyett and Thomas Fuhrman

Dramatic changes have occurred in the field of behavioral health care (formerly known as mental health and substance abuse services) in the past decade. Perhaps the most dramatic of these is the shift to the cost-containment strategy of managed care. Keigher (1995) defined managed care as "an alternative to fee for service [whereby] the financing and delivery of medical care are integrated through contracts . . . furnishing a comprehensive set of services to enrolled members, usually for a predetermined monthly premium" (p. 146). Managed care has developed primarily in urban areas, where integration of inpatient and outpatient services is geographically and fiscally feasible. Small towns and rural communities face a significant challenge in this shift from fee-for-service to managed care. As behavioral health care systems move to managed care as a way to contain costs, rural communities risk decreased access to care and the possibility that care will move further away from the local community. Preserving and strengthening small towns and rural communities' behavioral health care will require thoughtful design, implementation, and monitoring of managed behavioral health care systems.

PURPOSE OF STUDY

This study examines Carolina Alternatives, a Medicaid public-sector capitated managed behavioral health care program for children in North Carolina. In particular, the authors were interested in comparing rural, urban, and mixed rural–urban sites for Carolina Alternatives to answer the following questions:

- Were there differences in how managed care provider networks developed in the three types of sites?
- What was the impact of managed care on access to service in the three types of sites?

- Were there differences in service resource allocation patterns in the three types of sites as they worked to meet client needs in a managed care environment?
- Were there differences in total cost of care per client in the three types of sites?

BEHAVIORAL HEALTH CARE SERVICES IN RURAL AREAS

Behavioral health care is undergoing dramatic transformation in most locales, particularly in rural areas, where a unique set of needs must be addressed to adequately serve clients. Significant challenges exist in providing effective community behavioral health care services in rural areas. Rural behavioral health care systems have been described as overly costly, inefficient, and ineffective (Blank, Fox, Hargrove, & Turner, 1995). The primary issues in rural behavioral health care systems include limited availability of behavioral health care specialty services; geographic barriers to what are predominantly facility-based services; and excessive use of crisis services, which are more expensive than standard services.

Although the actual availability of behavioral health care specialty services in rural areas is difficult to determine (Office of Technology Assessment, 1990), the information available suggests that compared with urban and suburban areas, rural areas are less likely to have services (Shelton & Frank, 1995), that rural services are narrower in range (Grusky & Tierny, 1989), and that rural services are more poorly funded (Rohland & Rohrer, 1998). This decreased availability of specialty providers results in decreased utilization of behavioral health care services by rural populations (Lambert & Agger, 1994). The limited access to specialty providers in rural areas often is offset by primary care providers (Rost, Owen, Smith, & Smith, 1998). Primary care physicians, however, may not provide services that are as effective as those provided by specialists and may lack consensus with specialists on treatment choice, particularly antidepressant medication dosing (Wells, Katon, Rogers, & Camp, 1994).

Lack of transportation and long distances to facility-based care are significant barriers to behavioral health care services in rural areas (Blank, Fox, Hargrove, & Turner, 1995). Despite the rhetoric of the community mental health movement, much behavioral health care is still provided in office and facility settings, making services inaccessible for many rural populations. Comprehensive outreach and in-home services are not the norm; primary and secondary prevention are thereby limited, as are early intervention services, which could increase the efficiency and effectiveness of rural systems.

The lack of behavioral health care services in rural areas and barriers to their access result in an overutilization of crisis services (Sommers, 1989). Again, a lack of specialty providers exists, and local general hospital emergency rooms in rural areas are more likely than their urban counterparts to provide psychiatric care (Rost, Owen, Smith, & Smith, 1998; Shelton & Frank, 1995).

MANAGED BEHAVIORAL HEALTH CARE AND RURAL AREAS

Managed care is not new in this country or in rural areas; its origins can be traced both to "camp doctors" in mining towns, where miners contributed a fixed fee in return for guaranteed medical care (Ross, 1975), and to the prepaid group health plans of the 1930s (Bengen-Seltzer, 1995). Contemporary managed care is predominantly an urban phenomenon whereby employers have worked with insurers to contain health care costs. More recently, managed care has moved to the public sector, most notably through managed care waivers to contain the rapid rise in Medicaid costs. Behavioral health care has become part of the managed health care revolution. As of 1997, 43 states had some form of Medicaid managed behavioral health care waiver (Riley, 1997). Medicaid waivers are a strategy offered by the federal Health Care Finance Administration (HCFA) to provide individual states with an opportunity to develop managed care systems unique to their particular needs. The purpose is to allow states the greatest flexibility and control possible in addressing health care fiscal management and service provision. Although all waiver proposals must be approved by HCFA before implementation, it is assumed that states are in the best position to develop programs specific to and effective for their local needs.

In most rural areas, behavioral health care service use is limited, to a large extent, to public-sector services (Hargrove, Fox, Blank, & Eisenberg, 1995); the shift to managed public behavioral health care is thus particularly significant for rural populations. The creation of adequate provider networks with easy access to their services and the ability of rural areas to manage a managed care contract with a fixed amount of funding based on a per capita fee are significant issues.

Managed care technology may have significant limitations in rural areas, possibly resulting in ineffective or nonviable systems of care. Among the techniques used by managed care organizations to contain costs are the development of a provider network willing to accept a controlled and negotiated rate of reimbursement, careful control of access to such high-cost services as hospitalization and crisis care, and rapid response and access to low-cost services to prevent crises (Scheyett, 1997). As a result of limited specialty providers, high crisis-service utilization, and long distances to points of service, these technologies may be more difficult to implement in rural areas. Rural service networks do exist, but they are often linked with or are branches of urban care centers (Coburn & Mueller, 1995) and still face the challenge of providing timely access to necessary behavioral health care services.

At-risk capitated managed care systems (ones in which the managed care agency receives a fixed amount of funding, and agrees to provide all necessary care to a defined population for these funds) require a sufficiently large population base to generate an adequate pool of funds to operate a system of care. Sparsely populated rural areas may not be able to manage such risks; that is, as capitated systems allocate funds per capita, fewer covered lives may not provide for a sufficiently large fund to cover all client needs. Most state Medicaid programs employ primary care physicians as gatekeepers for specialty services in rural areas rather than fully capitated programs (Rural Policy Research Institute, 1995). Gatekeeping models, however, with their narrow focus on limiting access, may not be appropriate for rural populations that already underutilize behavioral health care services.

CAROLINA ALTERNATIVES

Carolina Alternatives is a Medicaid 1915(b) waiver (that is, a freedom of choice waiver) program begun in North Carolina in January 1994. It was designed as a capitated mental health and substance abuse service system serving Medicaid-eligible children under age 18. Unlike some state's Medicaid waivers, which allow participation by private, for-profit, managed care organizations, Carolina Alternatives is an exclusively publicly managed waiver. In other words, publicly administered agencies for mental health, developmental disabilities, and substance abuse (MH/DD/SA) services have carried out Carolina Alternative's managed care administrative functions. The North Carolina Division of Mental Health, Developmental Disabilities, and Substance Abuse Services (DMH/DD/SAS) entered into at-risk contracts (or contracts in which the agency will be "at risk" to provide all necessary care to a defined population for a fixed amount of funding) with public area authorities for mental health, developmental disabilities, and substance abuse services, called "area programs," which are local governmental authorities defined as single or multi-county catchment areas. For a monthly capitated payment per Medicaid-eligible enrollee, area programs coordinate, deliver, and fiscally manage covered mental health and substance abuse services for Medicaid-eligible children. North Carolina chose this managed care structure with the belief that "the use of the public system assures that accountability and decision-making will remain in the community, and that any savings generated through efficiencies and good management are reinvested into the local service system" (North Carolina Division of Medical Assistance, 1998, p. 3).

Services provided under the waiver include all mental health and substance abuse services in the State Medicaid plan previously paid for on a fee-for-service basis. Area programs are responsible for providing a single site for assessment, referral to providers, and care management to screen Medicaid-eligible children and determine medical necessity for behavioral health care services. In addition, they are required to have established a community-based behavioral health care delivery system that includes both in-house and external providers, offering clients a choice of providers whenever available and appropriate. Primary care physicians providing behavioral health care in their offices are excluded from the Carolina Alternatives network and are reimbursed through regular fee-for-service mechanisms.

Carolina Alternatives is a pilot program. The DMH/DD/SA has contracted with 40 public area authorities for area programs. Ten of the area programs were asked to participate initially in Carolina Alternatives, and the program was implemented in phases. Under Phase 1, which began in January 1994, only inpatient services were capitated. In Phase 2, which started in January 1996, the 10 area programs were capitated and at risk for all services.

In addition to the obvious goal of controlling Medicaid expenditures through managed care technologies, the specific goals of Carolina Alternatives include:

- increased access to behavioral health care services for Medicaid-eligible children,
- increased participation and cooperation among public and private providers through an expanded provider network, and

- provision of the most appropriate and least restrictive level of service to clients. (North Carolina Division of Medical Assistance, 1998)

To date, Carolina Alternatives has met those goals. By 1997, Medicaid expenditures in Carolina Alternatives sites were essentially flat, whereas expenditures in non–Carolina Alternatives sites had continued to increase. Carolina Alternatives increased access as measured by the penetration rate (that is, the number of eligible patients [known as "eligibles"] served divided by the total number of eligible people), which grew from 5.4 percent in 1992 to 8.5 percent in 1997. Resources shifted from inpatient to less restrictive community alternatives in Carolina Alternatives sites: 74 percent of dollars were spent on inpatient services in 1992, decreasing to 12 percent in 1997 (North Carolina Division of Medical Assistance, 1998).

METHOD

Design

To better understand the impact of managed behavioral health care, the authors conducted a retrospective, qualitative study of Carolina Alternatives. The authors sorted the 10 Carolina Alternatives pilot sites into three groups: rural, urban, and mixed (see below for definitions). Historical Carolina Alternatives performance data were used to compare the three groups and observe trends related to the research questions. In addition, the Carolina Alternatives coordinator at each site was interviewed.

Data Sources

The authors reviewed data from the following documents: the 1992 and 1996 clinical workload and performance reports, the 1997 Carolina Alternatives provider network quarterly report, and 1990 North Carolina census data. All data are for calendar years beginning January 1.

The clinical workload and performance reports are submitted regularly by Carolina Alternatives sites to the DMH/DD/SAS. They provide a quarterly and annual accounting of the average number of eligibles, the number of those eligibles actually using services, and the units of service provided for each type of service. All cost data included in this study are from 1992 or 1996. Although 1997 data have been collected, the state Carolina Alternatives office indicated that the 1997 data set is incomplete and not yet final. The 1996 data set is thus a more reliable source of information.

The Carolina Alternatives 1997 provider network quarterly report contained data for that year on the number of individual and agency contract providers by Carolina Alternatives site. Unfortunately, pre–Carolina Alternatives provider network data were not available, nor were these data collected within Carolina Alternatives until 1997.

Census data were drawn from the North Carolina State Data Center newsletter (North Carolina Office of State Planning, 1992). This newsletter distilled raw census data into urban and rural classifications by county. The questions asked during telephone interviews with Carolina Alternatives coordinators were as follows (the questionnaire was provided to the participants for their review in advance of the actual interview):

1. What strategy(ies) did you use when developing your provider network?
2. What sorts of challenges did you encounter as you went about building and maintaining a provider network?
3. What has been the best thing about creating a Provider Network?
4. What, if anything, would you change regarding this process?
5. How has your Crisis Services System changed as a result of the implementation of Carolina Alternatives?
6. What were the specific challenges you ran into as a result of being an urban versus rural area MH/DD/SAS program?

Subjects

All 10 of the Carolina Alternatives pilot site coordinators were invited to participate in the questionnaire portion of this study. A 70 percent response rate was realized; 75 percent of rural sites, 75 percent of mixed sites, and 50 percent of urban sites participated. Each telephone interview lasted approximately 35 to 45 minutes.

Definitions

Rural/Mixed/Urban

Using the North Carolina State Data Center definition of rural and urban (North Carolina Office of State Planning, 1992), the authors defined the three study groups as follows:

1. *Rural:* Each county within the catchment area is more than 55 percent rural.
2. *Mixed:* At least one county in the catchment area is more than 45 percent urban and the remaining counties are more than 55 percent rural.
3. *Urban:* At least one county in the catchment area is more than 45 percent urban and the total catchment area population is more than 65 percent urban.

Table 9-1 summarizes the rural/urban population distribution in the Carolina Alternatives sites.

Table 9-1

Rural/Urban Population Distribution in Carolina Alternatives Sites

Area MH/DD/SA Program	Counties in Area Program	Total Population 1990	Urban Population	% Urban	Rural Population	% Rural	Population in 1997
Rural 1	7	143,076	20,001	14.0	123,075	86.0	157,794
Rural 2	2	94,805	18,677	20.0	76,128	80.0	106,597
Rural 3	4	130,916	31,284	24.0	99,632	76.0	144,693
Rural 4	4	209,678	59,920	29.0	149,758	71.0	228,467
Mixed 1	3	162,790	67,741	42.0	95,044	58.0	187,565
Mixed 2	2	225,412	128,819	57.0	96,593	43.0	237,376
Mixed 3	4	221,626	107,642	49.0	113,984	51.0	244,083
Mixed 4	3	200,124	113,106	57.0	87,018	43.0	249,476
Urban 1	2	303,101	203,765	67.0	99,336	33.0	330,424
Urban 2	1	423,380	322,251	76.1	101,129	23.9	556,992

Service Categories

For this study, services provided under Carolina Alternatives were grouped into the following five categories:

1. *Inpatient Hospital:* 24-hour intensive treatment in a hospital setting.
2. *Intensive Services:* Includes day treatment or partial hospitalization and high-risk intervention–residential (HRI–R), a wrap-around service targeted to children with needs that require intensive service outside the child's home. (HRI–R services began in 1994.)
3. *Office Periodic:* Includes outpatient treatment, both individual and group, including counseling; psychotherapy; medication therapy; occupational, physical, and other specialized therapies; and collateral work with family members.
4. *Outreach Periodic:* Includes (a) case management and support; (b) client behavior intervention (a paraprofessional service for individuals with complex skill and behavioral needs begun in 1995); and (c) high-risk intervention–periodic (a community-based service begun in 1994 for children at risk of developing or exacerbating mental health, substance abuse, or developmental disability problems).
5. *Alternative Services:* Under the waiver, Carolina Alternatives sites could use a portion of capitated funds to provide alternatives to higher-cost and more restrictive services, such as transportation to appointments, basic supports (such as housing) to prevent family crises, and respite in the community to prevent the need for using institutions.

RESULTS

Provider Networks

A comparison of the composition of provider panels per thousand eligibles uncovered significant differences between groups (see Table 9-2). Differences were noted in the provider per one thousand eligibles ratio (P/E) for psychiatrists, other individual providers, residential treatment centers, and therapeutic homes. The mixed

Table 9-2

Providers Per Thousand Eligibles in Carolina Alternatives Network, 1997

Provider Type	Rural	Mixed	Urban
Psychiatrist	0.85	2.53	0.99
Other individual	7.14	12.05	4.70
Hospital	0.60	0.77	0.74
Residential treatment	0.60	0.79	0.18
Group home	0.58	0.31	0.58
Therapeutic home	1.43	5.09	0.33
Partial hospital	0.36	0.31	0.25

group had a psychiatrist P/E more than 2.5 times higher than either the rural or urban groups. The mixed group also had a P/E for individual providers 2.5 times higher than the urban group and 1.7 times higher than the rural group. The rural group's residential treatment P/E was 3.3 times higher and the mixed group's was 4 times higher than that of the urban group. Finally, the mixed group's P/E for therapeutic homes was 15.2 times higher and the rural group's was 4.3 times higher than that of the urban group.

Interestingly, although provider panel composition differed a great deal between the three groups, interviews with the seven responding Carolina Alternatives coordinators revealed many similarities between groups regarding network development and management. Coordinators described little variation in the manner in which they recruited providers and identified needs. Eighty-five percent used a combination of letters of invitation, questionnaires, and newspaper notices. One provider-rich mixed program was inundated with applicants without any recruitment. Coordinators used similar processes to identify the types of providers needed for their networks, including internal and community stakeholder feedback and historical service utilization data; some infrequently used services (for example, therapy for children who have been ritually abused) were developed on an "as needed" basis.

All groups reported some common challenges in provider network development. All indicated that they experienced difficulty finding sufficient residential treatment, particularly more intense, locked residential facilities. Culturally diverse network development was also a particular challenge for all three groups, which have significant Native American, Latino, and African American populations in their catchment areas. In addition to these similarities, some challenges were specific to rural groups and rural counties in mixed groups. Rural Carolina Alternatives coordinators reported a lack of behavioral health care specialists, intensive outpatient programs, and partial hospitalization programs within the catchment areas and a lack of inpatient providers within the catchment areas. Finally, transportation and access were problems at times, especially for patients in more remote areas. In general, solutions were viewed as adequate, although they were not perfect. Rural programs often used acute-care providers external to the area program. Care was closely managed while the patient was served in more urban settings; the lengths of stay were briefer, and the transition back to community support networks was more rapid than if the patient had been served in his or her own community. Transportation obstacles often were overcome using family or friends, community agency transportation, or capitated dollars for alternative services. Provider network challenges experienced by the mixed group revolved around a lack of providers in rural counties. Their solution was to increase in-home and outreach services and also to use capitated dollars for transportation.

Access to Services

A central question of this study was whether access to service, as measured by penetration rates, would increase in all three groups and whether it would increase at similar rates. A comparison of penetration rates in 1992 and 1996 revealed that rural, mixed, urban and non–Carolina Alternatives groups all increased (see Table 9-3). The increase was smallest for the rural group (26.3 percent); urban and non–Carolina Alternatives sites increased at similar rates (48.8 percent and 50 percent, respectively); and the mixed group increased the most (72.6 percent).

Carolina Alternatives coordinators were asked about their strategies to increase access to crisis services. Groups differed in their response. Rural coordinators reported using capitated dollars to significantly expand face-to-face crisis capacity after hours, whereas mixed group coordinators reported augmenting existing face-to-face capacity with more hospital diversion services. Urban coordinators reported that they expanded centralized crisis services to include the capacity for mobile outreach; that is, having crisis response staff who can go out into the community and respond at the site of the crisis.

Service Resource Allocation Patterns

How service patterns may have shifted in response to managed care and whether the shifts varied by group was another area of inquiry. The authors therefore looked at the dollars spent per service category in 1992 and 1996, as shown in Table 9-4. Because the total dollars spent increased in the four-year period, we also examined the percentage of total dollars spent in each service category to determine the focus and emphasis placed on different service types. The results are summarized in Table 9-5.

A dramatic shift in service resource allocation patterns can be seen in response to managed care. The percentage of total dollars spent on inpatient care decreased from a range of 64 percent to 70 percent in 1992 to a range of 5 percent to 20 percent in 1996 across the three groups. A concomitant increase occurred in other service categories, particularly in intensive services, outreach periodic services, and alternative services.

Differences in service resource allocation patterns under managed care can be seen between the three groups as well. Urban sites still spent 20 percent of their total dollars on inpatient services, compared with 9 percent in mixed sites and 5 per-

Table 9-3

Penetration Rates for Carolina Alternatives and Non–Carolina Alternatives Sites, 1992 and 1996

Group	1992 (%)	1996 (%)	% Increase
Rural	5.7	7.2	26.3
Mixed	6.2	10.7	72.6
Urban	4.1	6.1	48.8
Non–CA	4.0	6.0	50.0

Table 9-4

Service Resource Allocations for Carolina Alternatives Sites, 1992 and 1996 (dollars)

Service Category	Rural 1992	Rural 1996	Mixed 1992	Mixed 1996	Urban 1992	Urban 1996
Inpatient	3,136,084	589,963	4,786,720	2,580,587	3,099,780	1,900,353
Intensive	166,814	3,647,448	277,376	8,599,885	47,129	2,092,852
Office periodic	775,787	1,951,454	1,232,405	4,551,331	358,681	1,818,268
Outreach periodic	704,863	3,622,833	1,182,252	6,522,053	488,176	2,559,425
Alternate	0	3,173,693	0	5,051,006	0	1,356,502
Total	4,783,548	12,985,391	7,478,753	27,304,862	3,993,766	9,727,400

Table 9-5

Service Resource Allocation Patterns for Carolina Alternatives Sites, 1992 and 1996

	Percentage of Total Dollars Spent					
Service Category	Rural 1992	Rural 1996	Mixed 1992	Mixed 1996	Urban 1992	Urban 1996
Inpatient	66	5	64	9	78	20
Intensive	3	28	4	31	1	22
Office periodic	16	15	16	17	9	19
Outreach periodic	15	28	16	24	12	26
Alternate	0	24	0	18	0	14
Total	100	100	100	100	100	100

cent in rural sites. Conversely, urban sites spent 22 percent of their total dollars on intensive services, whereas rural (28 percent) and mixed (31 percent) groups spent higher proportions. Finally, rural sites spent a substantially higher percentage of their dollars on alternative services (24 percent) than did either mixed (18 percent) or urban (14 percent) sites.

Cost of Care

A final area of inquiry for this study involved an examination of the cost of care and how this changed under managed care for each of the three groups. Under Carolina Alternatives, area programs in all three groups were able to manage and contain their costs while remaining viable agencies. As seen in Table 9-6, before Carolina Alternatives the cost of care per client varied greatly among the three sites. In 1992 the cost of care per client in the rural group was much lower than for any other group and was 27 percent lower than in non–Carolina Alternatives sites. The mixed

Table 9-6

Average Cost of Care per Client in Carolina Alternatives and Non–Carolina Alternative Sites, 1992 and 1996

Group	1992 (dollars)	% Difference from Non–CA	1996 (dollars)	% Difference from Non–CA
Rural	2,282	−27	4,225	−19
Mixed	3,231	+3	4,885	−7
Urban	3,562	+13	4,174	−20
Non–CA	3,141	—	5,238	—

group had costs only 3 percent higher than non–Carolina Alternatives sites, while urban sites had costs 13 percent higher than non–Carolina Alternatives sites.

By 1996, after implementation of Carolina Alternatives, the cost of care per client had increased for all groups. This was to be expected, given inflation and the availability of new Medicaid-reimbursable services such as client behavior intervention and high-risk intervention. In 1996, however, the cost of care per client in all three Carolina Alternatives groups was lower than the non–Carolina Alternatives group: 19 percent lower for rural, 7 percent for mixed, and 20 percent for urban groups.

DISCUSSION AND CONCLUSION

In Carolina Alternatives all groups used similar strategies to develop provider networks, but their efforts resulted in very different compositions of provider panels. The data suggest that the urban area programs had the least-developed provider networks. With rapid access to inpatient settings, there may have been less incentive to develop residential alternatives. In addition, they reported that many local practitioners were not interested in being Medicaid providers and preferred to continue serving privately insured clients. The largest provider networks were developed in the mixed sites. Carolina Alternatives coordinators postulated that this situation was the result of a number of factors, including providers with less access to privately insured clients and area programs with assertive leadership in service continuum development. Rural area programs reported they had the most difficulty finding services within their catchment area, but compensated by contracting with services outside of the area and adding transportation, outreach, and other flexible services. Thus, although rural areas had the fewest providers in their areas, the flexibility of capitated dollars allowed them to build an adequate and responsive continuum of care.

It is significant that access to services increased in all three groups, even under the cost-containment pressures of managed care. The fact that penetration rates in the rural group did not increase as much as those in mixed, urban, or non–Carolina Alternatives sites is interesting and may indicate that the barriers to care in rural areas can hinder outreach more than in urban areas, even with the flexibility afforded by capitated dollars. It may be that rural areas can increase penetration rates more effectively under a fee-for-service system than under managed care, and that shifting to managed care will decelerate that process. This is an area for further study.

All groups reported that Carolina Alternatives was an opportunity to shift funds previously used for inpatient services to hospital diversion services and expansion of crisis services. As expected, transportation was cited as a challenge in all rural counties, in both rural and mixed groups. Flexible dollars allowed rural areas to provide some transportation as well as some creative supports (for example, paying for residential care that was not medically necessary so that a child could attend a needed partial hospital program for a few days) to prevent crises.

A dramatic shift was seen in service resource allocation patterns across all groups after implementation of Carolina Alternatives. The proportion of funds spent on inpatient care decreased, although urban areas, which have easy access to hospitals, spent more than the other two groups on this service. As might be expected, rural and mixed sites, having less inpatient access, used more intensive services for hospital diversion. Finally, rural sites compensated for many service limitations with creative use of alternative service dollars.

The cost of care was managed under Carolina Alternatives. Rural, urban, and mixed sites had a lower cost per client than non–Carolina Alternatives sites after full implementation of managed care. One concern about rural behavioral health care programs in managed care systems has been their fiscal viability in a capitated model with a small population base. All rural Carolina Alternatives sites remained financially sound, even under full risk.

Ironically, experts have noted that rural mental health services are underfunded, rather than too costly, and that rural populations are underserved (Rohland & Rohrer, 1998; Shelton & Frank, 1995,). This situation may explain the 1992 data, which showed that the rural group had a significantly lower cost of care per client than any other group. Under Carolina Alternatives, these costs increased a great deal, but they were still controlled and lower than costs in non–Carolina Alternatives sites.

This study demonstrates that a public-sector managed behavioral health care capitated model can be successful in rural areas. Costs of care can be controlled, and clients can be adequately served under this model. Crucial elements for success include access to intensive facilities in neighboring urban areas, including aggressive support and outreach and rapid return to the community, and flexible dollars for such alternative services as in-home services and transportation. One area of concern in rural managed behavioral health care is that of the penetration rate of services. This study suggests that rural penetration rates may not increase as rapidly under managed care as in fee-for-service environments and that rural areas' shifting to managed care may be slowing their penetration rate growth.

A significant positive finding regarding public-sector managed behavioral health care was seen across all groups when Carolina Alternatives coordinators were interviewed. In rural, as well as in mixed and urban sites, Carolina Alternatives coordinators strongly stated that the Carolina Alternatives model had improved the system of care, increasing both access and accountability. Across all groups, Carolina Alternatives was viewed as a catalyst for the development of a broad range of creative community-based services.

ACKNOWLEDGMENTS

The authors wish to thank the participating Carolina Alternatives coordinators for their significant input into this study: Bill Bailey, Glenda Brazell, Ron Gardner, June Kersey, Ralph Wright-Murphy, Anne Marie Lester and Vince Gallo. We are also indebted to Mike Schwartz at the DMH/DD/SA for his assistance in providing service utilization, provider panel, and cost data. Jim Nash was of great help with data organization and analysis. Finally, Amelia Roberts's editorial skills are greatly appreciated.

REFERENCES

Bengen-Seltzer, B. (1995). *Fourth generation managed behavioral health care: What does it look like?* Providence, RI: Manisses Communications.

Blank, M., Fox, J., Hargrove, D., & Turner, J. (1995). Critical issues in reforming rural mental health service delivery. *Community Mental Health Journal, 31,* 511–524.

Coburn, A., & Mueller, K. (1995). Legislative and policy strategies for supporting rural health network development: Lessons from the 103rd Congress. *Journal of Rural Health, 11,* 22–31.

Grusky, O., & Tierny, K. (1989). Evaluating the effectiveness of countrywide mental health care systems. *Community Mental Health Journal, 25,* 3–20.

Hargrove, D., Fox, J., Blank, M., & Eisenberg, M. (1995). Introduction to rural mental health theory and practice. *Community Mental Health Journal, 31,* 507–510.

Keigher, S. (1995). Managed care's silent seduction of America and the new politics of choice. *Health & Social Work, 20,* 146–150.

Lambert, D., & Agger, M. (1994). *Working paper #4: Access of rural Medicaid beneficiaries to mental health services.* Portland, ME: University of Southern Maine.

North Carolina Division of Medical Assistance. (1998). *1915(b) Waiver submission to the Health Care Financing Administration.* Raleigh, NC: Author.

North Carolina Office of State Planning. (1992). *North Carolina State Data Center Newsletter, 14,* 1–3.

Office of Technology Assessment. (1990). *Health care in rural America.* Washington, DC: Author.

Riley, T. (1997, January). *Medicaid directors' panel.* Paper presented at the Congress on Managed Medicaid and Medicare, Washington, DC.

Rohland, B., & Rohrer, J. (1998). County funding of mental health services in a rural state. *Psychiatric Services, 49,* 691–693.

Ross, M. (1975). Rural health care—Is prepayment a solution? *Public Health Reports, 90,* 239–240.

Rost, K., Owen, R., Smith, J., & Smith, G. (1998). Rural-urban differences in service use and course of illness in bipolar disorder. *Journal of Rural Health, 14,* 36–43.

Rural Policy Research Institute. (1995). *The effects of market-driven reform on rural health care delivery systems.* Paper for the House Rural Health Care Coalition. Washington, DC: Author.

Scheyett, A. (1997). *Making the transition to managed behavioral health care.* Milwaukee, WI: Families International.

Shelton, D., & Frank, R. (1995). Rural mental health coverage under health care reform. *Community Mental Health Journal, 31,* 539–552.

Sommers, I. (1989). Geographic location and mental health service utilization among the chronically mentally ill. *Community Mental Health Journal, 25,* 132–144.

Wells, K., Katon, W., Rogers, B., & Camp, P. (1994). Use of minor tranquilizers and antidepressant medications by depressed outpatients: Results from the medical outcomes study. *JAMA, 262,* 914–919.

CHAPTER TEN

A Crisis Intervention Program for Hurricane Fran Survivors in Rural North Carolina: Project HOPE

Deborah Zuver

On September 5, 1996, Hurricane Fran swept ashore in North Carolina. The storm and its aftermath devastated more than one-half of the state's counties and disrupted the lives of 3.4 million people.

In hard-hit beach areas, a number of communities were entirely destroyed. In areas farther north, where hurricanes seldom threaten, Hurricane Fran's heaviest rains resulted in widespread flooding throughout rural and urban areas. The eye of the hurricane collapsed over one county, producing deluges and historic flood levels that destroyed homes and rendered roads impassable for days. At least 400 flooded homes in a single county along the Neuse River displaced residents for an extended period of time; those with uninhabitable homes remained displaced for nearly a year. In many areas, destruction was compounded by tornadoes and a previous hurricane. The infrastructure was so damaged in one sparsely populated county that potable water was still being trucked in nearly seven months later.

Only one death resulted from Hurricane Fran, but much loss and suffering affected residents throughout all hurricane-damaged counties. Even in areas with less severe levels of destruction, people who were particularly vulnerable were left greatly in need of services. Many isolated, older adults were without power for days, producing a potentially life-threatening situation. People living in poor, rural areas had limited resources and scant access to helping services. Most children had no school for days or weeks, and once classes resumed, many were frightened and unable to concentrate. Non-English-speaking people were unable to understand information about recovery services, and members of the deaf community were without TTY or captioned news coverage. Many mental health consumers and medically fragile people were particularly affected when services, employment, and other aspects of their regular schedule were disrupted.

In the immediate aftermath of the storm, a range of agencies and organizations to ensure survival and safety provided relief services. The emergency services were withdrawn, however, after about two months, when the initial response period subsided. Survivors continued to need a wide range of services during the subsequent recovery phase. Their needs changed during this next phase and varied widely as individuals and communities worked toward achieving new forms of stability.

This chapter delineates the need for crisis counseling services several months after a disaster and describes how Project HOPE overcame the challenges inherent in providing such services.

THE NEED FOR LONG-TERM CRISIS COUNSELING

A long-term crisis-counseling program can support the process of adapting to the innumerable changes brought about by a disaster. Information, support, and awareness of available resources are critical during disaster recovery to assist survivors in developing a means of coping and to give themselves time to grieve. A community-based program that offers education and support services in a culturally acceptable manner aids emotional recovery (Substance Abuse and Mental Health Administration [SAMHSA], 1994). The communities as well as individuals benefit from such services as residents work together toward returning to previous levels of functioning.

Most victims of a disaster are normal people, who generally are capable of functioning well in everyday life. In the immediate aftermath of a disaster, people often are able to pull together effectively to help one another with basic needs. As disaster survivors begin to reconstruct their lives, however, emotional adjustment needs often surface in later phases of recovery. Once the initial severe stress caused by a disaster subsides, various indicators of emotional strain may begin to appear. Those signs can occur weeks or even months after the disaster and may include feelings of being overwhelmed, guilty, angry, lonely, and afraid. As stress builds in daily life, it is not unusual for survivors to experience denial, frustration, confusion, and even depression (SAMHSA, 1994). Survivors may find that they are unable to focus, have difficulty making decisions, or cry for "no apparent reason." In a misdirected attempt to cope, survivors may withdraw from others, become argumentative, or increase their use of substances. Such responses to a disaster are common, but they may not be understood as such by the survivor, who may simply note increased difficulty in coping with daily life.

It is particularly common for survivors not to recognize the link between stress-related symptoms and the disaster after some time has passed (SAMHSA, 1994). In fact, some secondary consequences may not even be recognized as stemming from the disaster. A family made homeless by the hurricane, for example, may find themselves living in cramped quarters with relatives for an extended period of time. The stress caused by this disruption can grow over the weeks, demanding strong coping skills that may not have been in place before the disaster.

After a disaster, people who lack or have limited coping strategies and support systems may be at particular risk for functioning poorly, such as the frail and elderly; adolescents and children who are under family, peer, or school pressure; active substance abusers or those in early recovery; and those who have a disability (SAMHSA, 1994). Most mental health consumers who are living in the community have the same capacity as the general population to rise to the occasion in the aftermath of a disaster. They should not require separate disaster recovery programs, but they may require specialized strategies for accessing the services they need (SAMHSA, 1996a).

Very young children may demonstrate a number of stress reactions, including regressive behaviors such as enuresis; elderly people tend to handle disaster stress more effectively than younger people (Webster, 1995). Some older adults tend to minimize the impact on their lives, for fear they will be perceived as unable to function independently. In addition, many older adults do not know how to access services if they have not previously done so.

Even when consequences are directly related to the disaster's destruction, such as job loss or home loss, survivors may have unrealistic expectations that they will be "back to normal" within a few weeks. Healing tends to actually take much longer. The six-month and, particularly, the one-year anniversaries of the disaster may trigger a reaction for survivors, who may be taken by surprise when strong feelings resurface (SAMHSA, 1994). This situation can be particularly true for people in areas with less pervasive destruction. In gratitude that their loss was minimal, some survivors have difficulty allowing themselves to grieve the loss that they did, in fact, experience. Such survivor guilt diminishes a person's ability to resume functioning at predisaster levels. Signs of stress need attention, or they may escalate to the point where long-term professional help is needed. A goal of long-term crisis counseling is to prevent such escalation through outreach and public education.

IMPLEMENTING PROJECT HOPE

Project HOPE (Helping Our People in Emergency) was a federally funded crisis counseling program that successfully provided outreach services to residents of 18 diverse North Carolina communities during the nine-month recovery phase. A grassroots, neighbor-to-neighbor approach was the single most important factor in effective service delivery. A well-designed training and strategizing process was arguably the most critical aspect of implementing the program, which in order to be effective had to be up and running in a timely manner (North Carolina Department of Health and Human Services Division of Mental Health/Developmental Disabilities/Substance Abuse [DMH/DD/SAS], 1997).

Project HOPE was funded by the Federal Emergency Management Agency (FEMA), which is best known for its immediate disaster response with shelter and funding after an area has been declared a disaster by the President. FEMA's response also has included crisis-counseling projects for nearly 25 years, although such programs are not as widely known. Crisis-counseling projects provide technical assistance and financial resources, so that added outreach services can be offered in recovering communities. For residents of the 18 North Carolina counties most severely affected by the storm, Project HOPE provided support, referrals, and public education.

Once a crisis-counseling project is approved, it is administered by the Center for Mental Health Services of the U.S. Department of Health and Human Services. In North Carolina, the DMH/DD/SAS coordinated the program. An immediate, short-term project served crisis-counseling needs in the early, two-month response phase of the disaster. Project HOPE provided the nine-month recovery phase program to the 10 area mental health programs that serve the 18 participating counties. Four state-administered projects that serve special needs populations were also included: Funds were provided to the Department of Public Instruction, to provide materials and support for school crisis teams; the North Carolina Mental Health Consumers' Organization, to provide peer counseling and support; Services for Deaf and Hard of Hearing, to provide information and support; and to CARE-LINE, the statewide information and referral phone line, to increase response capacity.

The main goals for Project HOPE were to educate the community about normal disaster reactions and the recovery process and to identify hurricane victims experiencing stress and assist them in accessing community resources in order to achieve predisaster levels of functioning. In this sense, Project HOPE was a prevention program. A secondary goal was to learn what may be helpful for communities in the event of future disasters (DMH/DD/SAS, 1997).

STRATEGIZING TO MEET DIVERSE NEEDS

A number of challenges exist in creating a program to address long-term disaster recovery needs. Project HOPE staff at some of the area mental health programs initially anticipated an overwhelming number of survivors suffering from post-traumatic stress disorder. Conversely, some staff felt that once basic needs had been met, counseling services would no longer be necessary. The first task, then, was to educate supervising staff about specific crisis counseling needs and how they differ from the traditional mental health services that the programs customarily provide.

After identifying the survivors in need, a major challenge lies in creating a delivery system that can effectively reach the residents to be served. The stigma attached to accessing such services can be a strong deterrent, even when need is great. Any association with mental health has a negative connotation for some members of the community. For those rural residents affected by Hurricane Fran who were inclined to seek out services, few had adequate information about existing community resources or how to access them.

A further challenge was identified among the agencies themselves. Community agencies in many areas do not have a history of collaboration with one another. Consequently, no system may be in place when the need for coordinating efforts arises after a disaster, a time when agency collaboration and coordination are particularly essential.

In small towns and rural areas, tightly knit communities tend to be particularly resistant to help from "outsiders." People in rural areas can feel misunderstood by outreach staff who may have (or are perceived to have) different norms, values, and politics than the community group. Moreover, outreach staff from outside the community may have difficulty locating people who need services and delivering those services in a culturally acceptable manner. Natural informal leaders within a given community, then, are best suited to serve a community that is recovering from a disaster. With training in disaster mental health and guidelines for designing a strategy, they are best equipped to reach survivors throughout the community (SAMHSA, 1994).

The cultural and economic diversity of the areas affected by Hurricane Fran was a major consideration in planning services. A large number of people who were affected lived in small towns and rural areas. Coastal fishing and tourist areas were affected, as well as inland agricultural areas. Disparity was noted in per capita income, racial make-up, and age. Poverty levels ranged from 8 percent to 24 percent. Many areas had large minority populations including African American and Hispanic residents; in one county, 68 percent of the population were American Indian. According to the 1990 census, 24 percent of the population in the affected areas were under age 18, and 12 percent were age 65 or older. Moreover, the effects and severity of storm damage varied from area to area (DMH/DD/SAS, 1997).

AN EFFECTIVE TRAINING PROCESS

With such a broad range of considerations, it would be difficult for coordinators to design a single strategy that could reach everyone in need of services. Moreover, research has shown that services are much less likely to be effective if they are imposed rather than derived from grassroots efforts (SAMHSA, 1994). For this reason, each area was given support in designing a specific approach to address the needs of that community; particular attention was given to cultural considerations.

The training process provided the structure for outreach staff to collaborate in creating a viable strategy. By the end of the two-week training and orientation period, staff had developed a profile of those in need and deliberated on how best to reach them.

Each of the 10 participating area mental health programs used paraprofessionals who were indigenous to the community. Local Project HOPE leaders either contracted with community agencies that were currently service providers or they directly hired temporary staff. Project HOPE funds did not cover salaries for existing mental health staff to ensure that services did not simply extend established mental health services.

A fundamental component of Project HOPE's implementation was the comprehensive and individualized training for outreach staff that was provided by state-level staff. Immediately after staff were hired, a two-week training and preparation period commenced at each of the 10 participating area mental health programs. By the end of this training period, local staff had designed their specific strategy to reach hurricane survivors in their communities. Follow-up meetings were held approximately one month later for additional problem solving and support. Teleconferences provided a format for staff from all 10 areas to be present to exchange information and ideas. An information sheet was compiled and distributed to outreach staff every few weeks to highlight innovative efforts and maintain momentum and a sense of collaboration among outreach staff.

Training sessions themselves were designed to do more than simply provide disaster outreach information. Through simulations, trainees were able to practice applying the outreach approach they were learning. Scenarios were enacted to simulate realistic situations that outreach staff were likely to encounter in the community. Such enactments allowed the paraprofessional staff to apply their newly learned skills in a workshop setting. The trainees practiced engaging "survivors" to tell their hurricane story and offering ideas for stress management and rehearsed talking with parents about children's disaster reactions and how to cope with them. Simulations also provided an opportunity to recognize when survivors' needs were beyond the scope of outreach staff and needed referral to a professional.

Simulations allowed trainees to explore ways to handle challenges before contacting actual hurricane survivors. From the staff who attempted to solve a survivor's every life problem to the staff who expressed helplessness to address even a single disaster-related problem, this preparation approach provided realistic practice opportunities. Staff could repeat a given scenario and try a different tactic or wording; staff enacting the survivor often reported gaining a more realistic sense of the survivor's needs and emotional state. In a few cases, simulations became somewhat diagnostic in terms of staff trainees who were themselves Hurricane Fran survivors and had their own need to seek additional support.

Initially, some staff members were frustrated to find that they were expected to tailor the program themselves to the specific needs and culture of a given area. They wanted to be provided with specific procedures from experts rather than given general guidelines. They responded well, however, when additional support was provided around planning and strategizing. In an activity used with some trainee groups, a "mythical" community was conceived with group input. Considerations included a breakdown of the community according to age, race, ability, economic level, available resources, and other factors. The group decided on the "damage" that was created by the storm and enumerated needs of its "residents." They then brainstormed ideas for providing services. The exercise seemed to provide momentum and the distance needed to gain perspective on their own community. Trainees then reassessed their own area's needs and resources. They were better able to think creatively and design a plan and timeline to effectively reach those in need of services.

Using an interactive style of learning throughout training and orientation had further positive benefits. With potentially stressful work of this nature, it was important to reduce the likelihood of "burnout" as much as possible. Giving staff the experience of interacting effectively with one another and offering mutual support laid the foundation for maintaining such support for the duration of the project. Moreover, this training approach modeled the collaboration that was advocated throughout Project HOPE's efforts.

RESULTS OF INNOVATIVE OUTREACH

Each of the 10 participating area mental health programs developed a specific strategy to provide services addressing the communities' specific needs. As described in the *Crisis Counseling, Regular Services Program FEMA–1134–DR–NC: Final Report,* staff adopted a nontraditional, creative, and resourceful stance that resulted in innovative ways to engage people (DMH/DD/SAS, 1997).

Project HOPE's success was measured by the number of survivors reached in each area through outreach efforts and public education. General demographics and information about the number of FEMA applications in each area provided a partial profile of the level of need and other considerations. Staff were required to document information about their contacts.

Project HOPE resulted in nearly 24,000 individual contacts. Of these, nearly 68 percent were members of minority groups, more than 18 percent were older adults, and 13 percent were children. A total of 529 schools were served, representing 330,133 students. The breakdown of those served is consistent with the demographics of those in need in the affected areas. A total of more than 96,000 residents were reached either individually or through group presentations. A range of printed materials was selected for distribution; more than 594,000 items were distributed through public education efforts. Materials included Spanish-language, low-literacy, and age-specific brochures and booklets (NCDMH/DD/SAS, 1997).

Specific examples of reaching survivors demonstrate the variety of strategies used by outreach staff to provide services to a diverse population in need. Many older adults were reached through the local Area Agency on Aging, which contracted with four participating area mental health programs. The elderly survivors were reached through churches, Meals on Wheels, caregiver meetings, and the media.

Young children were reached through extensive outreach at day care centers. This approach also proved to be an effective way to reach teachers and parents with information about children's disaster reactions and needs; after the interactive presentation, children were given a bag of related pamphlets and fact sheets to take home.

In some areas, Project HOPE staff became a familiar sight at malls, where people would pause, receive information, and have a chance to tell their story in a neighbor-to-neighbor interaction. Staff also attended county fairs, community events, and festivals. One staff member reported that she was often greeted as the Hurricane Lady; another was welcomed as Miss Hope.

A paraprofessional in one rural county was a retired postal worker. He enlisted former coworkers to visit homes from their rural routes with support and information. Spending time visiting country stores was an important way to contact people in a number of areas. Some areas conducted a door-to-door canvassing approach in especially hard-hit areas, leaving pamphlets if no one was home and returning to speak with the resident. In many rural areas, contact was made through Cooperative Extension, the Farm Bureau Extension Service, and church-related groups. One county was able to have information included in the water bill that was sent to all homes.

Some areas have a large Hispanic population. Catholic Social Services Hispanic Outreach was a contracting agency in one county and provided consultation in others. The organization contacted people at churches, in their homes, and at restaurants and laundromats. The state Hispanic ombudsman was an important resource. Spanish-language materials were distributed and public service announcements were aired on Spanish-language radio shows.

Outreach staff in one hard-hit county were concerned that school principals had discouraged addressing disaster issues in the classrooms. They concentrated their efforts on sending letters to principals and meeting with local educational committees, which resulted in widespread classroom dissemination of age-appropriate information by the conclusion of the project.

Special-needs populations were reached by strategies developed by four state-administered services. the Department of Public Instruction, the North Carolina Division of Services for Deaf and Hard of Hearing, North Carolina Mental Health Consumers Organization, and the North Carolina CARE-LINE Information and Referral Service.

The Department of Public Instruction served the disaster mental health needs of schools. The primary goal was to get disaster and recovery information into schools so that school personnel would be equipped to address the emotional concerns and stress-related symptoms of the students. Four workshops for teachers were presented with Tom Haizlip, PhD, chief of Psychiatry for Child and Adolescent Services at the University of North Carolina School of Medicine. Dr. Haizlip, an authority on childhood recovery from grief and disaster, is the co-author of *A Coloring Book After the Hurricane,* a booklet for parents and caregivers to use with young children (Corder & Haizlip, 1996). Another focus was to facilitate the process for schools to appoint a crisis liaison; nearly 75 percent of schools in the participating counties had a crisis liaison in place by the conclusion of Project HOPE.

The North Carolina Division of Services for Deaf and Hard of Hearing provided information and support to people with hearing impairments. Deaf, hard of hearing, and deafblind people often are not included in the full spectrum of information or services available to the general public, and this was the case in the initial disaster response. This omission caused confusion and isolation in addition to the safety risks that resulted. Members of the deaf community were hired and trained as Project HOPE paraprofessional outreach staff to provide information and counseling to groups and individuals.

The North Carolina Mental Health Consumers Organization offered peer-provided emotional support and information through the organization's support groups. Groups were provided with monthly workshops that focus on the life skills needed to manage stress and other disaster-related issues. They were able to discuss

frightening storm-related experiences in supportive group settings and normalize those feelings as separate from their mental health symptoms. The organization's efforts also provided a positive way to emotionally prepare for possible future
disasters.

The North Carolina CARE-LINE Information and Referral Service increased its
capacity to offer services to callers from all areas of the state. Printed disaster recovery information cards were developed and distributed in both English and Spanish.

LONG-TERM RESULTS

In addition to serving people, Project HOPE had a positive impact on communities.
As the community began to accept strong emotional reactions to disaster as normal,
the long-term impact of disaster and the remaining needs of survivors could be
addressed. Linkages were created or strengthened among local agencies and organizations. Newly opened lines of communication and strengthened collaboration
continue to benefit the community long after Project HOPE has concluded. In the
event of a future disaster, systems are now in place to expedite services, and an increased segment of the general public has a better and more realistic understanding of disaster stress and how to deal with it. Several area mental health program
staff in different sites commented that they felt a secondary benefit of Project HOPE
was the generation of a more positive attitude toward mental health. Perhaps the
stigma of mental illness has been diminished a bit, as disaster stress and other adjustment reactions became normalized in the eyes of the community.

CONCEPTS TO REMEMBER

Agency preparedness is vital to effective crisis counseling implementation in the
event of a disaster. In retrospect, a large portion of initial efforts through Project
HOPE went toward creating collaborative links that were needed to provide services.
The scope of this task varied from area to area.

Mental health centers would do well to review their understanding of and plans
for disaster response and recovery. The following fundamental concepts of disaster
mental health can serve as a reminder of the need for and scope of long-term crisis
counseling. In the event of a disaster, an understanding of the concepts can lay the
foundation toward creating procedures for a ready response to those survivors in
need of outreach.

- No one who sees a disaster is untouched by it.
- Most people pull together and function during and after a disaster, but their ef-
  fectiveness is diminished.
- Disaster stress and grief reactions are a normal response to an abnormal situation.
- Many emotional reactions of disaster survivors stem from problems of living
  brought about by the disaster.

- Disaster relief procedures have been called the "second disaster."
- Most people do not see themselves as needing mental health services following a disaster and will not seek such services.
- Survivors may reject disaster assistance of all types.
- Disaster mental health assistance is often more "practical" than "psychological" in nature.
- Disaster mental health services must be uniquely tailored to the communities they serve.
- Mental health staff need to set aside traditional methods, avoid the use of mental health labels, and use an active outreach approach to intervene successfully in disaster.
- Survivors respond to active interest and concern.
- Interventions must be appropriate to the phase of the disaster.
- Support systems are crucial to recovery.

A more comprehensive explanation of these concepts is provided in *Disaster Response and Recovery: A Handbook for Mental Health Professionals* (SAMHSA, 1994).

REFERENCES

Corder, B. F., & Haizlip, T. (1996). *A coloring book after the hurricane.* Raleigh, NC: North Carolina Department of Health and Human Services Division of Mental Health/Developmental Disabilities/ Substance Abuse Services.

North Carolina Department of Health and Human Services Division of Mental Health/ Developmental Disabilities/Substance Abuse Services. (1997). *Crisis counseling, regular services program, FEMA–1134–DR–NC: final report.* Raleigh, NC: Author.

Substance Abuse and Mental Health Services Administration. (1994). *Disaster response and recovery: A handbook for mental health professionals* (DHHS Publication No. 94–3010). Washington, DC: U.S. Government Printing Office.

Substance Abuse and Mental Health Services Administration. (1996a). *Responding to the needs of people with serious and persistent mental illness in times of major disaster* (DHHS Publication No. SMA 96–3077). Washington, DC: U.S. Government Printing Office.

Substance Abuse and Mental Health Services Administration. (1996b). *Training manual for human service workers in major disasters* (DHHS Publication No. 90–538). Washington, DC: U.S. Government Printing Office.

Webster, S. A. (1995). Disasters and disaster aid. In R. L. Edwards (Ed.-in-Chief), *Encyclopedia of social work* (19th ed., Vol. 3, pp. 761–771). Washington, DC: NASW Press.

FURTHER READING

Alameda County Mental Health Services. (1991). *How to help children after a disaster: A guidebook for teachers.* Oakland, CA: Federal Emergency Management Agency 219.

American Red Cross. (1991). *Disaster mental health provider's course* (ARC 3076A). Washington, DC: Author.

American Red Cross. (1991). *Disaster mental health services* (ARC 3050M). Washington, DC: Author.

California Department of Mental Health, National Institute of Mental Health, & Federal Emergency Management Agency. (1991). *Children and trauma: The school's response.* [Videotape]. Rockville, MD: National Institute of Mental Health, Center for Mental Health Services. (Available from Center for Mental Health Services, 5600 Fishers Lane, Room 16C–26, Rockville, MD 20857.)

DeWolfe, D. (1992). A guide to door-to-door outreach. In *Final report: Regular services grant, western Washington flood.* Seattle, WA: State of Washington Mental Health Division.

La Greca, A. (Ed.). (1993). *Helping children prepare for and cope with natural disasters: A manual for professionals working with elementary school children.* Miami: University of Miami Department of Psychology.

Myers, D. (1990). *Loma Prieta earthquake training manual.* Unpublished manuscript.

CHAPTER ELEVEN

Rural Suicide Survivors: An Exploration of Perceptions about Professional Support, Social Support, and Stigma

Ameda A. Manetta

It is well documented that talking with others in one's support network is a buffer against stress and contributes to emotional well-being (Reed & Greenwald, 1991). Confiding in others is extremely important when trauma or crisis, such as accidental death, homicide, or suicide, occurs (Pennebaker & O'Heeron, 1984). Interaction with support systems and the belief that there is someone to turn to helps survivors process the trauma and come to terms with an unanticipated death. Family care physicians and counselors often become confidants, as do family and friends. Yet little is known about the role of the professional and natural helpers of suicide survivors in small towns and rural communities.

The exact number of survivors is unknown; estimates are that at least six people are affected by the suicide of one person (Shneidman, 1972). Nationwide, the number of suicide survivors grows by approximately 180,000 each year, and more is known about survivors who live in cities than is known about survivors in rural areas. This chapter reports on research investigating suicide survivors' use of natural and professional supports in rural areas.

LITERATURE REVIEW

Depression

Successful adjustment to loss created by suicide is of major concern because suicide survivors often experience mental disorders (Wagenfeld, 1990) such as depression and are themselves at increased risk of suicide and suicidal behaviors (Lukas & Seiden, 1997). Reed (1993) described some characteristics of the adjustment process of survivors, including the following:

- The extent of grief is affected by the closeness of the survivor/victim relationship
- Gender differences exist in the adjustment process: male survivors tend to distance themselves from others, whereas female survivors seek support.
- Friendships are less stable than family ties after a suicide.

People react to death by suicide in different ways. Some people deny that suicide has affected them; they may say they are not bothered by the suicide, and they are not. Other people are not aware of and do not recognize the extent or source of their suffering. Acknowledging loss by being able to talk about a death from suicide is therapeutic for survivors. If the suicide is not talked about, emotional, mental, and physical problems may develop and continue for years (Moore & Freeman, 1995).

Depression is a common reaction to death from any cause and especially to death from suicide. Several links have been found that contribute to the extent of depression in survivors, including relationship to the deceased, length of time since the suicide, age of the victim, and closeness of the relationship. High rates of depression have been found in friends and acquaintances of persons who complete suicide. Brent and colleagues (1993) reported that 29 percent of adolescents who were exposed to suicide met the DSM–III diagnostic criteria for major depression. Faberow, Gallagher-Thompson, Gilewski, and Thompson (1992) conducted a longitudinal investigation of 100 suicide survivors. They found that $2\frac{1}{2}$ years after the suicide, survivors continued to report higher levels of depression when compared with spouses of natural death and a nonbereaved group. In a study on the survivor–victim attachment of 285 accidental deaths and 179 suicide deaths, Reed and Greenwald (1991) found that the age of the victim was significantly related to the self-esteem and amount of grief experienced by the survivors. In addition, they reported that the closeness of the relationship before death rather than whether the victim was a spouse or child was more significant with regard to the amount of distress felt by the survivor.

Professional Support Networks

In an effort to deal with traumatic events, survivors turn to both formal and informal networks. For rural suicide survivors, the formal helping network is composed of various professional services, including the primary care physician, counselors and other mental health professionals, and suicide or bereavement support groups. The use of support groups has been found to be beneficial for many survivors of suicide. Constantino and Bricker (1996) reported on 32 female (mean age = 43) spousal survivors of suicide who were assigned to one of two eight-week treatment groups. The first group, Bereavement Group Postvention, was designed to reduce depression and enhance social adjustment; the second group, Social Group Postvention, aimed to help survivors gain personal insight and behavioral change. Although they found no significant difference in outcomes between the two types of support groups, they did find that levels of depression decreased for both groups over the eight-week course of the treatment.

Gaffney, Jones, and Dunne-Maxim (1992) stated their belief that support groups for sibling survivors provide a secure place for children and adolescents to normalize their feelings regarding the death, including exploring their own thoughts of suicide. They stressed the need to encourage open communication among parents and siblings. The group setting also assists the adolescent in learning how to broach the subject of the suicide with their peers, who often feel that talking about the suicide may cause more trauma to the survivor and do not recognize the healing benefits of discussions.

Many school administrators oppose any suicide postvention because of their fear of contagion, or imitative suicidal behavior, in the rest of the adolescent populations. However, postvention, rather than denial of a suicide, is needed because providing information about the suicide is a vital first step to helping adolescents cope with the loss (Caplan, 1964; Mauk, Gibson, & Rodgers, 1994). Studies have found that students make better social and academic adjustments after receiving intervention in the schools (Sandor, Walker, & Sands, 1994). School counselors knowledgeable about the grief process following suicide can assist staff and students in sharing and dealing with their feelings surrounding the event.

Unfortunately in rural areas, those who seek professional help are often faced with a shortage of mental health resources and other similar local services (Bone, Cheers, & Hil, 1993; Whitener, 1996). Wagenfeld (1990), in his review of the research published in the past 20 years, reported that rural areas have higher rates of inadequate health care and services. In addition, compared with urban areas, small towns and rural areas tend to have fewer mental health centers, poorer quality of professional services, and less professionally prepared staff in the centers (Leaf, Brown, & Manderscheid, 1985). As previously stated, some suicide survivors develop major depression (Brent, 1994), yet many isolated small towns and rural areas do not have adequate facilities for people to receive inpatient psychiatric care (Goldsmith, Stiles, Wagenfeld, & Manderscheid, 1988). The facilities that are available are more likely to treat seriously mentally ill people. Thus, people who need help through the grieving process in order to avert development of long-term pathological grief are the least able to obtain the help they need.

Natural Support Networks

Following a suicide, many people turn to their natural support network. The natural support network in rural areas includes family, friends, neighbors, and clergy (Patterson, Memmott, Brennan, & Germain, 1993). Social support provided by a natural helping network has been assessed in many different ways, including measurement of instrumental and expressive support. Instrumental support measures focus on concrete events, such as running errands or providing transportation. Expressive support measures focus on abstract concepts, such as listening to another or just being there to show concern when a person is unhappy (Dean, Kolody,

Wood, & Ensel, 1989; Krause & Markides, 1990). Most suicide survivors need expressive rather than instrumental social support (Lukas & Seiden, 1997).

Most of the research on support from the natural network focuses on older people. Lee and Ishii-Kuntz (1988) studied the social interaction among 2,872 elderly people in Washington state. The marital status of the respondents did not significantly affect interaction with family or friends. Black (1985) found that perceptions of personal relationships with family, friends, and neighbors were significantly related to well-being among her sample of 48 elderly people. Morgan (1989) reported that 56 percent of the 41 participants in his study of social networks and widowhood expressed positive comments towards their friends, and 46 percent expressed positive comments toward their family. Only 20 percent, however, expressed any positive comments regarding nonspecific others (that is, regarding people in general, such as members of support groups, neighbors, friends of children or parents, doctors, ministers, bank tellers, car dealers, and so forth). Social support has also been shown to be a buffer against stress and depression for bereaved people (Krause & Markides, 1990).

Lowenberg (1988) stated that religious leaders should be included among natural helpers. Church leaders work to empower members of their congregations (Robbins, Chatterjee, & Canda, 1998), and religious affiliations contribute to psychological well-being and act as a buffer against stress (Ellison, 1991). To some people, however, suicide signifies a transgression against God or is a sin in the eyes of the church. Sin is then closely related to guilt and carries the implication that the survivor somehow should have been able to prevent this tragedy. As a result, people may be reluctant to consult with ministers or other clergy who might help them work through their guilt (Lowenberg, 1988).

Stigma

A rural lifestyle is often perceived as a healthy lifestyle. People are viewed as at one with nature, and the pace of life is generally less hectic than in urban areas. Life evolves around the seasons, which reflect a natural cycle of birth and death. As a result, life is often seen as sacred. When someone intentionally destroys life, the destruction goes against the traditional rural collective values. People in rural areas tend to be morally conservative (Martinez-Brawley, 1990). Given that social stigma exists toward suicide (Lazare, 1989), some people may lie about how a person died rather than say it was suicide. Range and Calhoun (1990) found that 44 percent of the college-student suicide survivors they studied lied about the cause of death. Other people just do not talk about a death by suicide, whereas they would had the death occurred in a different manner (Fraser, 1994). Stigma thus is present in the larger social environment and is sometimes self-imposed (Fraser, 1994).

A further stigma may occur for survivors: Not only the suicide but also feeling depressed about the suicide is stigmatized. The stereotype that rural living is an ideal way of life leads to the belief that less depression exists, therefore mental health services are not needed (Stallones, 1990). Depression, however, is the primary emotional reaction to suicide (Nelson & Frantz, 1996). Social stigma occurs from the insinuation that depression is a serious mental illness rather than a reaction to a sudden traumatic death. Consequently, people who are depressed fear that they will be labeled as crazy by others in their rural community. This fear is justified, according to Rost, Smith, and Taylor (1993), who found that rural people with depression felt the label associated with seeking mental health services, rather than the label of the mental health problem, was an even stronger deterrent to seeking help for treatable mental illness. The possibility of a mental illness diagnosis, in turn, prevents some rural people from seeking professional help after a suicide. Furthermore, the stigma may prevent people from reaching out to their natural helping network for assistance in coping with their loss.

Little research is available on the perceived availability and use either of professional helping networks or natural helping networks by rural suicide survivors (Patterson, Memmott, Brennan, & Germain, 1993). To add knowledge to this area, the author set out to identify the use of both formal and informal helping systems, as perceived by suicide survivors, by answering the following research questions:

1. Do rural residents who have survived a suicide of a relative/ friend/acquaintance experience depression?
2. Do rural residents who have survived a suicide of a relative/ friend/acquaintance express perceived stigma associated with the suicide?
3. Do rural survivors perceive the natural support network as being available to them?
4. Do rural suicide survivors use the natural helping network more often than the professional helping network?

METHOD

For the purpose of this research, rural is defined as a nonmetropolitan area with a population of less than 50,000 people (Daley & Avant, 1996). The criterion for inclusion in the study was self-identified suicide survivor, which was defined as any person who knew a person that had completed suicide. Participants for the study were self-selected in response to a newspaper advertisement that was placed in two rural newspapers and ran for two consecutive weeks. The advertisement invited people who knew someone who had completed suicide and who were willing to complete a questionnaire to telephone the researcher. Those who responded to the advertisements were mailed questionnaires. The questionnaire requested information on demographics and on the respondent's relationship to the person who completed suicide and included two measurement instruments (CES–D and SS–A) (see next section). The questionnaire also requested information on whether participants used the professional support network or the natural support network. Specifically, it asked whether the person talked with his or her primary care physician, consulted a mental health or other professional counselor, or attended a bereavement support group (that is, the professional support network). Questions concerning the natural helping network asked whether the person talked with his or her minister, family, friends, or neighbors. Participants completed the questionnaire and mailed it back to the researcher in an enclosed stamped envelope.

MEASUREMENT INSTRUMENTS

Two measurement instruments were used in the study. The first was the Center for Epidemiological Studies–Depressed Mood Scale (CES–D) (Radloff, 1977). The CES–D is a 20-item scale designed to measure current depression in the general population. The respondents are asked to indicate the number that best describes how they felt during the past week. The responses to these items are based on a four-point Likert-type scale (scored as 0 = rarely or none of the time; 1 = some or a little of the time; 2 = occasionally or a moderate amount of the time; and 3 = most or all of the time). The scores are added together to obtain a total score for each respondent. A predetermined arbitrary score is identified as the cutoff point, and people who score lower than the cutoff score are deemed to have less depression than people who score higher than the cutoff score. According to Fischer and Corcoran (1994), reports of the reliability of the scale show that it has an internal consistency alpha of .85 when used with the general population. This scale also has excellent concurrent validity and has the ability to distinguish between the general population and a psychiatric population. A small association with social desirability responses has been found (Fischer & Corcoran, 1994), but it does not appear to affect the utility of the scale.

The second measurement instrument was the Social Support Appraisals Scale (SS–A) (Fischer & Corcoran, 1994). SS–A is a 23-item self-appraisal scale that measures support. The respondents are asked to indicate the number that best describes statements about their relationships with family and friends. The responses to these items are based on a four-point Likert-type scale (scored as 1 = strongly agree; as 2 = agree; 3 = disagree; and four = strongly disagree). The scores are added together to obtain a total score for each respondent. A predetermined arbitrary score is identified as the cutoff point, and people who score higher than the cutoff score are deemed to have lower levels of perceived support than people who score lower than the cutoff score. According to Fischer and Corcoran (1994), the SS–A does not measure actual support, only the amount of support that others believe is available to them. Possible scores range from 23 to 92. The SS–A has a reported internal consistency that ranges from an alpha of .81 to .90. This scale has also shown validity and significant correlation with other measures of social support and psychological satisfaction.

Sixty-two questionnaires were mailed; of these, 47 were returned, for a response rate of 76 percent. Two questionnaires were not included in the analysis because the respondents lived in urban areas.

STUDY RESULTS

Table 11-1 provides demographic information about the respondents. Far more women than men responded (80 percent and 20 percent, respectively). The average participant was a 45-year-old married female with a university degree.

Suicide of an immediate family member (wife, husband, son, daughter, or parent) was reported by 51.1 percent ($n = 23$) of participants. An overwhelming number of people reported that the deceased used a gun as the method of suicide (66.7 percent, $n = 30$). Most survivors were close to the person who died (80 percent, $n = 36$).

CES–D

The reliability coefficient of the CES–D, based on 44 cases with scores ranging from 1 to 45, was alpha = .74. This alpha is lower than that reported by Radloff (1977) on the studies she conducted to test the reliability and validity of the scale. The mean

Table 11-1			
Demographic Information of Suicide Survivors ($N = 45$)			
	Mean	**SD**	**Range**
Age	45.0	13.1	21–72
Education	14.4	2.4	11–20
	n	%	
Gender			
Male	9	20.0	
Female	36	80.0	
Marital Status			
Married/common-law	25	55.6	
Divorced/separated	9	20.0	
Widow(er)	5	11.1	
Never married	6	13.3	
Race			
White American	43	95.6	
African American	1	2.2	
Other	1	2.2	
Religion			
Baptist	19	42.2	
Protestant	10	22.2	
Other*	9	20.0	
None	7	15.6	

*Includes Church of Christ, Jewish, Methodist, and Pentecostal.

CES–D score of the 44 cases was 20.8 (SD = 8.5). More than one-half of respondents (61.4 percent) reported low levels of depression (that is, scored 20 or less).

SS–A

The SS–A has been used with the CES–D in other studies (Vaux et al., 1986). In this study, the reliability coefficient of the SS–A, based on 43 cases with scores ranging from 23 to 76, was alpha = .94. Scores based on the 23 items ranged from 23 to 76. The cutoff score was 46, and scores higher than 46 indicate lower perceived levels of support. The mean score for this sample was 41.7 with an SD of 12.1 (N = 43). Most people (72.1 percent, n = 33) reported moderate to high levels of perceived support from family and friends.

Three subscales can be computed from the SS–A. "Family" and "nonspecific other" comprise eight questions and have a cutoff score of 16, whereas "friends" has seven questions and a cutoff score of 14. The mean scores for perceived support appear in Table 11-2. Most of the respondents (81.4 percent, n = 34) stated that they perceived their friends as more supportive than family (69.8 percent, n = 30) or nonspecific others (70.5 percent, n = 31).

High levels of depression were significantly correlated with low levels of perceived support from family ($r = .42$, $p < .005$) and others ($r = .40$, $p < .007$). There was no statistically significant finding between depression and perceived support of friends ($r = .13$, $p < .35$).

Stigma

Perceived stigma was measured by responses to three statements:

1. Others won't like me if they knew my relative/friend/acquaintance committed suicide.

Table 11-2

Perceived Social Support and Social Support Appraisal Scores

| | Perceived Support | | | | SS–A Score | | |
| | Yes | | No | | | | |
Variable	n	%	n	%	Cutoff Score	M	SD
Friends	35	81.4	9	18.6	14	12.3	3.7
Family	30	69.8	13	30.2	16	14.2	5.8
Nonspecific others	31	70.5	13	29.5	16	15.3	4.5

Table 11-3

Survivors' Use of Natural and Professional Networks (N = 45)

	n	%
*Natural Network**		
Family	27	60.0
Friends	29	64.4
Neighbor	2	4.4
Minister	0	0.0
No one	3	6.7
*Professional Network**		
Doctor	10	22.2
Mental Health Professional	16	35.6
Other Professional	8	17.8
Suicide Survivor Group	6	13.3
Other Bereavement Group	6	13.3

*Some respondents reported using more than one source of support; therefore the N totals more than the 45 cases in the sample.

2. I am ashamed to talk about the suicide.
3. Other people do not want me to talk about the suicide.

The three statements capture the feelings of the respondent. When measured together, the reliability coefficient was .74. The mean score was 9.0 (SD = 1.9). The cutoff score was 7 with a range of scores from 4 to 12. In spite of the high mean, only 16.3 percent (n = 7) perceived some type of stigma associated with the suicide. When the questions were measured separately, 17.8 percent (n = 8) stated they felt they would not be liked, 13.6 percent (n = 6) stated they were ashamed, and 48.8 percent (n = 21) stated that others did not want them to talk about the suicide. A fourth question was used as a control; it asked survivors if they felt their community was supportive at the time of the death, 76.7 percent (n = 33) responded yes.

Natural versus Professional Helping Network

Table 11-3 shows respondents' differences in utilization patterns of the natural versus the professional helping network. More respondents reported use of the natural helping network (86.7 percent, n = 39) than of the professional helping network (51.1 percent, n = 23). Some respondents talked with more than one person, and many respondents talked with people from both the natural and professional helping networks. Among those who used the natural helping network, friends were most often identified as the person talked to (65 percent, n = 29) and having no one to talk about the death was identified the least (7 percent, n = 3). One-third of the

Table 11-4

Spearman's r for Relationship Characteristics and Professional and Natural Helping Networks (N = 45)

	Professional Help	Natural Help
Gender	.29**	.45***
Marital status	.06	−.15
Relation to deceased	−.26*	−.03
Closeness to deceased	−.24	.18

*p < .10. ** p <.05. *** p < .00.

respondents (33.3 percent, n = 15) talked with both family and friends. A surprising finding was that none of the respondents reported talking with their minister. In the professional network, 35.6 percent (n = 16) stated that they talked with a mental health professional. Thirty percent talked with only one professional (n = 14), whereas 11 percent (n = 5) talked with three or more. No significant difference existed between the use of the natural helping network or the professional helping network (χ^2 = .88, p > .35).

A further comparison was made to identify survivors' characteristics that were associated with the use of the professional or natural helping network (see Table 11-4). Analysis was based on Spearman's r. Gender was significantly related to use of both networks (professional, r_s = .29, p < .05, and natural, r_s = .45, p < .00). Relationship to the deceased was significantly correlated with the use of the professional network (r_s = −.26, p < .08) but not with the natural network.

The time since death covered a wide range, from less than 1 year to 45 years. To determine whether the time since death contributed to the use of either network, this variable was condensed into two time periods (1 to 5 years and 6 years or more). Data were analyzed by comparing significance levels of the use of natural or professional helping networks and these two time periods. No significant differences were found.

DISCUSSION

The finding that most rural residents in the sample reported slightly elevated levels of depression may have been affected by their agreeing to participate in the study. Radloff (1977) stated that recent traumatic events affect the CES–D scores, and people who have been subjected to recent trauma have slightly higher scores. Agreeing to answer a questionnaire on the impact of suicide may bring back memories of the deceased, and these memories may cause elevated scores. Although the scores were higher than those that would normally be found in the general population, all respondents were reporting a negative life event, the suicide of a known person. In her comparison of three surveys, Radloff (1977) reported the CES–D scores for people who listed their marital status as separated were 16.83, 18.50, and 13.58. Thus, the depression scores in this study are comparable to the scores for people undergoing negative life events. Although the scores are relatively high, the scores are much lower than scores reported by people after receiving four weeks of treatment for psychiatric illness (Radloff, 1977).

The professional helping network was used less than the natural helping network. Even though previous studies (Bone et al., 1993; Whitener, 1996) indicate that fewer professional community resources are available in rural areas than in urban areas, this group of survivors was able to obtain professional help. The types of professional help the majority of survivors reported using were family care physicians and mental health professionals. It was not clear from the data why these two services were used the most; however, there are at least three plausible explanations. First, the majority of people who lose an immediate family member experience more trauma than those who lose an extended family member, friend, or acquaintance. More than 50 percent of respondents had lost an immediate family member. The negative correlation between distance in the relationship to the deceased and use of the professional network would support this explanation, because as the relationship to the deceased became more distant, the proportion of people who used the professional helping network decreased. Second, people in rural areas tend to turn to people they know and trust in times of stress. They often use the same family care physician for years; thus, it is likely that the physicians knew the deceased and were trusted by the survivors. Third, the survivors would have to seek the services of a mental health professional. In view of the fact that the respondents were a highly educated group of survivors, it seems likely that they would know which professionals to turn to and that they actively sought help from those professionals in working through their trauma.

The fact that no one spoke to a minister is an important finding. Social perceptions abound that many religions do not condone suicide. The rural church is commonly proclaimed to be the first place one can turn to in time of need, yet this group of suicide survivors did not consult their minister. Early and Akers (1993) stated that black pastors do not discuss suicide in their churches because they view suicide as "a white thing." Most of the respondents in this study were white, and although most identified a religious affiliation, they did not turn to that church for support. Those who did were met with rejection and felt that their ministers or pastors were not versed in how to counsel or listen to people who had lost a loved one to suicide. This finding warrants further inquiry.

The scores on the subscale regarding the perception that friends were perceived as more supportive than family or nonspecific others was consistent both with the finding that survivors talked with friends more often and with findings reported by other researchers. For example, Patterson and colleagues (1993) found that in rural areas, expressive support was given by friends more often than by relatives. Having people to talk with about the emotional turmoil that suicide survivors experience generally helps reduce feelings of helplessness, anger, guilt, and depression. Friends are at least one step removed from the death and may be less judgmental and more willing to listen than family members.

The findings reported here need to be interpreted cautiously for at least four reasons. First, respondents were self-selected, which limits the generalizability to other rural suicide survivors. Second, the study had a low number of participants. A larger sample would provide additional data on the variables under study, which in turn would be beneficial in differentiating the use of support networks. Third, the participants attained higher levels of education than would be found in the general population (most reporting having a minimum of a bachelor degree). Fourth, there was no control group. Further study is needed to compare the network use patterns. For example, suicide survivors could be compared with accidental death survivors in rural areas.

CONCLUSION

Many people who take their own lives are trying to escape unbearable psychic or physical pain. Yet, the act of suicide leaves a legacy of psychic pain for the survivors. Although researchers continue to search for links regarding the causes of suicide, suicide survivors often feel ignored by researchers. As one respondent stated, "I'm not in hiding and am glad that someone is taking a look at this issue." More research is needed on rural suicide survivors. Despite the belief that social changes may have deemed suicide more acceptable, the act of suicide continues to carry social stigma. Some rural ministers or pastors and professionals continue to stigmatize survivors and refuse to interact with them because of an act in which the survivor was not involved. As another survivor said "people need to realize 'it was not my fault,' it was his choice." Rural populations, including people in professional and natural helping networks, need education on the thoughts and feelings of people who are left behind as the result of a suicide. In their generalist capacity, social workers can use innovative pre- and postvention by conducting education seminars in rural churches, libraries, schools, rural mental health clinics and hospitals, and rural law enforcement agencies. Through education, social workers can build and strengthen the support networks of the at-risk population of suicide survivors.

REFERENCES

Black, M. (1985). Health and social support of older adults in the community. *Canadian Journal on Aging, 4,* 213–226.

Bone, R., Cheers, B., & Hil, R. (1993). Paradise lost: Young people's experience of rural life in the Whitsunday Shire. *Rural Society, 3*(4), 9–12.

Brent, D. A. (1994). Resolved: Several weeks of depressive symptoms after exposure to a friend's suicide is "Major Depressive Disorder." *Journal of the American Academy of Child and Adolescent Psychiatry, 33,* 582–584.

Brent, D. A., Perper, J. A., Moritz, G. M., Allman, C., Schweers, J., Roth, C., & Balach, L. (1993). Psychiatric sequelae to the loss of an adolescent peer to suicide. *Journal of the American Academy of Child and Adolescent Psychiatry, 32,* 509–517.

Caplan, G. (1964). *Principles of preventive psychiatry.* New York: Basic Books.

Constantino, R. E., & Bricker, P. L. (1996). Nursing postvention for spousal survivors of suicide. *Issues in Mental Health Nursing, 17,* 131–152.

Daley, M. R., & Avant, F. L. (1996, November). *Reconceptualizing rural social work practice.* Paper presented at the NASW National Conference, Cleveland, Ohio.

Dean, A., Kolody, B., Wood, P., & Ensel, W. M. (1989). Measuring the communication of social support from adult children. *Journal of Gerontology: Social Sciences, 44,* S71–S79.

Early, K. E., & Akers, R. L. (1993). "It's a white thing": An exploration of beliefs about suicide in the African American community. *Deviant Behavior, 14*(4), 277–296.

Ellison, C. G. (1991). Religious involvement and subjective well-being. *Journal of Health and Social Behavior, 32,* 80–99.

Faberow, N. L., Gallagher-Thompson, D., Gilewski, M., & Thompson, L. (1992). Changes in grief and mental health of bereaved spouses of older suicides. *Journal of Gerontology: Psychological Sciences, 47,* P357–P366.

Fischer, J., & Corcoran, K. (1994). *Measures for clinical practice: A sourcebook* (2nd ed.,Vol. 2). New York: Free Press.

Fraser, M. (1994). What about us? The legacy of suicide. *Rural Society, 4*(3/4), 7–10.

Gaffney, D. A., Jones, E. T., & Dunne-Maxim, K. (1992). Support groups for sibling suicide survivors. *Crisis, 13*(2), 76–81.

Goldsmith, H. F., Stiles, D. J., Wagenfeld, M. O., & Manderscheid, R. W. (1988, August). *Ecological patterns of inpatient mental health service availability in nonmetropolitan and metropolitan counties.* Paper presented to Rural Sociological Society, Athens, GA.

Krause, N., & Markides, K. (1990). Measuring social support among older adults. *International Journal on Aging and Human Development, 30,* 37–53.

Lazare, A. (1989). Bereavement and unresolved grief. In A. Lazare (Ed.), *Outpatient psychiatry: Diagnosis and treatment* (pp. 381–397). Baltimore: Williams & Wilkins.

Leaf, P., Brown, R. L., & Manderscheid, R. W. (1985). Federally funded CHMCs: The effects of period of initial funding and hospital affiliation. *Community Mental Health Journal, 21,* 145–155.

Lee, G. R., & Ishii-Kuntz, M. (1988). Social interaction, loneliness, and emotional well-being among the elderly. *Research on Aging, 9,* 459–482.

Lowenberg, F. M. (1988). *Religion and social work practice in contemporary American society.* New York: Columbia University Press.

Lukas, C., & Seiden, H. M. (1997). *Silent grief: Living in the wake of suicide.* Norvale, NJ: Jason Aronson.

Martinez-Brawley, E. E. (1990). *Perspectives on the small community: Humanistic views for practitioners.* Silver Spring, MD: National Association of Social Workers.

Mauk, G. W., Gibson, D. G., & Rodgers, P. L. (1994). Suicide postvention with adolescents: School consultation practices and issues. *Education and Treatment of Children, 17,* 468–483.

Moore, M. M., & Freeman, S. J. (1995). Counseling survivors of suicide: Implications for group postvention. *Journal for Specialists in Group Work, 20,* 40–47.

Morgan, D. L. (1989). Adjusting to widowhood: Do social networks really make it easier? *Gerontologist, 29,* 101–107.

Nelson, B. J., & Frantz, T. T. (1996). Family interactions of suicide survivors and survivors of non-suicidal death. *Omega, 33,* 131–146.

Patterson, S. L., Memmott, J. L., Brennan, E. M., & Germain, C. B. (1993). Patterns of natural helping in rural areas: Implications for social work research. In L. H. Ginsberg (Ed.), *Social Work in Rural Communities* (2nd ed., pp. 22–36). Alexandria, VA: Council on Social Work Education.

Pennebaker, J. W., & O'Heeron, R. C. (1984). Confiding in others and illness rate among spouses of suicide and accidental death victims. *Journal of Abnormal Psychology, 93,* 473–476.

Radloff, L. S. (1977). The CES–D scale: A self-report depression scale for research in the general population. *Applied Psychological Measurement, 1,* 385–401.

Range, L. M., & Calhoun, L. G. (1990). Community responses following suicide, homicide, and other deaths: The perspective of the bereaved. *Omega, 21,* 311–313.

Reed, M. D. (1993). Sudden death and bereavement outcomes: The impact of resources on grief symptomatology and detachment. *Suicide and Life-Threatening Behavior, 23,* 204–220.

Reed, M. D., & Greenwald, J. Y. (1991). Survivor–victim status, attachment, and sudden death bereavement. *Suicide and Life-Threatening Behavior, 21,* 385–401.

Robbins, S. P., Chatterjee, P., & Canda, E. R. (1998). *Contemporary human behavior theory: A critical perspective for social work.* Needham Heights, MA: Allyn & Bacon.

Rost, K., Smith, G. R., & Taylor J. L. (1993). Rural–urban differences in stigma and the use of care for depressive disorders. *Journal of Rural Health, 9,* 57–62.

Sandor, M. K., Walker, L. O., & Sands, D. (1994). Competence-building in adolescents, Part II: Community intervention for survivors of peer suicide. *Issues in Comprehensive Pediatric Nursing, 17,* 197–209.

Shneidman, E. S. (1972). Foreword. In A. C. Cain (Ed.), *Survivors of suicide* (pp. ix–xi). Springfield, IL: Charles C. Thomas.

Stallones, L. (1990). Suicide mortality among Kentucky farmers, 1979–1985. *Suicide and Life-Threatening Behavior, 20,* 156–163.

Vaux, A., Phillips, J., Holly, L., Thomson, B., Williams, D., & Stewart, D. (1986). The social support appraisals (SS–A) scale: Studies of reliability and validity. *American Journal of Community Psychology, 14,* 195–219.

Wagenfeld, M. O. (1990). Mental health and rural America: A decade review. *Journal of Rural Health, 6,* 507–522.

Whitener, L. (1996). Rural mental health care. *Journal of Rural Health, 12,* 235–239.

CHAPTER TWELVE

Enhanced Employee Assistance Program Services for Rural TANF Recipients

Amelia C. Roberts, Smith Worth, and Raymond Kirk

The new federal welfare reform law, Personal Responsibility and Work Opportunities Reconciliation Act (PRWORA) of 1996 (P.L. 104-193, 110 Stat. 2105), known in North Carolina as "Work First," mandates that welfare recipients enter the work force and become economically self-sufficient. Recent literature delineates numerous barriers that make it difficult for this population to find and keep jobs (Bush & Kraft, 1998; Young & Gardner, 1998). In small towns and rural areas, in which many of North Carolina's TANF recipients live, those barriers are more pronounced than in urban areas (Chasnoff & Burnison, 1994).

Because of the limited access of services and available programs that would facilitate enrollment into the work force, the focus on rapid entry into the work force presents additional challenges for Work First participants who are substance impaired and reside in rural communities. The 1995 North Carolina Household Telephone Survey of substance abuse prevalence found that 35 percent of the Work First population were at-risk for alcohol and drug problems throughout the state of North Carolina (North Carolina Department of Health and Human Services [NCD-HHS], 1996). Given that nearly 50 percent of North Carolina's residents live in rural areas, those estimates are alarming. Although policymakers recognize that employment is critical to breaking the cycle of dependency, they are increasingly aware that the fragmentation and lack of services create undue challenges and stresses for this population (Young & Gardner, 1998). The state of North Carolina Division of Mental Health, Developmental Disabilities, and Substance Abuse Services (DMH/DD/SAS), quickly recognizing the need for additional assistance to ensure labor force attachment and decrease relapse, has funded seven Employee Assistance Programs (EAP) with enhanced (EEAP) components to provide long-term support to this population.

This chapter suggests that whereas an EEAP can be a valuable resource and innovative model for both urban and rural counties, it has the potential to be of particular help in addressing the system gaps in small towns and rural communities.

The chapter first provides a brief overview of the new welfare law, barriers facing TANF participants, special issues in rural communities, and the use of EEAPs to address alcohol and drug issues. It then presents a case example of an EEAP model in a rural community, and discusses implications for policy.

NEW WELFARE-TO-WORK LAW

TANF is the nation's most recent attempt to help families who receive government resources become self-sufficient. When signed into law by President Clinton in August 1996, the law abolished existing welfare policy and dramatically changed the way in which welfare services are provided in this country. Before the TANF law, needy families were provided financial assistance through Aid to Families with Dependent Children (Social Security Act of 1935, Ch. 531, 49 Stat. 620), an open-ended federal entitlement program (with a state match) that had no time limits. In effect, the new law converts AFDC into a single capped entitlement to states. Although the eligible population remained essentially unchanged from previous policy (most recipients of benefits are single-parent families headed by women of child-bearing age), TANF emphasizes temporary support to families. The TANF program contains an explicit social contract between the government and the benefit recipients that requires transition off welfare within a specified time period. North Carolina's Work First program requires that this goal be reached within two years. This social contract is "enforced" through time limits on benefits. TANF is thus far more proscriptive than previous welfare policy and mandates labor force attachment.

Each state must develop a plan for the use of TANF funds. Though each plan is unique, the federal government has established certain expectations regarding work, which all states must meet. The expectations of work under TANF are twofold:

- Cash assistance is time limited, and it is expected that families will move toward work. States may not use federal funds to provide assistance to families who have received cash assistance for five cumulative years.
- Parents receiving cash assistance are expected to participate in work activities (including subsidized or unsubsidized work, training, or community service) 20 hours per week if the family is headed by a single parent, and 35 hours per week if the family is a two-parent family. Families that do not meet this expectation may have their cash assistance reduced through sanctions.

TANF RECIPIENTS: BARRIERS TO EMPLOYMENT

Several challenging and complex problems confront this population as they transition from welfare into the work force. Many TANF recipients will need assistance beyond what is specified in the TANF law. Among the barriers are the lack of child care and transportation resources, children with health or behavioral difficulties, family dysfunctional behaviors housing instability, past criminal histories, and domestic violence (Bush & Kraft, 1998; Pavetti & Duke, 1995; Quint, Fink, & Rowser, 1991; Urban Institute, 1998; Woolis, 1998; Young & Gardner, 1998). The most common barrier, which substantially contributes to the difficulty of obtaining and sustaining employment, is the lack of or low basic skills (Pavetti, 1993). The U.S. Department of Health and Human Services reported that 25 percent to 40 percent of TANF recipients have undiagnosed learning disabilities.

Psychological issues and mental health problems also impinge upon the ability of TANF recipients to perform adequately in the work force. Recent literature indicates that between 27 percent and 50 percent of TANF recipients are clinically depressed (Kelly, 1997). Moore, Zaslow, Coiro, and Miller (1996) reported that 42 percent of welfare recipients in Georgia had clinically significant levels of depression. Seventeen percent of participants in the Gain program (the California model of the Job Opportunity Basic Skills [JOBS] program) in Riverside, California, were deferred because they were identified as having substantial mental health or emotional difficulties (Maynard, 1995).

Additional problems encountered after participants enter the workplace include the lack of suitable clothing, the insensitivity of other employees and employers in addressing the needs of people in this group, the need for additional social support (Bush & Kraft, 1998), and the lack of awareness and understanding of workplace norms and culture (Rangarajan, 1996). All of these factors contribute to the difficulty in maintaining employment.

Many TANF recipients have significant problems with alcohol and other drugs that are likely to impair their ability to secure and maintain a job. The most recent estimates of the number of people receiving TANF who have an alcohol or drug problem that interferes with employment attainment and retention range from 5 percent (Strawn, 1997) to 16 percent to 37 percent (Center on Addiction and Substance Abuse at Columbia University [CASA], 1996) to 25 percent (Young & Gardner, 1998). Merrill (1994) reported that approximately 25 percent of recipients are so severely addicted that they cannot maintain employment. Additionally, Merrill reported that 20 percent of AFDC recipients have such severe alcohol or drug problems that they will require treatment before they can benefit from or engage in employment. Forty percent of the homeless TANF recipients are thought to have a problem with alcohol and drugs (Young & Gardner, 1998).

Obtaining accurate estimates is difficult because many states (approximately 40 percent) currently do not screen or assess TANF recipients for alcohol and drug problems. The underidentification of women substance abusers by professionals (for example, physicians, social workers, EAP counselors) (Beckman, 1994; Pape, 1993), the under-reporting that occurs in surveys and personal interviews because of possible stigma and judgment, and the diverse operationalization of the problem of alcohol and drug misuse also contribute to the underestimation of this problem (DHHS, 1994).

TANF RECIPIENTS IN NORTH CAROLINA

The evaluators of North Carolina's Work First program report approximately 80,000 TANF recipients in the state. Of this number, about 20,000 are "child only" cases, leaving about 60,000 "adult head-of-household" cases (personal communication with D. K. Orthner, associate professor, May 21, 1998).[1] The North Carolina Division of Substance Abuse Services estimates that 35 percent of those families (about 21,000 heads of household) have a problem with alcohol or other drugs that will interfere with their ability to move off welfare.

Orthner (1995) reported that nine out of 10 of the families are single parent, primarily female-headed households. The demographic characteristics reveal that the median age is 27, that 88 percent are female, that 70 percent are nonwhite, and that the median number of children is two. Work First recipients indicated that they are not satisfied with their life (46 percent) and the large majority (82 percent) are dissatisfied with the status of being on welfare (Orthner, 1995). Seventy-five percent worked full time in the past, but 65 percent lacked basic literacy skills or a high school diploma. Transportation is a major problem: Many recipients (42 percent) do not have a valid driver's license, and 62 percent do not have a personal vehicle.

PARTICULAR ISSUES IN RURAL COMMUNITIES

Rural communities are unique and challenging. The myth that all rural communities are the same must be disabused, for there is great diversity in ethnicity, cultural traditions, economic structures, types of available jobs, mores and values regarding alcohol or drug use, and divergent histories of discrimination and disadvantage (Wagenfeld, Murray, Mofatt, & DeBryn, 1994). Yet, several areas of similarity exist, which include sparsely populated areas with great distances between clients and services, fewer formal resources (Davenport & Davenport, 1995), inadequate transportation and communication infrastructures (Davenport & Davenport), and a lack of available professionals to provide services (Ginsberg, 1995). The required essentials for providing services that will be embraced by the rural community indicate that professionals must be aware of cultural values and community preferences and must be more creative and use more collaborative contacts than their urban counterparts (Bushy, 1997; Riggs & Kugel, 1976).

Although relatively little research has taken place on alcohol and drug use in rural communities, the 1993 *Monitoring the Future* survey (Johnston, O'Malley, & Bachman, 1994) indicated that nonmetropolitan youths were not substantially different from metropolitan youths in stimulant, barbiturate, tranquilizer, and alcohol use. Chasnoff and Burnison (1994) studied service needs and prevalence of substance abuse among pregnant women in North Carolina and found that 17 percent of the urinalysis toxicologies conducted in the rural areas of the state were positive

---

[1] "Child only" cases are cases in which the parent is not the designated payee and the child is in the care of a relative or nonrelative (that is, the care of a foster care provider or foster parent). "Adult head-of-household" means that the parent of the child is the designated payee.

for illicit drugs, three times higher than the positive rates for women in urban areas (5.9 percent). The rate of cocaine use in rural areas is eight times higher than the urban population (Chasnoff & Burnison, 1994). Other drug-use rates are similar in the two areas (Chasnoff & Burnison). The information gleaned from the 1993 *Monitoring the Future* survey and from Chasnoff and Burnison's findings about the higher prevalence of drug use in rural areas among low-income pregnant women may reflect greater problems in rural communities.

Many Work First participants entering the workforce, some for the first time, will experience a great deal of anxiety and stress. This new experience, coupled with the various barriers that must be addressed, has the potential to create chronic stress or, certainly, daily impediments for them and their families. Both chronic stressors and daily hassles are associated with higher levels of substance use (Moos, Brennan, Fondacaro, & Moos, 1990). Without additional and sustained assistance, these TANF participants are likely to cope with stressors through increased use of substances and thereby repeat the failure of previous attempts at welfare reform, during which 40 percent to 50 percent of recipients returned to welfare within one year (Rangarajan, 1996). This finding from the earlier welfare reform literature has ominous and serious implications for the current TANF populations because of the time-limited nature of the "reform" (Rangarajan). Substance use in the workplace could be a catalyst for premature job loss among TANF populations.

ALCOHOL AND DRUG USE IN THE WORKPLACE

The impact of substance misuse and abuse in the workplace gained national attention in the 1980s, when President Reagan issued an executive order to eradicate drug use among federal employees in 1986. The Federal Drug Free Workplace Act of 1988 required private employers with substantial government contracts to initiate and increase efforts to bring about a drug-free workplace (Tompkins, 1991). Alcohol and drug use in the workplace has serious direct and indirect negative consequences for both employers and employees (Gust, Crouch, & Walsh, 1991). Substance use interferes with employee job performance and contributes to workplace accidents and injuries, decreased productivity, absenteeism, involuntary job separation, additional health care and mental health costs, theft, loss of trained personnel, and costs associated with workers' compensation (Kopstein & Gfroerer, 1991; Lehman & Simpson, 1991; Tompkins, 1991). Hoffmann, Larison, and Sanderson (1997) found that workers who used illicit substances had more unexcused absences and voluntarily ended their employment or were terminated; some had held as many as three different jobs during that year. Substance abuse costs business approximately 140 billion dollars a year as a result of increased absenteeism, medical and health claims, and workplace accidents (Drug Strategies, 1996).

Substantial empirical evidence demonstrates that providing treatment to workers with alcohol and other drug problems is cost effective (CASA, 1996). In California, the benefits of treatment exceeded the costs and consequences of the misuse of alcohol and drugs (California Department of Alcohol and Drug Programs, 1994). The National Opinion Research Center and Research Triangle Institute

(1996) substantiated that treatment results in the reduction of alcohol and drug use, criminal activity, and risk of HIV/AIDS. Improvement in employment productivity, income, housing, and physical and mental health are also reported (Gerstein, Johnson, & Larison, 1997). The broad and powerful impact of substance abuse suggests the need for an innovative strategy of combining substance abuse treatment with comprehensive and unified services to TANF recipients who have been identified as having a substance abuse problem. Employee Assistance Programs (EAPs) may be an important solution in providing the additional supports that will be required for the TANF population to ensure success in the workplace.

EAPs

EAPs are employer-sponsored benefit programs primarily designed to identify problems early and implement intervention strategies for employees having difficulties performing their jobs (Hartwell et al., 1994; McCloskey, 1995; Roman & Blum, 1986). EAPs recognize that employees are the company's greatest resource, and their mission is to provide confidential assistance for employees and their dependents. Originally developed to help maximize recovery of employees who sought treatment for substance abuse, EAPs have grown to respond to numerous other personal issues that affect job performance. Frequently encountered problems include stress management, family and child concerns, depression, financial difficulties, health concerns, grief and loss, and legal difficulties (Goodwin, Geary, Meisel, & Chandler, 1997; Murck & Kamp, 1995). The referral (by self or others) of employees who are misusing substances continues to be the service most frequently used by businesses who have an EAP. Common practices of EAPs include developing an assessment and action plan, which may include referral services to community agencies and follow-up contacts. EAPs also provide training to assist supervisors in identifying performance problems and making early interventions (Mueller, 1996).

EAPs are recognized for their successful identification and treatment of those in the workplace who are misusing and abusing substances (McDonnell Douglas Corporation & Alexander and Alexander Consulting Group, 1990; Roman & Blum, 1986); for their contribution to increased performance and productivity (Trice & Schonbrunn, 1981), reduced tardiness and absenteeism (Amaral, 1998), higher retention rates and reduced health insurance costs (Bruhnsen, 1994; McDonnell Douglas Corporation & Alexander and Alexander Consulting Group, 1990; Oher, 1995). For every dollar invested in an EAP, employers save $5 to $17 (Normand, Lempert, & O'Brien, 1994). Amaral (1998) speculated that the positive outcomes of EAP result from rigorous client monitoring programs and the leverage offered by job retention.

Although the literature generally portrays EAPs as successful, success has not been conclusively demonstrated through the use of rigorous methodologies (Blum & Roman, 1995; French, Zarkin, Bray, & Hartwell, 1995). The lack of controlled studies and methodologically weak research designs are cited as the reasons for the lack of definitive findings (Blum & Roman, 1995). Studies have consisted of single-group pretests and posttests with no control group (Kurtz, Googins, & Howard, 1984; Walker & Shain, 1983).

NORTH CAROLINA EEAP MODEL

The EEAP is an innovative model unique to North Carolina that expands traditional EAP services. The program provides support to Work First participants who are identified as having problems with the misuse of alcohol and drugs that might interfere with their job performance. The North Carolina DMH/DD/SAS has a particular concern for assisting the Work First participants throughout the state; in addition, the department has a strong commitment to address the unique needs and challenges in the state's small rural communities. The EEAP model provides services within a framework that views addiction as a complex, progressive social problem that has biological, psychological, sociological, and behavioral components. Specifically, the EEAP model

- views substance abuse as a chronic, relapsing condition requiring long-term support for success;
- recognizes the impact of substances on many aspects of a woman's life, thus requiring an holistic approach to treatment;
- acknowledges the special needs of women substance abusers and the need to provide gender-specific services that address issues including child care and domestic violence;
- uses an integrated approach to substance abuse treatment and work, linking the two experiences to reinforce sobriety and maximize success in the work site;
- acknowledges the unique problems of the rural communities, including major gaps in services and the lack of professional support; and
- recognizes that substance abuse is an underidentified but a growing problem in rural communities. (Chasnoff, 1989)

Several services are provided by the EEAP counselor. First, EEAP counselors will take a proactive approach to their involvement with Work First participants. The aim of the initial EEAP contact is to provide support and encouragement at the workplace so that the participant has a known, readily available resource if there are any impending difficulties.

Second, experienced workplace employees or community persons will provide worksite mentoring for success for newly hired Work First participants. Mentoring has been found to be a critical component in helping women and minorities make significant advancements in the corporate world (Shimon-Craig, 1998). Mentoring programs are designed to provide support, direction, skill building, and encouragement to overcome obstacles related to the workplace.

Third, the EEAP will monitor participants' involvement in job performance through a defined process of client (that is, Work First participant) contact that is designed to monitor treatment and workplace activity of the person using EEAP services.

Fourth, extended two-year follow-up will be provided for Work First participants; a minimum of biweekly, face-to-face contact will take place during the first three months. After the first 90 days, biweekly contacts will continue with at least one face-to-face contact each month for up to two years.

To ensure successful entry into the workforce, developing literature indicates that comprehensive case management services are essential (Woolis, 1998). Mutual trust and development of strong relationships with volunteers or professionals has been identified as the most effective means of ensuring the successful transition of the participant from welfare to work (Weaver & Hasenfeld, 1997). The EEAP counselors will perform many, if not all of the functions of case-managers.

CASE EXAMPLE OF EEAP SERVICES IN A RURAL COMMUNITY

The TANF population in the rural North Carolina counties of Duplin and Sampson are confronted with additional barriers that add to the complexity of transitioning from welfare to work. Although large manufacturing corporations are located in some areas of the two counties, educational levels continue to be a major impediment, as most employers require employees to have at minimum a high school education. Statistics reveal that more than 33 percent of the adult population in these two counties did not graduate from high school. Second, the lack of financial resources are paramount, for one in five residents live at or below the poverty level; consequently, personal vehicles, money for childcare, and appropriate work-related clothing are not available. Third, as a result of sparsely populated areas and isolation within communities, issues of transportation are more difficult to resolve. The limited ability to find appropriate childcare in the vicinity of home or work is further complicated when personal vehicles and other sources of transportation are not available. Fourth, work is seasonal and unpredictable because of the agricultural nature of the economy and depends greatly on the kindness of the weather. The above issues alone are significant impediments, but when one factors in the lack of knowledge of workplace norms and cultures and the negative stigma held by some employees, the need for additional support is clearly indicated.

EEAP counselors are realistic but visionary in addressing the needs of TANF recipients in this rural community. In this community, the state-funded EEAPs have established collaborative relationships with the faith and school communities in developing means of transportation. Agreements have been established for the use of school buses and vans that are unused during the day to transport Work First participants to work. EEAPs have established strong collaborative networks which have evolved to provide services that are comprehensive (for example, childcare and transportation) and culturally and gender sensitive (for example, training local county and state personnel in using gender-sensitive interventions).

DISCUSSION: POLICY IMPLICATIONS

The recognition that multiple barriers face Work First participants is complicated by the reality of substance abuse and living in rural communities. The problems specific to rural communities indicate the need for policies that are comprehensive and realistic in meeting the service gaps in these communities. Specific policy implications resulting from this study may include recommendations for changes in treatment policies for substance-abusing Work First recipients. Treatment policies for such service providers as EAPs could include a mandate to provide long-term support for substance-abusing Work First recipients at the work site though group and one-to-one mentoring. The recommendations could include a mandate to provide holistic, gender-specific services that address various psychosocial issues Work First recipients face.

At the state level, the results of this study could lead to policies regarding services to Work First participants that include the following options:

- Mandate that integrative services and supports be provided in a collaborative manner (for example, cross-training to increase expertise in and recognition of substance misuse; interagency agreements that link all state agencies involved in service delivery to Work First recipients, including Department of Social Services, Substance Abuse Services, and Vocational Rehabilitation).
- Implement policy changes that require employers to provide EAPs or some form of on-site support for Work First recipients, to integrate treatment and work.
- Focus attention on rural areas to provide gender-sensitive interventions and services that are comprehensive and culturally and linguistically appropriate.
- Provide state funding for, at the very least, access to services for transportation and assistance for child care.
- Identify funding for long-term interventions and follow-up to reinforce sobriety and its maintenance into workplace. Orthner and Kirk (1995) reported successful interventions when sustained over time.
- Promote policies to include media coverage of successful Work First employees to diminish and counteract the negative social stigma surrounding hiring this population.

At the broadest level, this study could support a policy shift from defining substance abuse as a criminal justice issue (for example, the War on Drugs) to defining it as a public health issue. The study's implications for comprehensive public health policy involve moving from a unidimensional approach to alcohol and drug misuse, which focuses on abstinence but which fails to address multiple needs, including shelter, child care, mental health treatment, parenting skills, development, and preventive interventions with children (Chasnoff & Burnison, 1994). Second, the study could support state- and federal-level policy changes that view substance abuse as a chronic, relapsing disease state and that view treatment, rather than punishment, as an effective response to this national problem. Lastly, the study could solidify support from federal and state leaders to promote positive public attitudes towards TANF recipients who are attempting to sustain employment (Chasnoff & Burnison, 1994).

CONCLUSION

Numerous rural communities in North Carolina are isolated and have unique challenges and needs. Thousands of the state's residents, particularly rural poor people, have limited access to critical resources, the cause of which is the uneven geographic distribution of existing resources. The TANF law's mandate to have all welfare recipients become self-sufficient is unrealistic without providing additional long-term support. The state of North Carolina is attempting to provide support and address the need for services in these communities. Qualified professionals, some located in rural areas through the EEAP, are available and accessible to provide needed services to this population. EEAP counselors who are skilled in the early identification of substance abuse, addressing the needs of diverse populations, and assisting in the workplace will help close the gap for Work First participants in both rural and urban areas. Providing these additional supports will result in successful attachments to the work force and, one hopes, prevent the failures of previous welfare reform attempts.

REFERENCES

Amaral, T. A. (1998). *Benchmarks and performance measures for employee assistance programs: The employee assistance handbook.* New York: Wiley.

Beckman, L. (1994). Treatment needs of women with alcohol problems. *Alcohol Health & Research World, 18,* 206–211.

Blum, T. C., & Roman, P. (1995). *Cost-effectiveness and preventive implications of employee assistance programs.* DHHS Publication No. (SMA) 95–3053. Rockville, MD: U.S. Department of Health and Human Services.

Bruhnsen, K. (1994). Michigan study shows EAP clients use less sick leave, stay longer. *EAPA Exchange, 24,* 11–27.

Bush, I. R., & Kraft, M. K. (1998, Winter). The voices of welfare reform. *Journal of the American Public Welfare Association,* 11–21.

Bushy, A. (1997). Case management: Considerations for coordinating quality services in rural communities. *Journal of Nursing Care Quality, 12,* 26–35.

California Department of Alcohol and Drug Programs. (1994). *Evaluating recovery services: the California drug and alcohol treatment assessment (CALDATA).* Sacramento, CA: Author.

Center on Addiction and Substance Abuse at Columbia University. (1996). *Substance abuse and the American woman.* New York: Columbia University.

Chasnoff, I. (1989). Drug use and women: Establishing a standard of care. *Annals of the New York Academy of Science, 562,* 208–213.

Chasnoff, I., & Burnison, J. (1994). *Drug and alcohol use in pregnancy: A study of service needs and prevalence in the state of North Carolina* (Executive Summary prepared for North Carolina Department of Human Resources, Division of Mental Health, Developmental Disabilities and Substance Abuse Services). Raleigh, NC: North Carolina Department of Human Resources.

Davenport, J. A., & Davenport, J. (1995). Rural social work overview. In R. L. Edwards (Ed.-in-Chief), *Encyclopedia of social work* (19th ed., Vol. 3, pp. 2076–2085). Washington, DC: NASW Press.

Drug Strategies. (1996). *What we are getting for our federal drug dollars, 1996.* Washington, DC: Author.

French, M. T., Zarkin, G. A., Bray, J. W., & Hartwell, T. D. (1995). *Costs of employee assistance programs: Findings from a national survey.* Research Triangle Park, NC: Research Triangle Institute.

Gerstein, D., Johnson, R. A., & Larison, C. L. (1997). *Alcohol and other drug treatment for parents and welfare recipients: Outcomes, costs and benefits* (Final report to the U.S. Department of Health and Human Services from the National Opinion Research Center at the University of Chicago and the Lewin Group). Chicago: National Opinion Research Center.

Ginsberg, L. (1995). Public services management. In R. L. Edwards (Ed.-in-Chief), *Encyclopedia of social work* (19th ed., Vol. 3, pp. 1974–1981). Washington, DC: NASW Press.

Goodwin, S. N., Geary, C., Meisel, J., & Chandler, D. (1997). *The impact of behavioral health on employability of public assistance recipients: A technical assistance guide to the current state of knowledge.* Sacramento, CA: California Institute for Mental Health.

Gust, S. W., Crouch, D. J., & Walsh, J. M. (1991). Research on drugs and the workplace: Introduction and summary. In S. W. Gust, L. B. Thomas, & D. J. Crouch (Eds.), *Drugs in the workplace: Research and evaluation data* (Vol. 2, pp. 3–8) (National Institute on Drug Abuse Research Monograph Series, no. 91-1730). Rockville, MD: National Institute on Drug Abuse.

Hartwell, T. D., French, M. T., Potter, F. J., Steele, P. D., Zarkin, G. A., & Rodman, N. F. (1994). *Prevalence, cost and characteristics of employee assistance programs (EAPs).* Research Triangle Park, NC: Research Triangle Institute.

Hoffmann, J. P., Larison, C., & Sanderson, A. (1997). *An analysis of worker drug use and workplace policies and programs.* Rockville, MD: Substance Abuse and Mental Health Services Administration, Office of Applied Studies.

Johnston, L.D., O'Malley, P. M., & Bachman, J. G. (1994). *National survey results on drug use from the monitoring the future study, 1975–1993* (Vol. 1). Rockville, MD: National Institute on Drug Abuse.

Kelly, J. S. (1997). *Working with and motivating welfare recipients.* Washington, DC: Cygnus Associates.

Kopstein, A., & Gfroerer, J. (1991). Drug use patterns and demographics of employed drug users: Data from the 1988 National Household Survey on Drug Abuse. In S. W. Gust, L. B. Thomas, & D. J. Crouch (Eds.), *Drugs in the workplace: Research and evaluation data* (Vol. 2, pp. 11–24) (National Institute on Drug Abuse Research Monograph Series no. 91-1730). Rockville, MD: National Institute on Drug Abuse.

Kurtz, N. R., Googins, B., & Howard, W. C. (1984). Measuring the success of occupational alcoholism programs. *Journal of Studies on Alcohol, 45,* 33–45.

Lehman, W., & Simpson, D. D. (1991). Patterns of drug use in a large metropolitan workforce. In S. W. Gust, L. B. Thomas, & D. J. Crouch (Eds.), *Drugs in the workplace: Research and evaluation data* (Vol. 2, pp. 45–62) (National Institute on Drug Abuse Research Monograph Series no. 91-1730). Rockville, MD: National Institute on Drug Abuse.

Maynard, R. A. (1995). Subsidized employment and non-labor market alternatives for welfare recipients. In D. S. Nightingale & R. H. Havemen (Eds.), *Work alternative: Welfare reform and the realities of the labor market.* Washington, DC: Urban Institute Press.

McCloskey, K. (1995). *Workplace alcohol testing, a handbook for managers.* Horsham, PA: LRP.

McDonnell Douglas Corporation & Alexander and Alexander Consulting Group. (1990). *McDonnell Douglas corporation employee assistance program financial offset study, 1985–1989.* Bridgeton, MO: Author.

Merrill, J.C. (1994). *Substance abuse and women on welfare.* New York: Center on Addiction and Substance Abuse at Columbia University.

Moore, K. A., Zaslow, M. J., Coiro, M., & Miller, S. M. (1996). *How well are they faring? AFDC families with preschool-aged children in Atlanta at the outset of the JOBS evaluation.* Washington, DC: U.S. Department of Health and Human Services, Office of the Assistant Secretary for Planning and Evaluation.

Moos, R., Brennan, P., Fondacaro, M., & Moos, B. (1990). Approach and avoidance coping responses among older problem and non–problem drinkers. *Psychology and Aging, 5,* 31–40.

Mueller, T. I. (1996). Coerced treatment found to be effective for substance abusing employees. *Journal of Substance Abuse, 8,* 115–128.

Murck, M., & Kamp, J. (1995, June). American workers under pressure: Why EAPs are a valuable commodity. *EAPA Exchange,* 20–21.

National Institute on Alcohol Abuse and Alcoholism. (1990). Women and alcohol. *Alcohol Alert No. 10,* 3–8.

National Opinion Research Center and Research Triangle Institute. (1996). *National Treatment Improvement Evaluation Study (NTIES).* Rockville, MD: Center for Substance Abuse Treatment.

Normand, J., Lempert, R., & O'Brien, C. P. (1994). *Under the influence? Drugs and the American work force.* Washington, DC: National Academy Press.

North Carolina Department of Health and Human Services. (1997). *Substance use and need for comprehensive treatment and services in North Carolina's adult household population: 1995.* Research Triangle Park, NC: Research Triangle Institute.

Oher, J. (1995). *Survey results link EAP effectiveness to employer involvement, documentation and communication.* Chicago: Spencer.

Orthner, D. (1995, June). *North Carolina JOBS program: Impact evaluation executive summary.* (Report prepared for the State of North Carolina Department of Human Resources). Chapel Hill: Human Services Resources Design Laboratory at the University of North Carolina.

Orthner, D., & Kirk, R. (1995). Evaluation of welfare employment programs. In R. L. Edwards (Ed.-in-Chief), *Encyclopedia of social work* (19th ed., Vol. 3, pp. 2499–2507). Washington, DC: NASW Press.

Pape, P. (1993). Issues in assessment and intervention with alcohol and drug abusing women. In S.L.A. Straussner (Ed.), *Clinical work with substance-abusing clients* (pp. 251–269). New York: Guilford.

Pavetti, L. A. (1993). *The dynamics of welfare and work: Exploring the process by which women work their way off of welfare.* Cambridge, MA: Harvard University.

Pavetti, L. A., & Duke, A. E. (1995). *Increasing participation in work and work-related activities: Lessons from five state welfare reform demonstration projects* (Report prepared for the Office of the Assistant Secretary for Planning and Evaluation, U.S. Department of Health and Human Services). Washington, DC: Urban Institute.

Quint, J. D., Fink, B. L., & Rowser, S. L. (1991). *New chance: Implementing a comprehensive program for disadvantaged young mothers and their children.* New York: Manpower Demonstration Research Corporation.

Rangarajan, A. (1996, November). *Taking the first steps: Helping welfare recipients who get jobs keep them* (Report submitted to the State of Illinois, Division of Planning and Community Services, Department of Public Aid). Princeton, NJ: Mathematica Policy Research.

Riggs, R. T., & Kugel, L. F. (1976). Transition from urban to rural mental health practice. *Social Casework, 57,* 562–567.

Roman, P. M., & Blum, T. C. (1986, March). The core technology of employee assistance programs. *The ALMACAN, 18*(8), 17–22.

Shimon-Craig, V. C. (1998). Moving up through mentoring. *Workforce, 77(3),* 36–45.

Strawn, J. (1997). Substance abuse and welfare reform policy. *Welfare information network* [Online]. Available: http://www.welfarewatch.org/cgibin/printreport.cgi?18

Tompkins, C. P. (1991). Drug abuse among workers and employee assistance programs. In National Institute on Drug Abuse (NIDA), *Drug abuse services research series: Background pa-*

pers on drug abuse financing and services research (pp. 82–106) (DHHS Publication No. 91-1777). Rockville, MD: National Institute on Drug Abuse.

Trice, H. M., & Schonbrunn, M. (1981). A history of job-based alcoholism programs, 1900–1955. *Journal of Drug Issues, 11,* 171–198.

Urban Institute. (1998). *Personal and family challenges to the successful transition from welfare to work* (Executive Summary prepared for the Office of the Assistance Secretary for Planning and Evaluation and the Administration for Children and Families). Washington, DC: Author.

U.S. Department of Health and Human Services, Office of the Assistant Secretary for Planning and Evaluation, National Institute on Drug Abuse. (1994). *Patterns of substance abuse and substance-related impairment among participants in the Aid to Families with Dependent Children Program.* Washington, DC: U.S. Department of Health and Human Services.

Wagenfeld, M. O., Murray, J. B., Mofatt, D. F., & DeBryn, J. C. (1994). *Mental health in rural America: 1980–1993* (NIH Publication No. 94-3500). Washington, DC: U.S. Government Printing Office.

Walker, K., & Shain, M. (1983). Employee assistance programming: In search of effective interventions for the problem-drinking employee. *British Journal of Addiction, 78,* 291–303.

Weaver, D., & Hasenfeld, Y. (1997). Case management practices, participants' responses, and compliance in welfare-to-work programs. *Social Work Research, 21,* 92–100.

Woolis, D. (1998, Winter). Family works: Substance abuse treatment and welfare reform. *Journal of the American Public Welfare Association,* 24–31.

Young, N. K., & Gardner, S. L. (1998, Winter). Children at the crossroads. *Journal of the American Public Welfare Association,* 3–10.

CHAPTER THIRTEEN

Welfare Reform and Demand for Rural Public Transportation

Kenneth R. Wedel and Fran C. Butler

The Personal Responsibility and Work Opportunity Reconciliation Act of 1996 (PRWORA) (P.L. 104–193) embodies legislative changes that have been promoted to reform welfare. Although the measures contained in PRWORA cover numerous aspects of U.S. social welfare programming, this chapter focuses on the two programs most likely to affect rural public transportation—Temporary Assistance to Needy Families (TANF) and the Food Stamp program.

MAJOR IDENTIFYING FEATURES OF THE TANF PROGRAM

TANF replaced Aid to Families with Dependent Children (AFDC) in 1996. The AFDC program (Title IV of the Social Security Act of 1935) was a public assistance entitlement program with federal formula grant funding to assist states in providing cash assistance and certain services to needy dependent children and their parents (or caretaker relatives). Under the new TANF program, categorical federal formula grants to states for AFDC were replaced with federal block grants for TANF. The TANF program was designed to increase the flexibility of states in operating their public assistance programs to needy families with children (American Public Welfare Association, 1998).

TANF is a cooperative program between the federal government and the states. At the federal level, the Department of Health and Human Services (DHHS) oversees the program and monitors TANF as implemented by the state. At the state level, some TANF programs are carried out with state administration, whereas others are state supervised and administered by local governments (for example, counties, parishes, and towns). States are required to file a state plan every two years (amended as necessary) describing the operation of their TANF program; however, state plans are not subject to federal approval (Abramovitz, 1997). Funding is a joint effort with federal, state and, in some states, local monies. An annual total of $16.38

billion in federal block grants is being provided to the states in fiscal years 1997 to 2002. The block grants to individual states are based on previous federal expenditures for AFDC benefits and administration, Emergency Assistance (EA), and the Job Opportunities and Basic Skills Training Program (JOBS).[1]

Eligibility and Benefits

States have flexibility in determining eligibility for TANF and the benefits recipients receive. TANF block grant funds may be used in any manner reasonably calculated to accomplish the purpose of TANF. In general, however, the states tend to follow the broad eligibility standards that were set forth in the former AFDC program. Two critical features of eligibility are the presence of a needy child and family income and resources.

To be eligible for TANF, a needy minor child must be deprived of the support or care of at least one parent because that parent is deceased, incapacitated, or absent from the home. In the case of two-parent families, underemployment or unemployment may count toward meeting this criterion. Eligibility ends when the youngest child in the family reaches majority age (as determined by state statute). In addition to each needy child, the parent (or other caretaker relative) may be eligible to receive TANF. States may provide cash assistance, use grant funds to make payments, and provide job-placement vouchers for employment placement services (Wedel, 1998).

Cash Benefits

The amount of cash assistance benefits are calculated on the basis of need as determined in each state. In implementing TANF, many states are generally relying on previous formulas to determine essential living costs for necessities such as food, shelter, clothing, and transportation (Wedel, 1998). TANF also allows states to provide up-front "diversion payments" as an alternative to ongoing TANF assistance. Diversion assistance may be provided in different ways, including one-time lump-sum payments, health care, and other services. These short-term payments are generally intended to assist families or individuals in meeting critical needs for securing or retaining employment. Typically, states provide several months of payments in one lump sum or flat amount. By accepting the diversion payment, the family generally must agree not to reapply for cash assistance for a specified period of time (for example, three months if the diversion payment is equivalent to three months of benefits).

Child Care

Before TANF, three specific sources of child care funding were available for AFDC recipients: AFDC/JOBS Child Care, Transitional Child Care, and At-Risk Child Care

---

[1] The EA and JOBS programs were folded into TANF in 1996.

(formerly called "Title IV–A child care"). The three programs were repealed by the PRWORA legislation of 1996 and replaced by a single, integrated child care system under the former Child Care and Development Block Grant (CCDBG) to states. A newly established Child Care and Developmental Fund (CCDF) provides funding for child care.

Transitional child care under the old AFDC program was available as an entitlement for up to 12 months to families whose eligibility ended because of increased earnings or child support payments. Although the PRWORA law discontinued the 12-month entitlement, states are allowed to provide such care.

Work-related Services

In addition to cash assistance, medical services, and child care, other direct and indirect benefits and services may be available. For example, states are allowed to subsidize public- and private-sector employment for recipients. Typically, subsidized employment refers to "cashing out" TANF and/or food stamp assistance and providing funds to employers, who in turn pay wages to recipients.

States must perform assessments of recipients' work capabilities, although no guidelines are specified by the federal agency. Assessments under the JOBS program (Title IV-F) ranged from client self-assessments to various testing procedures. Personal responsibility contracts for recipients on their work and career goals are at the option of the state.

Examples of other job creation strategies already implemented or planned by the states are as follows:

- providing tax credits and other employer incentives
- creating industry partnerships and customized employment projects
- developing interagency task forces or linkages, typically among welfare, workforce, and economic development systems, for job creation, job development, or employer marketing
- using work force investment boards or councils
- supporting loans for entrepreneurial programs or small business
- convening a statewide employer job summit
- using one-stop career centers
- designing groups and positions responsible for soliciting employers to hire welfare recipients.

The arrangements for providing job-related and support services vary from state to state. Under the JOBS program, some states used a caseworker approach; each caseworker was responsible for coordinating basic services and monitoring a given number of AFDC cases. Other states used a case management approach for linking recipients to needed services. Another model is contracting with private and other public service providers for needed services.

Time Limit

In contrast to the former AFDC program, TANF is not an entitlement program (that is, clients are not entitled to receive cash assistance indefinitely if they otherwise meet all eligibility requirements). The federal limit for financial assistance to a family under TANF is a cumulative total of 60 months (five years).[2] This time limit applies to the entire household and to all forms of assistance under the TANF block grant. Exceptions to the time-limit requirement are child-only cases and certain hardship cases, including families with members who have been battered or subject to extreme cruelty.[3] States may use their own funds to provide assistance after the five-year time limit. Also, states may use Social Services Block Grant (SSBG) funds to provide vouchers to families who reach the time limit.

Maintenance-of-Effort

States must meet a maintenance-of-effort (MOE) requirement. The MOE requirement stipulates that each state continue to spend on TANF at least 80 percent of the state dollars it spent for AFDC programs in FY 1994. This level of spending is reduced to 75 percent of FY 1994 spending if the state meets work-participation rates discussed in the next section. A state's grant is reduced by one dollar for each dollar short of the MOE requirement.

Work-Participation Rates

States also must meet federal standards for the participation of TANF recipients in work-related activities, and this requirement is likely to have a significant impact on demand for transportation in both urban and rural areas. States must achieve minimum annual participation rates with respect to all families that include an adult or minor child head of household receiving assistance. The annual participation rate is the average of the participation rate for each month in the fiscal year. Not more than 20 percent of families may count toward the work rate by participating in vocational education. The incremental increases in work-participation requirements ratchets up 5 percent a year, from 25 percent in FY 1997 to 50 percent in FY 2002 and beyond.[4]

---

[2] States may enact a shorter time period.

[3] States are, however, limited to no more than 20 percent of recipient cases receiving exemption from work requirements.

[4] The participation rate for two-parent families is 75 percent in FY 1997 and 1998 and rises to 90 percent for FY 1999 and beyond.

Incentives and Penalties for States

Augmenting the requirements for increasing work-participation rates for TANF recipients, states can benefit financially through performance bonus funding. Cash
bonuses are available to "high-performing states" that meet the goals of the program
in fiscal years 1998 to 2002. The financial penalties against states for failure to meet
work-participation rates will result in a TANF grant reduction of 5 percent the first
year. For consecutive failures, penalties rise by 2 percent each year, up to a cap of a
21 percent reduction in the TANF block grant amount. DHHS can reduce the
penalty for missing the work-participation requirement based on the degree of non-
compliance or if a state is in an economic recession. In the latter situation a state can
be defined as "needy" on the basis of standards specified for federal contingency
funds available from the TANF program. The contingency fund provision allows
states to draw down additional funds during a period of economic downturn.
However, a state may only access the contingency fund by providing state match and
by having state expenditures in the TANF program at or above 100 percent of its historic state expenditures during the year in which the state seeks contingency fund
access.

Job Training and Work Requirements

Adults (parents or relative caregivers) in TANF cases are required to participate in
work activities after receiving assistance for a maximum of two years (24 months).
States may set a shorter time period, and in some states adult recipients are required
to begin a work-related activity immediately. In addition, if adult recipients are not
working within two months of receiving benefits, participation in community service
is required.[5] A phased-in minimum number of work hours is established at 20 hours
per week for FY 1997–98, increasing to 30 hours per week in FY 2000 and beyond.
For two-parent families, the work-hour requirement (for both able-bodied parents)
is 35 hours per week. Educational activities directly related to employment (or to
completing high school or obtaining a GED) is an allowable work activity but is not
counted toward the first required 20 hours per week (35 hours for two-parent families).[6] Examples of allowable work activities are as follows:

- unsubsidized employment
- subsidized public- or private-sector employment
- work experience and community service programs
- on-the-job training
- job-search and job-readiness assistance for up to six weeks
- vocational education training
- job-skills training directly related to employment

---

[5]States may opt out of the community service requirement.
[6]An exception is made for teen parents who have not finished high school or the equivalent.

- education directly related to employment
- satisfactory attendance at secondary school or course of study leading to the general equivalency diploma (GED), in the case of a recipient who has not completed secondary school
- provision of child care services to a person who is participating in a community service program.

Beyond the flexibility afforded states in setting eligibility standards, a number of other rules related to work activities apply:

- If a two-parent family receives federally funded child care, both parents must work, except for parents of severely disabled children or parents who are disabled themselves.
- A teen parent or head of household under age 20 will be counted as engaged in work if the recipient maintains satisfactory attendance at secondary school or the equivalent during the month or participates in education directly related to employment for at least the minimum average number of hours per week as specified above.
- States have the option to exempt single, custodial parents with a child less than one year old from the work requirement. A state may disregard the person when determining participation rates. A parent may only receive this exemption for a total of 12 months, although the months do not have to be consecutive.

For all families (except teenage heads of household), the following activities do not count as allowable work activities toward meeting the first 20 hours (35 hours for two-parent families) of participation:

- job-skills training directly related to employment
- education directly related to employment, in the case of a recipient who has not received a high school diploma or certificate of high school equivalency
- satisfactory attendance at a secondary school or a course of study leading to the GED, in the case of a recipient who has not completed secondary school.

Sanctions

States may sanction recipients for failure to cooperate with the required work-related activity standards. Sanctions may result in reduction of cash assistance or even closure of the case. A state must reduce assistance to a family pro rata (or more at state option) for any period in which an adult member of the family refuses to engage in work as required under the TANF grant. The state may waive the penalty subject to good cause and other exceptions the state may establish. The state may also terminate assistance completely and terminate Medicaid for the person whose cash assistance is terminated for failure to work. Minor children will continue to receive Medicaid. A state may not reduce or terminate assistance to a single parent with a child under age six, however, if the parent proves that failure to participate in work is a result of to lack of child care.

Provisions and Penalties

States may elect to deny assistance to unmarried teen parents and their children. In states that do not deny assistance, unmarried teen parents of minor children are eligible for TANF only if they are living at home or in an approved, adult-supervised setting. Also, if the age of a teen's child is 12 weeks of age or older, the teen parent must participate in educational activities directed toward achieving a high school diploma or GED or participate in an alternative education or training program approved by the state.

MAJOR IDENTIFYING FEATURES OF THE FOOD STAMP PROGRAM

The Food Stamp program is a federal food assistance program to provide access to a healthy diet for low-income people and family households. The program is funded through the U.S. Department of Agriculture (USDA) and administered through the cooperation of the states (and local public and private organizations). In contrast to TANF, it is an uncapped entitlement program. State and local governments pay one-half of the program's administrative costs, whereas the benefits portion of the program is 100 percent federally funded (USDA, 1997).

Eligibility and Benefits

U.S. citizens and some noncitizens who are admitted for permanent residency may qualify. To be eligible for food stamps, a person must meet an asset/resource limit of $2,000. Those age 60 and over have a $3,000 limit. A home owned by the applicant is not included in the asset/resource limit, and an automobile valued at less than $4,650 also is excluded. Deductions from income for eligibility purposes include shelter costs and earnings of elementary and secondary students age 17 and younger. States may operate a "simplified food stamp program" for households in which one or more members receive assistance under TANF. The simplified program allows for a single set of rules and procedures to determine eligibility and benefits for food stamps and TANF and standardizes the deductions for both programs. A state's simplified plan must not increase costs to the federal government.

The primary benefit of the Food Stamp program is the provision of food for a healthy diet. Coupons or electronic "smart cards" are used like cash to purchase food at participating grocery stores.

Job Training and Work Requirements

As in the case of TANF, welfare reform measures have brought about changes in requirements for food stamp recipients that are likely to increase the demand for rural public transportation. Able-bodied recipients age 18 to 50 with no dependents are ineligible for food stamps unless they meet the new work requirement specified under PRWORA. They may receive food stamp benefits for only three months in every 36-month period unless they are engaged in work or work programs. If the recipient finds work and then loses his or her job, however, an additional three months of benefits are allowed once in the three-year period.[7]

The definition of work for the Food Stamp program includes participating in a work program for 20 hours or more a week, averaged monthly. Qualifying work programs include the following:

- programs under the Job Training Partnership Act (JTPA) (P.L. 97–300) or the Trade Adjustment Assistance Act
- Trade Adjustment Assistance programs for workers who lose their jobs or whose hours of work and wages are reduced as a result of imports
- state or local programs approved by the governor, including a food stamp employment and training program
- a TANF workfare program.

Job search or job-search training programs do not qualify, but states may request waivers for areas with unemployment of more than 10 percent or with insufficient jobs. States may operate a work supplementation or support program where the value of public assistance, including food stamps, is provided to employers to be used for hiring and paying the recipient.

Transportation Issues

When welfare reform is fully implemented, it is estimated that an additional 1 million to 2 million people will move into the low-income work force (Kaplan, 1998a). For many people receiving TANF or food stamps, employment and child care will not be readily accessible using currently available transportation. For instance, it is estimated that only 6.5 percent of welfare recipients own an automobile (Community Transportation Association of America [CTAA], 1998b), and many jobs will require travel outside of peak times or at night, when public transportation is infrequent or unavailable

Nationally, about one in four families receiving public assistance live in rural areas, and a disproportionate share of nonmetropolitan residents reside in poverty-level households (U.S. Department of Transportation [DOT], 1998a). Further complicating the situation for rural residents is the lack of public transportation in many areas. Kaplan cites Goble and Bogren (1996) for an estimate that 38 percent of rural Americans live in communities unserved by any public transportation (Kaplan,

---

[7]States have received federal waivers from the work requirements where local labor markets are considered too weak to absorb otherwise eligible persons.

1998a). The next section identifies the major programs concerned with rural public transportation.

TRANSPORTATION PROGRAMMING AND LEADERSHIP

At the national level, DOT is the lead agency of the government for transportation programs. Responsibility for administering rural public transportation programming rests within a division of DOT, the Federal Transit Administration (FTA). In 1998 President Clinton signed into law the Transportation Equity Act for the 21st Century (TEA-21) (P.L. 105–178), within which is the Access to Jobs program. Access to Jobs projects involve developing transportation services to transport welfare recipients and eligible low-income people to and from jobs and other activities related to employment. If all authorized funds are appropriated, $150 million per year for five years will be available for Access to Jobs and Reverse Commute grants, which are for transporting people from the inner city to jobs in the suburbs. The distribution of these funds includes 20 percent to be spent in rural areas (DOT, 1998c).

Other programming and funding sources within DOT supporting rural public transit for workfare routes include the following (DOT, 1998b):

- JOBLINKS is a demonstration program funded by DOT and administered through the CTAA. The program funds projects that propose innovative methods of taking people to work, which range in scope from coordination efforts to new technology implementation. The funding level for this program is $1 million.
- The Livable Communities Initiative is a community-oriented transit-planning approach to producing jobs in low-income communities. The program provides local transit circulator services (rides to a series of points in a defined area, for example, a downtown bus service) and feeder services (rides to fixed-route public transit from origins and to destinations not accessible by fixed-route public transit). These services are meant to support local economic activity and joint-use facilities where transit and child care come together.
- The Nonurbanized Area Formula Program and the Rural Transit Assistance Program (RTAP), formerly known as "Section 18," provides formula funding to states to support public transportation in areas with a population of less than 50,000 through rural transit training and technical assistance. The funding level for the Nonurbanized Area Formula Programs is $115.1 million, and $4.5 million is designated for RTAP.
- The National Planning and Research Program, formerly known as "Section 26(b)," provides support for public transit research, demonstrations and special projects that are in the national interest, such as advanced technology; transit finance initiatives; transit accessibility; human resource training and development; and information initiatives, including the RTAP National Resource Center. The funding level for this program is $22 million.
- The State Planning and Research Program, formerly known as "Section 26(2),"

provides formula funding to states to carry out public transportation planning, research, demonstration, and technical assistance activities. The funding level for this area is $8.25 million.

OTHER MAJOR FEDERAL FUNDING SOURCES

In addition to DOT, five other important federal funding sources exist for welfare-to-work transportation needs. Listed below are the programs that focus on small town and rural public transportation (CTAA, 1998c).

DHHS

- DHHS funds the TANF program; some of those funds can be used for transportation purposes.
- Another DHSS funding source is the Community Services Block Grant program. States and Indian tribes may use those funds for transportation projects that improve the delivery and effectiveness of human services programs. The funding level for this source is $2.3 billion.
- Also through DHHS, the Substance Abuse Treatment for Rural and Remote Persons program supports project sites that use a coordinated approach integrating substance abuse treatment; health and social services; and related services, including transportation. The funding level for this area is $1.8 million.

U.S. Department of Housing and Urban Development (HUD)

HUD, through its Office of Community Planning and Development, funds several community-based programs.

- Some communities have used Community Development Block Grant (CDBG) funds to assist in transportation facility construction, operating expenses, and vehicle acquisition for community transportation services. The funding level for CDBG grants is $4.6 billion.
- The Supportive Housing (Homeless) Demonstration Program can fund transportation to link supported housing residents with other necessary services. The funding level for this area is $82.3 million.
- The Tenant Opportunities Program allows funding for transportation for public and American Indian housing resident organizations involved in job training. The funding level for this area is $5 million.
- Eighty percent of the funding in Welfare-to-Work/Economic Development Supportive Services (EDSS) grants will fund supportive services and economic development efforts that will enable residents of public housing developments to become

self-sufficient. Funded activities include employment training, counseling, transportation, and child care. The funding level for this area is $31 million.

USDA

USDA funds several rural development programs that include transportation services.

- The Intermediary Relending Program (IRP) is a program of revolving loans that finance businesses and community development projects in rural communities and towns with a population of less than 25,000. Nonprofits, public bodies, Indian tribes, and cooperatives are eligible participants, and transportation is among the eligible uses of borrowed funds. The funding level for this loan program is $37.15 million.
- The Community Transportation Development Fund (CTDF) can assist rural communities in improving or expanding local transit services, purchasing vehicles, building facilities, and promoting economic development. The program is funded through the Department's Rural Business and Cooperative Services Division. The funding level for this area is $2.1 million.
- The Business and Industrial Guaranteed Loan Program is designed to create and save rural jobs and improve the economic and environmental climates of rural communities with a population of less than 50,000 through direct and guaranteed loans. Loans may include financing for transportation-related facilities, vehicle acquisition, or other infrastructure investments. Any legally organized entity is eligible. The funding level for this program is $738.2 million.
- Rural Business Enterprise Grants (RBEG) support rural economic and community development projects, including transportation facilities, infrastructure improvements, and the capital costs of transportation services. The funding level for this program is $41 million.
- Rural Economic Development Loans and Grants are targeted to certain purposes, such as community development, medical care, educational technology, job training, business incubators, and technical assistance and can be used for transportation activities that fit with those purposes. The funding level for this area is $32.3 million.
- The Rural Empowerment Zones/Enterprise Communities program is an initiative designed to help distressed areas integrate local initiatives with federal support.

Department of Education (DoEd)

DoEd includes programming for vocational rehabilitation services to eligible individuals with disabilities. DoEd also provides funding through Even Start, which may include transportation services if necessary to ensure participation in the adult literacy component of this program. The funding level for this area is $102 million.

Department of Labor (DoL)

The DoL is actively involved in funding welfare-to-work programming.

- The Trade Adjustment Assistance program provides temporary benefits to workers whose employment has been adversely affected by increased imports including benefits for job training and necessary related services, specifically including transportation to training programs. The funding level is $8.5 million.
- The Employment Training Research and Demonstration Programs will support transportation services that are part of these projects. The funding level for this area is $10.2 million.

EXAMPLES OF RURAL PUBLIC TRANSPORTATION PLANNING INITIATIVES

At the national level the programming described above serves to stimulate state and local initiatives for transportation services. For example, the Livable Communities Initiative (LCI) funded by DOT seeks to make transit planning more responsive to the needs of neighborhoods and local communities by involving localities in the planning and design of transportation services and facilities that serve their communities (DOT, March 9, 1998a). One outcome of this process has been the incorporation of needed local customer services in or around local transit facilities. Services such as day care, shopping, banking, and other customer services are beginning to appear at transit stations. The LCI encourages job training, health care, and other employment services to be located at transit sites to make services more accessible to people dependent on transit and to make travel more convenient for customers who otherwise would be forced to take complicated trips. A similar approach is being taken in the One-Stop Shopping programs sponsored by DoL to transport welfare clients to and from the strategic one-stop locations (DOT, March 9, 1998a).

Finally, the DOT Access to Jobs program provides the flexibility to allow local planners and service providers to optimize their resources by combining federal, state, and local resources from multiple programs. The program seeks to build on existing networks of transportation providers and enhance integration with other human services supporting welfare reform efforts to provide economically disadvantaged people with affordable transportation to and from work (CTAA, 1998a).

STATE-LEVEL INITIATIVES

Transportation task forces are springing up at state and local levels. Typically, a task force comprises representatives from the state's transportation agency, public welfare agency, and other state and local agencies (Kaplan, 1998b). Some examples of proposals that are being considered are as follows:

- use of public school buses and other vehicles, such as senior center vans, to transport TANF or Food Stamp recipients to work and training sites
- Individual Development Accounts (IDAs), which are savings accounts for TANF recipients made by deposits from earned income, earned income tax credits, and public and private matching funds and which are used for education, buying a house, or purchasing a vehicle
- donation of vehicles by various organizations and social programs to selected recipients
- purchase by welfare agencies of surplus state and county vehicles for clients to lease, purchase, or use for travel to work.

Many states already pay for some clients' vehicle repairs, provide fuel subsidies, or issue a daily transportation reimbursement. In some cases, selected recipients are allowed to provide transportation services to other clients as part of their work-experience activities. The practice of changing the eligibility criterion by increasing the permitted book value of the first vehicle has been a popular practice among states.[8] Some states are purchasing public transit passes where public transportation is available.

Many of the transportation issues identified above may be addressed on an individual level through vouchers, donations, and volunteers. Community- or regional-based issues, however, require coordination of existing resources or development of new resources to address transportation needs. In many cases there is utility in developing interdepartmental task forces to involve human services in transportation planning, creating business/community partnerships, or using a single transportation broker. These issues will require more basic policy changes, such as providing transportation subsidies in welfare reform initiatives, creating more flexible insurance regulations, and exempting the value of cars in determining eligibility for benefits. States and communities addressing the issues will want to begin with a clear definition of need and a comprehensive inventory of potential resources. As with many aspects of welfare reform, the public agency may be both the convener and the catalyst, but resources will involve a wide range of public and private players. Important players may include the state agencies responsible for education, insurance, economic development and transportation (their local counterparts), public transit authorities, and employers.

CONCLUSIONS

It appears reasonable to project increased demand for rural public transportation, given the increased work requirements of TANF and the Food Stamp program coupled with the need for regular transportation to and from child care facilities. This

---

[8]Under the AFDC program, federal regulations limited the value of a vehicle to no more than $1,500 as recently as 1996, though some states had waivers to raise the value by the time the TANF program was implemented.

chapter has identified the heightened national interest in addressing those transportation needs. How well current rural public transportation initiatives will fit the populations described in this chapter may very well depend on simultaneously addressing the issues of child care arrangements, transportation needs of others in the household, social environment during rides, and amount of time spent away from home. To that end, further study and policy analysis is required and should include in-depth interviewing of TANF and Food Stamp recipients to learn their attitudes toward rural public transit, demonstration and evaluation of approaches to developing needed work routes, and increased coordination between human service and transportation professionals.

REFERENCES

Abramovitz, M. (1997). Temporary Assistance to Needy Families. In R. L. Edwards (Ed.-in-Chief), *Encyclopedia of social work* (19th ed., 1997 Supp., pp. 311–330). Washington, DC: NASW Press.

Aid to Families with Dependent Children (AFDC). Title IV A U.S.C. §401.

American Public Welfare Association. (1998, July 10). *Temporary Assistance for Needy Families (TANF) block grants (Title 1), August 22, 1996, revised* [On-line]. Available: http://www.apwa.org/reform/analysis.htm

Community Transportation Association of America. (1998a, July). *Access to jobs* [On-line]. Available: http://www.ctaa.org/welfare/innovative/

Community Transportation Association of America. (1998b, February 10). *II Determining transit needs* [On-line]. Available: http://www.ctaa.org/welfare/innovative/section2.html

Community Transportation Association of America. (1998c, February 15). *VII Funding sources* [On-line]. Available: http://www.ctaa.org/welfare/innovative/section7.html

Goble, R. T., & Bogren, S. (1996, April). Taking people to work: JOBLINKS success stories. *Community Transportation Reporter, 14*(3).

Job Training Partnership Act of 1982. P.L. 97–300, 96 Stat. 1322.

Kaplan, A. (1998a, February). *Transportation and welfare reform* [On-line]. Available: http://www.welfareinfo.org/transita.html

Kaplan, A. (1998b). Transportation and welfare: Addressing the "to" in welfare-to-work. *PA Times, 21*(11), 1–3.

Personal Responsibility and Work Opportunity Reconciliation Act of 1996. P.L. 104–193, 110 Stat. 2105.

Transportation Equity Act for the 21st Century. P.L. 105–178, 112 Stat. 107.

U.S. Department of Agriculture. (1997, October). *Food stamp eligibility and benefits* [On-line]. Available: http://www.usda.gov:80/fcs/stamps/fselig.htm

U.S. Department of Transportation, Federal Transit Administration. (1998a, March). *Keys to success* [On-line]. Available: http://www.fta.dot.gov/wtw/access-to-jobs-brochure.html

U.S. Department of Transportation, Federal Transit Administration. (1998b, March 11). *Access to jobs and training* [On-line]. Available: http://www.fta.dot.gov/library/legal/reauthissues/issues4.htm#at

U.S. Department of Transportation. (1998c, June). *Access to jobs program* [On-line]. Available: http://www.istea.org/docs/jun98/jobs.html

Wedel, K. R. (1998). *Programs of the Social Security Act.* Unpublished manuscript, University of Oklahoma at Norman.

CHAPTER FOURTEEN

Small Town Murals:
Remembering Rural Roots

Judson H. Morris, Jr., and Lynne Clemmons Morris

Never doubt that a small group of thoughtful, committed citizens can change the world. Indeed, it's the only thing that ever has.

—Margaret Mead

Small towns and rural communities are continually looking for ways to maintain, restore, and enhance their viability and visibility. One way in which those goals can be accomplished is to develop a community project that incorporates the factors that are critical for a rural community to sustain healthy growth: community involvement, pride, energy, and economic development.

Outdoor murals are one way in which people in rural communities can make a visible statement of what they think their community is all about, what they want to see, and what they want visitors to see, remember, and return again to admire. Some rural communities use current themes and farming scenes on their walls, whereas others use historical, turn-of-the-century scenes.

It is essential that people feel good about the place in which they live and feel that people who visit respect and have an interest in their community. Outdoor murals can be an effective way for communities to preserve and strengthen their identity, their sense of purpose, their linkages, and their renewal. One difference between urban and rural walls of pride is that urban walls of pride typically feature current neighborhood themes, accomplishments, affirmations of cultural identity, and illustrations of residents. In contrast, rural murals usually depict the community's past, traditions, and heritage. Rural walls of pride have been used to rekindle community spirit and pride in a town's heritage. Murals have also been used to rediscover rural towns' sense of purpose and direction.

REVIEW OF LITERATURE

Most rural communities in the United States are experiencing change and transition. Rural economies are becoming more diversified and less based on such traditional activities as farming, logging, fishing, and mining. During the 1990s most rural communities, particularly in the western United States, have experienced population growth resulting from an in-migration of newcomers (Johnson & Beale, 1998; Jossi, 1997). As a result of these social and economic changes, rural communities are recognizing the need to define and affirm their unique shared histories and identities. Developing a clear, collective vision of what residents value about their communities and what they would like to see their communities become is essential to processes of community development. In community development processes, rural people engage in community actions both to preserve their valued past and to shape the ways in which they grow and change.

The development of a mural offers an opportunity for community members to engage in the process of visioning, of creating a public image that visually represents a sense of what their community is or might become (Klein, 1993). The process also requires people to share their perceptions of community and to develop a consensus about how those perceptions should be publicly represented. Discussions of mural design provide an important forum for the exchange of ideas and development of relationships that can serve as the foundation for other community development efforts (McNeil, 1995). Mural projects often revive interest in local community history and frequently encourage residents to take on other projects that revitalize community arts and cultural heritage (Overton, 1997). Many rural communities also have discovered that creating murals can foster economic development by encouraging cultural and heritage tourism.

Mural development projects also require that communities engage in asset mapping to identify community resources such as potential sites for the mural, local donors of supplies, and local residents with artistic skills. The process of asset mapping, which encourages communities to discover and build on their strengths, is increasingly recognized as essential to successful community development (McKnight, 1992; Sullivan, 1994).

Identifying new forms of sustainable development is critical for the survival of rural cultures and communities (Kramer & Johnson, 1996; Johnson & Kramer, 1995). Sustainable development activities often require regional community collaboration (Bernard & Young, 1997; Murray & Dunn, 1996). Numerous cases exist in which communities in the same region have worked together to develop and publicize mural projects as a sustainable economic development activity. One example of those efforts is the Regional Heritage Area Mural Corridor, which is being created by 20 rural counties in southeastern Ohio.

MURAL DEVELOPMENT PROJECTS IN FOUR SMALL TOWNS

This chapter focuses on the use of street murals as a community project to create "walls of pride" for residents of four small towns in eastern Washington State to remember their rural roots, traditions, and connections. The small towns are Sprague (population 452), Chewelah (population 2,200), Uniontown (population 305), and Dayton (population 2,500). This analysis of the mural projects is based on a series of group interviews with town residents regarding the ideas, planning, designs, financing, painting, community involvement, decision making, time frames, and economic development that are essential for the development of a rural community's murals. After providing their name and town of residence, participants in the group interviews were asked to respond to the following nine questions:

1. What role did you play in the development of the mural?
2. How was the idea of the mural first developed?
3. How were the ideas, plans, designs, financing, and painting discussed, organized, and decided upon?
4. How was the design of the mural chosen?
5. How did community involvement, decision making, and time frames enter into the planning and success of the project?
6. Has there been any economic development benefit from the development of the mural?
7. What have been the positive outcomes of the project and the negative outcomes, if any?
8. How has the community benefited from a project that included and involved so many members of the town?
9. If you had to do it over again, what would you do differently and what would you do the same?

SPRAGUE

This small town is located near a lake at the edge of the rolling hills of the Palouse region of eastern Washington. The primary business of the area is wheat and lentil farming. Sixty-three percent of the town's residents are either low-income or retired people.

The entire community of Sprague was involved in the planning, design, development, and funding of its mural. Sprague's wall of pride reflects the way the main street of the town looked in 1889 and features a hardware store, bath house, hotel, saloon, stables, and barber shop. The catalyst for the mural was the 1989 Washington State centennial.

In 1988 several people in Sprague organized the Sprague Centennial Plaza Committee for the purpose of creating something for the centennial that would honor the state and also be good for Sprague. It was decided that the town would develop a mural on the side of an abandoned building and develop a town park on the site of a vacant lot filled with trash and the broken-up foundation from a building. This effort not only revived civic pride but also engaged the townspeople in a common project. Children in the town helped design the mural from old photos. Children, adults, and senior citizens worked on preparing the wall for painting by chipping away plaster and making the wall surface smooth.

Financing the project became a community responsibility. There were bake sales, spaghetti feeds, a turn-of-the-century fashion show, yard sales, and a small grant from the local utility company. The people in Sprague who were developing the mural came up with a creative way to raise money. Each child raised one hundred pennies, then one hundred nickels, then one hundred dimes, and then one hundred quarters. Through these fundraising events Sprague raised $25,000!

The mural was a truly a community project. Some people donated their time to work on the mural, others donated materials to help build the mural, and other people with building skills volunteered their time and labor. The only part of the project that was paid for was the artist. The town wanted a contractual agreement for the mural to be painted so that it would not have to rely on a volunteer who might not complete the project. The town paid $4,000 to an out-of-town artist to sketch and paint its mural, and it was completed on time. Sprague proudly features its mural on town brochures and postcards.

In addition to the mural, the townspeople cleaned up the adjacent vacant lot, planted grass, and built a gazebo. This gazebo displays historical wall plaques that people and businesses have purchased to help finance not only the wall but also the construction of the park and gazebo.

The Sprague wall of pride also became a Campfire Project. The children earned badges and won state and national awards for their efforts. To accept one of their awards, they traveled with several parent chaperons to Washington, DC. Because everyone was involved in the project, there is a great deal of local pride in the mural as well as no vandalism: The Sprague wall of pride belongs to everyone in the community.

CHEWELAH

Chewelah is located in the northeast section of Washington in the Panorama Valley, near the Huckleberry Mountains. Chewelah has two tourist attractions: a golf course and a nearby downhill ski mountain. Its major industries are farming and timber logging. A major state highway, which has a great deal of traffic, runs through the middle of the town. Sixty-five percent of Chewelah's residents are low-income or retired people.

The idea for a mural was something the people of Chewelah have thought about for a long time: Discussion of murals can be found in community newspaper articles published more than 60 years ago. Current residents had talked about creating a mural for several years. The Chewelah Chamber of Commerce was interested in economic development and the town's image. Its members thought a mural would be a way of making the town more attractive to people driving through and to those who might stay for golf or skiing. The chamber formed a mural committee to raise money, select a design, and find an artist to paint the mural. The mural committee was hopeful that a mural beside the state highway would interest people in stopping to look at the mural and spend their money in town. The chamber saw a mural not only as a symbol of pride but also as a springboard for economic development.

The mural committee got the local communications company to let them use a wall on the company's building. The mural committee had to decide whether the mural was going to depict what Chewelah used to look like, what it looks like now, or what they would like the town to be. The scene that was finally decided on, which reflected the community's roots, was a 1920s farm scene with rolling hills and pasture. The scene was created from old photos in the local museum.

The mural committee raised about $1,700 for the mural and found a local artist who would paint it. Local stores donated the painting materials. A problem arose when the artist moved out of town. In response, the mural committee contracted with a sign painter to finish the mural. In the end the mural cost the committee $1,200, but the experience of the artist leaving was disappointing to the mural committee members.

Even though the mural was not a community project, the mural committee members received a great deal of input from the town residents. The mural committee was also well connected and networked with the town so that the painting was not seen as "only" a Chamber of Commerce venture. The mural committee is now planning on using the remaining $500 to paint other murals depicting historic objects, such as an old printing press. The mural committee is also considering getting information and consultation from Toppenish, Washington, a small town in the south central part of the state that has made its murals a huge tourist attraction, complete with a dinner theater.

One of the outcomes of painting the mural was that a mural committee member became interested in painting a mural on an outside wall of her hair-styling salon business. She designed it herself. Some people in the town were "nervous" because they did not know what would be painted. She hired a painter for $1,600, materials included, and then worried about the painter falling and her insurance not covering the injuries (he did not fall).

The completed mural was a painting of modern townhouses in pastel shades. Many people in the town breathed a sigh of relief when they saw the final product. Now people in the town compare the two different murals, and few people like both of them. "Why can't they be more alike?" is a common complaint, but the owner is happy with her mural. She has also built a pocket garden park around the painting. The park and mural have become something of which she is proud, and she feels that they are improvements the whole town can enjoy.

UNIONTOWN

Uniontown is in the heart of the rolling Palouse hills of eastern Washington. The primary business of the community and surrounding rural area is wheat and lentil farming. Uniontown is also a bedroom community for Washington State University, which is approximately 25 miles away. The Uniontown mural was a project of several newcomers to the community who formed an informal organization named "The Uniontowners." The project was undertaken by people representing about 24 households who wanted to show that they had pride in their new community. The project itself was a good example of using group dynamics to create cohesion, group purpose and focus, and group strength and identity. The project brought the

Uniontowners together for the entire summer, and created a basis for future projects, friendships, and successes. The newcomers learned they could work together and get along, too. The Uniontowners also used the mural project as a way to connect with the community, build credibility, and show the old-timers that they cared about Uniontown. The mural project was their was of becoming part of the community.

The project began when one of the Uniontowner members approached the owner of the barn, herself a newcomer, with the idea of putting a sign on the barn, which was on the highway between Lewiston, Idaho, and Spokane, Washington. The sign would say, "Welcome To Town." The owner liked the idea, but was unfamiliar with what would be involved in creating a sign. By the end of the mural development project, the "Welcome" sign had evolved into a wall of pride.

The proposed sign evolved into a colorful farming scene that is reminiscent of the art of Van Gogh and Cezanne. The farm scene that evolved features rolling, planted hillsides being harvested by a peapicker (gleaner) combine. The design was a combination of several designs from a contest that the Uniontowners held for the local schoolchildren. The barn owner contributed the money ($876) for the paint and rental equipment needed. The Uniontowners did not hire an artist to paint their mural; rather, they worked on the project not only because it was fun but also because they wanted to give something positive to Uniontown. The wall of pride took more than a thousand hours of the members' time to design and paint; it became everyone's summer weekend project.

Several of the town's old-timers were quite impressed and expressed a sense of "wonderment" with the mural and what the Uniontowners had done. However, one old-timer said, "Didn't they have anything better to do?" The old-timers did not participate, but they did watch, and two contributed money to the project. The town's old-timers developed respect for the newcomers not only because they created something for the town but also because they stuck to it and completed the project. The mural has also had a positive response from many highway drivers, who often stop to admire the wall of pride and take photos.

The newcomer wall of pride project had many positive spin-offs for Uniontown. The community applied for a grant to build a town park, and it used the mural as an example of how it could get a project accomplished (the town got the grant). The Uniontowners used their newfound momentum to paint the community church, and then put up welcome signs around town, thus eventually carrying out the original project idea that spawned the mural. They also believe that their learning to work together on the mural was instrumental in getting the highway through town paved. Because of their wall of pride, Uniontown is now "more than a slow spot in the road."

The process of painting the community's mural created many relationships, connections, and linkages. An interesting outcome of the project was a realization by the townspeople that the newcomers really did care about what happened to Uniontown and that they had infused the community with new energy. One of the Uniontowner members has been elected Uniontown mayor, and another Uniontowner, the owner of the barn on which the mural was painted, has been appointed to the town's planning commission. The outsiders have become insiders.

DAYTON

Dayton is located near the Snake River at the edge of the Palouse. The Touchet River runs through Dayton, a golf course is nearby, and ski slopes are in the Blue Mountains. The primary business of the surrounding rural area is wheat and pea farming, and a Green Giant processing plant is in Dayton. The town has an active historical society and has restored the train depot, which is now on the National Register of Historic Places. Dayton is the county seat for Columbia County and has a uniquely designed courthouse; it holds two festivals annually to celebrate its community heritage.

In 1994 several members of the Broughton family, who own a land company, and their friends got together and decided that they were going to make Dayton a brighter place by painting a mural on one of the walls of their company's building, which is located on the town's main street. They received many design suggestions and decided on four building scenes from Dayton in the 1890s to honor their community. The project reflected a family's pride in the roots of their town. The mural depicts the history of a small town and is an attempt to preserve that history for residents and future generations.

The Dayton mural began as a family project, but it quickly involved friends and many residents of Dayton. The mural was totally financed by the Broughton family, at a cost of $8,000. Although the Broughton family initially planned the project, almost the entire town worked on the mural. Both the townspeople and family members prepared the wall. Dayton residents were proud of their participation in the project and the way it turned out. The family chose a well-known artist to design the mural, because they wanted to be sure that the mural would be of professional quality. The artist supplied the paint and directed the townspeople in the painting of the mural.

The family chose four buildings (Fraternity Hall, the Dayton Hotel, the Mercantile, and the Portland Flour Mill), all of which had great historical significance to Dayton and to the family. Some family members remembered the buildings from their youth, before they were burned or torn down, or had been told stories about them by their parents and grandparents. To design the mural, old photos were used to determine what the buildings had looked like. The mural became a visual reminder of Dayton's history and the residents' pride in that history.

During the painting of the mural, the family constructed a grandstand and a local club developed a concession stand, so that residents of Dayton and the surrounding rural community could sit and watch the mural being painted on the company wall. One of the benefits of painting the mural was that even though it was hard work, everyone had a good time and enjoyed working together for a project that would benefit the town. The town took on the project with a great deal of enthusiasm.

The Broughton family chose the mural scenes because they wanted current and future residents of Dayton to know and be proud of the history of the town. Various family members therefore used the painting of the mural as an opportunity to teach classes of schoolchildren an engaging history lesson about Dayton and the town they lived in. The field trips to the mural were an excellent example of using a visual aid to tell and enhance an oral history.

Almost as an afterthought, and because they had a little bit of money left over, the mural painters decided to paint another mural on the town's main street. One purpose of this new mural was to cover up a building's glittering cinderblock front. Originally the building had been a J.C. Penney store, so the mural painters decided that this mural would depict J.C. Penney's store windows in the early 1900s. This design shared the historical theme of the other mural. The family used its own money again, but this time another person helped finance the mural. Most of the money was donated by an out-of-town resident who had a strong appreciation for the town of Dayton and all that had been generated by the painting of the first wall of pride. Both murals were completed in 1995.

Out of the two projects the Dayton Mural Society was formed. The society has advised two other small towns which are interested in painting their own walls of pride. A related family project was the publishing of a brochure detailing the development of the mural and the history of each building on the Dayton mural. The brochure is available just outside the Broughton Land Company office on Dayton's main street.

One of the natural outcomes of the ways in which the family involved the children of the town is that the children felt that they "own" the mural. The children wanted to take care of the town mural, because they felt there was something good about the place and they were the keepers of the town history. Because the community had participated in the painting of the mural, the townspeople had feelings of ownership. As a result, no acts of vandalism have been directed at the Dayton walls of pride. The family has succeeded in passing on to the next generation their pride in Dayton and the history of their community.

COMMUNITY SIMILARITIES AND DIFFERENCES

Many similarities and differences exist among the four rural communities that used murals to show their community pride. None of the organizers of the four walls of pride knew of the other towns' murals until this information was shared with them by the interviewer. All the people interviewed wanted a video copy of their group interview as well as the other towns' interviews to see how each town did its mural project and to get new ideas for future projects and funding. The people in Dayton are particularly interested in their interview as a way of preserving the oral history of not only the painting of the mural but also the history of the buildings on the mural.

Even though the primary purpose of the projects—the creation of murals—was the same in each small town, the motivation of the organizers was different in each community. In Sprague the motivation was to clean up the town. In Chewelah the motivation was economic development. In Uniontown the motivation to show the town that the organizers were part of the community. In Dayton the motivation was to preserve part of the town's history.

The intentions of the organizers with regard to using the mural development process to create linkages and relationships also differed. In Sprague the organizers' intention was to encourage community involvement. The Chewelah organizers wanted to use the mural as a way of making the town attractive to tourists passing through. In Uniontown the newcomers wanted to establish credibility with the old-timers. In Dayton the organizers wanted to share the town's history with current and future residents.

Because the mural organizers' motivations and intentions all were different, the processes for developing the walls of pride were also different in each town. In Sprague, the Centennial Plaza Committee involved the whole town and made it a community project, but in Chewelah the participation was mostly from the Chamber of Commerce and business community. In Uniontown participation was limited primarily to newcomers who were members of the Uniontowners, but it also appears that the old-timers were hesitant to participate. In Dayton, the Broughton family created opportunities to involve many of the community residents.

Despite their differences, all four towns have many similar feelings about their murals. All the towns' murals are truly walls of pride. The organizers and the towns are proud of what was represented about their towns on the murals. Some of the purposes that the organizers shared were that the murals would help bring their community together, renew community spirit, and strengthen community pride. All the murals reflect each town's roots. Even though two of the murals are town scenes (Sprague and Dayton) and two of the murals are farm scenes (Chewelah and Uniontown), they all reflect the heritage of their roots. In the four rural communities the farms and towns are interdependent. Consequently, the mural scenes are truly shared histories and a successful projects that encourage small towns to remember and affirm their roots.

IMPLICATIONS FOR RURAL SOCIAL WORK PRACTICE

What implications for rural social work practice and community organizing can be learned from the four community interviews regarding the development of the murals? First, most rural communities are individual social systems that have their own unique structure, communication patterns, rules, and ways in which projects get accomplished. Unlike most urban communities, which have policies, procedures, and union contracts that give a certain uniformity, consistency, and predictability to planning and projects, small rural towns have fewer established planning structures. Thus, small communities exhibit considerable variation in the ways in which they go about the process of change.

It is essential for rural social workers to know how the community that in which they are working (and, possibly, living) successfully organizes; they need to know who has power, how decisions are made, what process must be followed for a plan to succeed, and who needs to be involved and when (Kahn, 1991). How does a rural social worker learn these essential community organization processes? By observing, listening, asking, and learning about the present and past of the community, including its history of failure and success.

Another critical factor that can be learned from the experience of the four rural communities in the development of their murals is that the broader the base of support, involvement, and participation of the town residents is, the more likely it is that the mural will be completed and that there will be high positive community satisfaction with the completed project. Residents want to be informed and have their ideas considered, even if they do not participate directly in the project.

Community organizing leadership and skills can be found in a variety of people in small towns. Leadership can come from informal leaders, as in Sprague (neighbors and friends), and recognized community leaders, as in Dayton (a founding family), or leadership can come from a formal organization (Chewelah Chamber of Commerce) or a "semiformal" organization (Uniontowners/newcomers). The key to success for the rural social worker is to have an understanding of the community and to work with the community to use its energy and talents to successfully identify and accomplish the tasks at hand. The murals are as symbolic of how communities can accomplish tasks as they are of the communities' pride in showing their heritage to the world.

Finally, rural social workers can learn how proud rural community residents are of their accomplishments. The residents appreciate the recognition given to their towns for their murals and the community heritage that the murals represent. The experience of creating a mural can lay the foundation for ongoing community participation in development activities. They are visible evidence of residents' pride in their communities and in their ability to work together to make their vision a reality.

REFERENCES

Bernard, T., & Young, J. (1997). *The ecology of hope: Communities collaborate for sustainability*. East Haven, CT: New Society Publishers.

Johnson, C., & Kramer, J. (1995). Sustainable development and social development: Necessary partners for the future. *Journal of Sociology and Social Welfare, 23,* 75–91.

Johnson, K., & Beale, C. (1998). The rural rebound. *The Wilson Quarterly, 22*(2), 16–27.

Jossi, F. J. (1997). Small town survival strategies. *Planning, 63*(10), 4–8.

Kahn, S. (1991). *Organizing: A guide for grassroots leaders* (Rev. ed.). Silver Spring, MD: NASW Press.

Klein, W. (1993). Visions of things to come. *Planning, 59*(5), 10–15.

Kramer, J., & Johnson, C. (1996). The global economy, global sustainability and social development. *Social Development Issues, 17*(2/3), 19–37.

McKnight, J. (1992). Redefining community. *Social Policy, 17*(3), 54–58.

McNeil, L. B. (1995). The soft arts of organizing. *Social Policy, 26*(2), 16–22.

Murray, M., & Dunn, L. (1996). *Revitalizing rural America: A perspective on collaboration and community*. Chichester, NY: John Wiley.

Overton, P. (1997). *Rebuilding the front porch of America: Essays on the art of community making*. Columbia, MO: University of Missouri Press.

Sullivan, W. P. (1994). The tie that binds: A strengths model for social development. *Social Development Issues, 16*(3), 100–111.

CHAPTER FIFTEEN

Building Support for Rural Elderly People with Mental Illness: The Carolina Companions Project

Anne-Linda Furstenberg and Denise Gammonley

Mental illness in old age is a serious problem in terms of the number of people affected, treatment complications arising from coexisting physical and psychiatric illnesses, impediments to service response, and stigma associated with receiving mental health care. Resource limitations, organizational constraints, and attitudinal barriers particularly affect older people receiving services through publicly funded community mental health systems (Swan, Fox, & Estes, 1989). These features hinder mental health service delivery to older people even more in the rural South. In these communities barriers are exacerbated by the region's high rates of illiteracy, poverty, and substandard housing and by the persistence of negative racial attitudes (Abraham & Neese, 1993).

The Carolina Companions Project was designed to increase access to services, community integration, and long-term well-being of older mental health consumers in one rural North Carolina county. Based on a model of community supportive care developed in rural Wisconsin (Cannady, 1982; Sullivan, 1989), the project provided a sustained, informal companion relationship to older people receiving outpatient services through the local mental health center. This chapter examines the significance of mental illness among older people in rural areas, and describes the theoretical foundations, program components, and preliminary outcomes of this project.

BACKGROUND

Past studies have estimated that between 7 and 25 percent of the population age 65 and older have a serious mental disorder (George, Blazer, & Winfield-Laird, 1988; Regier et al., 1993; Roybal, 1988). This statistic includes about 1 percent of the older population that have schizophrenia (Gurland and Cross, 1982). In addition, community-dwelling older adults also report high rates of psychiatric symptoms, particularly depressive symptoms (Blazer, 1989; National Institutes of Health, 1991). Elderly people nevertheless receive significantly less treatment for depressive disorders when compared with younger adults (National Institutes of Health, 1991). Minority status diminishes even more the likelihood of receiving treatment (Kessler et al., 1996), despite comparable prevalence rates for non-whites and whites (Regier et al., 1993; Somervell, Leaf, Weissman, Glazer, & Livingston-Bruce, 1989; Williams, Takeuchi, & Adair, 1992).

Although they represent 12 percent of the population, people over age 65 comprise only 6 percent of the clientele of community mental health centers and only 2 percent of private mental health care clients (Roybal, 1988). Older adults experiencing a mental illness are more likely to seek care in the general medical sector than in specialized mental health services (Waxman, 1986). At the same time, however, they consume psychotropic medications at the highest rates (Blazer, 1989; Burns & Taub, 1980; Waxman, 1986).

A variety of factors accounts for the under-representation of elderly people among recipients of mental health services (Furstenberg & Koons, 1995). These factors include:

- the reluctance of elderly people to seek mental health care labeled as such;
- limitations in physical mobility;
- difficulties with transportation (Bachrach, 1977; Heussy, 1972; Prue, Kinane, Cornel, & Foy, 1979; U.S. General Accounting Office, 1982);
- difficulty locating appropriate services (Wood & Parham, 1990);
- the failure of health professionals to recognize the need for mental health services (Butler & Lewis, 1982; Waxman, 1986); and
- the lack of psychiatrists, social workers, or psychologists with specialized training in gerontology (Roybal, 1988).

In addition, limited reimbursement mechanisms for aging-specific mental health services (Swan, Fox, & Estes, 1989) and increased targeting of services to youths with serious emotional disturbance have further reduced access and outreach services to elderly people (Estes, Binney, & Linkins, 1994).

In addition to the lack of fit between their needs and the mental health system, rural elderly people with mental illness are also poorly served by the aging service system (Rathbone-McCuan, 1993). Most rural area agencies on aging (AAAs) are not able to give high priority to the funding of services for elderly people with mental health problems (National Resource Center for the Rural Elderly, 1994).

Social support, social integration, and full community participation have been identified as important predictors of long-term functioning among elderly people with severe and persistent mental illness (Harding, Brooks, Ashikaga, Strauss, and Breier, 1987; Meeks et al., 1990). Despite the importance of social support, older people with mental illnesses may have access to few social support resources. Stigmatizing attitudes, support network attrition because of long-term mental illness or the loss of age peers, diminished mobility as the result of age-related decrements, and lack of access to transportation pose critical barriers. Participation in the life of the community remains even more elusive for older people residing in rural residential care settings. Neglect of socialization needs, coupled with a lack of daily activities or opportunities for productive roles, affects both the functional status and self-esteem of seniors residing in these facilities (Gottesman, Peskin, & Kennedy, 1991). When opportunities for structured social contact between stigmatized people and their neighbors are available, however, these negative attitudes have been found to change (Desforges et al., 1991).

Innovative service models that take account of the special needs of elderly people and the rural character of the community have demonstrated success both in reaching under-served elderly people and in maintaining their residence in the community (Buckwalter, 1991; Raschko, 1991; Snustad, Thompson-Heisterman, Neese, & Abraham, 1993). Rural geriatric outreach models in Iowa and Virginia (Abraham et al., 1993) both emphasize in-home assessment and treatment by professional multidisciplinary teams with nursing as the lead discipline. The Virginia model serves a racially diverse southern population and emphasizes the use of informal resources such as neighbor and friend networks to overcome significant resource limitations. The Senior Adult Growth and Enrichment (SAGE) Program in rural North Carolina demonstrated the effectiveness of providing nonstigmatizing day programming for older consumers, as well as outreach to elderly people with mental illness in their own homes (Atkinson & Stuck, 1991).

Descriptions of peer companion projects have underscored their utility not only for reducing inpatient psychiatric hospitalization (Thwing & Cannady, 1979), but also for improving quality of life and consumer satisfaction (Greenberg, Greenley, & Benedict, 1993; Skirboll, 1994). In rural locales, given the scant resources spread over large areas, case manager extenders(paraprofessionals used as outreach workers and peer counselors) may be a particularly effective strategy for serving elderly people whose physical mobility and transportation problems diminish their access to mental health treatment (Buckwalter, 1991).

The "Rhinelander Model" (Cannady, 1982; Sullivan, 1989) trains and pays well-functioning community members to provide companionship for people with serious mental illness. Use of these paid case manager extenders—in the Rhinelander model called "community workers"—has been found to enhance functioning and promote social integration of clients. Community workers serve as role model, friend, and coach in the development of social competence. Descriptive data indicate that the Rhinelander service model has been successful in reducing total inpatient psychiatric days by 74 percent to 92 percent and hospitalization costs by 97 percent in three rural Wisconsin counties (Cannady, 1982). The model has also produced substantial gains in independence from expensive mental health services and in consumer self-esteem (personal communication with M. L. Galli, Clinical Director, Community Supportive Care, Rhinelander, WI, August 17, 1995).

Despite the demonstrated usefulness of models such as the ones just reviewed, AAAs have cited use of trained volunteers to assist older people with mental illness as one of the least available service modalities (DeCroix-Bane, Rathbone-McCuan,

& Galliher, 1994). Peer companion models have been slow to spread, perhaps because these programs have lacked the rigorous outcome evaluations that specify service elements and demonstrate their connection with particular consumer outcomes.

THEORETICAL FRAMEWORK

Mechanic's (1989) coping and social adaptation theory of chronic mental illness provides a framework for understanding the performance of geriatric outreach models and peer companion or case manager extender models. The coping and adaptation treatment framework emphasizes education in pro-social activities within the community, rather than treatment of deficits in a separate medicalized setting.

Mechanic's (1989) model uses a problem-solving orientation in its definition of successful adaptation as effective coping, which "involves not only the ability to react to environmental demands but also the ability to anticipate and plan events and the capacity to influence and control both the demands to which one will be exposed and the pace of exposure" (p. 122). Mechanic outlined the requirements for successful coping of people with mental illness as follows:

1. effective problem-solving skills
2. accurate cognitive appraisal of social situations
3. motivation to try out new behaviors
4. maintenance of an adequate level of equilibrium in psychological functioning
5. adequate formal and informal resources in the community.

Models using nonprofessional helpers may offer one cost-effective means for assisting elderly people with mental illness in underserved rural areas acquire the skills and resources required for successful coping.

DESCRIPTION OF PROGRAM

The Carolina Companions Program was a collaborative project of the School of Social Work at the University of North Carolina at Chapel Hill, the Vance-Warren-Franklin-Granville Area Mental Health/Developmental Disabilities/Substance Abuse (MH/DD/SA) Program, and the Coordinating Council for Senior Citizens of Warren County. The program matched retired people with mental health consumers in a paid companion relationship and provided services from September 1996 through February 1998. A North Carolina foundation, local corporations, and private donors provided funding both for the companion program and for a comprehensive evaluation to determine the program's outcome. Medicaid funding covered the companion services for people who met eligibility criteria.

Program Model

The Carolina Companions Program used the Rhinelander program just described as its model (Cannady, 1982; Sullivan, 1989). The Rhinelander Project was developed in the mid-1970s to increase access to mental health services for residents of three northern rural counties of Wisconsin. (Through providing companion services, the Rhinelander program seeks to prevent psychiatric hospitalization; to improve psychiatric status and social functioning, performance of daily-living tasks, and overall quality of life; and to increase community acceptance of people with mental illness. The model emphasizes the natural abilities of competent and caring community members to help adult mental health consumers build the skills and motivation necessary for effective community functioning.

The model rests on several assumptions. Competent community members have built up skills for managing their own lives and "taking care of themselves." If a community member can take care of him- or herself by setting limits on the mental health consumer's demands and by communicating more adult expectations to the consumer, the consumer will benefit. The model posits that supporting the companions' competencies and skills and their growth will lead to increases in the competencies of the consumers with whom companions have a relationship.

An accessible and supportive supervisor, group meetings, and cohesiveness among the companions have been found to be critical requisites for successful service to consumers and for the long-term commitment of community workers (companions) to the program. While promoting the companions' own personal growth, the program also increased their awareness and acceptance of mental illness, and; the companions in turn have influenced others in the community (personal communication with M. L. Galli, Clinical Director, Community Supportive Care, Rhinelander, WI, August 17, 1995). Most important, the richness of the support provided to the community workers, the personal growth they experienced, and the prevention of burnout through encouraging them to take care of themselves and to limit consumers' demands on them resulted in the workers' long-term commitment to and participation in the program.

Although the Wisconsin program used and served adults ages 18 to 60, Carolina Companions focused on retired people as companions for older adult mental health consumers. We focused on older consumers out of our shared concern about the inability of overburdened mental health staff to provide the continuous support that might have improved consumers' psychosocial functioning. Participating consumers continued to receive mental health services. We thought, however, that providing a companion, although not a substitute for mental health services, might reduce the need for services and augment their effectiveness as well.

We chose to recruit retired people as companions for several reasons. Like the community members working in the Wisconsin program, retired people can draw on the skills they have built up over a whole lifetime, as well as their direct acquaintance with the challenges of old age. In addition, many retired people want opportunities to contribute to their communities. A program like this, in which the companions are paid, may also help meet financial and leisure needs.

Whereas the Wisconsin counties have a mixture of white and Native American populations, the county we selected had a racially mixed population including African Americans and Native Americans. We wanted to test the usefulness of this project in a more racially mixed region and in the context of the culturally distinct traditions of the rural Southeast.

Setting

Of the counties served by our mental health center collaborators, we selected Warren County, the county poorest in human services resources. Sixty percent of its 18,000 residents are African American, and 39 percent are white. Eighteen percent of county residents are age 65 or older (North Carolina Office of State Planning, 1998) in a state where only 12 percent of residents fall in that age group (U.S. Bureau of the Census, 1998). The county has the highest poverty rate in the state—28 percent (North Carolina Office of State Planning). The racial disparities in economic status in Warren County are clear: Thirty-nine percent of African Americans, but only 10 percent of whites, are living in poverty. Of Warren County residents 65 years of age and older, 32 percent live below the poverty line.

Consumers

From among the consumers age 60 and older served by the mental health clinic in Warren County, the mental health staff selected those who they thought would benefit from the program. The inclusion criteria we used were as follows:

- serious psychiatric illness;
- age 60 or older;
- risk for psychiatric hospitalization;
- residing independently or in domiciliary care;
- lack of threat of violence;
- absence of current alcohol or substance abuse;
- absence of significant cognitive impairment; and
- physical capacity to participate in activities.

In part, the research constrained the criteria used in selecting consumers, because we wanted to select people with a good chance of improving their functioning. For this reason, we excluded people in nursing homes and people with significant cognitive impairment. For the retired people we recruited, however, these consumer criteria created the conditions for a relatively rewarding relationship in terms of the consumer's ability to communicate and potential for improvement and the moderate level of challenge these consumers' mental problems posed. Twenty-one of the consumers meeting selection criteria and considered appropriate by the staff accepted the invitation to participate in the program.

Fourteen of the 21 participating consumers were age 74 or younger; seven were age 75 or older. Fourteen were African American, six were white, and one was Native American. Nineteen were women, and two were men. Eleven were eligible for Medicaid, meaning that Medicaid reimbursed their companion services. Ten were not eligible for Medicaid. Fourteen lived in the community, and seven lived in domiciliary care facilities. Fifteen of the participating consumers had depressive disorders, four had anxiety disorders, and two had schizophrenia. Thirteen of the 21 consumers had required at least one psychiatric hospitalization in the past; nine of these occurred during the preceding 10 years, and seven of the nine during the five years before the program began.

Companions

The Carolina Companions Program recruited, hired, and trained a total of 17 companions—all retired individuals. To find companions, we used the senior center, the local newspapers, contacts we had had with seniors during the planning phase of the project, and key people in the community. The newspaper ads, mandated by state hiring policy, did not attract anyone; companions later explained to us that "people over 60 don't read the want ads." Most people heard of the project by word of mouth. People whom the senior center director approached became interested and then recruited their friends and, in some cases, family members.

In interviewing potential companions, we looked for mental competence, warmth, tolerance of differences, and a sense of humor. We probed for applicants' comfort with people with mental illnesses and imaginativeness about how they might feel. Driving ability, availability of a car, and knowledge of the community culture were also important requisites. We also assessed ability to report observations and to follow instructions. Discomfort with mental illness, judgmental attitudes, and pay as the prime motive for applying raised red flags and were a basis for rejecting an applicant.

The companions were a heterogeneous group. Nine (64 percent) of the companions were African American, and five (36 percent) were white. Six (43 percent) were between ages 60 and 69, and the remainder (57 percent) were age 70 or older. Eleven (79 percent) were women, and three (21 percent) were men. Half (50 percent) had 12 or fewer years of education; the rest had business school, college, or graduate training.

A few companions signed on to the program to counter their own loneliness, but most had provided help to others in their community before. For them, participating as a companion was a logical extension of their life pattern. Most companions reported receiving adequate levels of social support; a few expressed the desire to provide more support to others. Most companion and consumer participants in the Carolina Companions Project had either resided in Warren County all their lives or had returned there following earlier migration to the North in search of employment opportunities.

Training and Supervision

A two-day training, provided by a consultant from the Wisconsin program, built on the premise that companions knew how to take care of themselves and prepared them to use this skill in their relationship with the consumer. The training provided a simplified framework for understanding consumer behavior and for guiding their own behavior. Specifically, the training introduced companions to the parent–adult–child schema from transactional analysis (Berne, 1964) and the concept of a truck that can carry two tons, but no more, as a metaphor for preventing companion overload.

The project director, an experienced social worker with local ties, held supervision two times a month for one hour. The case manager and the adult services director often attended. One of the two meetings was in good part devoted to administrative matters and assistance with and discussion of record keeping. Companions were paid for supervisory time and for mileage traveling to and from the meetings and for their time and mileage traveling to, from, and with their consumer. The rate per hour was $6.14, and companions generally earned $100 to $125 per month. Companions had to keep time sheets, travel records, and logs, in which they described their activities in relation to the clinical goals for the consumer. Managing these tasks, particularly for the companions with less education, consumed a good deal of administrative and supervisory time. After a short period, however, the supervisor and mental health staff were able to limit these matters to only one of the two meetings per month.

The other meeting could then be used for discussion of the companions' experiences with their consumers. Supervision in this program model embodied the assumptions of the program model described previously: that companions have good judgment, competence, and life skills; that promoting the growth of the companion will result in the growth of the consumer; and that with adequate support, the companions will be able to work long term with their consumers. The purposes of the supervision were to provide support to the companions, to help them solve problems that came up with consumers, and to help them develop new skills. Clinical staff from the mental health center participated with an occasional didactic presentation and with contributions to the discussion of issues and problems the companions brought to the meetings.

The group supervision meetings reinforced the concepts communicated in the training, helped develop collegiality between the companions and the mental health staff, and melded the companions into a highly productive group for support and problem solving. Companions offered suggestions and commiseration, reminded one another about practice principles learned in the training, and supported each other through personal crises. The following excerpt illustrates the importance of the supervision meetings for the companions.

> I have enjoyed meeting the other companions. I love our time—we all like our time together in which we ask each other questions about what to do. . . . The supervised meetings were very informative. It lets you know that you're on the right track, that

you're thinking along the same lines and doing—handling some of the same problems that they have.

Sharing their experiences with the others and seeing that they faced common problems was a useful tool for group supervision and led to frequent collective problem solving.

As it turned out, the injunction to the companion to "take care of yourself" was clearly a critical component of the training. Without help to the companions in learning to set limits to their own benevolence, these companions—so accustomed to helping others—would have quickly burned out in dealing with the intense dependency needs of the consumers. The words of this companion illustrate her commitment to her consumer and the importance of the idea of self-care.

> I don't know if I should say it, the other part I like about it. My supervisor says that when you feel like you need to, you know, take a break, you can do it. Most jobs you can't. [laughs] So, that's what I like. That's one thing I like about it, 'cause for almost the month of April I was in El Paso, Texas, with my daughter, and I was thinking what's gonna happen to her and what's gonna happen, maybe I might have to forget my job, you know, but when I talked to my supervisor, she said, . . . "Good, you need a break. We'll have someone to look in on her while you're gone." She is, she's alright. And I kind of hated to leave her for that long. But I couldn't go that far and just come right back.

Without this support for taking time off, this companion would have had to choose between her work and family obligations.

The supervisor identified a number of factors that contributed to creating a supportive environment for meeting with an older group. The area had to be easily accessible physically, comfortable, and private and had to have adequate parking. Regular, predictable times for the supervision group meetings were important for setting up a routine. The payment to companions for supervisory time helped underscore its importance. Prompt beginning and ending of the supervision provided needed structure.

The availability of the supervisor outside the planned meetings seems to have been a critical ingredient of the project. The supervisor sometimes needed to help people with paperwork or provide immediate consultation when a companion was uncertain what to do or when crises occurred. A considerable number of the companions sought advice from the supervisor about such problems as personal illness or illness of a family member, difficulties with impaired adult children, or financial problems. The companions depended on this confidential, concerned attention of the supervisor, and her assistance with problem solving no doubt facilitated their continuation in the program.

Companion–Consumer Activities

Companions and consumers negotiated a wide range of activities, such as assistance with travel to appointments with doctors, dentists, and other medical professionals;

joint participation in such senior center activities as exercise programs and line dancing; discussing symptoms and negotiating communication with the mental health case manager or other staff; and shopping, attending church services together, going out together to eat, visiting the companion's home to share a holiday meal with companion's family, visiting the consumer's relatives, helping consumers get places they needed to get, working together on household tasks, and going out for other recreational activities such as fishing. An important activity for some consumer–companion pairs was just driving around together. Several companions spent time taking consumers to see familiar places from their past, sometimes discovering common past experiences and sharing reminiscences. This was found to be a comforting and distracting activity when the consumer's spirits were particularly low. Another companion–consumer pair discovered a mutual interest in quilting and spent time together doing this activity. One companion, paired with a visually impaired consumer, found a program to teach people how to cope with and compensate for visual problems, transported her consumer to it, and attended with her.

Yet another companion took her consumer to a local senior center where she got her involved in line dancing. At the holiday party during the second year of the project, they and a few others demonstrated their line dancing steps, to the delight of all present. When one companion visited her consumer in the domiciliary care facility, their conversations gradually began to involve other rest home residents. This not only benefited the other residents, but it also stimulated increased interaction between the participating consumer and the other residents in the home.

As might be expected in this elderly population, health crises were not uncommon. When consumers were hospitalized or moved to a nursing home, companions visited and provided support. Companions and consumers became attached to one another, and the presence of the companion eased transitions for consumers experiencing moves, even when the move would necessitate termination of the companion–consumer relationship.

There was a fair amount of attrition among consumers. Two consumers died, and two moved to facilities outside the county and were phased out of the study. At the time of the second interview, three other consumers were unable to be interviewed because they were too ill, too stressed, or in a nursing home. On the other hand, three new consumers had entered the program—one in late 1996, and two in 1997, because we continued to accept consumers until July 1997. Companions were able to manage these changes both emotionally and in terms of the way that they handled transitions from one consumer to another.

Payment for Services

Services for Medicaid-eligible consumers were paid for under the Client Behavioral Intervention (CBI) program. This program pays for mental health interventions delivered by nonprofessional workers under the supervision of a case manager. Services for the other consumers were covered under the foundation grant that provided the bulk of financial support for the project and its evaluation. School of

Social Work resources and charitable donations from corporations and individuals supported other expenses and some of the project staff time.

EVALUATING THE IMPACT OUTCOMES OF THE PROGRAM

To evaluate the program, we measured changes in perceived social support, health, psychiatric symptoms, social functioning, and quality of life for consumers. We also examined alterations in perceived social support, health, well-being, and age self-concept of the companions. These measurements were gathered in structured interviews at baseline and at six-month intervals during the project. Qualitative interviews at the same time probed companions' and consumers' experiences in the program. In addition, tape recordings of the first year of supervision meetings and several in-depth case studies provided additional information about consumers' and companions' responses.

Our most important finding is that none of the consumers required psychiatric hospitalization or psychiatric emergency visits during the 18 months of the program. The avoidance of hospitalization alone could establish the cost-effectiveness of this program. In addition, a few outcome findings, based on measurements at 12 months, are interesting and statistically significant. The project rested on the assumption that provision of a companion would increase perceptions of social support among the consumers. This perceived support would in turn lead to improved functioning. The scale we used measures three types of received social support: informational, emotional, and tangible support. Consumers did report an increase in receiving tangible support, and satisfaction with tangible support showed a consistent trend of improvement. The total of all three types of support received also showed a consistent trend of increase.

Although not a predicted outcome, consumers also reported increased satisfaction with the support they provided to others. Certainly, there was give and take between the consumer and the companion. When the companions shared details of their lives, consumers were able to express concern about them. Having this experience, rather than that of only receiving help, may have been a very helpful change for the consumers.

Among objective measures, the number of daily activities showed a consistent trend of increase, an indicator we hope companion services affected. In the earliest stage of the program, there was also an appreciable jump in the number of doctor visits between the pre-program and the six-month measures. It seemed from our qualitative observations that with the help of the companions, many consumers were able to obtain services they had previously been unable to obtain. This leveled out by the 12-month interview.

Discussions with the case manager and review of the consumers' clinical records yielded qualitative evidence of changes in consumers' functioning. We observed that one consumer became more independent, whereas previously she would not venture out of the rest home without another resident. Another consumer copied the behavior, dress, and gestures of her companion; indeed, the grooming and appearance of many of the consumers improved. Therapists reported how positive their patients were about participating in the Carolina Companions Program and how much they enjoyed the companion and the activities they engaged in together. Therapists whose clients came to appointments accompanied by the companion also noted the closeness of the relationship between the two and noted the services that companions had been instrumental in brokering for the consumer.

A more thorough appraisal of all the evaluation data awaits processing of the fourth wave of interviews and analysis of the qualitative data. We will be examining changes both in consumers and in companions. Evaluation findings will be limited by the very small samples and by the difficulty in obtaining measures at all four time points.

IMPLICATIONS FOR PRACTICE

The model of care, training, and supervision is applicable to other programs using lay helpers, whether as volunteers or as paid employees. Lay helpers—retirement age or younger—can supply invaluable resources in many different types of human service systems and with care recipients of varying functional levels and of differing ages. Lay helpers working with very challenging care recipients require intensive training and continuing supportive supervision so that they can provide a successful service and so that they will be motivated to continue as helpers. Reducing turnover naturally results in increasingly successful functioning of the companions and boosts the cost-effectiveness of a program.

Our experience in the Carolina Companions Project suggested a number of provisions that may facilitate the use of retired people as lay helpers. Attention to the physical environment—both its comfort and its accessibility—is important for avoiding potential barriers to attendance or participation. Travel needs, recreation needs, and health problems of the retired lay helper and his or her family members are realities to be anticipated. In our project, group supervision, with its discussion of consumers, made it easy for one companion to fill in for another. Selection criteria for care recipients and the matching of care providers to recipients must take into account the somewhat diminished resilience and physical stamina of the older lay helpers.

The use of groups has many advantages for the supervision of lay helpers. Helpers can pool information, share data about community resources, exchange emotional support, and provide feedback to one another. In ways that are often more difficult for the professional supervisor, group members can confront, remind, and assist one another with problem solving. Although the professional may model desired behaviors for the group, the greater similarity of status and the parallel experiences of the lay helpers may increase the effectiveness of members serving as models for one another.

EPILOGUE

The Carolina Companions Project demonstrates the viability of the program model for mental health consumers in the rural Southeast. The mental health center staff were sufficiently satisfied with the results, particularly the absence of hospitalizations, that they decided to institutionalize the program as part of their regular services. The companions continued their employment with the mental health center after the end of the project.

Presentations and workshops about the project have found an interested and responsive audience. A manual that provides a template to guide other mental health centers and aging programs in creating a companions project is in production. Future plans include completion of the evaluation research and dissemination of findings that adequately document the changes in consumers and in companions. When a number of programs using the Carolina Companions model are in place, a larger-scale evaluation can be mounted that will test the efficacy of this intervention more rigorously.

REFERENCES

Abraham, I. L., Buckwalter, K. C., Snustad, D. G., Smullen, D. E., Thompson-Heisterman, A. A., Neese, J. B., & Smith, M. (1993). Psychogeriatric outreach to rural families: The Iowa and Virginia models. *International Psychogeriatrics, 5,* 203–211.

Abraham, I. L., & Neese, J. B. (1993). Outreach to the elderly and their families: Focus on the rural South. *Aging, 365,* 26–31.

Atkinson, V. L., & Stuck, B. M. (1991). Mental health services for the rural elderly: The SAGE experience. *Gerontologist, 31,* 90–94.

Bachrach, L. (1977). Deinstitutionalization of mental health services in rural areas. *Hospital and Community Psychiatry, 28,* 669–672.

Berne, E. (1964). *Games people play.* New York: Grove Press.

Blazer, D. (1989). The epidemiology of psychiatric disorders in late life. E. W. Busse & D. Blazer (Eds.), *Geriatric psychiatry* (pp. 235–262). Washington, DC: American Psychiatric Press.

Buckwalter, K. (1991). Mental health services for the rural elderly outreach program. *Gerontologist, 31,* 408–417.

Burns, B., & Taub, C. (1980). The epidemiology of dysphoria and depression in an elderly population. *American Journal of Psychiatry, 137,* 439–444.

Butler, R. N., & Lewis, M. I. (1982). *Aging in mental health.* St. Louis: C. V. Mosby.

Cannady, D. (1982). Chronics and cleaning ladies. *Psychosocial Rehabilitation Journal, 5,* 13–16.

DeCroix-Bane, S., Rathbone-McCuan, E., & Galliher, J. M. (1994). Mental health services for the elderly in rural America. In J. Krout (Ed.), *Providing community-based services to the rural elderly* (pp. 243–266). Thousand Oaks, CA: Sage Publications.

Desforges, D. M., Lord, C. G., Ramsey, S. L., Mason, J. A., Van Leeuwen, M. D., West, S. C., & Lepper, M. R. (1991). Effects of structured cooperative contact on changing negative attitudes toward stigmatized social groups. *Journal of Personality and Social Psychology, 60,* 531–544.

Estes, C. L., Binney, E. A., & Linkins, K. W. (1994). *Proceedings of the 47th annual scientific meet-*

ing of the Gerontological Society of America. Washington, DC: Gerontological Society of America.

Furstenberg, A. L. & Koons, C. (1995). *Mental health care for the elderly: Views from the other side of the barriers.* Unpublished manuscript.

George, L. K., Blazer, D. G., & Winfield-Laird, I. (1988). Psychiatric disorder and mental health service use in later life. In J. A. Brody & G. L. Maddox (Eds.), *Epidemiology and aging* (pp. 188–192). New York: Springer.

Gottesman, L. E., Peskin, E., & Kennedy, K. M. (1991). Research and program experience in residential care facilities: Implications for mental health services. E. Light & B. Lebowitz (Eds.), *The elderly with chronic mental illness* (pp. 245–284). New York: Springer.

Greenberg, J. S., Greenley, J. R., & Benedict, P. (1993). *Client satisfaction with mental health services in the Rhinelander system.* Mental Health Research Center. University of Wisconsin–Madison.

Gurland, B. J., & Cross, P. S. (1982). Epidemiology of psychopathology in old age. *Psychiatric Clinics of North America, 5*(1), 11–26.

Harding, C. M., Brooks, G. W., Ashikaga, T., Strauss, J. S., & Breier, A. (1987). The Vermont longitudinal study of persons with severe mental illness, II: Long-term outcome of subjects who retrospectively met DSM-III criteria for schizophrenia. *American Journal of Psychiatry, 144,* 727–735.

Heussy, H. R. (1972). Tactics and targets in the rural setting. In: S. E. Golann & C. Eisdorfer (Eds.), *Handbook of community mental health* (pp. 699–710). New York: Appleton/Century-Cross.

Kessler, R. C., Berglund, P. A., Zhao, S., Leaf, P. J., Kouzis, A. C., Bruce, M. L., Friedman, R. M., Grosser, R., Kennedy, C., Narrow, W., Kuehnel, T., Laska, E., Manderscheid, R., Rosenheck, R., Santoni, T., & Schneier, M. (1996). In R. W. Manderscheid & M. A. Sonnenschein (Eds.), *Mental health, United States, 1996* (pp. 59–70). Rockville, MD: U.S. Department of Health and Human Services.

Mechanic, D. (1989). *Mental health and social policy* (3rd ed.). Englewood Cliffs, NJ: Prentice Hall.

Meeks, S., Carstensen, L. L., Stafford, P. B., Oltmanns, T. F., Brenner, L. L., Weathers, F., & Welch, R. (1990). Mental health needs of the chronically mentally ill elderly. *Psychology and Aging, 5*(2), 163–171.

National Institutes of Health. (1991). *Diagnosis and treatment of depression in late life.* Washington, DC: U.S. Government Printing Office.

National Resource Center for the Rural Elderly. (1994). Survey of need and availability of mental health services. *Rural Elderly Networker, 5*(1), 1–3.

North Carolina Office of State Planning. (1998). Warren County. *LINC county profile* [On-line]. Available: http://www.ospl/state.nc.us/osplbin/crpmain.cgi?county=WARR

Prue, D., Kinane, L., Cornel, J., & Foy, D. (1979). Analysis of distance variables that affect after care attendance. *Community Mental Health Journal, 15*(2), 149–154.

Raschko, R. (1991). Spokane community mental health center elderly services. E. Light & B. Lebowitz (Eds.), *The elderly with chronic mental illness* (pp. 232–244). New York: Springer.

Rathbone-McCuan, E. (1993). Rural geriatric mental health care: A continuing service dilemma. In C. N. Bull (Ed.), *Aging in rural America* (pp. 146–160). Thousand Oaks, CA: Sage Publications.

Regier, D. A., Farmer, M. E., Rae, D. S., Myers, J. K., Kramer, M., Robins, L. M., George, L. K., Karno, M., & Locke, B. Z. (1993). One-month prevalence of mental disorders in the United States and sociodemographic characteristics: The Epidemiologic Catchment Area Study. *Acta Psychiatrica Scandinavia, 88*(1), 35–47.

Roybal, E. R. (1988). Mental health and aging: The need for an expanded federal response. *American Psychologist, 43,* 189–194.

Skirboll, B. (1994). The Compeer Model: Client rehabilitation and economic benefits. *Psychosocial Rehabilitation Journal, 18*(2), 89–94.

Snustad, D. G., Thompson-Heisterman, A. A., Neese, J. B., & Abraham, I. L. (1993). Mental health outreach to the rural elderly: Service delivery to a forgotten risk group. *Clinical Gerontologist, 14*(1), 95–111.

Somervell, P., Leaf, P., Weissman, M., Glazer, D., & Livingston-Bruce, M. (1989). The prevalence of major depression in black and white adults in five United States communities. *American Journal of Epidemiology, 130,* 725–735.

Sullivan, W. P. (1989). Community support programs in rural areas: Developing programs without walls. *Human Services in the Rural Environment, 12*(4), 19–23.

Swan, J. H., Fox, P. J., & Estes, C. J. (1989). Geriatric services: Community mental health center boon or bane? *Community Mental Health Journal, 25*(4), 327–340.

Thwing, N. E., & Cannady, D. (1979). *Community supportive care.* Rhinelander, WI: Human Service Center.

U.S. Bureau of the Census. (1998). *County population estimates* [On-line]. Available: http://www.census.gov/population/estimates/county/ca/canc97.txt

U.S. General Accounting Office. (1982). *The elderly remain in need of mental health services* (Publication GAO/HRD-82–112 ed.). Washington, DC: Author.

Waxman, H. M. (1986). Community mental health care for the elderly. *Public Health Reports,* 294–300.

Williams, D. R , Takeuchi, D. T. & Adair, R. K. (1992). Socioeconomic status and psychiatric disorder among blacks and whites. *Social Forces, 71*(1), 179–194.

Wood, J. B., & Parham, I. A. (1990). Coping with perceived burden: Ethnic and cultural issues in Alzheimer's family caregiving. *Journal of Applied Gerontology, 9,* 325–339.

SECTION V

ACKNOWLEDGING AND CELEBRATING DIVERSITY

Rural communities and small towns are not homogeneous but are characterized by differences ranging from socioeconomics to race to religion. Although rurality is a unifying characteristic, that trait alone does not totally eliminate issues of rural diversity. Furthermore, racial tension has a strong history in rural communities. Acknowledging the existence of that tension and friction is imperative if effective social work practice is to take place. The authors in this section present content that describes and celebrates rural diversity.

Robert Blundo, Clyde McDaniel, and Frank Wilson present a glimpse of life in a small, multiracial, southern town through the eyes of its mayor. Through their intriguing qualitative inquiry in chapter 16, the authors provide a look into the ongoing flow of life in that community; they describe racial relationships, politics, and government. Any new social worker moving to a rural or small town community should conduct a similar inquiry in order to understand the community and its history, traditions, and ethos.

Eugenia Eng, Mary Altpeter, and Edith A. Parker address in chapter 17 the need to share knowledge about building community competence with people in small towns and rural communities. The authors discuss a new way of thinking about demonstration projects for research studies and evaluations in health promotion and community competence. They present two examples of community health promotion programs in the rural South to illustrate the implementation of a community-based research approach and to share what they learned from the experience.

Cheryl Waites and Iris Carlton-LaNey discuss elderly African American return migrants' use of senior centers in chapter 18. As elders retire, many desire to return to their hometown roots for a more peaceful and tranquil lifestyle. Senior centers, an important component in the continuum of elder care, can play a critical role in seniors' adjustment to their new environment. To determine the extent to which elders use senior centers, the authors gathered information from a sample of elders in two counties in North Carolina. The results were mixed and showed that some elders were highly involved, whereas others knew little about the centers' services and programs.

In chapter 19, Rosemary Clews presents the results of an exploratory qualitative study of members of four First Nations communities in Canada. Clews' study was designed to provide information for the development of social work curricula that would assist individual healing processes and contribute to initiatives to preserve and strengthen indigenous rural communities. The author found that the indigenous people wanted social work students to focus more on learning about First Nations people and less on understanding social work theory.

CHAPTER SIXTEEN

Change and Survival in a Small, Rural, Multiracial Southern Town

Robert Blundo, Clyde McDaniel, and Frank Wilson

The character of rural life has changed over the centuries and continues to change today, but at a different pace and with potentially different consequences. Small rural communities are facing rapidly shifting economic, technical, social, and political forces as our nation enters the next century. Many small communities are experiencing pressures that are challenging their viability as communities. In fact, they stand in jeopardy of disappearing as physical entities or as "communities as understood and felt" by the generations that have lived out their lives in these special places (Beaver, 1986, p.168). Change has always been a part of all communities, both rural and urban. The significance for us today is the rapidity and nature of that change. Fitchen (1991) noted that the "cumulative effect of this quickening pace challenges not only what goes on in rural communities but also what people think about their communities and about their lives. In many rural places, the entire image of rural life is being called into question, and rural identity is becoming blurred" (p. 2). The implications of such rapid change for any specific community will vary according to the confluence of geography and history of a particular economic and social life of a group of people living in a particular place. Yet, each unique situation provides insight into the nature of rural community life and the attempts of community residents to preserve and strengthen that sense of place and of a life to be lived.

It is significant to our understanding of this changing circumstance that we have a chance to look inside small towns in rural areas of this country. What follows is an attempt to stop and look into the life of a small, multiracial, rural Southern town through the eyes of its mayor. This chapter is intended to provide a glimpse into a place many people merely pass by on the way to someplace else.

JUST A QUIET LITTLE PLACE OFF THE HIGHWAY

Most people traveling to the coastal beaches and resorts in southeastern North Carolina drive along North Carolina state highway 74/76, or what the local people call the "new highway," and take little notice of the small green sign on the side of the road inscribed with the name "Bolton." The travelers are on their way to bigger cities and coastal resort towns. If they happen to think about the passing landscape, they might think only of the seeming simplicity of the "country": farmers living solitary lives or poor people living in trailers here and there perched up on blocks back in the trees along the side of the road. Few travelers venture off the main highway, and they probably never consider the lives of the many people who live behind the passing pines and underbrush that line the road mile after mile. Yet, like most small towns, Bolton is a community of history, memories, and hopes for the people who make it their home. It is important for those of us who pass by to stop and take in this vitality, the threats to its existence, and the efforts to maintain its presence.

The mayor of Bolton has his office in a used but newly acquired side-by-side trailer. It is set up on blocks in the sandy soil out among the tall Long Leaf pines that have played such a significant role in this town's development for the past 100 years. It is a new and proud addition to this community's efforts to grow and prosper. Like many small rural southern towns over the past decades, progress has taken many people and opportunities elsewhere. But the mayor, those who have remained, and those who are moving back in order to return to earlier family roots are hopeful that they will continue to maintain the autonomy, self-determination, and sense of identity or belonging that this small community provides.

The mayor is optimistic about his town and all 531 citizens who live within its official boundaries. The community has a pride and an optimism that appears to sustain the mayor and his commitment to his hometown and the people with whom he grew up:[1]

> I think that Bolton is going to survive, because in just being out there talking to people, I'm not hearing negative things. I'm hearing: "Let's make Bolton progress again. Let's do something for Bolton. Let's do those things necessary to make life livable for all the citizens." I hear this from everybody. That is what is good about Bolton. You're not just hearing it from a small group. I smile and I really feel good when I see a diverse group of people get together and work on problems. (personal communication with F. Wilson, mayor of Bolton, North Carolina)

BRIEF HISTORY OF BOLTON

The rich timber lands of southeastern North Carolina all had been harvested during the 1800s except for a large and inaccessible virgin stand of Long Leaf pines in the region surrounding what would become Bolton Township. The Great Green Swamp, with its waist-deep water, protected the region from exploitation and limited growth until the means to harvest the timber were available at the turn of this century. It was a region unsuitable for anything but marginal subsistence farming, lumbering, and small-scale pine-sap harvesting. Settlement was sparse, and relatively

---

[1] Much of the material for this chapter is based on the authors' interviews and conversations with Mayor Frank Wilson, Bolton, North Carolina, from June 1997 to September 1998.

few people could succeed in such an inaccessible area. The records show that the first public school in the area of Bolton was established in 1886. It was described as a wooden frame "Colored" school with 124 students. Public records also show that the first church in Bolton was the African Methodist Episcopal Zion Church, which was deeded land in July 1887. But with the advent of new industrial technology and American progress, this remote region of poor blacks and whites living a subsistence existence would change.

As the story is told by members of the Bolton community, in the summer of 1907 a long train loaded with lumber milling equipment stopped on the tracks of the Wilmington and Manchester Railroad in what was then no more than a post office known as Bolton, which dated back to 1866. The Waccamaw Lumber Company purchased the large stands of Long Leaf pines in the Great Green Swamp and began the construction of one of the largest lumber mill operations in North Carolina. The work relied on human capital; an estimated 800 people were employed at the mill site, and another 800 worked to cut and transport the lumber to the mill. In 1909, Bolton was incorporated as a township and boasted a Company Commissary, a dozen stores, two hotels (one for "Colored" and one elegant, three-story frame hotel for whites, which was built and owned by the lumber company), a boarding house, a doctor, a law officer, and approximately 800 residents living within the town limits (Dorward, 1980). In 1916, a fire destroyed the milling operation. Although a new mill was built, the town never regained the development it had attained so briefly. By 1930, the mill had run its course and no longer needed the laborers it once had supported. Bolton sustained itself for the next several decades with a small commercial center and a state-controlled liquor outlet (ABC store). Local farmers and workers in the paper company, which had taken over the milling operation, kept the small businesses of Bolton going through the decades leading to the 1980s. Travelers en route to the coastal communities stopped for gas and refreshments. But even this small economic trade was not to last; rapidly changing economic and social conditions brought further challenges to the community and its leaders.

In 1990 the "new highway," state route 74/76, was completed. It bypassed many small towns that had depended on the traffic for business, including Bolton. The new highway diverted traffic to the northeast of town by several miles and sealed off the main street from the usual traffic and business generated by travelers. It also enabled people living in the region to more easily make longer trips to larger towns for business and pleasure. Construction of the new highway followed the loss of the Trailways bus route through Bolton, which had been eliminated in the early 1980s, effectively cutting off residents from public transportation to distant relatives and larger cities in the region. The small businesses that had served the travelers and local needs began to close, and the buildings housing them were abandoned with the departure of the bus line and the completion of the new highway.

What remains today is an all-purpose gas station/convenience store, another smaller gas station that serves "the best dipped ice cream around," and the ABC store. The old frame buildings built for commerce at the beginning of this century have long since been torn down. The small rows of brick-faced storefronts built in the 1960s are now abandoned. There are no traffic lights in the center of the town, and there is no charming courthouse or other public building except for the cinder-block volunteer fire station and the town's new "used" side-by-side trailer that sits next to the station and the ABC store. The mayor, his assistants, and the new police chief work in the offices located in the fire station and the side-by-side trailer. This is the public center of the community, the official town of Bolton and its surrounding areas.

MULTIRACIAL CITIZENS OF BOLTON

Bolton is a multiracial community, and the mayor is one of its black citizens. The mayor does not make reference to any distinct group when he discusses the community, its citizens, or the issues he and they are attempting to address. When asked specifically about the racial composition, the mayor usually describes the community in this manner:

> Racially, Bolton has three distinct groups of people. Our black population makes up about 61 to 65 percent. We have a 25 to 30 percent white population, and the remaining citizens are American Indians of the Waccamaw group. There seems to be more of a closeness between the Indians and whites than between either of these groups and blacks. You would think that since both Indians and blacks are minorities, there would be more closeness. This is not the case. For instance, whites can marry easily into the Indian community, whereas blacks are not as acceptable. Yet, all of us have managed to pull together as a community in many other ways to support our town and all the people here. (personal communication with F. Wilson, mayor of Bolton, North Carolina)

Bolton has maintained a black majority for most of its history except for the "boom" era, which lasted from 1907, when the first mill was constructed, to the late 1920s. It was not until the Voting Rights Act was passed in 1965 and implemented on the local level that black citizens ran and were elected as mayors of Bolton. The mayor's father has been described by some people in the town as an important figure in the community, but he was never able to hold public office in his lifetime. Bolton is one of several towns in the region that have similar histories.

The town council has both black and white members, but no one from the Waccamaw Indian population. Only a few Waccamaw Indian families live within the town itself, but in the township more than 400 Waccamaw Indians live in what is called the "Buckley community."

Although Bolton is small, the residents of the town proper and the surrounding township view themselves as residing in different parts of town. Residents who identify with a particular section of town or the township feel an affinity for their "part of town." Even though outsiders may think that Bolton is too small to have different "ends of town," for the residents of Bolton the designated areas play a part in their relationships both to the community as a whole and to individual citizens. The areas are distinguished by the ethnicity of the people who live there, although the distinction is not based solely on racial differences. Most of the people living in what is referred to as the "Outback" (the area just outside the town limits, near the Waccamaw Indian community on the northern edge of the township) have closer ties with the Waccamaw Indian residents. Another group of people live in the "Eastern section," the area of the township toward the larger community of Wilmington and several other communities with similar or larger populations than Bolton. Finally, residents of the town proper live in what the community refers to "up in Bolton." Each section has special differences, and sometimes friction exists between the sections of the township. For example, the mayor recalls a town picnic:

> The town decided to have a picnic at the town's recreation facility, the Reverend Maxwell Park, a rather nice little park. The park is located in a place (mostly black) that many of the people from the "Outback" section of the township do not consider a good place to go. Instead of coming to the town picnic at Reverend Maxwell Park, the people from "Outback" packed up and went to the town of Leland. Their rationale was that they didn't really want to come to a park that was not suitable for them. But, you know, in spite of our differences, for some reason or another, people are attracted to Bolton. And after a while, after we get past all our self-interests we are able to pull ourselves together and work for the good of the town. That's hard, to try to work together when we have different ideas. But, generally we do just that, work together for the town. (personal communication with F. Wilson, mayor of Bolton, North Carolina)

During the last election, some citizens brought up the issue of the mayor's attending the National Conference of Black Mayors. Some people suggested that the mayor's association with other black mayors could have a negative effect on white citizens. The voters of Bolton generally rejected this implication, and the mayor received good support from the white citizens. The mayor believes that the support was evidence that the whole community is trying to "get past the problems we have had and to move forward together as a community" (personal communication with F. Wilson, mayor of Bolton, NC, 1997–1998).

Even with the differences, the mayor sees further changes that have added to the diversity of the community and are bringing in new and different ideas. This small community is experiencing shifts in personal relationships and in the meaning of community. The mayor notes that in his community there are

> 200 households in the town of Bolton, with a population within the town limits of 531 people. Now, when you talk about the Bolton community, or the Bolton township, there are quite a lot more than that. In fact, there are about 1,600 people. It used to be that you knew everybody; that used to be very easy to do. If you saw some kid from one of the households or families walking out there on the street, you could say: "That's a member of the Smith's [*sic*] family" or "That's Mrs. Smith's kid." But, increasingly, it's getting to be harder to do that, and a lot of it has to do with the influx of people coming into the community from the north. (personal communication with F. Wilson, mayor of Bolton, North Carolina)

Over the years, young people have moved away from Bolton to the north for jobs and school. Today, many of them and their children are returning to Bolton. Many of the children were born in the north but have always been told about the family home down south in Bolton. Their parents have told stories about "home" all their lives, and they have grown to feel a sense of family roots in Bolton. In many cases, families maintained property to which they could return. They have, in many ways, always thought of this community as their home. This group of returning families has helped bring new members to the community, members with different experiences and new ideas on what is important for a community. Mayor Wilson believes that this return to roots presents a challenge to the community and town government.

MAYOR WILSON AND THE TOWN GOVERNMENT OF BOLTON

The Bolton town government consists of a mayor and five town aldermen. The mayor serves a two-year term, and the aldermen serve staggered four-year terms. The town has a part-time town clerk, finance officer, and tax collector; a full-time police chief, who is also the only full-time police officer for the town; and a secretary for office management.

The mayor's post is a part-time position. Throughout its history, Bolton's mayors have worked full time at other jobs in the area. Mayor Wilson has a full-time job with the local chemical plant, which serves as one of the area's main sources of work. Although the position of mayor is part time, Mayor Wilson puts in long hours to maintain and advance his community. It is a demanding and complex job, which sometimes surprises outsiders. What looks like such a simple life on the surface has many demands, intricacies, and nuances to which the mayor and the community leaders must attend. The following material is Mayor Wilson's perspective on the complexity of managing and working for this small, multiracial rural town government:

> *Small town politics:* Openness and truth is not only demanded, but the right thing to do. Officials should be open to ideas from all members of the community, never worrying about party affiliation, race, or gender. Everyone should be able to bring something to the table. If you disagree with a person's point of view, let that person know, but only after you have heard their complete thoughts and have thanked them for their ideas. Then, if you disagree, explain why you disagree and back up your position with evidence or information to support your reasoning. Your whole term in office is judged by how open and truthful you are with the community.

> *Rumors and misinformation:* Rumors can get started very fast and spread quickly in a small community. It is important to tackle this misinformation or story as quickly as possible. If you are not able to intervene quickly, things can develop to a point that situations that are only speculations arise and become divisive for the community. If these rumors are not caught early, it is hard to then establish what is fact and what is not for the people of the community.

> *Fairness:* Try your best to be fair with all members of the community. People expect a lot from us, and sometimes they do not think things that are done are fair or equitable. This is why it is important to be open and to have decisions made in public

ways so that everyone will understand why things were done the way they were. Public meetings are very important, even though community members don't always show up. But the word gets around about what happened. You never want to deal with major complaints out on the street.

Conflicts of interest: Considerable conflict can arise as a result of the immediacy of family and friendship relationships in a small community. It is hard not to have family members involved or affected by decisions being made in a small community such as ours. For example, in such a community you may have a relative applying for a job or awaiting a decision from the town. Since nearly everyone is at least known to (if not a relative) most members of the town government, this becomes a difficult situation for all concerned. Again, openness and public decisions must be fostered. In many cases, members of the government must remove themselves from the decision-making process. In North Carolina, the General Statutes state that towns under 5,000 in population can hire relatives to work in public offices. However, close members of a family should not be in a direct supervisory relationship.

Town board: Doing business as a town board has restrictions. The state regulations do not permit three or more board members to discuss town business outside of a regular or special call meeting. The same regulation does permit a single board member to talk with one other board member (that is, one at a time) about town business. This is helpful in preparing for the meetings. It gives board members a chance to understand what issues might be coming up and what support or lack of support there is for items on the meeting agenda. Here again, it is a good law because it helps keep the decisions open to the public meetings.

Managing the town business: The mayor cannot do it all his- [*sic*] or herself. You have to make sure you have competent and reliable staff and citizens. Ultimately, the mayor is responsible for what happens. Therefore, you must have confidence in the people working with you. Most importantly, the mayor must keep up with what the staff is doing. Keeping up to date with the necessary paperwork required by the county, state, and federal government programs and departments is a very demanding job. In a small town, there are no department heads who juggle all the programs, funding sources, and required reporting on the town's status. There are no full-time town bookkeepers or auditors or grant writers. A part-time mayor and his or her part-time staff must undertake these tasks as well as many others. You must be creative and seek out assistance from other mayors, residents, local and state officials, and supportive organizations such as neighboring town officials, community colleges, consulting firms, legislators, and many other resources with whom the mayor must cultivate working relationships.

Making connections outside of the town: It is important for the mayor to be involved in county, regional, and state organizations. These connections provide information and access to support systems for the town. Visibility for the mayor is important in order to gain access to services and assistance from other agencies and government departments. The mayor attends conferences and workshops conducted by the League of Municipalities, Mayor's Association, Institute of Governments, State Officials Conferences, as well as state and federal programs for public officials. These contacts and training help the mayor know what grants, services, allotments, and any other resources might be available for the town. This awareness of potential resources is necessary in maintaining Bolton and essential services for its residents. (personal communications with F. Wilson, mayor of Bolton, North Carolina)

PRESERVING, CARING FOR, AND STRENGTHENING THE TOWN OF BOLTON

Small towns must be creative as they grapple with many issues and relate to county, state, and federal departments and agencies. For example, Bolton has successfully regained some of the revenue that was once produced by the ABC store in its old location. The ABC store provided a small but significant percentage of its income to the local community. When the new highway diverted business away from the center of town and the ABC store, the store lost considerable revenue, so efforts were initiated to regain this lost income. The mayor and others conceived and initiated a plan to move the store closer to the new highway to provide more visibility and accessibility. The mayor put together a grant proposal for the town to buy the building from the Bolton ABC Board. Technically, the town would be buying the building from itself. This approach was a creative way of generating the money the Bolton ABC Board needed to relocate the store. The new location has increased sales and has produced additional money for the Bolton community to use for services and programs. A secondary benefit was the foresight of the mayor and members of the community to address other needs by converting the store building previously housing the ABC store into a community center for programs to help and assist its citizens.

Recently, the community held the formal opening of this new center, The Bolton Senior and Youth Center. Attending the opening ceremony were a wide range of state, county, and local officials whose presence demonstrated the range of connections and cooperation needed by the mayor to accomplish this effort. Services to be offered will include such programs as an innovative collaboration with the University of North Carolina at Wilmington School of Nursing, which will provide medical services at the community center through student interns in the practical nursing masters degree program. Other programs will provide residents with special literacy and GED courses during the evening as well as programs for its senior citizens and its youth.

This innovative and creative management is helping keep Bolton a distinct, autonomous, and successful community, but it requires many forms of help. For instance, the Cape Fear Council of Governments can offer expertise in grant writing that enables communities like Bolton to attempt innovative financing for projects such as moving the ABC store and to compete for other funding for projects important for their survival.

In the day-to-day operations of the town, Mayor Wilson has engaged the assistance of the North Carolina League of Municipalities and the Institute of Government at the University of North Carolina, Chapel Hill. These organizations provide the mayor with timetables on when state offices require reports and information on the filing deadlines for state and county services and monies.

Taking care of Bolton also requires personal and hands-on judgments that can only be made in a small community. In one such incident, a member of the community was delinquent in paying his property taxes to the town. This particular person did not have the money to pay, but he did have a bush hog, a large mower used to cut heavy underbrush. The town decided to forgive his tax debt in exchange for his using his bush hog to clear property owned by the town and that of residents who could not afford to clear their own lots, which was required by town ordinance. In another incident, an elderly resident had his water turned off. The mayor found out from the man's neighbors that the man's son had taken off with his father's monthly check. The mayor called the son into his office, had a talk with him, and extracted a promise from the young man to take care of his father. As a result, the check was returned, the bills were paid, and the water was turned back on.

Sometimes these personal encounters have resulted in the development of services for the people in the community. On one occasion, Mayor Wilson was approached by a young woman who told him that she was addicted to crack and was thinking of killing herself. As the mayor went about finding the necessary resources for her, he and others in the community were helped by the County Drug Coalition. Out of this grew a community effort led by the mayor to develop the present Neighborhood Action Council of Bolton. The members of the council have focused on helping people with drug problems as well as initiating health fairs, community picnics, and clean-up campaigns.

A particular irony for many small rural towns like Bolton is the reluctance of land owners to give up any part of their land. As a result, the young people who want to remain in Bolton have trouble finding affordable housing and land to live on. The town is now trying to find ways to help them buy town-owned land so that they can stay in Bolton. The Bolton community faces a different set of needs with yet another significant segment of its population, elderly citizens, who make up nearly one-third of the population. In response to the needs of those citizens, the town has developed and located programs for elderly members of the community in the new community center. Efforts are being made to address this group's growing demand for health and social services. Plans are underway to provide these services as well as increased support services, such as the town's "meals on wheels" program.

Being a good neighbor is an important part of life in Bolton. Mayor Wilson speaks proudly of his brother as he tells of the spirit of helping in Bolton:

> Let's speak a little about my brother. He is doing the kinds of things my father did here many years ago. For example, last year my brother grew a lot of collards and other vegetables in his garden. When they were ready, he backed his van up, filled it with collards, sweet potatoes, and whatever. He went around to all the houses and gave the produce away. He is not the only one who does that. I can name many others who do this sort of helping all the time. This is where community spirit can be seen and felt. (personal communication with F. Wilson, mayor of Bolton, North Carolina)

At the same time, Mayor Wilson recognizes that the town must find other ways to help its citizens address ongoing issues through government services and programs. These efforts are what the mayor refers to as "keeping up" with grants, loans, and programs to support community efforts and funding for those ideas and plans. Doing so brings the mayor back to maintaining extensive relationships outside the town in order that the necessary resources and expertise can be gathered to achieve Bolton's goals.

BOLTON AND ITS FUTURE

The mayor and people of Bolton are working hard to maintain their viability and their sense of autonomy. Doing so is difficult when so much of the context of their lives is changing in terms of economic, demographic and, literally, physical alterations on the landscape. The regional shifts in population growth along the coastal areas of North and South Carolina are bringing in people from different parts of the nation and changing the regional politics and economic base of what were once small towns, fishing communities, and farms. Two groups separated in many ways by race and, to an increasing extent, socioeconomic factors are contributing to this shift.

Stack (1996) described part of this shift in the title of her ethnographic study *Call to Home: African-Americans Reclaim the Rural South*. She stated that "by 1990 the South had gained more than half a million black Americans who were leaving the North—or more precisely, the South had *regained* from the cities of the North the half-million black citizens it had lost to northward migration during the 1960s [italics in original]" (p. xiv). Stack found that this "returning" is challenging old communities with new ideas and that only the future will determine the consequences for those returning as well as the communities and societies to which they are coming back.

Generally, wealthy white retirees and entrepreneurs are moving into the coastal regions because of the climate, beaches, and recreational opportunities. Land and home prices have risen enormously. The new residents are paying relatively low state taxes as well as low property tax, compared with Northern states and larger urban communities, but the services needed to sustain the increasing numbers and the amenities demanded by this new group keep expanding.

Bolton is located on the eastern edge of Columbus County and is adjacent to the western edge of Brunswick County, which is experiencing some of the greatest population increases in the immediate region, in the beach towns of Southport, Long Beach, and Holden Beach. According to the North Carolina Office of State Planning, Brunswick County has grown from 50,985 people in April 1990 to 65,200 in July 1997. This represents an increase of 27.9 percent, of which 25.3 percent is the result of people moving into the beach communities from outside the state (North Carolina Office of State Planning, 1997). In nearby Columbus County, the population has grown from 49,587 to 51,942, a growth of 4.7 percent, of which 2.2 percent is the result of migration. The projected county population growth for the period 2010 to 2020 is 18.8 percent for Brunswick County and 1.0 percent for Columbus County (North Carolina Office of State Planning, 1997). This evidence demonstrates the extent of the present changes in the region and the continued changes that will take place in the future.

Bolton, located in the interior flatlands an hour's drive from the coast, is on the outer margins of this in-migration along the coast. Unlike some towns that have literally been engulfed by larger communities and "suburbanized," Bolton has sustained its physical integrity because it is just outside the prime coastal lands and is within the large tracts of cultivated pine forests farmed by the local paper company that replaced the original lumber mill. Thus, Bolton and the neighboring small towns are buffered from the rapid expansion by both distance and present land use.

The impact of this population change is that Bolton is becoming less significant in relation to the wealthier and larger communities that are being developed along the coastal areas. State, regional, and county governments are grappling with this shift and are becoming more focused on the growing service demands of the coastal communities. Thus, Bolton is being affected by the political and economic power shifts that are evolving. The allocation of services is growing more competitive between communities. For Mayor Wilson, ensuring adequate services for Bolton requires that the town become increasingly connected to the outside and to the resources that can help sustain the community. For the citizens, it means that sustaining their way of life is increasingly dependent on maintaining an influential town government.

Operating against this effort to sustain the community of Bolton are the changing economic realities, which mean that more and more jobs outside the town are drawing people away from traditional income sources, like farming and small businesses, to larger opportunities elsewhere. As Martinez-Brawley (1990) noted, "the pull of internal and external forces constitute one of the major dilemmas of the small community" (p. 5). In Bolton, the communal or horizontal ties are being strained by the necessary connections people must make to places of work and other activities no longer sustainable within the town. In addition, new community members who are returning "home" have not shared the *participation locality encourages* and are therefore introducing different behaviors, attitudes, and interests. These external and internal dynamics place considerable pressure on those who want to maintain a certain sense of identity and a connection to their family's roots and traditions. Ultimately, the political autonomy of the town, which permits Mayor Wilson to advocate for services and town control of necessary services, could be challenged as vertical ties, or what has been described as "differentiation of interests among people in the locality and differential association based on respective interests" (Warren, 1963, p. 59), disrupts the horizontal ties produced through locality and interdependency. These changes and challenges are all part of Bolton's future.

CONCLUSION

Bolton is a unique, complex, and vital community that to most travelers is no more than a name on a small green sign on the side of the highway. What is being lived out in this small rural community, like many other similar places along the road, is what Fisher and Karger (1997) described as an "epochal transformation equal to the industrial revolution of the nineteenth century [with] much of contemporary life [seeming] very different and detached from that of only a few decades ago" (p. 3).

This chapter has been an inquiry into the public life of a black mayor and his community as they come together to address the survival of their home during this time of change. It has been presented in the tradition of a naturalistic or qualitative inquiry with the intent to provide a look into the ongoing flow of life in a particular town in a particular region of the country, reflective of the traditions and history of that region. Although similar communities within southeastern North Carolina share similar economic and social histories, we have found that in daily existence, sometimes only the broadest issues can be viewed as being in common. The significance of this ethnographic process of getting to know a place is, we think, the renewed appreciation of both the uniqueness and the complexity of even the smallest of communities who are attempting to preserve and strengthen their existence in the face of an uncertain future.

REFERENCES

Beaver, P. D. (1986). *Rural community in Appalachian South.* Lexington, KY: University Press of Kentucky.

Dorward, K. (1980). Bolton township. In A. Courtney & W. Little (Eds.), *Recollections and records: Columbus County, North Carolina* (pp. 323–338). Whiteville, NC: Columbus County Commissioners and Columbus County Public Library.

Fisher, R., & Karger, H. J. (1997). *Social work and community in a private world.* New York: Longman.

Fitchen, J. M. (1991). *Endangered spaces, enduring places: Change, identity, and survival in rural America.* Boulder, CO: Westview Press.

Martinez-Brawley, E. E. (1990). *Perspectives on the small community.* Washington, DC: NASW Press.

North Carolina Office of State Planning (1997). *Certified County population estimates and County population growth 2010–2020* [On-line]. Available: http://www.ospl.state.nc.us/demog/projbdm1.html

Stack, C. (1996). *Call to home: African-Americans reclaim the rural South.* New York: Basic Books.

Warren, R. L. (1963). *The community in America* (2nd ed.). Chicago: Rand McNally.

CHAPTER SEVENTEEN

Listening for a Change:
Strategies for Community-Based Health
Promotion Research in Rural Communities

Eugenia Eng, Mary Altpeter, and Edith A. Parker

Community competence is a concept that has been derived from practitioners' experience and observations from working with communities, particularly those that have been marginalized, such as rural and ethnic minority communities. Cottrell (1976), who was the first to use the term, drew on his work in community psychiatry and concluded that the more competent a community, the more mentally healthy the people. He defined a competent community as

> one in which the various component parts of the community: (1) are able to collaborate effectively in identifying the problem and needs of the community; (2) can achieve a working consensus on goals and priorities; (3) can agree on ways and means to implement the agreed-upon goals; and (4) can collaborate effectively in the required actions. (Cottrell, 1976, p. 197)

Community competence emanates from different social structures. Kretzmann and McKnight (1993), community organizers from the Midwest, found that the source of power for building the capacity of communities lies with the citizen associations that people create for themselves. Kark and Steuart (1962), a social epidemiologist and a health educator in South Africa, found that social groups based on friendship in rural Zulu villages were the most significant unit of identity, practice, and solution for achieving community health development. Geiger (1971) and Hatch and Eng (1984), the crafters of the first rural community health center in the United States, uncovered the strengths of rural African American communities in the Mississippi Delta. Those strengths resided in the role of the Black church in nurturing leadership and community competence.

Despite the rich public health history and community organizing experience that have pointed toward the importance of community competence, the concept still eludes research and theory. We do not know either the determinants of community competence or its effects. We do not agree on how to operationalize the definition of community competence in order to detect its presence. Instead, we talk of "images of a good community" that represent both objective characteristics as well as subjective feelings and ideals (Fellin, 1995).

Nevertheless, we continue to go forward with community-based programs and capacity-building agendas in rural communities, intending to increase their competence and to promote healthy lives. Indeed, we should. If we are to learn more about communities' competence, then it will be through public health and social work practice that strives to build on the assets and talents of community people. This type of practice establishes a kind of trust between professionals and communities that offers a unique opportunity for generating new knowledge. Too often, however, this opportunity is not taken or, if it is, the wealth of practitioners' experience in building community competence is not documented, interpreted, or disseminated.

This chapter addresses the need to share knowledge about building community competence with people in small rural towns. We also want to stir up a new way of thinking about demonstration projects for health promotion and community competence research studies and evaluations. We and others propose *community-based research* as a viable approach to reducing the gap between theory, research, and practice (Alary, Beausoleil, Guodon, Lariviore, & Mazer, 1990; Eng & Parker, 1994; Hall, 1981; Israel, Shultz, Parker, & Becker, 1998; Yeich & Levine, 1992). We offer examples of two community health promotion programs in the rural South to illustrate how the community-based research approach was implemented and to share what we learned from this experience. We conclude with a discussion of principles for public health and social work practitioners to guide their community-based research efforts, all of which are appropriate for rural communities. To begin, we provide an overview of community-based research.

CHARACTERISTICS OF COMMUNITY-BASED RESEARCH

Table 1 summarizes characteristics of community-based research in terms of the roles of the researcher and the research purposes, processes, and products. This approach relies on the program participants to act as full partners with the investigators in (1) uncovering the range of natural and unplanned determinants of each community's social, political, and physical environment; (2) anticipating change to occur simultaneously in multiple social entities, such as organizations, communities, kin and non-kin networks, and individuals; and (3) building a competent community able to mobilize the talents and resources of people to analyze and accommodate change. Perhaps our professional field needs to consider program planning and implementation as a unique research opportunity. As a profession, social work has only to reflect back on its early survey and settlement house efforts to recapture its rich heritage of using research as a vehicle for social change (Altpeter, Schopler, Galinsky, & Pennell, in press; Simon, 1994; Tyson, 1995; Wagner, 1991; Zimbalist, 1977). With the resurgence of attention to community–agency–academic partner-

Table 17-1			

Community-Based Research Characteristics

Role of Researcher	Purpose	Process	Product
Collaborator	To build a team of researchers, program staff, local practitioners, and funders to develop trust	Meet personally with each stakeholder in the program about their vision of success and potential barriers	Conceptual framework Evaluation plan
Insider	To acquire privileged information on internal dynamics of agencies and private lives of communities	Stay informed about intervention design decisions on needs and strategies	Identification of data sources as intervention responds to changing needs and conditions
Co-Learner	To build a theory about the intervention, ensure mutual feedback, and revise research methods and tools	Exchange with stakeholders their understanding of specific determinants of and effects from change	Conceptual and operational definitions of key factors and outcomes from *planned* change Identification of *natural* and *unplanned* determinants of stability and change
Advocate	To amplify the voices of participants	Use methods and tools authentic to the values and principles of the intervention	Findings that are immediately beneficial to participants

ships and coalition building, the field of public health education can reaffirm its roots in community participation and community organizing to effect meaningful change in the distribution of power and resources that affect health (Steckler, Israel, Dawson, & Eng, 1993; Trostle, 1986). People in communities, particularly marginalized ones, may be more willing to participate in research when they can experience the immediate benefits from collaborating in a program of planned change.

CASE EXAMPLES OF COMMUNITY-BASED RESEARCH

The values that underpin the characteristics of community-based research include the rights of community members to have self-determination, equality, and educa-

tion; to make informed choices; and to take actions that transform their environment and social structure. But how can we ensure that those rights are secured in
our community-based practice? The following sections describe two health promotion programs, one in North Carolina and the other in Mississippi, and detail how
those rights were folded into the implementation process. Throughout these illustrations, we share both our successes and mistakes.

Both projects shared characteristics typical of community-based research
efforts:

- Both programs were intended to be immediately beneficial to multiple communities. In North Carolina, four African American communities residing in one urban and three rural towns, each in a different county, participated. In Mississippi,
the participants were three African American communities in three different
rural towns in the same county. In all seven towns, historical patterns from the era
of segregation were reflected in that African Americans resided in one part of
town and identified themselves as a distinct community.

- Both programs shared the values of community participation, shared decision-
making between community associations and professional organizations, and
partnership to effect fundamental changes in the distribution of power and resources.

- Both programs were committed to starting with the needs identified by communities. Neither program began with a previously determined categorical health
problem, thereby rendering baseline and health outcome indicators as "moving
targets" for the evaluation.

- The outcome of increased community competence was explicitly stated in the
projects' objectives and had equal importance to the goal of improving health outcomes. Both programs viewed conditions of poverty and discrimination as the underlying causes of poor health. Hence, activities that engaged the community's
distribution of resources and intrinsic power structure (for example, food banks,
job training, mobile libraries, and voter registration drives) were considered to be
as related to health as health fairs and neighborhood drug patrols.

- Both programs designed the evaluation at the same time as they designed their respective interventions. Hence, the program staff and the evaluators agreed at the
beginning that the values underlying an agenda to increase community competence would need to be reflected in the evaluation.

- Funding came from two different private foundations (W.K. Kellogg Foundation
and Freedom from Hunger Foundation), each of which stipulated that the evaluation could use no more than 10 percent of the total budget.

- An academic institution was responsible for the evaluation for both programs.
Specifically, faculty and students from the Schools of Public Health and Medicine
at the University of North Carolina at Chapel Hill participated.

These program characteristics functioned as a driving force for using a community-based approach to research.

A key element of community-based research mandates that the program evaluators need to be accepted by the participants as trusted collaborators, not as distant observers. This crucial relationship is necessary in order to acquire privileged information about the process of building community competence and its effects on both the internal dynamics of organizations and the private lives of communities.

For any study, a certain amount of tension enters into the relationships among investigators, funders, program staff, and community participants. The difference with community-based research is that differences in perspectives and social inequalities are made explicit so that the research process can struggle with the differences and their implications. Throughout the community-based research process, the researcher thus engages in reflexivity, that is, constantly scans his or her value base and motivations. Reflexivity is essential to ensure that the different points of view and cultural contexts of participants and communities are recognized, honored, and championed.

To begin the process of implementation in Mississippi and North Carolina, two of the authors spent the first three months meeting with foundation representatives and program directors, who then introduced us to practitioners and residents at the sites. The purpose was to define our relationship as collaborators on the evaluation. In Mississippi, the products generated through consensus were a conceptual framework, a set of program objectives with accompanying evaluation questions, indicators, sources of data, and a data collection schedule. In North Carolina, where the program is significantly larger than Mississippi's, six months were needed to interview 41 participants about their vision of changes that could come from the program. Separate evaluation plans were produced for each program partner: the four county coalitions, the School of Public Health, the School of Medicine, and the consortium.

Next, to make "in-flight" adjustments to data collection methods and indicators, the evaluators sought to gain an "insider's" view of local service needs and strategies. Before implementing a noncategorical health program in North Carolina and Mississippi, we made a "best guess" at anticipated health outcomes by arranging with each state's Center for Health Statistics for access to secondary data. In Mississippi, the health department service encounter data and county high-risk birth counts were tracked longitudinally by the Center for Health Statistics. Focusing on those data was a mistake, because the anticipated program focus on needs of mothers and children changed after Year 2 to a focus on teens and elderly people. In large part, the shift could be associated with a critical incident in this small rural county—a highly publicized drug raid. With few services offered by county health departments for adolescents and the elderly, the sources of relevant secondary data were quite limited. Moreover, with only two years remaining for implementation, there was not enough time to detect statistically significant change.

Acquiring information about community competence, however, required evaluators not only to be accepted as insiders but also to become co-learners with program participants. That is, everyone was a stakeholder in the success of the program, but no one was an expert on knowing why the program would or would not be effective. Hence, to begin building a theory about the intervention, another step in the process was to review concepts in the literature that were relevant to community competence. We distributed important publications to the Mississippi program staff and arranged for them to meet with scholars who had done work in community-based health promotion. The purpose was for program staff to provide us with their assessment of the relevance of the concept to the program's communities. This meeting was followed by half-day workshops, held separately with groups of residents from each community, on what they consider to be characteristics of a community that can "get it together." In Mississippi, a workshop was also held with the county's Interagency Council.

The workshops generated nine dimensions of community competence and were used to develop a 41-item questionnaire, which trained Community Health Advisors (CHAs) administered once a year to key informants from each community (Eng & Parker, 1994). The CHAs in Mississippi, who were paid to conduct these interviews, decided to put the money into a fund for community projects. Another instrument, developed with program staff to measure changes in referral patterns among agencies, was self-administered. Two interview questionnaires to measure changes in natural helping patterns in communities also were developed with program staff.

As implementation progressed, the findings were presented to participants during regularly scheduled meetings. The intent was for them to interpret the findings and reflect on why the effects were occurring. Their insights were invaluable for identifying aspects of the intervention to be emphasized or changed and for generating hypotheses about potential determinants of or effects from increased community competence. For example, in Mississippi, conflict containment and accommodation, which is one of the dimensions of community competence, was virtually nonexistent after one year of implementation. Explanations from program staff found that this skill had not been included in the training of CHAs. The CHAs themselves explained that representation of African Americans among elected officials was a critical issue that divided their communities on how to reduce racial tension. This information suggested that in the context of discrimination, dimensions of community competence based on a community's internal social interactions may need to improve in order to improve the externally focused dimensions involving mediating with outside institutions.

Another feature of the researcher as co-learner was to elicit critiques from participants on the data-gathering methods in order to adjust the format or timing of our methods according to changes in circumstances. It would have been naive to expect that programs to initiate community change would not affect or be affected by political and social conditions. During the months of racially motivated election campaigns, for example, it became prudent to postpone interviewing so that participants could focus on political organizing and so that interviewers would not be suspected of political organizing.

Although an intervention strategy may represent a *planned* attempt to induce social and behavioral change, the actual design almost always depends on *natural or unplanned* determinants of stability and change (Steuart, 1969). Therefore, the justification for continually revising our research methods and tools throughout our implementation process was to help programs respond to natural or unplanned social and political conditions. This underscored, for the Mississippi and North Carolina evaluations, the value of a qualitative research component to capture effects that were broader than changes in individual behaviors and health outcomes.

For the evaluation component of the process, the perceptions, stories, and explanations from program participants about effects and their determinants were gathered systematically through document review, participation observation, focus group interviews, and in-depth individual interviews. Using a text analysis software program called Nota Bene, the transcribed responses and field notes from each community were coded and summarized to describe three levels of change that were attributed to the program: (1) communities' interactions with agencies, (2) agencies' interactions with other agencies, and (3) individual residents' relationships with agencies and their communities.

The qualitative findings in Mississippi, for example, revealed two important effects from increasing community competence. One was that in a community—agency partnership, communities can provide care to complement the services offered by an agency. For instance, the CHAs organized a food bank that assisted social service clients who had to wait two weeks for approval to receive food stamps. Another effect was improved race relations. During the first two years of the program, citizens from the white communities avoided participating as CHAs. The explanation uncovered through interviews with white key informants was their need to observe whether the program intended to benefit all people in need, regardless of race. This intent was demonstrated through community projects, such as a white church's active participation in the food bank organized by the CHAs, who were all African American, and the training of two white health department staff who wanted to become CHAs.

DISCUSSION

Through the two case examples, we have attempted to demonstrate how community-based research straddles both research and practice even though neither the research community nor the practice community clearly names the research as their own. We believe that practitioners can readily equip themselves for this research methodology because it builds on the skills and values they have acquired in their training and experience. From the point of view of social work, Goldstein (1994) argued that

> doing practice and studying practice are variations on a similar humanistic theme and process [and that this process] shares common philosophical assumptions and similar procedures in how we understand people and their predicaments and find meaning in their thoughts, language, behavior, and life circumstances. (p. 42)

Hence, community-based research is part of a continuum of practice that is based on a set of core values and goals that permeate the entire intervention process. Based on the case examples in North Carolina and Mississippi, as well as a review of the literature related to participatory research (for example, action research, participatory action research, collaborative inquiry, collaborative action research, participatory evaluation, and empowerment evaluation), we propose a set of principles for conducting community-based research in small towns and rural areas. The principles incorporate fundamental values and goals (in italics) (Altpeter et al., in press):

- Community-based research focuses on *exposing and addressing social or practical problems* in order to stimulate *action for social change;* a secondary aim is to develop theory that is "grounded in action" (Flynn, Ray, & Rider, 1994; Pareek, 1990; Smith, Pyrch, & Lizardi, 1993; Wagner, 1991). Findings are regularly disseminated as feedback to participants to inform their action (Israel et al., 1998).
- Community-based research *involves collaboration, cooperation, and co-learning* (Flynn et al., 1994; Hugentobler, Israel, & Schurman, 1992; Israel, Schurman, & House, 1989; Israel et al., 1998; Ketterer, Price, & Politser, 1980; Pareek, 1990; Peters & Robinson, 1984; Sarri & Sarri, 1992b; Smith et al., 1993). Collaborative relationships may be established between the researchers and community residents (Flynn et al., 1994), practitioners (Ketterer et al., 1980), or workers or program participants (Hugentobler et al., 1992). Fully participating members ultimately can become co-researchers (Chesler, 1991; Hicks, 1997).
- Community-based research, conducted as a *scientific method of investigation,* promotes high validity because the participation of the community generates a "more accurate and authentic analysis of the participants' social reality" (Hall, 1979). Such validity can be ascertained through "member check-ins" to determine whether the research methods used and the interpretation and use of findings are relevant, credible, and useful to participants (Lincoln & Guba, 1985; Rappaport, 1990; Ristock & Pennell, 1996).
- Community-based research is a *cyclical process* that includes problem diagnosis and analysis (fact-finding), planning and implementation (action), and feedback (evaluation), followed by a new cycle (Chesler, 1991; Hugentobler et al., 1992; Israel et al., 1998; Ketterer et al., 1980; Peters & Robinson, 1984). In this process, the community is actively engaged in the origination, definition, and analysis of the problem and the subsequent solutions (Hall, 1979).
- Community-based research *creates competencies* within a community (Sarri & Sarri, 1992a), building capacity and fostering self-empowerment (Chesler, 1991; Flynn et al., 1994; Israel et al., 1998; Schoepf, 1993; Wagner, 1991).
- Community-based research *follows an ecological orientation to health promotion* (Israel et al., 1998; Stokols, 1996) in that research questions and units of observation examine naturally occurring strengths and social entities that people create for their well-being. Special worth is accorded to longitudinal designs and using multiple sources of data to capture changes in information, attitudes and behaviors, policies, cultural norms, and the physical and social environment. An important assumption is that interventions designed from an interdisciplinary perspective and which plan for change to occur at multiple levels are likely to achieve higher levels of scientific and social validity than more narrowly focused interventions.

CONCLUSION

In sum, both social work and public health not only require but also benefit from the participation of people in addressing problems that affect them. Community-based research methods can be highly effective in customizing interventions that enhance personal growth, improve program services, strengthen organizations and community groups, and promote social action to transform the lives of the marginalized. It is a comprehensive approach that maximizes the interplay between research and practice. Community-based research has roots in empowerment and feminist theory and in progressive social work perspectives; it thus includes an ideological commitment to social progress; intervention that considers individual and collective strategies within the context of economic and political factors; and goals that seek changes ranging from small increments through complete reorganization of society (Midgley, 1995; Simon, 1994). Sarri and Sarri (1992b) noted that the decade of the 1990s was "unlikely to be a time in which many more resources become available for the human services" (p. 120) and posited that community-based research can be a "cost-effective approach because it allows consumers an active role in setting priorities and in controlling many aspects of service delivery so as to maximize the allocation of resources to populations in greater need" (p. 120).

The grounded approach of community-based research ensures that the research endeavor stays focused on the realities of participants' lives in rural small towns and that the participants "own" the study with the researcher. The research questions, the process, the interpretation of the findings, and the manner in which the results will be used are decided within a democratic process (Kondrat & Julia, 1997; Ristock & Pennell, 1996). With its interplay between research and practice, community-based research is an ideal approach to maximizing the capacity and competence of people living in rural and small towns to create new knowledge about how they can be healthy and achieve human potential with dignity.

REFERENCES

Alary, J., Beausoleil, J., Guodon, M.-C., Lariviore, C., & Mazer, R. (Eds.). (1990). *Community care and participatory research* (S. Usher, Trans.). Montreal: Nu-Age Editions.

Altpeter, M., Schopler, J. H., Galinsky M. J., & Pennell, J. (in press). Participatory research as social work practice: When is it viable? *Journal of Progressive Human Services.*

Chesler, M. A. (1991). Participatory action research with self-help groups: An alternative paradigm for inquiry and action. *American Journal of Community Psychology, 19*(5), 757–768.

Cottrell, L. S. (1976). The competent community. In B. H. Kaplan, R. N. Wilson, & A. H. Leighton (Eds.), *Further explorations in social psychiatry* (pp. 195–209). New York: Basic Books.

Eng, E., & Parker, E. (1994). Measuring community competence in the Mississippi delta: The interface between program evaluation and empowerment. *Health Education Quarterly, 12,* 81–92.

Fellin, P. (1995). *The community and the social worker.* Itasca: F. E. Peacock.

Flynn, B. C., Ray, D. W., & Rider, M. S. (1994). Empowering communities: Action research through healthy cities. *Health Education Quarterly, 21*(3), 395–405.

Geiger, H.J. (1971). A health center in Mississippi—A case study in social medicine. In L. Corey, S. E. Saltman, & M. F. Epstein (Eds.), *Medicine in a Changing Society* (pp. 157–167). St. Louis: C.V. Mosby.

Goldstein, H. (1994). Ethnography, critical inquiry, and social work practice. In E. Sherman & W. J. Reid (Eds.), *Qualitative research in social work practice* (pp. 42–51). New York: Columbia University Press.

Hall, B. L. (1979). Knowledge as a commodity and participatory research. *Prospects, 9,* 393–408.

Hall, B. L. (1981). Participatory research, popular knowledge and power: A personal reflection. *Convergence, 14*(3), 6–19.

Hatch, J., and Eng, E. (1984). Community participation and control. In V. Sidel & R. Sidel (Eds.), *Liberal reforms in America* (pp. 223–244). New York: Pantheon.

Hicks, S. (1997). Participatory research: An approach for structural social workers. *Journal of Progressive Human Services, 8*(2), 63–78.

Hugentobler, M. K., Israel, B. A., & Schurman, S. J. (1992). An action research approach to workplace health: Integrating methods. *Health Education Quarterly, 19,* 5–76.

Israel, B. A., Schurman, S. J., & House, J. S. (1989). Action research on occupational stress: Involving workers as researchers. *International Journal of Health Services, 19*(1), 135–155.

Israel, B. A., Shultz, A., Parker, E. A., & Becker, A. (1998). Principles of community-based research. In *Annual Review of Public Health,* 173–202.

Kark, S. L., & Steuart, G. W. (1962). *A practice of social medicine: A South African team's experiences in different African communities.* Edinburgh, Scotland: E & S Livingston.

Ketterer, R. F., Price, R. H., & Politser, P. E. (1980). The action research paradigm. In R. H. Price & P. E. Politser (Eds.), *Evaluation and action in the social environment* (pp. 1–15). New York: Academic Press.

Kondrat, M. E. & Julia, M. (1997). Participatory action research: Self-reliant research strategies for human social development. *Social Development Issues, 19*(1), 32–49.

Kretzmann, J. P., & McKnight, J. L. (1993). *Building communities from the inside out: A path toward finding and mobilizing a community's assets.* Evanston, IL: Center for Urban Affairs and Policy Research.

Lincoln, Y. S., & Guba, E. G. (1985). *Naturalistic imagery.* Beverly Hills, CA: Sage Publications.

Midgely, J. (1995). *Social development: The development perspective in social welfare.* London: Sage Publications.

Pareek, U. (1990). Culture-relevant and culture-modifying action research for development. *Journal of Social Issues, 46*(3), 119–131.

Peters, M., & Robinson, V. (1984). The origins and status of action research. *Journal of Applied Behavioral Science, 20*(2), 113–124.

Rappaport, J. (1990). Research methods and the empowerment social agenda. In P. Tolan, C. Keys, F. Chertok, & L. Jason (Eds.), *Researching community psychology: Issues of theory and methods.* Washington, DC: American Psychological Association.

Ristock, J., & Pennell, J. (1996). *Community research as empowerment: Feminist links, postmodern interruptions.* Don Mills, Ontario: Oxford University Press.

Sarri, R. C., & Sarri, C. M. (1992a). Organizational and community change through participatory action research. *Journal of Administration in Social Work, 16*(3/4), 99–122.

Sarri, R., & Sarri, C. (1992b). Participatory action research in two communities in Bolivia and the United States. *International Social Work, 35,* 267–280.

Schoepf, B. G. (1993). AIDS action research with women in Kinshasa, Zaire. *Social Science and Medicine, 37,* 1401–1413.

Simon, B. L. (1994). *The empowerment tradition in American social work.* New York: Columbia University Press.

Smith, S. E., Pyrch, T., & Lizardi, A. O. (1993). Participatory action-research for health. *World Health Forum, 14,* 319–324.

Steckler, A. B., Israel, B. A., Dawson, L., & Eng, E. (1993). Community health development: An overview of the works of Guy W. Steuart. *Health Education Quarterly* (Suppl. 1), S3–S47.

Steuart, G. W. (1969). Planning and evaluation in health education. *International Journal of Health Education, 2,* 65–76.

Stokols, D. (1996). Translating social ecological theory into guidelines for community health promotion. *American Journal of Health Promotion, 10*(4), 282–298.

Tyson, K. (1995). New foundations for scientific social and behavioral research: A heuristic paradigm. Boston: Allyn and Bacon.

Trostle, J. (1986). Anthropology and epidemiology in the twentieth century: A selective history of collaborative projects and theoretical affinities, 1920 to 1970. In C. R. James, R. Stall, & S. M. Gifford (Eds.), *Anthropology and Epidemiology* (pp. 59–94). Norwell, MA: D. Reidel Publishing.

Wagner, D. (1991). Reviving the action research model: Combining case and cause with dislocated workers. *Social Work, 36*(6), 477–482.

Yeich, S., & Levine, R. (1992). Participatory research's contribution to a conceptualization of empowerment. *Journal of Applied Psychology, 22,* 1894–1908.

Zimbalist, S. E. (1977). Historic themes and landmarks in social welfare research. New York: Harper & Row.

CHAPTER EIGHTEEN

Returning to Rural Roots: African American Return Migrants' Use of Senior Centers

Cheryl Waites and Iris Carlton-LaNey

In recent years North Carolina has become a preferred destination for streams of retirees moving south. An attractive retirement state for affluent and less prosperous elders alike, North Carolina has the fourth highest net in-migration of people over age 60, preceded only by Florida, Arizona and Texas (Center on Aging Research and Educational Services, 1995). The state's attractive quality of life, combined with the relationships that African American elders have maintained with their homes of origin throughout the years, partly explains why African American elders are returning to North Carolina for retirement. Longino and Smith (1991) noted that the higher prevalence of return migration among older African Americans bolsters a scenario of African American labor force migration during youth, followed by a return to one's state of birth upon retirement.

Wiseman (1980) identified three categories of migration of elderly people: amenity, assistance, and return migration. Amenity migration involves long-distance moving in order to change lifestyles to a more leisure- and recreation-oriented way of life. Assistance migration involves moving because of a perceived or anticipated need for assistance, whereas return migration is going back to the place where one was born or grew up. The African American elders returning to North Carolina seem to fall into those three categories. As Longino and Smith (1991) observed, they are returning after an employment-related out-migration during their youth, and they are seeking the safety, comfort, and peace of the small town and rural life that they remember. Because some family members who never left the small communities often exist, return migrants also have some sense of family connection and social support that encourages their return. Their bonds with close kin and extended family have remained intact throughout their absence through events such as family reunions, vacations, funerals, and weddings (Hill, 1997). Many return migrants are bringing resources to their home communities that contribute to the area's economic development, and others are coming back to their places of birth with very few resources (Center on Aging Research and Educational Services, 1995).

Whatever their situation, they are also bringing with them the normal problems and needs of aging.

Because African American elders are returning to North Carolina in large numbers, we were interested in learning more about them. In particular, we wanted to explore the extent to which elderly return migrants use senior centers in their rural communities. Senior centers are facilities established to help elders to deal with some of the needs of aging. The Division of Aging of the North Carolina Department of Human Resources (NCDHR, 1995) defines the senior center as a facility in which older adults and their families can access services and activities such as information and case assistance, local and extended trips, health counseling, exercise classes, health screening, assistance with housing choices, employment and volunteer opportunities, arts and crafts classes, congregate meals, personal counseling, and other programs designed to provide social, educational, or health support. Senior centers have become an important component in the continuum of elder care.

The need for senior center programs in rural areas is well documented (Ralston, 1986). Senior centers provide an opportunity for social participation, which has been shown to have a strong relationship to the well-being of elders. Senior centers also provide needed social support for rural elders who may otherwise be isolated from family and friends. Elders in rural areas lack social outlets, which senior centers can provide. Finally, senior centers in rural areas provide places for coordination of services, which is a significant benefit where distance and travel are issues (Ralston, 1986, p. 77). Krout (1988) argued that research on senior center use suffers from several weaknesses, including the practice of conceptualizing and operationalizing senior center attendance as an act rather than as a continuum ranging from nonuse to former use.

This chapter looks at African American elders who have left northeastern and midwestern cities and moved back to their rural or small-town roots in North Carolina. Essentially, the chapter focuses on their adjustment to life in smaller towns in the rural south and their use of the senior centers as a mechanism instrumental to that adjustment.

METHOD

Design

This qualitative study was conducted with North Carolina's senior centers and their elderly African American return migrants. A total of 132 senior centers are in the state and can be found in 91 of the state's 100 counties. Public monies support some centers, whereas others are privately funded and run. Nine counties have no senior centers (NCDHR, 1995). For the purposes of our exploratory study, we conducted focus groups and individual interviews in Cumberland and Duplin Counties. Cumberland County has three senior centers, and Duplin County has one. Cumberland County is larger than Duplin and encompasses a small city, two towns, and several very rural communities; Duplin is the more rural and poorer of the two counties. Cumberland County is home to Fort Bragg Military Reservation and Pope Air Force Base, two of the largest military installations east of the Mississippi River. Duplin County boasts no such facilities. Slightly more than 85 percent of all residents of Duplin County live in rural areas, and the county's major industries are agriculture and manufacturing. Because of the military installations, Cumberland County's residents are relatively young; most people are under age 34. Both counties are located in southeastern North Carolina, which is a relatively less industrialized region than other parts of the state. Both Duplin and Cumberland Counties' elder populations are growing at a rate faster than any other age group.

Identifying and selecting return migrant subjects was a difficult task. To recruit participants, we used the following four data collection strategies:

1. A survey of directors of senior centers in selected counties in North Carolina
2. A survey of elders participating in senior centers in selected counties in North Carolina
3. A focus group of elders in Cumberland County
4. Telephone interviews with four elderly return migrants in Duplin County.

The same questions were asked of all the return migrants through a questionnaire, focus group discussion, or telephone interview. Senior center directors were selected using the North Carolina *Senior Center Directory* (NCDHR, 1995). The directors were asked to identify African American return migrants who participated in activities in their centers.

Surveys

Surveys consisting primarily of open-ended questions were mailed to select senior center directors to obtain information about return migrants' involvement in senior center programs and activities. A total of 81 director surveys were mailed to directors of senior centers in counties that had approximately a 20 percent African American population. One follow-up mailing was conducted three weeks later. Along with the survey instruments, directors were sent survey forms for African American return migrants and were asked to distribute them to each of their members who fell within this category. Return stamped envelopes were provided. The surveys were mailed before the focus group meeting and telephone interviews.

Focus Group

The focus group was the third data-gathering method. Focus groups are group interviews in which a small group of participants from similar backgrounds discuss topics that are guided by a moderator (Morgan, 1997). The four key elements of a focus group include: (1) careful planning of the focus group meeting, as well as identification of purpose and objectives; (2) recruiting and screening appropriate participants; (3) effective moderating during meetings; and (4) analyzing and interpreting the results in clear and detailed ways (Aaker, Kunar, & Day, 1995). We conducted one focus group in Cumberland County, which followed the model described above. We selected this particular center in Cumberland County because the assistant director was interested in this study and was able to identify many return migrants who were active at that senior center. The other centers, although interested, had access to a smaller percentage of return migrants.

In preparation for the focus group meeting, a preliminary consultation was conducted with the senior center director and assistant director to discuss the topic and to plan the focus group meeting. The director and assistant director played a key role in identifying prospective participants. Flyers were designed and distributed inviting African American return migrants to participate in the focus group meeting at the senior center. The center's assistant director followed up by identifying and reaching out to key seniors and inviting them to participate, and the meeting was also announced at two predominantly African American churches in the community. The focus group participants were given an agenda that identified specific topics to be discussed, and the meeting was video- and audiotaped.

Telephone Interviews

Individual telephone interviews were conducted with four elderly return migrants in Duplin County. The interviewers used guided open-ended questions and asked the same questions covered during the focus group. The interviewees were identified using snowball sampling; three males and one female were interviewed. The interviews lasted about one hour each. Each respondent was between age 65 and 74. They had been "back home" between three and 15 years.

FINDINGS

Data were collected from the surveys, focus group, and interviews. The survey responses were coded and provided descriptive and qualitative information. We also transcribed and analyzed the tapes from the focus group and interviews.

Directors' Survey

The senior center directors' survey response rate was somewhat disappointing, in that of the 81 surveys mailed, only 34 were returned, for a response rate of 42 percent. Most directors who completed the survey were located in midsize centers with a mean membership of 279. The respondents' senior centers sponsored an average of 22 programs. They had an average of 110 African Americans and 9 African American return migrants who attended the center. Many directors did not have information on the number of African American return migrants who attended their centers and therefore were unable to provide meaningful details about this group.

The directors who completed the survey had various responses when questioned about the return migration of African American elders. When asked why this group had returned to the South, the director's most common responses were that they did so to be closer to family and to return home to the South. They also indicated that they believed their members enjoyed the slower pace of life in the South. Essentially, the directors believed that the elders' decisions to move back to their communities of origin also could be classified as amenity and assistance migration. Directors indicated that their members were glad to be out of northern cities. The directors reported that the elders sometimes noted that there were fewer services in the towns in which they now live, but they were pleased with the lower crime rates, affordable costs of living, and warmer climate. Overall, center directors suggested that most migrants had expressed satisfaction with their return. One director, however, indicated a divergent view and wrote that her elders had indicated that "it was different than they expected, more expensive, . . . some culture shock. . . . [T]he people here are more closed-minded than they thought, they have not experienced different ways of doing things and thinking."

When reviewing use of senior centers and the specific activities and programs in which African American return migrants participated, many directors stated that they did not specifically monitor this subgroup. They said that African American return migrants participated in all the center's activities:

> "Our programming is to encourage all seniors regardless of race or sex."
> "Same as any participant, these older adults are no different than any who attend our center."

Many directors seemed not to consider that this population might have different interests or needs. There were a few directors who acknowledged that they did recognize diversity issues when engaging in program planning and tried to accommodate their members. One director stated that their African American return migrants "are involved in clubs that form their own activities i.e., annual fashion shows, black history trips, oral histories, a choral group, they do not see themselves as set apart."

Directors reported that African American return migrants have attempted to remain active and maintain regular involvement with their local senior centers. Most of their members' attendance averaged twice weekly. Popular activities for these elders were the variety of fitness and health programs offered at the centers. They also participated in lunch programs, parties, trips to the mall and restaurants, grocery shopping, and tours. Some indicated that elders at their centers attended regularly to play games and just to interact with others. They were also active in other senior organizations, namely, the American Association of Retired Persons (AARP) and church-related activities.

When asked whether senior centers were offering the programs and services that appeal to African American return migrants, some directors reported that they do have programs that might appeal to this group. Of the 22 directors who responded to this question, 15 said yes and seven said no.

Senior center directors most often indicated that their elders had no complaints about the services offered at the center or in the community. A few suggested that their elders wanted centers to offer local and overnight trips, health classes, trips to concerts, programs on African American history, transportation to the center, and a community information center.

Elders' Survey

The directors were asked to give the elders' surveys to their members who were African American return migrants; 20 surveys were returned. Most of the respondents indicated that they made a decision as retirement approached to return to the South and enjoy the small-town atmosphere. The feeling of safety and the atmosphere of benevolence that are part of the small community were major factors that contributed to their contentment. They also appreciated their families who have stayed in the South. The two respondents who indicated difficulties seemed to feel that the people were not as friendly as they had anticipated. They also longed for the level of activity found in larger cities and the access to public transportation. They also missed cultural activities, such as plays and concerts, as well as the family and friends who they left in the North. In spite of these issues, most elders indicated no regrets with their decision to return home.

Although they have basically adjusted to life in small towns, the respondents seemed to want their centers to offer more trips or tours and more educational classes. They also suggested that the community would benefit from improved systems of public transportation, more cultural activities, and a program that would provide friendly support and assistance for senior return migrants and newcomers. Other activities enjoyed by return migrants included traveling, trips to interesting places, activities that emphasize fitness and wellness, and educational classes.

Focus Group

The focus group was composed of seven participants: six women and one man. After 25 minutes, the only male left the meeting to join a planned activity, and his wife took his place. The participants had been back in their home communities for between three and eight years. The assistant director sat in on the meeting and was graciously welcomed by the participants. The meeting was held in a small conference room at the senior center; the atmosphere was comfortable for the participants because all were members of the center. The meeting began with introductions and an explanation of the focus group process. The group briefly reviewed the questions, and the discussion began.

The moderator facilitated the discussion around each question. After the initial orientation, the participants began exploring reasons for returning to their rural roots. Most indicated that they had easily made a decision to return but did yearn for some aspects of life in cities. One elder shared the following:

> I had to leave Detroit because of the weather. . . . I miss the snow. Detroit was good to me for job opportunities. I did really well in Detroit. I have no qualms about it, living in the northern cities, but I'm glad to be back.

One participant was not very happy with the outcome of her move to North Carolina and stated, "I jumped out of the frying pan into the fire." Others added that they moved to the North for a specific purpose, and their goals and needs have changed. They moved north in their youth, searching for a good education for their children, better employment opportunities, and higher salaries. Jobs that paid good salaries were limited for African Americans in the South, and the group attributed the scarcity to discriminations and the lack of unions. Many were union members and reported that their retirement income and benefits are good because of the employment they found in the North. They concluded that they left for a better life, and now they are returning in search of a comfortable retirement.

When asked what they liked about their return to the South, several elders said, "I like it because it is home." They also talked about the family members with whom they now spend time. Many added that their children have followed them to the south and live close by. Several elders indicated that they have been able to stay close to their children and extended family, and the closeness has been beneficial to all.

Most participants described themselves as leading active lives when they lived in the North. They expressed some disappointment in how difficult it had been to connect with their communities upon their return to the South. One participant said that she had not been readily accepted. The following exchange reveals some of the group's feelings:

Helen	I lived in Worcester, Massachusetts, and I was involved in the church and I had two different teen clubs from two different churches. They were two different denominations [the churches]. I was director of two teen clubs. I went to cosmetology school. I went to nursing school. I worked in the church with the Sunday school choir and junior choir. I was head of the traveling group at our church and here you can't get active because someone already has the job.
De	Yeah . . . someone has been in that position for so many years that they think. . . . [laughter]
Mary	I know, I know. . . .
De	They don't want to share it.
Helen	All the work is there but they don't want to share it.
Moderator	You feel like the outsider there.
Helen	Yes.

One participant reported that she was always active and has worked hard to remain active. The following exchange describes the group's attitude:

De	In Detroit as I said before, it was good to me, my husband and me. When I was there I worked for the criminal investigation division of IRS for 32 years in all. I was involved in my church choir and usher board. We traveled to Europe, and to the islands and I was with the youth of my church as far as the choir is concerned. And I was into bowling and dancing and all the things that I love to do. . . .
Helen	Yes.
De	I'm still trying to stay involved in those things that will keep me physically fit.
Mary	She won gold at the Senior Games.

All the participants attend the senior center regularly. They plan their weekly schedule and pack it with a variety of activities. Although their leisure pastimes varied somewhat, all expressed interest in some form of exercise, including dancing, Senior Games, aerobics, and bowling. They all reported doing some form of volunteer work with local organizations through the Retired Seniors Volunteer Program (RSVP). Several also indicated that the center had recently begun to plan tours and trips and that they planned to participate. All reported attending the center at least weekly to participate in a specific activity that they enjoyed. They also discussed their involvement in their churches and the time they spent with family members.

Essentially the focus group participants stated satisfaction with their return to their hometowns but complained about the limited cultural activities available in the area. They missed the easier access to cultural activities that the cities provided. One member noted that she had to be resourceful in locating stimulating enterprises. She reported that she carefully scans the newspaper every day for things to do and also fills her time with athletic activities. She helped organize a senior bowling club several years ago and is an active member.

The participants were ambivalent about the programs offered at the center. When asked about their satisfaction with the activities, the respondents were lukewarm but went on to discuss the issue carefully. Many participants expressed a need for a variety of cultural activities that would relate to the "black experience." They mentioned a recent trip to see Bill Cosby and cited that as an example of the kind of activities that they would like to do more often. They were pleased that upcoming trips were scheduled to New York and Alaska. They were seasoned travelers, having traveled abroad to Europe, the Caribbean, and other places, and they welcomed the opportunity to travel with other elders.

These elders also discussed segregation in senior programs and activities. One elder commented, "I like line dancing but [the white members] don't want you to participate . . . they will say oh you are doing it wrong and just give you a hard time when you are first learning." The assistant director commented that this center is a "predominantly Black center." She explained that they do have whites that participate in activities like line dancing, beach and concert trips, and other excursions. Most of the regular participants, however, are African Americans. The focus group participants agreed that because the senior center is close to a predominantly African American community, many white seniors did not participate in many activities at the center.

The participants also discussed the differences that they have noticed with some African Americans who have not left the South but have aged in place. They indicated that many seemed to be satisfied with the assortment of activities at the center and enjoyed "sitting around, playing games and knitting and sewing."

This group went on to discuss the closeness of the core group of elders that regularly attended the center. They indicated that they all tried to reach out to each other. A participant who had just moved to this area added that she did not know anyone at the meeting because she had just moved from Wilmington but enjoyed the discussion "tremendously." She stated, "It was nice to get together with people you have something in common with."

These elders indicated that their major concern with the senior center was a lack of variation in programming. They generally recognized that the problem was partially caused by the center's insufficient funding. One elder stated, "I have to beg for food for our activities." They also said that transportation was a big problem and called for more support in helping elders get around to grocery stores, medical appointments, and to the center. Transportation services were provided in the past; with budget cuts, however, they have been curtailed. The assistant director added that they could now only provide transportation three times a month for each member and that the transportation is limited to assistance in getting to the center.

The elders also suggested that communities should establish an official welcome committee with a support network. A participant recalled:

> I remember when . . . George [the former director] was in charge and I first came here, he took me around and explained everything to me. He asked me where I lived and I said I lived in P—. . . . And he said "I'm going to put you in touch with someone who can run you down to the center." And he did and they lived three houses down from me. And I told him that I did not know how to get back down here and he said "you follow me down" and I did. And that's how my husband and I started to come down here.

The focus group return migrants generally wanted to return home and have a comfortable retirement. They were active participants of the senior center but advocated for more variety in the center's programming and activities.

INTERVIEWS

After several telephone interviews with the director and staff at Duplin County Services for the Aged, which houses the senior center, we were informed that the center did not keep any records and had no way to identify whether center participants were return migrants. We decided to locate and interview return migrants who lived in the county and who may or may not attend the senior center. Four return migrants were identified and interviewed by telephone.

All the respondents said that they had enjoyed their lives in the cities. They led active lives and had lucrative employment, both of which had been their primary motives for moving to the cities. None of the respondents had completed college, although one attended college for three semesters before joining the army. Returning to a more peaceful life was their reason for coming back home. Each respondent said that they always considered this their home, even though they had been away for more than 25 years. In anticipation of his retirement, one man and his wife had built their home more than 20 years before their return. Others recalled their high expectations regarding their preparation for and return to their place of birth.

Two of the four respondents said that they had used the services at the senior center. One man said that he used the center's tax preparation service but had not used any other services. He said that he did not enjoy bus trips. He further indicated that the center's other services and programs were things that his mother, who was in her eighties, would enjoy because she knew the people. The respondent said that he did not do any volunteer work, although he had been asked to become a volunteer at the senior center. When asked what he did as a pastime or for enjoyment, the same respondent said that he was involved in his church and that he and his wife also enjoyed driving to the casinos in Atlantic City.

The one woman who was interviewed said that she attended the annual dance that the senior center sponsored. She said that she enjoyed that activity but could not get her husband to participate. She did not participate in any other center-sponsored activities. She worked part time in the kitchen at a local long-term care facility and did not express any desire to engage in additional activities.

The third male respondent said that he had gone to the senior center to visit the other participants, but he was "not really a senior" and did not participate in center-sponsored activities. When asked about his social activities, he said that he missed New York because he and his wife enjoyed travel to Canada and the Catskills and dining at fine restaurants. He further indicated that he has found an active social life since returning home. He and several other couples of return migrants engage in group activities that include fishing on the Atlantic Ocean, cooking out, and taking regular trips together. He spoke fondly of the other return migrants with whom he socializes.

The fourth man said that he had never used the services at the senior center. He said that visiting the senior center "never crossed his mind" and that he was too busy and simply didn't have time; nor did he enjoy bus tours and those types of activities. He is in his mid-sixties and regularly travels back to the northeastern city where he lived for more than 45 years. For social activities, this respondent organized a community club, goes to church, plants and tends a garden, and takes care of his livestock.

All the respondents said that their children and grandchildren were still in the cities where they had lived and that they maintained regular contact with their children through telephone calls and visits. Although the return migrants said that they missed being close to their children, they had no regrets about their return home for retirement. They were comfortable in their homes and with their social involvement. They all said that they could enjoy the "peace and quiet" and "wide open spaces" of the country.

DISCUSSION

The African American return migrants strategically planned and carried out their return home. Overall, they were pleased with this decision. Those who regularly attend senior centers indicated that they had made a conscious effort to stay active with the centers. They were advocates for the center and wanted to expand the variety of programming and increase the funding.

Sometimes they felt like outsiders and were trying to find their place in their community. They were ambivalent about the slower pace; they enjoyed the close-knit religious-oriented community yet missed the convenient and constant activity of city life. Others had found or created social outlets and had little or no interest in the services and programs of their senior center.

The elders suggested the following community support to help with their transition back into their communities of origin:

- a welcome committee for return migrants
- information networks
- acknowledgement of diversity when planning activities at the center
- adequate budget to support active programming and resources
- transportation services.

IMPLICATIONS

As Longino and Hass (1993) indicated, migration is a complicating factor in planning for a rural elderly population because it adds to the population's diversity (p. 29). Return migrants present a special complication because their return is viewed as a family member returning home after being away for several years. This perspective ignores the fact that they are not like the elders who have aged in place and that they are indeed migrants. As this study indicates, the elderly African American return migrants are not a homogeneous group. They are characterized by diversity.

Perhaps of greater importance is the fact that this study highlights the invisibility of elderly African American return migrants. Their invisibility is partly a result of their underuse of certain services designed exclusively for seniors. An examination of health care service use, in contrast, may provide a different picture from this study with regard to use of social services—specifically the senior center. Hass and Crandall (1988) noted, for example, that physicians in two rural North Carolina mountains communities felt that retirement migrants' effect on rural health care system had altered them in positive ways. Krout (1991) found that many senior centers in rural areas reported growth in resources and staff. This growth may result from elders' requests for additional resources as well as from the strategic role that senior centers play in service delivery and information and referral in rural areas.

Our study of elderly African American return migrants was hampered by their invisibility. Even though we used several mechanisms for gathering information from this group we actually reached a smaller sample of the population than desired. We believe that conducting focus groups in several communities that have high rates of return migrants and various levels of senior center funding could strengthen our work. Because the snowball sampling method was used to identify the interviewees in Duplin County, we talked with people who were more alike than different. Perhaps a purposive sampling method would give more diversity to the pool of interviewees and provide a different picture of rural elders' use of senior centers.

Although the response rate of nearly 42 percent from the senior center directors was adequate, we suspect that the senior center directors were reluctant to respond to our survey for a number of reasons, including fear that their programs would be criticized. Moreover, they were probably also reticent because the sensitive issue of race was broached. Several center directors suggested that their programs were color-blind and served all elders equally. We know, however, that color-blindness is not ideal; it tends to discriminate because all people are not alike, and culturally sensitive practice means taking "difference" into account respectfully. The ultimate consequence of this group's invisibility is that they are at high risk of being excluded from county and state strategic and long-range plans for serving rural elders. We believe, nonetheless that this study begins to provide useful information for the state Division of Aging and for others who work with rural elders, including policymakers, planners, social service agencies, and professionals practitioners.

Furthermore, we suggest that the issue of return migration is an important phenomenon among elders regardless of race and that their continued return to their places of birth will have a critical effect on these communities' development, service delivery, and public policies. This study focused on rural North Carolina, but rural communities throughout the South are experiencing similar in-migration of retirees, many of whom are return migrants. We advocate additional research with this population to ensure that an important part of the country's citizenry is recognized and served. Research that is helpful in policymaking and program planning and that includes heretofore excluded people is always in demand, particularly when the focus of social services is on inclusion, cultural competence, and strength-based practice.

REFERENCES

Aaker, D., Kunar, V., & Day, G. (1995). *Marketing research* (5th ed.). New York: John Wiley & Sons.

Center on Aging Research and Educational Services. (1995). *The North Carolina aging services plan: A guide for successful aging in the 1990s.* Raleigh, NC: Author.

Hass, W., & Crandall, L. (1988). Physicians' views of retirement migrants' impact on rural medical practice. *Gerontologist, 28,* 663–666.

Hill, R. (1997). *Strengths of African American families: Twenty-five years later.* Washington, DC: R&B Publishers.

Krout, J. (1988). Senior center linkages with community organizations. *Research on Aging, 10,* 258–274.

Krout, J. (1991). Senior center participation: Findings from a multidimensional analysis. *Journal of Applied Gerontology, 10,* 244–257.

Longino, C., & Hass, W. (1993). Migration and the rural elderly. In C. N. Bull (Ed.), *Aging In Rural America* (pp. 17–29). Newbury Park, CA: Sage Publications.

Longino, C., & Smith, K. (1991). Black retirement migration in the United States. *Journal of Gerontology: Social Sciences, 46,* S125–S132.

Morgan, D. L. (1997). *The focus group kit: Planning focus groups.* London: Sage.

North Carolina Department of Human Resources, Division of Aging. (1995). *Senior center directory, 1996–1997.* Raleigh, NC: Author.

Ralston, P. (1986). Senior centers in rural communities: A qualitative study. *Journal of Applied Gerontology, 5,* 76–92.

Wiseman, R. (1980). Why older people move theoretical issues. *Research on Aging,* 2, 141–154.

CHAPTER NINETEEN

Antiracist Social Work Curriculum Development for Preserving and Strengthening Indigenous Communities in Rural New Brunswick, Canada

Rosemary A. Clews

This study sheds light on how a social work curriculum should develop if it is to enable social work graduates to assist individual healing processes as well as contribute to initiatives to preserve and strengthen indigenous rural communities. The participants in this study consider it crucial for social workers to understand the realities of life for First Nations people. This understanding involves appreciating the legacy of the past on individuals and their communities; it also involves possessing an awareness of individual and community issues that First Nations people currently face as well as understanding how the past and the present influence different hopes, fears, and expectations about the future. First Nations participants in the study considered that this knowledge is far more important than extensive knowledge of existing social work theory and practice wisdom. The findings have implications for antiracist curriculum development in other schools of social work in the United States and Canada.

RACISM, SOCIAL WORK CURRICULA, AND INDIGENOUS PEOPLE

A need exists for social work educators in both the United States and Canada to develop curricula to assist social work students in developing knowledge, skills, and values for social work with indigenous people, including American Indians and First Nations Canadian people.[1] Views about the appropriate knowledge, values, and skills

---

[1] Many different terms are used to refer to indigenous people in the United States and Canada. I use the term *American Indians* to refer to indigenous people in the United States because it is a term which appears frequently in the literature. The term *First Nations* is that most favored by the Canadian indigenous people who were participants in the research described in this chapter.

for social work have mainly been developed from the experiences of those who have immigrated to these countries over the past five centuries. A "colorblind" approach often has been adopted by social workers "through the concept of 'universality of treatment,' whereby equality is assumed rather than proven because all individuals and groups are treated as if they were 'all the same'" (Dominelli, 1997, p. 37). Until the past decade many of the large social work texts that provide the basis for social work curricula were colorblind because they ignored differences that resulted from ethnicity, culture, and race. People from diverse ethnic and racial backgrounds often experience "colorblind" approaches to working with them as racist. Antiracist social work curricula confront the bias of colorblind approaches and seek alternatives.

More recently a number of social work texts have provided references to ethnic and racial differences. The subject index of the third edition of a major text has a section on "American Indians" (Hepworth & Larsen, 1993, S2). This index refers the reader to one page that discusses alcohol abuse among American Indians. Similarly, the book has one page on child abuse reporting and one page on child rearing in relation to American Indians. On other occasions authors devote entire sections to American Indians and explain concepts such as "Indian time" to the non-Indian reader (Morales & Sheafor, 1995, pp. 5–7). Authors sometimes mention the diversity among indigenous people (Kirst-Ashman & Hull, 1993, pp. 4–7; Morales & Sheafor, 1995, pp. 5–6). Nevertheless, there is a danger that when books provide social work students with a small amount of information, this can produce or reinforce stereotypical ideas.

Furthermore, the implication seems to be that once nonindigenous people can understand some of the ways in which indigenous people differ from other people, a culturally competent modification of social work practice can be developed. This approach has several problems. First, existing social work curricula usually have been developed from nonindigenous perspectives and are treated as a model that can be adapted for work with indigenous people. An assumption is made that an adaptation to existing curriculum is sufficient, but perhaps more than adaptation is needed. Second, often the adaptations to social work curricula are made by social work curriculum developers who have learned about indigenous people by studying nonindigenous interpretations of history and present-day life of indigenous people. Alternative ways of viewing the world, as expressed by indigenous people themselves, are rarely placed in a central position when social work curricula are developed. Consequently, the danger exists that ethnocentric bias or even racism is built into our social work curricula.

CHALLENGES OF WORKING WITH INDIGENOUS PEOPLE IN RURAL COMMUNITIES[2]

Both indigenous and nonindigenous social workers may have difficulty gaining acceptance in communities of indigenous people. Newly appointed indigenous social

---

[2] I define a community as rural if it is a distinct community and has a small population. The four First Nations communities from which participants were drawn in this study had populations of 400, 700, 800, and 2,500.

workers who originate from the community where they become employed are likely to have been known to local people since childhood. It may be hard for these social workers, particularly those who have experienced troubles in their past, to establish credibility. Another difficulty is that indigenous social workers can be shunned by their home communities and treated as defectors to "the other side." Social workers who are not from a First Nations or American Indian heritage, and even indigenous social workers from outside the particular province or state where they find work, may be viewed as outsiders and treated with suspicion.

Many social work graduates can expect to work with indigenous people. Social workers who work with indigenous people in rural communities often lack the specialized resources, services, or expertise that is available in cities, and models for working with First Nations people in urban communities may be inappropriate (Herberg, 1993). In these circumstances social workers need to inform their practice by developing a knowledge base about the experiences, lifestyles, and beliefs of local indigenous people. Different social work skills and practice theories from those taught in the social work classroom may be needed to enable graduates to work effectively in such an environment (Goldstein & Bornemann, 1975, p. i).

Canadian First Nations people often live in "difficult and impoverished conditions that are unimaginable to the average person in Canada" (Mawhinney 1995, p. 214). Levels of suicide, violence, infant mortality, shared homes with poor sanitation, unemployment, and low incomes are much higher than the Canadian average (Mawhinney 1995, p. 215). Similar situations often exist in the United States (Dana, 1981, p. 3). People who experience these social problems are likely to encounter social workers, who need knowledge, skills, and commitment to work in a culturally competent and antiracist manner.[3]

Indigenous people are writing accounts of their experiences of oppression. Their suffering is reflected in the graphic titles of books. A Mohawk woman writes of the "thunder in my soul" (Monture-Angus, 1995), a Metis activist refers to his people as "a tortured people" (Adams, 1995), and a social historian writes about "the dispossessed" (York, 1990). Autobiographies, novels and poetry are other media through which indigenous experiences are expressed. (Campbell, 1973; Joe, 1978, 1988, 1996). As I read these accounts, I am constantly reminded about the necessity of providing social work students with a social work curriculum that addresses these experiences.

The experiences of indigenous people in different parts of North America differ enormously. Historical, geographical, and climatic differences are just three of many influences on the development of different cultures and lifestyles. Consequently, the experience of Inuit people in Labrador differs greatly from experiences of indigenous people in Alaska or rural parts of the southern United States. In addition, people within each region will not all have the same views. Although the same process of developing a curriculum may be used in different North American regions, the cur-

---

[3] By *culturally competent* social work with indigenous people, I mean social work that is relevant to their needs and their ways of meeting these needs. By *antiracist* social work I mean social work that confronts racism at the level of individual interactions and biased cultural assumptions and social structures.

riculum content that is developed for work in each region should reflect the unique characteristics of each community and the people within it.

The absence of locally relevant resource material that could assist me to develop a curriculum for work with indigenous people led me to conduct some research. In this chapter, I describe the research process and outline views of research participants regarding what social workers should know if they are to work with indigenous people. I invite the reader to consider whether a similar process would be appropriate in other communities and whether the views of participants in the study have applicability elsewhere.

CURRICULUM FOR WORKING WITH FIRST NATIONS PEOPLE IN RURAL NEW BRUNSWICK

New Brunswick is a province of Canada located in the Atlantic region in Eastern Canada. It is bordered by the state of Maine, the province of Nova Scotia, and the Atlantic Ocean. With a population density of 10.1 people per square kilometer, New Brunswick is the second most rural province in Canada.[4] Most of New Brunswick is forested, and the province has almost 1,000 miles of coastline. Fishing, forestry, pulp and paper, mining, and agriculture, along with manufacturing, are the principal industries (Colombo, 1997, p. 27).

Of a New Brunswick population of 723,000 in 1991, 12,185 people self-identified as having some First Nations origins. Seventy percent of New Brunswick First Nations people live in one of the 15 rural First Nations communities. The First Nations population is young[5] and has an estimated fertility rate of 2.7, which is almost 60 percent higher than the average for all New Brunswick people (Government of New Brunswick, 1996, p. 2). The proportion of First Nations people in the total New Brunswick population is likely to increase, meaning that social workers will experience an increased need to develop knowledge and skills to work with them.

Atlantic Canadian social work educators in rural areas struggle to apply non-Canadian "urban" literature or, at best, literature about antiracist social work developed several thousand miles away in Western Canada, the United States, England, and other countries to their different rural realities. Atlantic Canada has had more than 400 years of contact between European settlers and First Nations people. Many traditional ways have been lost, and the number of people who can speak the Micmac and Maliseet languages of New Brunswick is declining rapidly. With the loss of language comes a loss of culture. The first phase of this research is designed to enable First Nations people in rural New Brunswick to share their views about the necessary knowledge for social work. Once this has occurred, a dialogue between First Nations people and social work educators can inform the development of curriculum content and teaching and learning methods for antiracist social work practice.

---

[4] Prince Edward Island has the lowest population density in Canada.

[5] Fifty-six percent of New Brunswick's indigenous population is under age 25. Those over age 55 make up 20.4 percent of the provincial total population and only 7.1 percent of the New Brunswick indigenous population.

RESEARCH METHOD AND ETHICAL ISSUES

Eight First Nations research participants and a Caucasian social worker who practices in a First Nations community individually reviewed a preinterview questionnaire that asked participants what they thought social work students needed to learn to practice in an antiracist way. I subsequently met with each participant to discuss his or her views about the topic. We considered the questionnaire, cultural bias in the questionnaire, and other questions that participants thought should be asked. We explored methods of teaching and learning that would enable social workers to develop the commitment and the knowledge, values, and skills that the participants considered important. From the discussions and questionnaires, I identified key themes mentioned by participants.

I selected First Nations participants who have had a variety of life experiences to inform the first stages of development of a curriculum that would be relevant to a broad range of First Nations people. Six of the eight live in four different New Brunswick First Nations communities, and two participants live in a rural community that is not a First Nations community. Many participants have lived and worked in other urban and rural communities. Three have lived in Eastern United States, and one participant has lived in "every major Canadian city." The sample included an elder, a politician (band councilor), social workers, and others with an interest in social work education, including previous social work clients. Several participants had fair skin and blue eyes and referred to themselves as "mixed blood" but identified with their First Nations heritage over any others. Although a number of First Nations people in New Brunswick are angry and hostile toward social workers and therefore would not participate in a study of this nature conducted by a white social work educator, people with many different ideas agreed to participate in it (Clews, in press, explores these issues in greater depth).

I asked participants what antiracist social workers should know, believe, and be able to do as well as how they should learn. I explored whether white social workers could work effectively with First Nations people. I also asked participants about the questions I was asking: Did they capture what it is important about antiracist social work, or were there other questions and answers that were more important?

I experienced a number of difficulties as I attempted to apply traditional ethical research principles of "informed consent," "avoidance of harm," and "confidentiality." Many social workers, particularly non–First Nations social workers, are greeted with suspicion in First Nations communities. As a non–First Nations social work researcher with a strong English accent, I realized I was unlikely to gain access to many potential participants because of a suspicion about my motives. I therefore consulted three First Nations people who were well accepted in First Nations communities. I told them about the issue I wanted to research and asked for their assistance in finding a sample of research participants.

I have been told that my research was discussed around a First Nations "sacred fire" in Fredericton, the capital of New Brunswick. Apparently, my proposed research and I, as the researcher, were considered honorable. As a result, people who had many different viewpoints generously gave their time to share ideas with me. Participants who had been introduced to me through this process rarely paid much attention to the consent forms that I asked them to sign. They listened patiently when I explained the reasons for my research. Often I thought that consent to participate had really been given as they sat around the sacred fire. I asked myself whether this was the "informed consent" referred to in human subjects protection guidelines and decided that it probably was not. A community of people, rather than individuals, gave consent to a researcher who was judged to be honorable.

My first participant was a volunteer who was not on my initial list of potential participants. He told me that he had heard about my research plans and wanted to help and that he did not want to discuss what he was consenting to in offering to participate, because he said he knew enough. I consulted with First Nations people and was reassured that First Nation ethical principles had been satisfied by the sacred fire discussions, even though this would not satisfy ethical standards developed in a European context. This experience highlights the need to develop research ethics that are relevant for work with First Nations research participants.

The remainder of this chapter outlines the views of the First Nations people who participated in the study on the knowledge base necessary for antiracist social work. Not surprisingly, First Nations participants focused mainly on knowledge they believe is needed for work with First Nations people.

WHAT SHOULD SOCIAL WORKERS KNOW IF THEY ARE TO WORK IN AN ANTIRACIST WAY?

> They should know the people . . . who they are . . . where they're coming from . . . where they came from . . . how they got here . . . where they want to go . . . not where social workers want them to go.

The above quotation encapsulates the responses from many participants. Participants told me that it is most important for social work students to learn about the reality of life for Canadian First Nations people in the past and the present as well as their different hopes for the future. They were not asking for social workers who were skilled in applying complex theories to the difficulties they face, but rather social workers who spend time getting to know about First Nations lifestyles. One participant explained it in an amusing way:

> They don't want to be told university big words . . . they want to be told "Hi, how are you? What can I do for you today?" I can't walk in and say, "Mr. Aboriginal Man of Canada, can I help you with your psychological problem?" They don't want to hear that, they want a cup of tea and a cigarette.

"The Phoenix Rose"

During the past 30 years, particularly during the past decade, indigenous people in North America have tried to reconnect with their culture, language, and traditions. One participant described this rebirth in the following way:

A long time ago they used to have the talking circles [and] the sweat lodges. Then along came the European society and they said no, none of that, [they] destroyed the whole structure of the Native way of life. We ended up in little plots here and there . . . some of us in swamps. Because of the dominant race saying, "No, you're no good," lording it over the unsuspecting people of the land, they begin to lose sight of who they are, why they're there. If you tell a person for long enough that they're no good they begin to believe it. Back in the sixties it started coming back. (You have to remember that in the fifties a person could be jailed for practicing their culture.) People were kind of weary. Then something happened, maybe the phoenix rose and rejuvenated those ones that were selected to go out and teach and give them the spirit to do so. In the sixties and seventies people met in small groups. After 500 years of not doing this . . . they had to begin to trust themselves. They didn't know what an eagle feather meant, they probably didn't know what this meant . . . [pointing at a smudge stick]. Anything that you're born with, that's inside you, your spirit somehow knows. And maybe within that group, could have been two or three people there who had knowing spirits, and those people connected, and there began the resurgence of Native spirituality.

THE PAST

Many people I talked to said that only when social workers can understand the past and how it influences the present will they be able to help First Nations people plan for their futures. Frequently mentioned issues from the past were the Indian Act and education. Education was considered to be a possible means of escape, but educational experiences at primary, secondary, and university levels were often sources of considerable pain. The Indian Act was much hated Canadian legislation that gave First Nations people an experience of bondage and separation from their beliefs and lifestyles.

Indian Acts: "Apartheid" and "Imprisonment"

Indian people have been isolated to a community geographically and they only qualify for certain programmes and services living on this reserve.[6] If I was to move outside of the boundaries of this reserve, I would qualify for no service. We have legislation, the Indian Act which dictates to how things are going to unfold for the Indian people. If I use an analogy in terms of the apartheid legislation in Africa, it's similar to the Indian Act, it dictates to you where you live, who can be Indian and who can't, what services you qualify for [and] when the Bands have lawmaking authority it has to be approved by the Minister of Indian Affairs. . . .

---

[6] *Reserve* is a term that was frequently used in the past and is sometimes still used to refer to a First Nations community.

The First Nations social worker who expressed this view about legislation reflected views of many others. Another participant likened the legislation to imprisonment. I asked her how she had been disadvantaged, and she pointed to the questionnaire and said:

> Well, by that word [pointing to the word 'Reservation' on her answer to a question]. I feel that because of that my beginnings started off as not being a free person. I was only allowed to stay on a small little land and I was not allowed to venture off, or my ancestors were not.

A third participant pointed out that "they don't have an Italian Act . . . they don't have an Irish Act."

"And This was Supposed to be a Place of Learning"

Many First Nations people considered education a possible way to improve life for themselves, their children, or their community. Educational experiences themselves, however, were often very painful:

> The residential school system has done . . . a great harm . . . when they were educating us Indians, they wanted us to conform to society. And then they saw that education was a vehicle for that. The kids were uprooted from their communities and taken into residential schools, they were abused in some way if they didn't conform . . . [parents] want the children to speak English so that we don't experience what they experienced . . . the Mi'kmac and Maliseet language is almost extinct . . . Language is important because it's the only form of communication we have.

When a Canadian military base was built in New Brunswick in 1953, a large part of a First Nations community site was taken by the federal government. First Nations people living there were required to relocate:

> There were some people that moved up here that didn't have anything at all. [They had] no running water . . . and when they came to school some of their hands were dirty and the teachers made them wash up or send them back home. I've seen the teachers hit those kids on the fingers and they come to school with no mittens, when your fingers are cold and the teacher hits you with a ruler on the fingers, that must really hurt.

Two participants spoke about their experiences of going off the "reserve" for secondary education. One went to the high school each day by bus:

> All barriers broke down and I was able to go to school outside the reserve . . . our grades went up to grade eight and anything after that you had to go off the reserve. I remember that first day . . . the new ones "us" . . . there were ten or eleven of us . . . when we got off that bus in Richibucto . . . we were . . . just a little group . . . all by ourselves . . . didn't know what the hell was supposed to be going on . . . and this was supposed to be a place of learning.

The other participant lived in a First Nations community in another part of New Brunswick. In this location, students who entered grade nine had to leave the community and attend boarding school:

> It's my first time of leaving the reserve and it was very scary. I cried when my parents left me. The nuns were very strict, we had to get up at six in the morning and do chores. [We] weren't allowed to go anywhere, it was like a prison. My parents always pushed me to get my education. I got my Grade Ten and then I didn't want to go back there anymore.

Often high school students' grades fell because they were stereotyped as academically weak:

> There were some teachers that were so young that they could not figure me out, so in those classes I excelled. Some of the older ones, they'd figure out that, "yeh, she's from Big Cove so she's Native," and obviously they have to teach me manners. I was not judged as a person, I was judged as a group. I was an "A" student until I hit Richibucto, then I became a "C" student . . . even my parents questioned that because they knew I was smart.

High school students experienced racist behavior from other students:

> They pulled my hair, they called me "squaw." Several times I had to go and talk with the principal, children were really nasty. I was the only Native girl in the whole class. I would go home and I would cry to my parents, but they always made me go back. I'm glad they made me go back now. These are the struggles you have to go through.

RACISM IN ACADEMIA

Some went on to higher education. Experiences with other students could be difficult:

> I felt like I was an outsider. We had to break into groups. There was a girl there, she was part-Native too, when they formed their group they left us out. [The professor] had to fit us in . . . I felt really bad.

> Racism does exist, even in academia. I think that it's a journey that a social work student should be prepared to go through, to come to the realization that this is what we have been taught, this is the world we live in, these are the people that we oppress. To acknowledge that . . . and then go on to say, well, what can I do to work towards a more egalitarian system.

Sometimes comments were made in classrooms that were amazing to First Nations students because they showed a total lack of understanding about life in a First Nations Community. One participant reported, "We were talking about . . . how

Natives get funding. She couldn't figure out why, if the government is giving Natives all this money . . . they aren't doing anything with it." The student failed to understand that education was needed because many people had no qualifications at all for their jobs; she did not realize that people were given any job in the community that was available.

> That lady thought that the funding was to send them to school and get them out of that place. These people wanted to be carpenters but the carpenter jobs were full so they had to throw them somewhere else. So here, you be a cop and you be a drug and alcohol worker.

Several participants alluded to little understanding about First Nations issues by professors:

> There were some institutional prejudices. I guess that they had bad experiences with an [indigenous] community, they were using that experience in regards to how they would treat [indigenous] students . . . stereotyping. To teach at the university . . . I think that they need to be aware of their own prejudices.

The same participant also stated, "You need to have a team of educators that believe in a certain goal." In contrast, one participant was pleasantly surprised by her experience at university:

> I went in there expecting to get beat up, put down by both teachers and students. None of that happened. I have been shown more respect than I have anywhere. I think it's only a minority of students who are racist.

THE PRESENT

"What Happened in the Past is in the Past, It's Now Time that People Can Start Working Together"

Some participants spoke about their past sufferings; others thought that the past should be placed firmly behind them so that non–First Nations and First Nations people could work together. I asked one participant: "Does each individual white person that's trying to work with each individual Indian person need to say, 'I acknowledge what went on, I want to move forward?'" This was her reply:

> The Indian people and the white people need to stop fighting over the past and need to get together, not just to right the wrongs but to make the changes. I think that posters or something should be put on walls everywhere to start educating the people, to stop looking at each other as different and to stop thinking of the past.

> It's time now that people can start working together. [Social workers need to be aware of what went on in the past] in order to understand why people are in the situation they are in today, but not to carry the burden or the guilt. It builds walls, barriers between the two. There's no need of that today.

Participants spoke about what social workers need to know about the present experiences of First Nations people in order to work with them. Themes that occurred most frequently were First Nations spirituality and healing, the way of life in First Nations communities, mistrust of the government, the experience of racism, and the effect of unemployment on First Nations families and communities.

Linear or Circular?

I was told that social workers need to understand that the Western linear method of thinking is just one possibility, one that contrasts with the circular thinking of many First Nations people. Participants spoke about how people were related to each other, to other living creatures, to the world, and how the past related to the present:

> There is a difference between linear and circular thinking, for myself life is a ceremony and it's very circular. I begin as a child and I am going through specific stages of my life, as we get older we go back to our childhood and it just keeps on. Everywhere you walk your ancestors are there, have been buried before you and so each step you take you need to be conscious of that.

Another said, "There are many powers . . . there's Glooscap . . . there's the eagles . . . there's animals. They're all our higher spirits, our higher powers."

"I Believe Our Community Needs a Lot of Healing"

Participants thought that social workers should understand about pain and about healing processes. Several spoke about their own painful past experiences. Many experienced abuse or alcohol and drug problems. After conquering these problems they tried to help others.

> [Healing is] recognizing mistakes in the past and fading them out. It's not like one of those things where once you get converted you become holier. It's [not] just something for me, me going to university it's like a job. The reserve's paying for my education, so once I get educated it's best to go back to the reserve and give back what you learned from off-reserve. [Healing is] letting go . . . [of] your anger, not to be negative. Because people say one thing [it] doesn't mean you have to believe

them. Learn for yourself. You've just got to learn not to cross that line and be a preacher [and] put them down because of something you don't do. They say "I shouldn't drink," and you just listen . . . when they're in good shape, you tell them. "Did you mean what you said here? Do you want to talk about it?" I see a lot of changes in the reserve lately and I'm glad to be part of that change. . . .

Some participants embraced First Nations spirituality as a way of promoting healing for themselves and for others. These participants spoke with sorrow about "reverse racism" and how it prevented bridges of understanding being built between First Nations people and others. As one participant said, "If someone says you [*sic*] white . . . whatever . . . they're going to feel that sting that the Indians felt and that's counterproductive . . . it builds walls."

"Two Ears but Only One Mouth"

Many participants considered that social workers must understand something about life in First Nations communities and that they can learn most effectively by listening. The following statements are representative of their thoughts on the subject:

I think non-Natives can be very effective in [indigenous] communities but first they need to be aware of the community, the political structure . . . programming.

I think also that they should be told what really goes on on a reserve. Most people think that they get free housing and don't have to pay taxes. The government and most people look down on the reserves as if they're just welfare recipients. . . .

Social workers come in that are not Native and they try too hard. I think that they should learn first that, just go in, sit back, listen. I learned more by them coming to talk to me than me asking them questions.

Participants stressed that the lifestyle in First Nations communities differed greatly from other lifestyles:

It should be required that, let's say a student is invited to stay with me a week at my home . . . find out how I live, what kind of foods I eat. How do I pray? How do I interact with my people? What are those things that I share with my neighbors?

Social workers and social work students should be quietly respectful and learn from what they see. Only when they understand about the lifestyle should they presume to intervene in people's lives.

Being there . . . watching people interact with each other, and you're sort of on the outside looking in. There's a joke that goes around, it's a teaching joke. The question is "Why do we have two ears but only one mouth?" "Because we're supposed to listen more than we talk." We learn by what we hear and what we see. Sometimes you're allowed to ask questions, but the questions are not that important, you learn more from observing than you do by asking questions.

Community Care

Some participants thought that it was crucial for social workers to know about differences between First Nations and other communities regarding community and nuclear family responsibilities.

> When we're dealing with families, normally the non-Native agencies work directly with the client. Here we work with the heads of families who will be the most significant other in that family relationship. We would give them the responsibility. . . .

A non–social worker expressed the same sentiment in more simple terms: "On the reserve it's family oriented. You need help, your family's there. If you're not receiving help you're giving help."

Another participant said that social workers should learn to look at actions in context because "what appears wrong can be right." There are important differences between indigenous and non-indigenous people in their child-rearing practices. One participant noted, "Here, in this community . . . the tendency is to roam quite freely in the community, there's always someone looking after the child. [The social worker needs to] move away from this kind of individualistic notion to much more of a community-based. . . ."

"Don't Trust the Government"

Many mentioned the importance of social workers understanding current Canadian federal, provincial, and community politics. There was much mistrust of both federal and provincial governments. Participants also talked about corruption that occurs within First Nations Communities.

> Don't trust the government but learn to trust your neighbors . . . the white neighbors because we are all ruled by the same government . . . they should be aware of what the dependence on the government has done. They call it the management regime, which the federal government is cramming down our throats. For populations from one thousand you get 100 percent funding, and it goes down the line. Anywhere from 500 to 251 you qualify for a minimal amount of money. There's only 217 kids in that category from 0 to 18 [here] so we qualify for nothing.

> They need to know who the leaders are [and] what kind of corruption goes on [and] who is behind it.

Participants thought that social workers should be aware of current important political issues for Aboriginal people. The disruption of life that occurs during band elections was mentioned as an important community issue. At a provincial level, issues related to logging and fishing were important. If social workers become aware of these issues, they will go far in earning trust from First Nations people.

"I Know What a Cherry Tomato Is . . . And I Can Read!"

All participants spoke about personal racism[7] that they experienced on a daily basis. As children, many of them had not been conscious of the fact that they were subjected to racism. As adults, they reflected on their experiences when young and they realized that racism was all around them.

> It doesn't bother me that I'm a different color, they call us redskins. It used to bother me but it doesn't now. The other day I went to buy some tomato plants, and I picked cherry tomatoes and the lady came running up to me and said, "Those are cherry tomatoes you know" . . . and she repeated herself . . . and I said, "Lady, I can read." I started thinking [that] because I'm Indian [she thinks] I can't read or I'm stupid. . . . Then I let that go because I was reverting to my old self.

In spite of attempts to accept that racism was around them, it was still associated with "pain, shame, and degradation." Many said that living in a context of racism had an effect on self-images. One participant noted that "you lived in shame being defined as stupid and taking that definition to yourself, feeling you were stupid." Another said:

> When you are growing up people are making you feel that you are inferior to them, that you are stupid because you are of a different race, because you speak a different language . . . the teachers did that to me and, of course, the students because they followed the teachers' examples.

Sometimes racism was overt and clear; on other occasions it was subtle. One participant referred to the more subtle forms of racism as "read-in-between-the-lines racism." This racism took the form of a lot of politeness but involved, for example, jobs suddenly becoming unavailable when the people doing the hiring learned that the job applicant was from a First Nations community. Those who had lived in both urban and rural settings thought that this type of racism was more prevalent in the rural settings. One participant told the following story:

> The term *closeted* was used to contrast rural racism with urban racism: I come from a very small community, so if there's any racism there it's very closeted. . . . My biggest reality check was when I was in Quebec a few years back, we had a thing called a "tax card" where you wouldn't pay taxes . . . and I approached to use that in Quebec. It was the first time I've ever had "out of the closet racism." The lady told me . . . I'm charging you taxes . . . you can take your receipt and mail it to the federal government and let them reimburse you with your taxes. She was very rude about it. I've never been treated like that. Around here it's not out. "I hate Indians." Around here they keep it to themselves if a Native walks among them.

---

[7] Generally participants spoke indirectly about the racism of ethnocentric cultural assumptions and about institutional racism. Their main focus was the racism they encountered in interactions with others.

Occasionally participants spoke about the loss of culture, usually through the loss of languages:

> The Official Language Act in this province creates duality . . . English and French . . . but there are other specific groups here, Mi'kmac and Maliseet . . . so do we give up our language just for the sake of speaking English or French? I don't think so.

"Like a Chameleon"

Some fair skinned or blue-eyed First Nations people could choose to hide their First Nations identities. These people were particularly aware of racism in the community:

> I kind of slid in. I can go through cracks. I'm not exactly of color and my hair was lighter than most, but if I made myself known as a Native person you can see all the barriers go up.

> Well, I'm not full blood. I'm a mixed blood. Because of that you kind of learn to dance between both worlds. I think I can do very well in an urban community and I also think I can do well in a rural community. I guess you're like a chameleon, sometimes you don't have acceptance from either. To gain acceptance I think that you're watched quite closely.

> To me, it means that I don't really belong anywhere. I have adopted the Indian culture and it's more or less adopted me. But the sense of belonging isn't there. Not in the French, or the Indian and certainly not in the white world.

> You would never know I was a Native . . . blue eyes, brown hair . . . so a lot of times I've walked into these [racist] conversations. They won't know I'm Native and I'll get the real . . . until someone actually speaks up and says, "Did you know that young fella was Native?" And then they're sitting there, biting their tongue or putting their head down and walking away.

"It's Not Their Fault They're Not Working"

Participants who had considered that education was a way to escape poverty and unemployment were saddened that despite their painful educational experiences, they were unable to secure employment outside of their First Nations community. Employment within the community had problems of its own. They were keen that social workers should know about these difficulties. One participant has a job as a social assistance administrator on a First Nations Community. She advises people to get training so that they can leave social assistance support. She believes that education is important for First Nations people despite the experiences of her son and her daughter.

> My daughter, she's a financial comptroller now, before she got that job she put her name in everywhere . . . everywhere . . . and they always say "well, no." She went for

an interview and she got a letter saying "someone else got the job who had more experience," but she was educated and her job was in finance. She never did get the job. Finally she had to go to her own people and get a job. She thought that she would get a good job, that was her goal, to be like everyone else. It didn't work out. She does finances for the Union of New Brunswick Indians. To me that's oppression. When my son graduated from community college he couldn't get a job . . . he went to St. John . . . he gave up . . . he joined the army in the States . . . now he's out of the army, he's back at the house . . . he's been trying to get a job.

First Nations bands try to create employment, but many people are without work:

Employment is one [problem], and the majority is relying on our welfare department. We have to look to try to create jobs. It's not their fault that they're not working. We try to accommodate as many people as we can. In town nine times out of ten they will not hire a Native. If you get a job in town you have no car to get there.

People who secure employment in their community often face resentment from others.

They always say . . . you think that you're the big boss, because you got that education you think that you can control people here. They look down on me because I have my education. It's hard because the people are hurting.

THE FUTURE

Participants agreed that social workers should know about future aspirations of each First Nations person they were trying to assist. There were differences in views about the probable future for First Nations people. As the following excerpt indicates, one participant was pessimistic:

What makes me mad is whenever we think we're on to something good and start to make a living for ourselves . . . then they try to put a stop to it. They're saying all along, "Oh Natives, all they want to do is stay on reserves, collect welfare and they don't want to work" . . . but then you have something that comes in good for them, they say "hey, what's going on here?" Then right off, they're trying to put a stop to it. You'd be surprised how many Native women, Native men, went out to work. Actually the women went out into the woods and did some cutting, and they were able to buy new clothes, new toys, cars, TVs for their homes. Before they were on welfare. All this is now down the drain and it took the fight out of us"[8] Everything is changing, some prescriptions they will fill and some they won't. Some drug stores

---

[8] This participant was referring to disputes between the province of New Brunswick and the Federation of Indian Nations about whether indigenous people have a right to harvest wood on crown land.

will not accept our cards. The dental is a charge for us, only some dentists will take our cards. One by one we are losing our services, and first thing you know I guess we won't exist as Natives. It looks like we won't be considered a reservation, we're all going to be a municipality . . . it's not going to matter to us because we are going to be old and die off but what about the young kids that are coming up?

Other participants were hopeful for the future.

The white race taught me to be racist. They taught me to hate . . . but now, over the last few years I would say that the white race is teaching me to not be racist and not to hate . . . A couple of years ago I would walk into a store and I found that I was being followed . . . and I think yeah, it's only because I'm Indian . . . you think I'm trying to steal something . . . that still happens on and off . . . but not as much . . . people are more respectful in the public sector it seems . . . probably because my attitude has changed, I'm friendlier than I was.

When participants reflected on their hopes for the future, they generally expressed hopes for their communities rather than hopes for themselves and their immediate families. They hoped that First Nations communities would not have to rely on funding from the government and that they would become financially self-supporting. They hoped that their healing processes would be encouraged rather than impeded by their social workers. They hoped that their social workers would have the necessary knowledge about their communities and lifestyles to offer realistic help.

CONCLUSION

Participants spoke clearly. They told me that social work educators should focus on helping students learn about First Nations people rather than existing social work theory. Indeed, none of the participants emphasized the value of existing social work knowledge for preserving and strengthening First Nations rural communities. This outcome is not really surprising, given that existing practice wisdom has been developed in a Eurocentric context. Some social workers might try to apply existing knowledge to the different reality of work with First Nations people. Others, in their efforts to be fair, might adopt a colorblind approach. Neither approach is appropriate, and both are likely to be experienced as racist. The words of the participants in this study emphasize just how different rural First Nations experiences, beliefs, and lifestyles are from those of the dominant majorities. Adapting existing practice wisdom is not enough.

One major difference between First Nations people and social work textbooks is in the language used. Social work texts refer to problems, needs, and intervention. The First Nations participants spoke about pain and healing. The concepts introduced by local indigenous people should form the building blocks for the development of social work theory and curriculum for practice with their cultures.

Social work educators who want to help students preserve and strengthen indigenous rural communities must first familiarize themselves with the lifestyles in them. This step is crucial if indigenous social work students are not to be further oppressed by the education that they hope will liberate them. Social work educators and students who are not from local indigenous communities need to learn to use their "two ears rather than the one mouth" to help them gain understanding.

If social workers, social work educators, and students clearly acknowledge that they want to learn about social work that is really relevant for local indigenous people and their communities this is an important beginning. Such an acknowledgment would help to build the trust that is needed to help individuals to heal and communities to be preserved and strengthened. The alternative is to practice in a way that perpetuates colonial oppression.

Social work educators and students need to find ways of understanding the legacy of the past in each local context. Participants in the study have suggested elements of the past that should be studied by present generations of students in New Brunswick, including the Indian Acts and the residential school experience. Literature from elsewhere suggests that similar themes may be important to other North American indigenous people (Kirst-Ashman & Hull, 1993, p. 404). Students must understand the impact on and the legacy of these experiences for First Nations people.

Students will be unable to acquire the necessary learning through library study alone. The voices of local indigenous people should be brought into the social work classroom. For this to occur, social work educators and their students must be willing to set aside ideas that the only worthwhile learning occurs through the study of traditional textbooks or through the formal classroom lecture. There are many alternatives. For example, study of first-person accounts of experiences may assist students who seek to develop empathy with indigenous people (Adams, 1995; Campbell, 1973; Monture-Angus, 1995; York, 1990). Reading novels and poems about indigenous experiences also can be of benefit in this regard (Joe, 1978, 1988, 1996). Many elders, as well as other indigenous people who have experienced the cultural genocide promoted through residential school systems, are willing to help them to learn.

Educators and students need to know what issues concern local communities of indigenous people. At the same time, it is arrogant and potentially oppressive for people to intervene in those issues unless they have been invited. As Collier points out, "The only reason for a social worker to be in your community . . . is to help place the means of survival in the hands of the people themselves" (Collier, 1993, p. xix). Social workers need to understand people's visions for the future and find culturally relevant ways of helping them to realize those visions. They will then have a knowledge base that may allow communication with indigenous people and participation in activities that aim to promote individual or community healing. In this way, they can strengthen indigenous communities.

When social work educators design curricula intended to prepare students to work in indigenous communities, they should try to find ways to help students know what it is really like to live in one of those communities. They must avoid the risk involved in attempting to adapt existing social work theory and practice wisdom that use "big university words" that distance social workers from the people they are trying to help. Social work students must learn to understand ways of helping and healing in local indigenous communities.

A blueprint for developing social work curricula that will provide the knowledge needed for antiracist social work in rural communities of indigenous people is not feasible. Nevertheless, similar processes of learning about these communities possibly can be adopted in different locations. The processes would begin with a commitment by social work educators to reduce ethnocentric bias in existing curricula and a willingness to be imaginative in seeking new methods to facilitate student learning. The educators would work to develop a dialogue with local indigenous people to identify the needed curriculum content as well as teaching and learning opportunities that are relevant and feasible. Throughout this dialogue, social work educators and students should seek opportunities to assist indigenous people in strengthening and preserving their lifestyles.

New Brunswick First Nations people have generously given time and ideas during this research process. They have offered to continue a dialogue with non–First Nations social work educators to devise learning opportunities for students. The goal is for social work students to gain knowledge in order to contribute to individual healing as well as to processes that will preserve and strengthen First Nations communities.

Many mutually beneficial relationships between indigenous people and social work educators in different parts of North America already exist. For those who have only recently begun a process of building bridges between schools of social work and local indigenous people, time is needed to develop trust so that indigenous people can be assured that social work educators are acting in good faith. When trust is established, I am sure that First Nations people in other parts of North America would offer to work with local schools of social work. We should eagerly accept those offers.

REFERENCES

Adams, H. (1995). *A tortured people: The politics of colonization.* Penticon, British Columbia: Theytus.

Campbell, M. (1973). *Half-breed.* Toronto: McClelland and Stewart.

Clews, R. (in press). Cross-cultural research in First Nations rural communities: A Canadian case study of ethical challenges and dilemmas. *Rural Social Work* (Vol. 4).

Colombo, J. R. (1997). *The 1998 Canadian global almanac.* Toronto: MacMillan.

Collier, K. (1993). *Social work with rural peoples.* Vancouver, British Columbia: New Star.

Cox, C. B., & Ephross, P. H. (1998). *Ethnicity and social work practice.* New York: Oxford University Press.

Dana, R. H. (1981). Editorial introduction. In R. H. Dana (Ed.), *Human services for cultural minorities* (pp. 3–4). Baltimore, MD: University Park Press.

Dominelli, L. (1997). *Anti-racist social work* (2nd ed.). Basingstoke, Hampshire, England: Macmillan Press.

Goldstein, H., & Bornemann, S. (1975). Editorial. *Social work in Atlantic Canada* (Vol. 1, pp. i–iii). Halifax, Nova Scotia: Maritime School of Social Work.

Government of New Brunswick. (1996). *New Brunswick at the dawn of a new century: A discussion paper on demographic issues affecting New Brunswick*. Fredericton, New Brunswick: Author.

Hepworth, D. H., & Larsen, J. A. (1993). *Direct social work practice: Theory and skills*. Belmont, CA: Wadsworth.

Herberg, D. C. (1993). *Frameworks for cultural and racial diversity*. Toronto: Canadian Scholars Press.

Joe, R. (1978). *Poems of Rita Joe*. Halifax, Nova Scotia: Abanaki Press.

Joe, R. (1988). *Song of Eskasoni: More poems of Rita Joe*. Charlottetown, Prince Edward Island: Ragweed Press.

Joe, R. (1996). *Song of Rita Joe: Autobiography of a Mi'kmaq poet*. Charlottetown, Prince Edward Island: Ragweed Press.

Kirst-Ashman, K. K., & Hull, H. (1993). *Understanding generalist practice*. Chicago: Nelson Hall.

Mawhinney, A. M. (1995). The First Nations in Canada. In J. C. Turner & F. Turner (Eds.), *Canadian Social Welfare*. Scarborough, Ontario: Allyn and Bacon.

Monture-Angus, P. (1995). *Thunder in my soul: A Mohawk woman speaks*. Halifax, Nova Scotia: Fernwood.

Morales, A. T., & Sheafor, B. W. (1995). *Social work: A profession of many faces*. Needham Heights, MA: Simon and Schuster.

York, G. (1990). *The dispossessed: Life and death in Native Canada*. Toronto: Little, Brown & Co.

SECTION VI

ENHANCING SERVICE DELIVERY THROUGH TECHNOLOGY

Technology brings rural communities and small towns much closer to both their urban counterparts and each other. Many of the problems of isolation that have existed in rural communities can be eliminated with the use of technology. The authors in this section present innovative ways to use technology to improve the quality and types of services available. Through technology, both individuals and organizations can have access to a much wider range of services.

Lynne Clemmons Morris, Robert O. Rich, and William C. Horner, in chapter 20 address four issues raised by the growing demands on rural social agencies for information and their capacity to provide information. The authors ask several questions that guide their discussion of management information systems (MIS) in rural communities: (1) Who owns MIS? (2) To what extent should the capacity of MIS be used to track consumers and providers? (3) What ethical standards should govern the visual presentation of information? and (4) What appropriate roles should social workers take in rural communities?

In chapter 21, Laura Zimmerman and Natasha K. Bowen describe the implementation of a computerized Information and Referral (I&R) system for providers of services for the aging in 16 rural counties in eastern North Carolina. The authors describe the steps involved in developing this regional I&R: technology assessment, standardizing information, gathering data, entering and reviewing the data, distributing the data, training system users, updating the system, and data analysis and reporting. They also discuss strategies that helped the counties overcome barriers to the use of I&R services.

In chapter 22, Paul K. Dezendorf and Ronald K. Green discuss the use of technology as a way to respond to the needs of rural elders, who are often disregarded in human service delivery. They suggest that practitioners address those needs through the development of "community support networks" (CSNs) based on in-

269

formation technology. The authors discuss various CSNs and describe other applications of computer-mediated communications, including electronic support groups and electronic self-help groups. The authors encourage social workers to recognize the societal changes that are taking place and to focus on opportunities for involvement at the group and community level.

CHAPTER TWENTY

Information Needs of Rural Agencies: Ethical and Practice Considerations

Lynne Clemmons Morris, Robert O. Rich, and William C. Horner

Social service agencies have a responsibility to represent their constituencies in the public discourse of local communities and to advocate for rural needs and interests in discussions with external funders and policymakers. To fulfill those responsibilities, agency representatives need the technological capacity to effectively present their positions in forums with people who represent competing interests and ideologies or who may have little understanding of social service delivery in rural areas. Many urban agencies have developed the resources and capacity to stay current with information technologies. They have been able to use their technological capacity to participate in the civic debate of their communities and to influence the priorities and directions of community development. Until recently, most rural service agencies have been limited in their ability to use information technologies because of their costs and personnel requirements. Information technologies and the people trained to use them have resided primarily in urban centers.

Today, the rapid expansion and declining costs of information technologies have made the capacity to persuade audiences through the use of integrated spreadsheets, statistical analysis, and multimedia presentation software available to computer users worldwide. Access to information technologies has created new opportunities and conflicting demands on small town and rural social service agencies. Even small or formerly isolated rural agencies now have the potential capacity to tell their stories aided by sophisticated software available on site. This new ability to persuade, however, is a two-edged sword in today's highly competitive environment where an agency's continued existence often depends on its ability to convince others of the efficacy of its programs and services. On the one hand, even small agencies now have the potential internal capacity to track service delivery outcomes, evaluate the effectiveness of their programs, and make sophisticated and persuasive reports and presentations to stakeholders. On the other hand, the need to market programs to community leaders, funders, and oversight bodies in today's increasingly competitive service environment can place increased stress on agency personnel charged with evaluating services, who are faced with multiple ethical decisions when preparing reports or presentations.

Large, well-resourced agencies with long-standing internal research and data-management protocols always have been confronted with the tension between the need to sell their programs and the ethical proscription against misrepresentation through distorting research outcomes. This ethical challenge, however, is new for many small rural agencies that have only recently acquired the capacity for integrated data analysis and presentation.

Once largely isolated from intense scrutiny and aggressive competition for resources, welfare reform and managed care funding models have left rural agencies with little choice other than to compete with other agencies for scarce resources. To compete successfully, rural agencies must now track and evaluate service outcomes. They must also develop persuasive presentations for their funders, consumers, and the public.

Affordable integrated software applications now give social agencies the ability to create persuasive reports and presentations that combine the power of spreadsheets, graphics, limited statistical analysis, sophisticated word processing, and desktop publishing. These applications also provide an enhanced ability to select which elements of data to highlight and which to push into the background. Sophisticated graphical capacities place in the presenters' hands the ability to clearly illustrate or distort reporting of outcomes. Modern spreadsheet-based applications can blur or even erase the boundaries between research, administration, fundraising, and clinical practice. With integrated software capability, the same database may provide information on the effectiveness of a program, the economic value of a given employee to an organization, the need for continued or enhanced funding, and the efficacy of continuing a given treatment approach with a specific consumer. Given that demands on rural social agencies are increasing concurrent with their burgeoning capacity to collect, store, organize, and persuasively present data about their programs, it is little wonder that new ethical dilemmas are emerging for social workers engaged in research.

Rural human service systems provide an excellent environment in which to examine the advantages and disadvantages of agency-based information technology, the expertise required to effectively use it, and the ethical issues raised by its potential uses. Rural service systems frequently have limited resources to allocate to data collection, analysis, and use in ongoing program planning and evaluation. Agencies must carefully select appropriate software applications for information management and then develop staff competencies for using the software selected. Schools of social work, correspondingly, need to work with rural human service systems to develop learning experiences that equip students with information technology competencies that meet rural human service agencies' needs, including competencies for making ethical decisions regarding the use of information technologies.

This chapter addresses four issues raised by the growing demands on rural social agencies for information and agencies' concomitant enhanced capacity to provide such information:

1. Who owns the data in management information systems (MIS), and who controls MIS design and development?
2. To what extent should the capacity of MIS be used to track individual consumers and individual providers?
3. What ethical standards should govern the visual presentation of information through the use of computer-generated graphics?
4. What roles are appropriate for professional social workers working with rural communities to develop useful, ethically responsible agency and community information systems?

COMPUTERS AND COMPUTER NETWORKS IN RURAL HUMAN SERVICE PRACTICE

Social workers have found three uses for computers in social agencies: (1) financial and personnel administration, (2) client and management information systems, and (3) the creation and dissemination of information (Rafferty, 1997, p. 292). The first use is commonly accepted as legitimate and useful. The second and third uses, although commonly used today by social agencies, continue to be somewhat controversial in the profession.

Paradoxically, although in most peoples' minds computers are probably associated with technology-rich and progressive urban environments, some of the most innovative uses of information technology in health care and human services have been in rural settings. Wellman (1996) asserts that electronic networks can link not just computers but people, and when they do they create social networks. These virtual communities were first created by the exchange of text, but today they are increasingly supported by graphics, animation, video, and sound, thus increasing the social presence of network members. Virtual communities seem to emphasize shared interests more than social similarities and provide enough anonymity to permit the kind of transitory trust people often exhibit in bars or with seatmates on airplanes. Such communities can be of value to some of their members who feel socially or geographically isolated (Wellman).

Technology-based therapy or support groups have proven to be efficacious for some people who, because of circumstance or choice, find it difficult to be part of a face-to-face group (Galinsky, Schopler, & Abell, 1997; Schopler, Abell, & Galinsky, 1998). For example, technology-based groups can be helpful when social stigma, geographic distance, or disability make face-to-face groups untenable. Among the problems noted in technology-based groups are decreased social cues and less social bonding. A specific limitation found in computer-based groups is the need for group members to have access to a computer and to be computer literate.

Cybercommunities of professionals facilitated through the Internet provide for some of the professional and personal needs of their members (Albritten & Bogal-Albritten, 1996; Kelly & Lauderdale, 1996). Cybernetworks support the exchange of empirical findings and practice knowledge among professional social workers in a socially unstratified medium in which the merit of ideas counts for more than reputation or power (Giffords, 1998).

Telemedicine applications in social services were developed more than years ago when the University of Nebraska used black-and-white television transmitted by microwave to provide psychotherapy to rural populations (Redford & Whitten, 1997). The Internet and fax machines are being used to transfer information from health care and social service records to other providers, insurance companies, and managed care organizations (Dowd & Dowd, 1996; Redford & Whitten, 1997). Telecommunications technologies are now promoted and are generally accepted as integral to the provision of rural human services and the development of rural communities (Galston & Baehler, 1995).

Consumer records can now be transferred in seconds rather than hours or days, transmission speed that can benefit consumers and sometimes even save lives. The use of these technologies is not without risk, however. Files can be misdirected to unintended recipients, and receiving devices can be left unprotected or in public areas. Health insurance and managed care companies require that certain types of clinical information be faxed or e-mailed to them for purposes of utilization review. The Medical Information Bureau (MIB) is a central database for medical information on Americans and Canadians accessible by member insurance companies. The MIB contains information about a wide range of health care information on people, including psychiatric diagnoses, drug dependency data, information about sexually transmitted diseases, and results of genetic testing (Dowd & Dowd, 1996).

Davidson and Davidson (1995) suggest that managed care provisions and employee assistance programs make it impossible for clinical social workers follow the ethical standards for confidentiality. The demands of the marketplace require that not just diagnoses, but intimate details about a service consumer's behavior, thoughts, and lifestyle be divulged by clinicians for determination of eligibility for reimbursement and to meet cost-containment requirements. The data are then entered into the databases of the insurance or managed care company and, sometimes, the consumer's employee records as well. The problem is exacerbated by the ease with which the data can be stored and transmitted electronically. The end-user of the data is frequently not a service provider, and the end-use of the data is frequently cost-containment (business interest) rather than treatment (therapeutic interest). With the data stored in multiple locations and, in some cases, in the custody of persons who do not share the provider's or consumer's interest in confidentiality, the information may be accessed by persons who intend to use it against the consumer's interest (Davidson & Davidson).

Issues regarding confidentiality of health care records represent a general concern, and they are of particular interest in rural populations, particularly in locales in which the information would be stigmatizing. McGinn (1996) and Heckman and colleagues (1998) found that the fear of stigma through the loss of confidentiality was a major concern for rural persons with HIV/AIDS and rural parental caregivers of adult children who were seropositive for HIV. Rural caregivers in McGinn's sample reported social isolation, inability to find competent health care, inability to sell the house where they had provided care and, in some cases, awareness of other families of patients with AIDS who were forced to leave their rural community when confidentiality about the family member's HIV status became compromised. The rural caregivers also reported that the informal helping networks so often present in rural communities did not mobilize on their behalf, often leaving them isolated from both formal health care and informal supports.

MIS TECHNOLOGIES

MIS, which have become a fact of life in most human services during the past 20 years, have provided staff with new opportunities and new methodological and ethical challenges. MIS technology has evolved from tracking staff activity only to a focus on client services and service outcomes (Carrilio, Kasser, & Moretto, 1985). MIS development has been driven by three forces: (1) reduced funding for social services, (2) increased demands for objective accountability for social programs, and (3) the development of computer technology with the capacity to support complex information systems. With multiple forces driving MIS development and usage, social workers are confronted with a system that can have political, economic, administrative, and clinical implications for the agency and its staff (Carrilio, Kasser, & Moretto). MIS can be used to track and reinforce staff behavior. As a control device, MIS is a powerful tool that can work to the advantage or disadvantage of given services and activities.

MIS technologies can also have subtle and unintentional consequences. Yeager and Morris (1995) encourage historians not to select data that fits their methodology and technology, but rather to focus on the content and purpose of their inquiry. Carrilio, Kasser, and Moretto (1985) describe how early MIS program technology had limited utility because it tended to dictate the nature of the data collected. Those systems typically recorded data as undifferentiated service units so that a clinical office interview, a home visit, or negotiating a housing contract on behalf of a client were all counted as a service unit and were not differentiated in the MIS database.

CURRENT INFORMATION NEEDS IDENTIFIED BY RURAL AGENCIES: THE SHIFT FROM PROGRAM EVALUATION TO UNDERSTANDING SYSTEM CHANGE

As part of the ongoing process of developing curriculum content that prepares students with appropriate research competencies for practice in rural settings, the authors carried out exploratory interviews with a purposive sample of six regional agency service providers regarding their current and anticipated future information needs. The agencies provide services to multiple rural counties in the areas of health, mental health, aging, and services to children and families. Through the exploratory interviews, a shift was identified in current rural agency information needs. In the past, the agencies focused on research related to specific program planning and evaluation. Typically, the research was shaped by the information requirements of funding agencies. Increasingly, however, agencies report a growing focus on research that improves their understanding of service system change, particularly the effects of managed care and welfare reform. Several types of research questions emerged in the course of our exploratory interviews:

- What are the effects of managed care on the agency's own service system? To what extent has the provision of ongoing services or long-term services been replaced with multiple, short-term, repeated "service events?" One agency that identified information needs such as these is a regional health care provider serving multiple rural counties. The agency wants to develop research to analyze its hospital readmission rates and the factors associated with what it perceives to be high readmission rates and increases in readmission rates.

- What types of information does the agency need to collect and analyze on an ongoing basis in order to remain competitive and to define and expand its service markets? What are the agency's current and potential future client populations? In what ways is the area's population changing, and how can the agency be responsive to these changes? Several agencies indicated that they needed information that could be used as a basis for planning services relevant to the needs of the area's growing number of older persons. One agency's research priority was to understand the decrease in use of its inpatient geropsychiatric unit and its geropsychiatric consultation services to nursing homes and to study the potential for expanding those services to adult family homes. An agency in a different service area indicated an interest in a regional needs assessment for an inpatient geropsychiatric facility, which it would develop.

- In what ways is the overall rural community or regional service system changing? Are specific parts of the system currently overloaded as a consequence of increasing numbers of clients or changes in client population? Examples of these research interests included proposed studies of impacts of welfare reform on access to quality childcare and possible mental health training needs of adult family home providers.

- How effective are interagency relationships and communication and coordination mechanisms in supporting an effective and efficient flow of clients through the service system? One example of interest in these types of questions is a proposed research project to assess mechanisms of communication and coordination between a regional mental health inpatient facility and multiple rural community mental health centers.

- What are the effects of these changes on clients? To what extent are clients moving out of and into different parts of the service system? To what extent are clients moving (a) from social services to self-sufficiency, (b) from public social services to community services and greater reliance on family supports and natural helping networks, and (c) into greater involvement with more social control–

oriented—and more expensive—organizations such as protective services, courts, and corrections? A variety of organizations indicated the need for research assessing the effects of welfare reform on clients, families, communities, and community service systems.

- To what extent do specific agency programs and services support long-term changes in client functioning? To what extent are specific agency programs and services associated with effects on communities and on the functioning of the social service system? Several agencies indicated an interest in research that would help them to assess the effects of their services on long-term client and community functioning.

ETHICAL DILEMMAS RAISED BY CURRENT INFORMATION NEEDS

The information needs identified by the rural agencies in these interviews share a common theme. Information needs are shifting from research related to the planning and functioning of programs largely internal to the agency to research related to an understanding of changes in the larger service system, effects of those changes on current agency functioning, ways to strengthen the agency's current and future position within the service system, and ways to assess and assist others in understanding the effects of an agency's program on the community and on the larger system within which the agency functions. Such systems-focused research will generate information that has potential consequences not only for the specific agency with which a school of social work and its students might develop a collaborative research activity but also for rural communities and a regional service system. Systems-focused research therefore raises a variety of ethical issues that need to be addressed by agencies and by school of social work faculty and students in the development of collaborative research projects.

Systems Change—Whose Information Is It?

The study of systems change raises important questions concerning rights of access to information. Typically, in university–agency collaborations in which students carry out evaluative research in agency settings, research reports are developed for the use of the agency and are shared with funders, consumers, other agencies, and community groups at the discretion of the agency. Research focused on system change, however, often requires collecting information from a variety of system sources and generates information that may have implications for multiple service providers. The types of research needs identified in our interviews suggest the need for a careful stakeholder analysis carried out by university faculty, students, and potential agency and community participants; this analysis would identify (a) interest groups and organizations that would be affected by the research-generated information in terms of costs and benefits, (b) the range of groups and organizations that should participate in formulating the research questions which will guide the study, and (c) the range of groups and organizations who should have access to the information produced by the study. The importance of stakeholder analysis has been emphasized as central to engaging agencies in the process of what is called "empowerment evaluation" (Fetterman, Kaftarian, & Wandersman, 1996). At the same time, systems-focused research also requires a stakeholder analysis that can be used to make ethical decisions regarding what information should be part of a community information system, what information should be retained internally as part of the management information system of individual agencies, and what the rights are of individual clients and community members to access information in both agency and community information systems.

A related ethical issue concerns the implications of schools of social work forming research alliances with specific agencies or groups of agencies within a community. The research needs identified in this study are related, at least in part, to agency concerns about functioning in a competitive environment. The development of effective computer-based information systems can strengthen agency abilities to provide and to market services. Social work faculties need to engage themselves and their students in discussions with agencies regarding the effective and fair allocation of university research resources in an increasingly competitive agency environment.

The Ethics of Tracking: Linking Data from Multiple Systems

Essential to the development of community information systems (CIS), which can increase understanding of systems change and its consequences for people, is the ability to link data from multiple systems. The CIS must be designed to collect information that follows clients through the multiagency service system. A well-designed community database technologically permits several types of tracking. First, the outcomes of services to clients provided by individual agencies can potentially be tracked and compared with other agencies' outcomes; such information could be accessed on a communitywide basis. One agency interviewed as part of the exploratory study identified this ability to generate information that could be used to publicly compare agency service outcomes as the primary impediment to its efforts to develop a regional information system.

Second, clients themselves can be tracked over time and in multiple agency settings. The research questions posed by agencies with respect to the systemic consequences of welfare reform are examples of the ethical dilemmas raised by the technological possibilities for client tracking: To what extent will former welfare recipients and their families experience greater risk of involvement with protective services or the criminal justice system? Gathering information to address such questions requires using shared client identification numbers to track clients over time in terms of their involvement with social control–oriented agencies. The research questions are important, and the privacy issues raised by the tracking systems required for data collection are also important. This issue is particularly salient for rural communities, where the numbers of clients are smaller and where much family history, including social service history, is essentially public knowledge.

Consequently, clients may be individually identifiable in research focused on the flow of persons through multiple service systems unless careful attention is paid to presenting information in ways that protect individual privacy. An important consideration, then, is who should participate in decision making related to the development and use of these types of community information systems.

Third, both agency and community information systems have the technological capacity to track and compare the performance of individual employees who are service providers. The ability to engage in relatively autonomous professional practice has historically attracted many competent, creative, independent persons to careers in rural communities. Although the capabilities of information technologies offer professionals in rural areas expanded opportunities to access needed information and reduce isolation, they also increase the possibility that data indicators of one's professional performance will be monitored and evaluated by others. Agencies, faculty and students in schools of social work, and professional associations need to become involved in the development of ethical guidelines for creating information systems that permit the monitoring of employees' professional behavior.

Ethical Considerations Related to Editing, Producing, and Displaying Information

Contemporary multimedia technologies enable researchers to present information in a variety of interesting ways using colorful visual graphics. Segments of videotapes, photographs, clip art or drawings, and audio effects can be added to enhance presentations. Multiple forms and sources of information—video, audio, text, tables, and graphics—can be integrated into a report or presentation. People engaged in research now have both the technological capacity and the responsibility to produce research reports and presentations that are credible, useful, and engaging. Multimedia technologies have been developed and applied to the presentation of information specifically for the purposes of (1) making information more understandable to people through use of visual graphics rather than tabular presentation of numbers; (2) using graphics, color, and audio effects to engage and interest the reader or listener; and (3) using color, audio effects, and the enlargement or reduction of graphs to draw attention to specific points of information contained in the report or presentation.

Multimedia technologies provide the researcher with the ability to edit a research report or presentation in new ways to influence the conclusions that the reader or listener will draw from the information. In working with social service agencies and in educating students in the use of multimedia technologies, special emphasis needs to be placed on the development of ethical guidelines for the editing and production of research reports and presentations. Several agencies expressed an interest in working with faculty and students not only in the development of research questions, selection of research instruments, and data collection, but also in thinking through the political and ethical implications of presenting information to various agency and community groups using multimedia technologies. One agency staff member participating in our exploratory study also expressed interest in working with staff, consumers, and community groups to build skills in evaluating information presented through the use of multimedia technologies.

The need for ethical guidelines becomes particularly critical when developing community information systems. Research findings can be presented to and accessed by a wide range of audiences. The growing technological capacities for visually highlighting and displaying information can be used both to educate and empower community members (Massat & Lundy, 1997; Schwab, 1997) and to edit and manipulate information in ways that shape community perceptions of needs and services. Little work has been done to develop ethical guidelines for the presentation of research findings using contemporary multimedia technologies (Dragga, 1996; Kienzler, 1997).

PROFESSIONAL ROLES FOR PEOPLE ENGAGED IN RESEARCH

Carrying out applied research in agency settings always includes establishing appropriate professional roles and boundaries for people engaged in research. Under the current conditions of major system change, however, the roles of the range of possible participants in the development of CIS are not clear; they are, in fact, in the process of formation. Researchers need to be open, flexible, and willing to assume a variety of roles in working with communities who want to increase their understanding of the effects of change along with their ability to manage change while respecting individual needs for privacy and confidentiality. Researchers need to be intimately involved with communities in order to increase their understanding of the critical questions that need to be asked regarding system change and the effects of service systems on the lives of people. At the same time, researchers also have the responsibility to use the research process to create CIS that are open to new ideas, generate useful information, are responsive to the needs of diverse groups and organizations, and are not selectively biased in the collection and presentation of information. Unless research activities are fully integrated into the field experience and include appropriate supervision, the typical social work curriculum provides few opportunities for students to engage in professional development and discussion of ethical issues related to their future roles as staff who will be involved in development and use of CIS.

CONCLUSION: IMPLICATIONS FOR COMMUNITY COLLABORATION IN THE DEVELOPMENT OF INFORMATION SYSTEMS

Contemporary rural agency information needs for understanding system change require the development of complex databases that integrate information from multiple sources. Without such databases, rural agencies are seriously disadvantaged in evaluating service outcomes, identifying changes in service systems, presenting program needs to funders and other stakeholders, or influencing public discourse about community priorities. Today, software that integrates spreadsheets, graphics, multimedia technologies, and statistical analysis provides even small rural agencies with the capacity to effectively tell their stories. Rural social agencies thus now have the ability to compete with urban agencies and other interests for funding and influence. This new capacity has also presented rural agencies with the ethical challenge of deciding at what point presentations go beyond sophistication and become misleading or violate clients' rights to confidentiality. In spite of this challenge, rural agencies and their communities can profit greatly from the wide distribution of integrated software capacity.

The development of useful agency and community agency information systems requires ongoing involvement of agency staff and community stakeholders in creating and reviewing guidelines for the use of information technology. CIS should be designed with community input, so that they collect information that helps agencies improve services and be responsive to local needs. Agencies need to work together to create resources such as Web sites for sharing research reports with each other and with their communities. Just as agencies have begun to develop ethics committees to discuss service dilemmas resulting from the use of technologies in health care, agencies need to create interagency and community forums for the discussion of ethical guidelines regarding the use of information technology. These processes will create new roles for agency staff and community stakeholders in the design and dissemination of social service research. The absence of community forums for the discussion of issues raised by information technology also suggests the need for people with more traditional responsibilities and expertise for carrying out research to engage in developing partnerships with local agencies who are creating CIS.

The software capacity now available to rural agencies provides a unique opportunity for them to partner with schools of social work to train agency staff in applying the new integrated software options in their work as well as to study both the technology's most effective uses and its potential for misuse. In working with rural agencies to develop collaborative research partnerships, social work faculty need to emphasize the importance of stakeholder analysis, which identifies the range of community groups and organizations that are potentially affected by systems-focused research. Schools of social work can assist rural agencies by creating forums for discussing issues related to the development of agency and community information systems. The forums can provide a venue for the development of ethical guidelines and technical protocols for the effective and ethical use of integrated software packages by social agencies and service systems.

Rural communities offer some of the best opportunities for creating truly appropriate information systems. Rural communities and their service systems often provide a more manageable size and level of complexity for investigating service systems and how they change. Examination of rural social environments can increase knowledge concerning system change and its human consequences and support the sharing and use of this knowledge to improve agency services and the quality of life for rural people.

REFERENCES

Albritten, B., & Bogal-Albritten, R. (1996). What's happening in Washington? The Internet can provide answers. *Human Services in the Rural Environment, 19*(4), 28–30.

Carrilio, T., Kasser, J., & Moretto, A. (1985). Management information systems: Who is in charge? *Social Casework: The Journal of Contemporary Social Work, 66*(7), 417–423.

Davidson, T., & Davidson, J. (1995). Cost-containment, computers and confidentiality. *Clinical Social Work Journal, 23*(4), 453–464.

Dowd, S., & Dowd, L. (1996). Maintaining confidentiality: Health care's ongoing dilemma. *Health Care Supervisor, 15*(1), 24–31.

Dragga, S. (1996). "Is this ethical?" A survey of opinion on principles and practices of document design. *Technical Communication, 43*(3), 255–262.

Fetterman, D. M., Kaftarian, S. J., & Wandersman, A. (1996). *Empowerment evaluation: Knowledge and tools for self-assessment and accountability.* Thousand Oaks, CA: Sage Publications.

Giffords, E. (1998). Social work on the Internet: An introduction. *Social Work, 43*(3), 243–251.

Galinsky, M., Schopler, J., & Abell, M. (1997). Connecting group members through telephone and computer groups. *Health and Social Work, 22*(3), 181–188.

Galston, W. A., & Baehler, H. J. (1995). *Rural development in the United States: Connecting theory, practice, and possibilities.* Washington, DC: Island Press.

Heckman, T., Somlai, A., Peters, J., Walker, J., Otto-Salai, L., Galdabini, C., & Kelly, J. (1998). Barriers to care among persons living with HIV/AIDS in urban and rural areas. *AIDS Care, 10*(3), 365–375.

Kelly, M., & Lauderdale, M. (1996). The Internet: Opportunities for rural outreach exchange and resource development. *Human Services in the Rural Environment, 19*(4), 4–9.

Kienzler, D. (1997). Visual ethics. *Journal of Business Communication, 34*(2), 171–187.

Massat, C. R., & Lundy, M. (1997). Empowering research participants. *Affilia, 12*(1), 33–56.

McGinn, F. (1996). The plight of rural parents caring for adult children with HIV. *Families in Society: The Journal of Contemporary Human Services, 77*(5), 269–278.

Rafferty, J. (1997). Shifting paradigms of information technology in social work education and practice. *British Journal of Social Work, 27*, 959–974.

Redford, L., & Whitten, P. (1997). Ensuring access to care in rural areas: The role of communication technology. *Generations, 21*(3), 19–23.

Schopler, J., Abell, M., & Galinsky, M. (1998). Technology-based groups: A review and conceptual framework for practice. *Social Work, 43*(3), 254–267.

Schwab, M. (1997). Sharing power: Participatory public health research with California teens. *Social Justice, 24*(3), 11–32.

Wellman, B. (1996). Computer networks as social networks: Collaborative work, telework and virtual community. *Annual Review of Sociology, 22*, 213–238.

Yeager, E., & Morris, J. (1995). History and computers: The views from selected social studies journals. *Social Studies, 86*(6), 277–285.

CHAPTER TWENTY-ONE

Rural Information and Referral Services: Serving North Carolina's Elderly Population

Laura I. Zimmerman and Natasha K. Bowen

In meeting the needs of their clients, human service providers often help clients and their family members gain access to services and resources provided by other agencies in the community. The ability of providers to link clients to appropriate services may depend on providers' personal experiences with and knowledge of other service providers in the community and on the accessibility of more formal sources of information about available services and resources. In the past decade, the proliferation of low-cost computers, user-friendly software, and access to the Internet have placed computerized information and referral (I&R) services within the reach of many communities. Human services practitioners in small towns and isolated rural communities with limited local resources may find such services especially useful. At the same time, however, small towns and rural communities may face unique barriers to obtaining and exploiting I&R technology.

This chapter describes the implementation of a computerized I&R system for providers of aging services in 16 rural counties in eastern North Carolina. The project, called "The Planning and Implementation of Information and Referral in Eastern North Carolina" (the eastern North Carolina I&R project) represents the first known comprehensive attempt to coordinate I&R services across a large rural region of a state. Strategies that helped the counties overcome barriers to the implementation of I&R services, such as high startup costs and geographic dispersion of resources, may help other provider networks plan similar services. The project was organized and funded by North Carolina's Mid-East Area Agency on Aging with the collaboration of the North Carolina Division of Aging, the Duke University Long Term Care Program, the East Carolina University Center on Aging, and the Job Training Partnership Act (JTPA) in Region R Council of Government.[1] The Human Services Smart Agency (HSSA) of the School of Social Work at the

---

[1] The Region R North Carolina Council of Government includes Camden, Carteret, Chowan, Currituck, Dare, Gates, Hyde, Pasquotank, Perquimans, Tyrrell, and Washington counties.

University of North Carolina at Chapel Hill implemented the project. The chapter begins with an overview of I&R services and then describes the counties targeted in the project. Subsequent sections provide a description of the stages and procedures of the project. Finally, although the project is still being implemented and therefore has not yet undergone an outcome evaluation, the strengths and limitations of the implementation procedures and of the I&R system itself are identified.

INFORMATION AND REFERRAL SERVICES

Background

In the past, human services providers have relied on their own knowledge of community services, the knowledge of co-workers, telephone directories and, possibly, information gathered by designated community resource experts in their agency. Some communities also benefited from more formal and centralized information resources, such as community referral guides published at regular intervals by state, regional, or community agencies. In contrast to these sources of information, I&R as discussed in this chapter refers to a formal, computerized database that is accessible to providers and, often, to clients themselves. Levinson (1988) provided the following comprehensive description of I&R services:

> I&R is an organized set of systems of services, agencies, and/or networks that aims to facilitate universal access to human services. Through its use of an updated and readily retrievable resource file, trained I&R staff link inquirers in need of information and/or services to appropriate resources in accordance with acceptable standards of professional practice. Of equal importance to direct client services is the capacity of I&R to provide a reliable and retrievable database for advocacy, policy, programming, and social planning in the interest of promoting and improving access to human services. (p. 9)

A number of constituents are interested in I&R services. Human service providers benefit from I&R services because the services allow providers to spend less time researching available resources and more time with clients. The information enhances services to clients, and having the data collected and updated centrally by a service is more cost-effective than having each organization maintain its own database. Employers may find the services useful sources of support for employees and their families (Levin, 1990). State and national groups are also becoming advocates of the services. For example, I&R services are mandated as part of the aging service provisions in the North Carolina Administrative Code (1991). As a funder of regional services to the aging with an interest in cost-effective ways of helping clients in local communities, the National Association of State Units on Aging (NASUA) has promoted the development of I&R services (NASUA, 1993). Finally, the resource information provided by such services is also in demand by citizens who believe the information should be available through the Internet.

Until the early 1980s, access to I&R services tended to be primarily by telephone. As computers became more prevalent, they were increasingly used to store the resource information available through the call lines. Computers not only helped reduce the cost of updating the information but also allowed many more resources to be included in the data bank. Using computers for I&R systems made updating, sharing, and distributing the information easier, and it permitted more sophisticated search-and-retrieval procedures (Manikowski, 1995).

During the 1990s, IRIs (Benchmark Enterprises, 1993/1999), a software program written specifically for I&R purposes, appeared on the market and promoted more widespread use of I&R by human service providers. The software allows resource data to be collected centrally and distributed to human service organizations. Virtually any organization with a computer can provide the data in a searchable format to its practitioners and clients. The IRis software also allows the database to be translated into HTML format, meaning that the resource database can be viewed and searched through the Internet.

Getting an I&R service up and running with a core of resource data can be expensive. Planning and creating the database for the original five-county region targeted in the eastern North Carolina I&R project, for example, cost almost $40,000. Startup costs depend on a number of factors, including the number of resources in an area, the size of the geographic area, the cooperation of the community organizations, and the levels of experience of personnel working on the system. The more resources and services there are, for example, the more time is required to obtain the resource data, enter it into the central database, and categorize it for database searches. The larger the geographic area, the more participation is needed to obtain and categorize information from localities. Rural regions, in which the population is dispersed across multiple counties and a large geographical area, may therefore confront higher costs and organizational difficulties in their efforts to establish I&R services. Typically, communities are more cooperative when community members are working on the project. Community members who have experience with I&R systems may be aware of extra tasks that can help the information-gathering effort, such as using public service announcements to publicize the project or obtaining letters of support from area leaders.

The ability to distribute a central database and the development of the Internet format are two I&R innovations that have had a major impact on reducing costs and increasing access to data. Costs associated with updating, distributing, and marketing the information are the only ongoing data expenses of I&R services once a system is in operation. Therefore, once an I&R service is established, its data costs drop dramatically. Of course, the referral and assessment are ongoing services with or without a computerized data system.

MODELS OF INFORMATION AND REFERRAL

Four basic models or types of computerized I&R exist. In the most basic and most popular model, resource information is collected and stored in a single database. A community provider or citizen calls a central number and speaks to a trained I&R specialist, who searches the database for resources appropriate to the client's needs. The I&R specialist gives the caller referral information and records information about the transaction along with follow-up suggestions. Responsibilities of the I&R service with this model include providing telephone consultation and assistance, maintaining the database, and marketing the service.

In a second model, the I&R service maintains a central database, provides telephone consultation and assistance, and provides human service agencies across the region with a copy of the database. Practitioners in organizations with computers are able to gain access to the data on-site. This arrangement reduces the number of calls to the I&R service and thus the number of skilled phone consultants required at the central I&R office. Only individual citizens and providers without computers need to call the central system. In this model, documentation of referrals may be less uniform because users obtain information from the database with or without the assistance of the central service.

A third model of I&R includes the central call-in service, resource updates, and database distribution discussed above as well as a standard client data collection system. Information about contacts with callers and direct service cases can be collected when the providers not only have the resource data but also a client database to collect case information. The information allows providers to document their services and permits communities to assess unmet needs and common problems across a community or region. For this model to work successfully, a minimum amount of data must be recorded about each contact or individual receiving a referral. The I&R service provider, users in agencies, and the community decide on what data will be recorded and stored in the client database associated with the I&R database. The client data are exported on a regular basis, merged, and analyzed by personnel at the central site.

The most recently developed model of I&R services is the online Internet model. In this model, agencies are able to update their online databases through the World Wide Web. Currently, this type of system is available only in a few areas of the country to agencies who have signed up for the service and paid for an Internet Service Provider (for example, America Online, AT & T Worldnet, and Mindspring).

INFORMATION AND REFERRAL SERVICES IN NORTH CAROLINA

The first three models of I&R have been implemented in North Carolina in a variety of forms. In North Carolina, some I&R services, such as those provided by a number of United Way organizations, serve general populations. Others serve more specific populations, such as the aging or children. "CARE-LINE" is a state-funded general I&R service that serves the entire state; it is operated by the North Carolina Office of Citizen Services, which is under the North Carolina Department of Health and Human Services. CARE-LINE provides information through an 800 number. Most local I&R services only provide local numbers.

I&R services are not as prevalent in rural areas of North Carolina as in urban areas. Initial startup costs put formalized I&R systems beyond the reach of many rural communities. One I&R effort targeting a large rural area in Canada started as the extension of a service provided by a large urban area (Crampton, 1997). Another problem in rural communities is disseminating information about existing I&R services. Even when they are established, providers and citizens in rural areas may be unaware of the services (Haynes, 1995).

The I&R project described in this chapter represents a major collaborative effort to bring the benefits of I&R services to providers of aging services in a large rural region of eastern North Carolina. A goal of the project was to develop and test data standards so that in the future, resource data can be shared statewide through the Aging Network, a partnership of all agencies serving the aging population in North Carolina. The network includes the Area Agency on Aging (AAA) in each locality and its partner programs. There are 18 AAAs in North Carolina serving regions containing three to 10 counties. These agencies receive funding from the State Units on Aging (SUA) and administer federal, state, local, and private funds through service contracts with local service providers (National Association of Area Agencies on Aging, 1998). Area Agencies on Aging (AAAs) typically do not provide direct services; in addition to administering funding, they develop county and community-based aging service plans and advocate on behalf of older adults.

TARGET REGION OF THE EASTERN NORTH CAROLINA I&R PROJECT

Sixteen counties[2] were included in the pilot project. These counties lie in the eastern portion of the state, from the Virginia border to Pamlico Sound. Although they represent 16 percent of North Carolina's 100 counties, they are home to only 5.7 percent of the state's population (North Carolina Office of State Planning, 1998). In 1996, the population density of the region was less than one-half that of the state as a whole (North Carolina Office of State Planning, 1997). The two largest cities in the region, Greenville and Elizabeth City, had approximately 56,000 and 17,000 inhabitants respectively. The rest of the population centers had fewer than 10,000 inhabitants, according to 1996 data (North Carolina Office of State Planning, 1997). The region relies somewhat more on extractive industries (agriculture, forestry, and fishing) than the state as a whole, but like most counties in the state, the targeted counties tend to have retail trade as their major employer. Because of the beach economy, there are income disparities in many of the counties. Inland farm areas have much lower per capita income than communities along the shore.

Compared with the rest of the state, the targeted counties are more rural (83.1 percent vs. 49.7 percent), poorer (18.7 percent in poverty vs. 13.0 percent), older (15.3 percent 65 or older vs. 12.7 percent), have larger African American populations (32.2 percent vs. 22.0 percent), and face higher unemployment (6.1 percent vs. 4.3 percent) (North Carolina Office of State Planning, 1997, 1998; U.S. Census Bureau, 1990). Statistics notwithstanding, there is a great deal of diversity among the counties. The percentage of African American residents, for example, ranges from 3.7 percent to 61.4 percent, and poverty rates range from 8.3 percent to 25.9 percent among the counties (U.S. Census Bureau, 1990).

---

[2] The counties were Beaufort, Bertie, Camden, Carteret, Chowan, Currituck, Dare, Gates, Hyde, Martin, Pamlico, Pasquotank, Perquimans, Pitt, Tyrrell, and Washington counties.

The poverty and low population densities common in rural communities in general and in the targeted region in specific have implications for the provision of human services. Social workers and other human services personnel providing services in small towns and rural areas are typically employed in the public sector, work in "relatively isolated, small local and county offices and confront a host of complex problems" (Davenport & Davenport, 1995, p. 2081). A flexible, generalist approach to practice is most effective under the conditions faced by rural social workers, according to Davenport and Davenport. Not only may rural social workers potentially confront a broader array of client needs than their counterparts in more specialized urban agencies, they also may require knowledge of resources within a broader geographic area. In this context, it appears that I&R services may serve a valuable function for social workers and other practitioners in small towns and rural communities. Through databases of regional resources and services, clients with a broad spectrum of needs may be linked to specialized services beyond the typical geographic range of most practitioners' knowledge and experience. Without easily accessible I&R data, practitioners may spend inordinate amounts of time seeking out information about appropriate services in distant towns or cities.

Although the absence or geographic dispersion of specialized services in small towns and rural communities may make I&R services especially useful to rural practitioners. Poverty and less-developed infrastructures or infrastructures weakened by social and economic change (Martinez-Brawley, 1987; Morris, 1995) represent barriers to establishing the services in rural areas. High startup costs of I&R services, for example, and the need for regional collaboration in the creation of centralized databases were issues that had to be confronted in the pilot project.

EASTERN NORTH CAROLINA I&R PROJECT

The collaborative I&R project implemented in eastern North Carolina drew on the third and fourth I&R models described above; in addition to a central resource database, a data collection component, and a data distribution system, an Internet-based update system was developed. Because of the goal of sharing data with additional counties in the future, the project also focused on developing standardized data elements. By working together to develop a standardized database, the region was able to afford the startup costs that often deter individual rural communities from establishing I&R services. The effort to coordinate I&R standards and a shared database in North Carolina began in a five-county area and then expanded to include 11 more counties. The standardization efforts and cost-effective aspects of the system will promote the system's expansion through the Aging Network into additional counties in North Carolina and into neighboring states.

Standards for information and referral programs are available in two slightly different but comparable forms from the National Alliance for Information and Referral Systems (National Alliance for Information and Referral Systems & United Way of America, 1991) and the National Association of State Units on Aging (NASUA, 1993).

The standards were used in the development of the pilot system and will continue to be used to help standardize systems across the state for the Aging Network.

Project Components

The project was initiated in 1997, and the implementation process is continuing at this writing. Implementation of the project involves the following eight steps:

1. technology assessments
2. standardizing information
3. gathering data
4. entering and reviewing the data
5. distributing the data
6. training system users
7. updating the system
8. data analysis and reporting.

Each step is described in more detail below.

Technology Assessments

Technology assessments were conducted in nine AAAs and organizations providing services to the aging. Some of the technology assessments took place within the subsequent I&R project region; others took place in the central (Piedmont) region of the state. The goal of the technology assessments was to determine the availability of hardware and software in agencies providing services to the aging, the computer skills of employees in the agencies, and other factors related to the ability of agencies to benefit from computerized systems.

A team of two to three staff members from the HSSA at the University of North Carolina at Chapel Hill and the Duke Long Term Care Program spent from one to three days at each site. The duration of the visit depended on the size of the organization and the number of computers at the site. Technology assessments included the following steps:

- an interview with the agency director to assess his or her goals, understanding of technology, perceptions of technology needs for the organization, and philosophy about budgeting for technology in the organization;
- a focus group with supervisors and agency personnel, which was designed to gain understanding of each organization's training needs and political issues in the organization that enhanced or limited the use of technology;
- an inventory of the agency's computer hardware and software resources and how they were used; and
- a computer knowledge survey assessing agency employees' experience with computers, software skills, knowledge of Windows operating systems, and familiarity with Windows-based software.

Each organization was briefed at the end of the site visit and received an outcome report. Outcome reports to organizations included summaries of the computer knowledge surveys and individual strategic technology plans (Zimmerman, Broughton, & Bratesman, 1998b–j). Additional reports based on all the technology assessments were prepared for the Aging Network consisted of a comprehensive report providing aggregate results from the computer knowledge survey and results by region (Zimmerman, Broughton, & Bratesman, 1998a) and a curriculum for computer skills training for the Aging Network (Zimmerman & Broughton, 1998).

The technology assessments represented an important fact-finding step that facilitated the implementation of the eastern North Carolina I&R project. The information helped providers and the regional AAAs understand their technology and training needs and promoted the acquisition of hardware, software, and training necessary for using computerized systems.

Standardizing Information

The IRis (Benchmark Enterprises, 1993/1999) I&R data system has two components, the database of resource and referral information (resource file) and the database containing client information (client data file). For information to be shared across a region, the databases used by providers must contain the same data elements and standards for database searches.

To develop and coordinate a standardized data system, providers of aging services from the original six counties involved in the project held a series of meetings. During the first meeting, different software packages were reviewed and demonstrated by HSSA personnel. IRis (Benchmark Enterprises, 1993/1999) was ultimately agreed upon for use across all agencies involved. IRis was chosen for a number of reasons. First, it allows users to distribute and share the database. Second, it contains several additional useful features, including a follow-up module, a client case management module, an Internet translator, and a read-only version. The follow-up module can be used to send reminders to service providers to check in with clients to determine whether referral information was used and the requested services or resources were obtained. The client case management module allows providers to retrieve information organized by case (for example, information about referrals given, services provided, and other case notes). The availability of read-only versions of the database (versions that do not have the client data tracking features) allow multiple sites to obtain relatively inexpensive copies of the resource database. The software also permits users to have a common set of data fields as well as additional fields customized to the documentation needs of providers. Finally, IRis was already being used for I&R services in numerous counties in North Carolina and for the statewide CARE-LINE, increasing the potential for future integration and sharing of I&R systems across the state.

At a second meeting, three forms were developed; they contained a list of suggested data fields for the information on (1) agencies, (2) programs or services (for the resource file), and (3) client information (for the client data file). IRis (Benchmark Enterprises, 1993/1999) accommodates different types of data fields, such as memo fields, check lists, pop-up lists, numeric fields, date fields, and financial fields. Users can define custom field names in addition to certain common fields that are built into the software. After the service providers reviewed how the different types of fields function in the software package, the forms with suggested data fields for the I&R system were distributed and explained. The providers were asked to take the forms back to their agencies, discuss the possible database format with their associates, and choose or add fields they thought would be useful. Subsequently, the forms were returned to HSSA staff, and the information was analyzed in preparation for the third meeting.

During the third meeting, agency input about the data fields was discussed and the provider representatives agreed on a set of data fields to be used across the region. Individual agencies had the option of providing data unique to their interests or record-keeping in any fields that remained unassigned in the common database.

Gathering Data

After the fields in the database were standardized, forms were developed by HSSA staff to collect data on resources and services for entry into the resource database. In the first of four mailings, forms were mailed to approximately 800 human service agencies across the original five project counties and in some bordering counties. The mailing included a letter from a county commissioner or manager supporting the project, detailed information about the project, and instructions about how to complete the agency information forms. To generate support for the data collection process, the AAA agreed to make public service announcements by radio and newspaper. Of the 800 mailings, 200 forms were returned. A follow-up mailing went to 400 providers and resulted in approximately 100 additional forms. As new counties joined the project, 500 more forms were mailed, followed by another follow-up mailing. As forms were returned, it was necessary to call many agencies to validate the information provided or to obtain vital information that was missing. Currently, the I&R database contains records on 400 providers and almost 700 programs.

Entering and Reviewing the Data

Data on agencies and on individual programs within agencies were entered into the I&R database. Programs were also assigned keywords to facilitate user searches. For example, a meals-on-wheels program might have the keyword "home-delivered meals." Each agency and program was also linked to a standardized taxonomy of human services. Two major taxonomies, or formal classification schema, of human services are available in software packages and in written form. For this project, the Info-Line taxonomy (Sales, 1994) was used, which is the classification system used to organize and search human services and resources in Los Angeles, California. The taxonomy is a software add-on that was incorporated into the IRis (Benchmark Enterprises, 1993/1999) database as an alternative to the keyword search option.

After the data entry process was completed, services providers for the aging from the targeted communities met to review and enhance the keyword system.

They discussed the utility of each keyword, and decisions were made about which services should or should not be linked to each keyword.

Distributing the Data

Service providers who took part in the pilot program received either the complete system, which included the resource database and the client data depository, or a read-only version of the software, which contained the resource data file but not the client data depository. As the data entry phase neared completion, the I&R system was installed at all locations that received the complete system. The read-only resource file is also available through the Internet.

Training System Users

In implementing any new computer system, adequate training of users is essential. The importance of training may be even greater for agency personnel from rural areas, who may be less comfortable with computers than their urban colleagues. In the pilot project, training took place at the Council on Aging in Greenville, North Carolina, which has a computer training room equipped with 10 computers. HSSA staff conducted the training sessions for personnel from agencies and providers who will be using the I&R system. Each training session was five hours long and included a lunch break and short morning and afternoon breaks. In order to maximize the hands-on experiences of the training, sessions were limited to 10 participants.

All participants received a software manual and videotapes for reference after training. Trainers provided instruction on how to use those additional training tools. Participants also received a comprehensive outline of the training session, which included detailed instructions for selected activities and information about two listservs available through the Internet as sources of support for I&R system users.

The hands-on training component focused on how the software works from the end-user's perspective and on how to make modifications, update information, and generate reports using the system. Trainers stressed the users' ownership of the I&R system, including their responsibility to notify HSSA personnel in Chapel Hill about problems or inaccurate information encountered in the system.

Updating the System

The most difficult part of maintaining an effective I&R system is keeping the data updated. Because caseloads, program offerings, and demands for services change frequently in the typical human service organization, maintaining up-to-date I&R information for human service providers may be especially challenging. Changes that occur in the services or programs offered by agencies necessitate changes in the central database. If an agency enters new information onto its local computers and not the central database, the changes will not be available to other sites and will be lost when a new version of the main database is distributed. Ideally, updates should occur whenever agency or program changes occur, and new versions of the database should be distributed to all sites. More typically, I&R databases are updated once a year.

To facilitate database updating in the rural region in the eastern North Carolina I&R project, several cost-effective and efficient options and features were developed. Providers can report changes in their programs to the central organization maintaining the database (currently HSSA) by telephone, fax, mail, or by typing in changes on a form available through a Web site. HSSA staff members then enter the changes into the central database.

The updated database also be distributed in several ways. Most providers prefer to receive regularly (for example, monthly or quarterly) updated versions on a diskette sent through the mail. It is also possible, however, for providers to call the central organization and ask for the updated data file to be sent by modem. When providers call in to request receipt of the database by modem, they receive the most current version of the file available. In addition, providers and agencies with Web browsers and Internet connections can view and search the most updated version of the file at any time through the Web.

Data Analysis and Reporting

A schedule for data analysis and reporting has not yet been established for the pilot project. Analysis of the contact and client information entered by providers and the I&R central service serves to document use of the system, the provision of services, and the degree to which client needs were met by providers of services to the aging. Analyses of client data recorded in the client data file component of the I&R system, for example, will help AAAs determine who used services in the region, what services were in demand, and what client needs were and were not adequately met by available services for the aging. The specific analyses conducted will be based on the information needs of agencies and providers and driven in part by the reporting demands of their funders. A software program that is currently being modified to link with the IRis database (Benchmark Enterprises, 1993/1999), called "service outcome screen" (SOS) (Maddox, Bolda, & Breschel, 1991), provides a mechanism for client screening and assessing the needs of aging clients through an on-screen interview.

In summary, the eastern North Carolina I&R project has progressed successfully through seven of the eight steps described: technology assessments, standardizing information, gathering data, entering and reviewing the data, distributing the data, training system users, and updating the system. The data analysis and reporting step remains to be implemented.

PROJECT OUTCOMES

The true test of any I&R system is the extent to which it can be efficiently and effectively sustained over the long term and the extent to which it provides users with accurate, up-to-date information. Although the pilot project described in this chapter is still being implemented in rural eastern North Carolina and therefore has not yet been evaluated, a number of strengths and limitations have been identified.

Strengths

The eastern North Carolina I&R project enabled a large rural region to establish an I&R service for providers of services to the aging. Project participants were able to overcome high startup costs that are a common barrier to the implementation of I&R systems in rural regions by developing a single service for organizations in multiple counties across a large geographical area. Through their collaboration and cost-sharing, participating providers of services for the aging were able to create a system that was affordable to all.

A significant strength of the project was the use of technology assessments to determine the availability of hardware, software, and computer skills in the agencies providing services to the aging. Information collected in site visits to providers was key to the development of appropriate strategies in the subsequent planning stages of the I&R project. A second strength of the project was the development of common standards that will facilitate the addition of new organizations to the system in the future.

The most difficult aspect of maintaining a successful I&R system is keeping the data current. A third strength of the pilot project was its use of multiple low-cost technologies to keep the I&R database up-to-date and to distribute the updated data file. Telephone, fax, a Web site, and regular mail can be used to report database changes. Diskettes, modem files, and a data file available on the Web are among the strategies used to keep users equipped with up-to-date information. These modes of updating and distributing the data are low-cost and efficient.

A fourth strength of the project was the high level of support it received from multiple organizations, and their sense of ownership and investment in the ongoing success of the system. A fifth positive aspect of the project was the use of hands-on training for users of the system. Training users with actual service provision examples from their own system was an effective teaching strategy. A sixth notable strength was the availability of several options for technical support. Rapid resolution of problems is promoted through the existence of multiple technical support options, including e-mail and telephone access to I&R system personnel and other providers in the area.

Limitations

As the process of implementing the multiple-county I&R system unfolded, two barriers to success were identified. First, many of the small town and rural human service organizations in North Carolina still have limited access to computers. Although practitioners in agencies providing services for the aging appear to have greater access to computers than practitioners in other human service organizations in rural North Carolina, many do not have computers readily available to them in their offices, especially computers with Internet connections (Zimmerman et al., 1998a). Many organizations that did have access to the Internet had only one computer with the connection. Although some agencies and providers still need additional computer equipment, the project promoted the acquisition of new computers, software, and Internet capabilities in many sites. Participation in the project provided justification for including technology in budget requests. It also gave many providers access to computer consultation that helped them determine specifically what kinds of hardware and software they needed to obtain.

Another barrier was the difficulty of educating potential system users and marketing the system across such a wide demographic area. Lack of familiarity on the part of the public about what I&R services do meant that interest in the system was mainly on the part of human service providers in the region.

CONCLUSION

The eastern North Carolina I&R project, conducted by the HSSA at the University of North Carolina at Chapel Hill School of Social Work, provides an example of how organizations dispersed over a large geographic area can work together to create an affordable I&R system. The sequence of steps presented and the strategies used successfully in the project are instructive for designers of future collaborative I&R services. Collaboration and cost-sharing among regional organizations and individual providers, the solicitation of input from future users of the system, comprehensive training of future users, the selection of cost-saving system features and data update mechanisms, and an initial technology assessment all contributed to the successful implementation of the system in a large rural region. We believe these steps can serve as a guide to others who may wish to implement similar services in other small towns and rural areas.

ACKNOWLEDGMENTS

The authors gratefully acknowledge the contributions to this chapter of Louisa Cox, James G. Griffith, Vanessa L. Mitchell, Mary Anne P. Salmon, Angela K. Scott, and Jerrol David Weatherly.

REFERENCES

Benchmark Enterprises. (1993/1999). *IRis Information and Referral Software.* Lake Worth, FL: Author.

Crampton, C. (1997). I & R which covers a wide service area: Expanding an agency's service area to an entire province. *Information & Referral, 19,* 69–76.

Davenport, J. A., & Davenport, J., III. (1995). Rural social work overview. In R. L. Edwards (Ed.-in-Chief), *Encyclopedia of social work* (19th ed., Vol. 3, pp. 2076–2085). Washington, DC: NASW Press.

Haynes, K. S. (1995). Information and referral services. In R. L. Edwards (Ed.-in-Chief), *Encyclopedia of social work* (19th ed., Vol. 1, pp. 1464–1469). Washington, DC: NASW Press.

Levin, R. (1990). *Public/private partnerships in aging working with the business community on eldercare: A primer for the aging network.* Washington, DC: Washington Business Group on Health.

Levinson, R. W. (1988). *Information and referral networks: Doorways to human services.* New York: Springer.

Maddox, G. L., Bolda, E. L., & Breschel, E. F. (1991). *Training manual for the Duke SOS profile.* Durham, NC: Duke Long Term Care Resources Program.

Manikowski, D. (1995). Making referral file automation decisions. *Information & Referral, 17,* 85–107.

Martinez-Brawley, E. E. (1987). Rural social work. In A. Minahan (Ed.-in-Chief), *Encyclopedia of social work* (18th ed., Vol. 2, pp. 521–537). Silver Spring, MD: NASW Press.

Morris, L. C. (1995). Rural poverty. In R. L. Edwards (Ed.-in-Chief), *Encyclopedia of social work* (19th ed., Vol. 3, pp. 2068–2075). Washington, DC: NASW Press.

National Alliance for Information and Referral Systems and United Way of America. (1991). *National Standards for Information and Referral Systems.* Seattle, WA: Author.

National Association of Area Agencies on Aging. (1998). *National directory for eldercare information and referral.* Washington, DC: National Association of State Units on Aging.

National Association of State Units on Aging. (1993). *National Standards for Older Americans Act information and referral services.* Washington, DC: Author.

North Carolina Administrative Code. G. S. 143B–181.1(c); G.S. 143B–181.1 (a)(11) (1991).

North Carolina Office of State Planning. (1997). *State data center, LINC county profiles* [On-line]. Available: http://www.ospl.state.nc.us/sdn/cntyindx.html

North Carolina Office of State Planning. (1998). *State demographics, 1997: County age groups* [On-line]. Available: http://www.ospl.state.nc.us/demog/c97sage.html

Sales, G. (1994). *A taxonomy of human services: A conceptual framework with standardized terminology and definitions for the field.* Los Angeles: Information and Referral Federation of Los Angeles County and the Alliance of Information and Referral Systems.

U.S. Census Bureau. (1990). *Database C90STF3* [On-line]. Available: http://venus.census.gov/cdrom/lookup

Zimmerman, L., & Broughton, A. (1998). *North Carolina area agencies on aging information technology project: Computer training curriculum for aging network in North Carolina* (Technical report). Chapel Hill: Human Services Smart Agency, School of Social Work, University of North Carolina.

Zimmerman, L., Broughton, A., & Bratesman, S. (1998a). *North Carolina Area Agencies on Aging Information Technology Project: Overall technology results of the information technology site visits* (Technical report). Chapel Hill: Human Services Smart Agency, School of Social Work, University of North Carolina.

Zimmerman, L., Broughton, A., & Bratesman, S. (1998b). *North Carolina Area Agencies on Aging Information Technology Project: Report on the information technology site visit to Beaufort County Department of Social Services* (Technical report). Chapel Hill: Human Services Smart Agency, School of Social Work, University of North Carolina.

Zimmerman, L., Broughton, A., & Bratesman, S. (1998c). *North Carolina Area Agencies on Aging Information Technology Project: Report on the information technology site visit to Martin County Senior Center* (Technical report). Chapel Hill: Human Services Smart Agency, School of Social Work, University of North Carolina.

Zimmerman, L., Broughton, A., & Bratesman, S. (1998d). *North Carolina Area Agencies on Aging Information Technology Project: Report on the information technology site visit to North Carolina Division on Aging* (Technical report). Chapel Hill: Human Services Smart Agency, School of Social Work, University of North Carolina.

Zimmerman, L., Broughton, A., & Bratesman, S. (1998e). *North Carolina Area Agencies on Aging Information Technology Project: Report on the information technology site visit to Mid-East Commission Area Agency on Aging* (Technical report). Chapel Hill: Human Services Smart Agency, School of Social Work, University of North Carolina.

Zimmerman, L., Broughton, A., & Bratesman, S. (1998f). *North Carolina Area Agencies on Aging Information Technology Project: Report on the information technology site visit to Northwest Piedmont Area Agency on Aging* (Technical report). Chapel Hill: Human Services Smart Agency, School of Social Work, University of North Carolina.

Zimmerman, L., Broughton, A., & Bratesman, S. (1998g). *North Carolina Area Agencies on Aging Information Technology Project: Report on the information technology site visit to Pitt County Council on Aging* (Technical report). Chapel Hill: Human Services Smart Agency, School of Social Work, University of North Carolina.

Zimmerman, L., Broughton, A., & Bratesman, S. (1998h). *North Carolina Area Agencies on Aging Information Technology Project: Report on the information technology site visit to Senior Services of Winston-Salem* (Technical report). Chapel Hill: Human Services Smart Agency, School of Social Work, University of North Carolina.

Zimmerman, L., Broughton, A., & Bratesman, S. (1998i). *North Carolina Area Agencies on Aging Information Technology Project: Report on the information technology site visit to Yadkin Valley Economic Development District* (Technical report). Chapel Hill: Human Services Smart Agency, School of Social Work, University of North Carolina.

Zimmerman, L., Broughton, A., & Bratesman, S. (1998j). *North Carolina Area Agencies on Aging Information Technology Project: Report on the information technology site visit to Yadkin County Council on Aging* (Technical report). Chapel Hill: Human Services Smart Agency, School of Social Work, University of North Carolina.

CHAPTER TWENTY-TWO

Using Electronic Social Work to Serve the Rural Elderly Population

Paul K. Dezendorf and Ronald K. Green

The recent development of electronic social work (ESW) provides practitioners with opportunities for new approaches to practice that lend themselves to strengthening and preserving small towns and rural communities and addressing the special needs of the rural elderly. Social workers should learn to use these new ESW approaches in their practice to improve their ability to meet client needs, as professionals in other fields have been doing in the 1990s. In addition, social work practitioners should go beyond the use of individual ESW tools by integrating these tools to create "electronic Hull Houses." Electronic Hull Houses would provide community support networks (CSNs) offering a range of ESW tools (for example, electronic support groups [ESGs]). CSNs would focus on a geographic area (rather than a "virtual" community), be dedicated to social change, and offer opportunities for practitioners, fieldwork students, and academics to vigorously apply the new ESW practice approaches to the special needs of the rural elderly.

This chapter analyzes the factors in rural communities that negatively affect the elderly and identifies ways in which ESW can address the needs of this population. It outlines obstacles to achieving the benefits of ESW and describes approaches to overcoming these barriers. The chapter ends with recommendations for social work education and the profession.

FACTORS AFFECTING WELL-BEING AMONG RURAL ELDERLY PEOPLE

By 1990, 8.2 million elderly lived in small towns or other rural communities. Rural elderly make up about 25 percent of all the elderly in the United States, 50 percent of the elderly living below the poverty level, and 19.8 percent of the South's population (Coward & Dwyer, 1998). Research has identified a range of factors that contribute to the difficulty faced by these rural elderly in securing needed community services and supports.

Compared with nonrural elderly, five factors influence to a greater extent the health and social well-being of the rural elderly: a higher level of health and mental health problems, fewer community-based services, less proximate services, less awareness and less use of services, and increased distance from family members.

Health studies suggest that rural residents are less healthy than urban residents; this difference is especially clear in terms of acute and chronic health conditions (Sumner, 1998). The differences may be a result of the higher proportion of poor and nonwhite elderly, who have less health insurance and schooling than their urban counterparts (Coward & Dwyer, 1998). The incidence of poor mental health also appears to be higher in rural areas (Coward & Dwyer, 1998). Given lower educational levels, the rural elderly likely represent a less sophisticated population when it comes to health promotion and maintenance. The differences suggest that the rural elderly pose a greater challenge regarding monitoring client health conditions and securing adequate health care.

Even though their incidence of serious ill health is proportionately higher, the rural elderly have access to fewer and a more limited range of health services than the urban elderly, particularly community-based services such as adult day care, homemaker services, hospice services, respite services, foster care, and home health services. The higher incidence of health problems and lower level of in-home and community-based services mean that the rural elderly are at an increased risk of premature institutionalization (Coward & Dwyer, 1998). In addition, the fewer services that are available are less proximate because of geographic distance, limited public transportation, and insufficient household income for private transportation (Coward & Dwyer, 1998; Ward, 1977).

Even though the level of chronic and acute health problems are greater among the rural elderly, there appears to be common agreement that this population does not use formal health care services, when available, to the same degree as their urban counterparts (Coward & Dwyer, 1998; Sumner, 1998). In fact, this group is among the lowest of all the subpopulations in the United States regarding mental health utilization (Coward & Dwyer, 1998); one study found that rural elderly African Americans who needed mental health counseling services used counseling only 14 percent of the time (Spense, 1993).

The reduced number of services, lack of proximity, and transportation problems may contribute to this lower usage. However, at least two studies focusing on the African American rural elderly in southern states found a widespread lack of awareness of the availability of services and a failure to use information and referral resources, in some cases up to 60 percent of the time (Spense, 1991, 1993; Waring & Kosberg, 1980). A third study identified four specific causes for underutilization of human services by rural elderly African Americans: (1) lack of awareness of the range of available services; (2) lack of involvement in service planning and service provision; (3) lack of involvement in the political process, which spawns services; and (4) lack of a sense that those services were really "theirs" (Carlton, 1991).

Despite popular belief, extensive kinship networks with members located near one another do not offset the reduced level of service availability. Although a greater proportion of rural than urban elderly depend exclusively on family members, rather than formal services, for help, the nonfarm elderly (90 percent of the rural elderly) are less likely to either live with their children or have a child within 30 minutes of their residence than the general elderly population (Coward & Dwyer, 1998).

These five factors suggest the existence of three major barriers to meeting rural elderly human service needs, even when services are available. The first barrier is the significant level of poverty, which restricts the purchase of home-based supports that can offset the lack of community-based services and social support and limits the ability to obtain transportation.

The second, related, barrier is lack of proximity. Proximity issues include the location of the service itself, the nature of public transportation in rural areas, and the location of friends and relatives. The distances to be traveled in rural areas hinder access to services and impede public and private transportation. As a result, the formal and informal supports that could overcome some of the effects of poverty are not available.

The third major barrier is lack of awareness. Contributors to this barrier include isolation and the less frequent use of information and referral systems. Low population density reduces the time spent by older adults with other poor elderly and thus decreases the opportunity to share information about available human services.

RATIONALE FOR ESW

The magnitude and intractability of the factors affecting the well-being of the rural elderly challenge social workers in rural communities to go beyond "doing more of the same." The nature of the barriers to addressing these factors means that current and developing technologies can be used to make significant inroads to overcoming them. In particular, information technology (IT) offers the potential for overcoming distance barriers, raising awareness, and even partially offsetting the barrier of poverty as a result of IT-based improvements in efficiency and effectiveness of interventions and agency delivery systems.

During the past 25 years, literature from a growing number of disciplines addressed the social aspects of IT at five levels: individual (see Turkle, 1996, on changes in personality), group (see Finn & Lavitt, 1994, regarding use with clients), organizational (see Lucas, 1996, on the transformation of organizations), community (see Jones, 1995, on the meaning of community in cybersociety), and society as a whole (see Kelly, 1994, on neobiological civilization). Social workers' interest is now being spurred as other disciplines apply IT to a rapidly growing number of areas. Applying the experiences of other fields to social work, it appears that IT can be used in ESW to (1) mediate the interaction between the social worker and clients (for example, direct practice with electronic support groups); (2) mediate the actions of the social worker with the clients' environment (for example, media advocacy through the Internet); (3) empower the client to use IT in changing their own environment (for example, creation of self-help groups); (4) bring changes by the social worker in their own environment (for example, altering agency policy).

Of the variety of possible ESW approaches, the authors believe that rural social workers should first look at using IT at the community and group levels to mediate interaction between social workers and clients and between the clients and their environment. Those two ESW applications may promote strengthening of small towns and rural communities and address the barriers to the well-being of the rural elderly discussed in the previous section.

At the community level, rural social workers should take responsibility for the development of community support networks (CSNs), which use IT to create links among people and provide information. The development of CSNs will be an "innovation in environment" that will produce systemic changes in how social work is practiced in rural areas. Practitioners and agency administrators will have to change their conceptualization of IT from simply providing practice supports, such as management information systems, to IT as a major vehicle of practice.

At the group level, a generic ESW approach called "electronic support groups" (ESGs) is a tested approach to practice. ESGs rely on computer-mediated communication (CMC; see Hiltz & Turoff, 1993). Although social work literature is limited on this subject (see group work articles by Finn & Lavitt, 1994, and Weinberg, Schmale, Uken, & Wessel, 1995), a growing literature in other disciplines suggests uses of these applications in public health (see Brennan, Schneider & Tornquist 1997; Harris, 1995), consumer medicine (Ferguson, 1996), psychosocial nursing (see Ripich, Moore, & Brennan, 1992), public policy (see Sussman, 1997), innovation diffusion research (see Rogers, 1986), gerontology (see Smyth & Harris, 1993), and in the popular press (see Godwin, 1994).

The next two sections describe CSNs and ESGs; the changing environment for ESW with individuals, organizations, and society is briefly discussed in a third section.

ESW AT THE COMMUNITY LEVEL: CSNS AND THEIR USES

Computer networks are common; what types of networks offer potential for ESW? CSNs enhance client access to resources by integrating people and organizations with a network of communications designed to increase client ability to help themselves and encourage social change. Current CSNs vary in their focus, from single areas of activity (such as aiding seniors in going online) to an electronic network that attempts to provide an electronic surrogate for an entire community (such as the Electronic Village of Blacksburg, Virginia). At present, many so-called networks described by social workers are simply information repositories; they are archives of useful information but not robust tools for addressing client needs and bringing about social change. Examples of this kind of network are the federal government sites containing information about seniors using computers.

Ideally, CSNs include people from all parts of the community in developing the network's policy and process and act as a change agent in the community. For example, community networks can make provision for those without computers at home or even those without homes by advocating for public access terminals in libraries or kiosks in public spaces. However, some CSNs not only are indifferent to social issues but place an entrance fee on the network to gain revenue and to increase the attractiveness of the audience to advertisers.

A major concern for ESW is the rapid increase in the percentage of the U.S. population using networks, such as America Online, and the increase in hours per week that people devote to those networks. As with the growth of other communications media in this century, national or regional networks may attract prospective users of local CSNs and resource contributors. In this way, the large national networks may impede the efforts of a CSN dedicated to strengthening specific small towns and rural communities.

No prescriptive specification exists for an ideal CSN; the examples in the next section illustrate existing patterns and highlight desirable characteristics. The examples include FreeNets, wired cities, local government networks, nonlocal government networks, and private networks. In the following section, the authors argue that prospective developers must address four essential criteria in using CSNs in ESW.

EXAMPLES OF CSNs

FreeNets are loosely organized, community-based, volunteer-oriented electronic network services that provide local and other information sharing and discussion, generally without charge. Some typical areas inside a FreeNet include an administrative area, a "post office" for communications, a government center with archives, an arts building with announcements and information, and a schoolhouse with educational information, online courses, and areas for professional groups. FreeNets are intended to be a network for the whole community and strongly emphasize participatory democracy and social change. FreeNet activities often are concerned with improving public participation in civic activities.

Wired cities are more tightly organized, private sector–oriented networks that attempt to provide an electronic version of a geographic area. The emphasis is on consumerism, that is, shopping, films, clubs, and entertainment. Wired city networks may provide useful information similar to public service announcements on radio and TV (volunteer activities or support group meetings), but they are not oriented to social change; the networks appear to serve the business community's interests and thus reflect the existing power and class structure.

Local governments sometimes sponsor networks, often as a community relations activity. Sometimes their creation is motivated by an interest in making government records more accessible and improving the speed and amount of citizen input into the community. Other motivations include improving business communications within the town and to consumers. In California, for example, a bill has been introduced that would establish state grants to support the development of new or existing community Internet networks. The author of the bill is hoping to stimulate the development of "virtual town squares," which would provide citizen access to government services, leisure, business, education, workforce training, health care, and emergency response systems ("California Senator," 1998).

Nonlocal government networks are typified by the federal government's efforts this decade to provide consumer information through Internet access (for example, resources for seniors provided by the Administration on Aging). These sources of information are powerful tools for rural social work to use in gathering information, but they are not as helpful in strengthening and preserving small towns and rural communities; in fact, these massive federal networks may work against local networks by drawing users from local aging agency sites to the federal networks.

Private networks are rapidly developing as a result of general access to computers and to the Internet. They attempt to attract people with certain characteristics (for example, lifestyle networks for affluent singles in New York City). Those networks will proliferate. Some networks may focus on specific geographic areas and strengthen communities (such as AIDS activities in New York City), but most appear likely to draw resources away from rural communities. Large private networks will pull advertising dollars and revenue away from networks based in rural communities, much as national radio networks left local AM stations with limited revenue and audiences.

DESIGN CONSIDERATIONS FOR CSNs

Prospective CSN developers face four formative issues. The first is spatiality: Will the network be oriented to a specific geographic territory (spatial) or oriented to a non-geographic community, whose members may live anywhere (nonspatial)? Nonspatial communities are collections of people in a socially created space (in this case, "cyberspace") operating without regard to a defined spatial area of concern (for an excellent description of nonspatial communities, see Jones, 1995). In spatial communities, CSNs address the particular needs of people in a geographic area, (for example, specific Appalachian counties).

After an early period of telephone network-based growth, which favored CSNs serving spatial communities, the influence of Internet-based communications encouraged nonspatial networks, or "cyberspace communities," which provided benefits to selected types of people (for example, marginalized groups). Adverse effects of this enthusiasm for nonspatial communities are beginning to be develop; for example, nonspatial CSNs may decrease civic engagement and social capital (Blanchard & Horan, 1998). CSNs originally used the public telephone system. The cost of long-distance calls led to a spatial community orientation such as Cleveland's FreeNet. CSNs shifted to the Internet as it grew, in part because of the absence of cost for communications at a distance. The shift to a new medium led to the growth of nonspatial community orientation, such as America Online's thousands of electronic groups. These "cyberspace communities" do provide benefits to marginalized groups. However, adverse effects of this enthusiasm for nonspatial communities are beginning to develop; for example, nonspatial CSNs may decrease civic engagement and social capital (Blanchard & Horan, 1998).

Because program funding for social work often emphasizes reaching particular groups rather than strengthening entire communities, the spatiality issue is an important one. The authors believe that spatially based community networks should be the primary focus of rural social workers and that nonspatial networks should be used only when a specialized need exists (for example, a national AIDS network that has expertise in rural issues).

The second issue faced by ESW is the nature of the proposed intervention(s) to be included in a CSN. Is the proposed network to be focused on a single intervention (or type of intervention, such as school social work), or will the CSN's focus be holistic? In general, once networks are set up, they are not easy to shut down. As a result, single-focus networks may compete in the long term for funding and community priorities against CSNs with a communitywide focus.

A third issue is the degree of government involvement. Government ownership or sponsorship may result in additional resources but at a high price in terms of restrictions on advocacy and social change. This issue will be of particular concern in rural areas with monolithic political structure.

A final issue is ownership. Will a single powerful organization or a coalition of organizations run the network? Single organizations are often able to create and oversee networks more expeditiously than coalitions. However, most single organizations that have the resources to establish a community network usually have vested interests that influence the nature and operation of the network.

IMPLICATIONS OF CSNs FOR PRACTICE WITH THE RURAL ELDERLY

The impact of CSNs on current practice with rural elderly will be to improve the access of rural elderly citizens to services, improve the quality of service, and control costs, much as predicted for telemedicine in rural areas (Harris, 1995). CSNs will provide a major resource for raising awareness of available community services and will provide the capacity for much greater involvement of the rural elderly in providing data and opinions regarding service development such as online polling.

Social workers will participate in the CSN, either voluntarily or involuntarily, because CSNs will become the first source of information that the elderly in rural areas consult. CSNs will provide links to resources, facilitate development of social networks, and be the repository for answers to frequently asked questions and information on service availability and eligibility. As a consequence, rural practitioners will become more involved with coalition-based activities, increase their communication across organizational boundaries, and be better organized for the delivery of service.

ESW AT THE GROUP LEVEL

Of the five levels of IT interaction with society, one that appears to lend itself to immediate adoption by rural elderly social work practitioners is work at the group level. IT for groups began in 1971 with task groups (Rapaport, 1993) and expanded to general public use beginning with the development of electronic bulletin board systems (BBSs) in 1978 (Rheingold, 1993). Information on BBS development and their use for those without a technical background is readily available (see Bryant, 1994); the literature on ESW at the group level should grow rapidly in the near future. This section describes a generic example of ESW at the group level, that of an electronic support group (ESG).

An ESG

During the 1980s, caregivers of Alzheimer's patients were the subject of much attention. Interventions to reduce caregiver burden were developed or expanded, but problems with support groups became apparent (Office of Technology Assessment, 1990; Wright, Lund, Pett, & Caserta, 1987). Potential users were kept away by barriers similar to those faced by the rural elderly: poverty, distance, and lack of awareness.

In the late 1980s, the Cleveland (Ohio) Area Alzheimer's Association was aware of these problems. The group teamed up with the University Hospitals of Cleveland/Case Western Reserve University Alzheimer's Center to address the issue. The Center's research director, Dr. Kathleen Smyth, reviewed the Alzheimer's literature, the growing body of CMC literature, and the developments during the 1980s in applying innovation diffusion theory to CMC as well as to the flourishing field of BBSs. She was convinced that if tens of thousands of BBSs could reach people with minimal computer expertise with inexpensive, simple equipment, then she could use the same approach to reach poor, housebound caregivers in the Cleveland area.

The result of her and other people's efforts was the creation of the Alzheimer's Disease Support Center (ADSC) in 1989 (see Smyth & Harris, 1993). The ADSC provides a long-term demonstration of the viability of ESGs to serve a home-bound, low-income population burdened by a common problem in rural areas, caregiving. In 1995, the ADSC was awarded the first National Information Infrastructure Award in the community service category.

The ADSC was intended to complement existing services and had electronic versions of information and referral services, health education counseling, support groups, and self-help groups. The primary target for the ADSC project was low-income households with minimal access to conventional support groups and community resources. The ESG provided social support in order to delay institutionalization and improve the health of both the caregiver and the sufferer. The ADSC demonstrates the basic components of ESGs and provides a clear use of the two major theories of assistance, computer-mediated communications theory and innovation diffusion theory, for social workers intending to develop an ESG. Assessment of results are also available and suggest evaluation approaches for ESG developers (Brennan & Moore, 1994; Brennan, Moore, & Smyth, 1992; Ripich, Moore, & Brennan, 1992).

The ADSC had the support and involvement of three major organizations, substantial funding, and the insight and creativity of Dr. Smyth and others. For many rural agencies, ESG-like activities could be take place with fewer resources through electronic self-help groups. Establishing a electronic self-help group (ESHG) may be the best first step in acquiring resources and expertise for work with ESGs in rural locations.

One typical mental health problem is recovery from abuse; elder abuse is increasingly recognized as a major problem among older adults, particularly where physical isolation is involved. Use of an electronic meeting ground for survivors could substantially increase access of the rural elderly to self-help groups and provide specific advantages for sexual abuse survivors. An ESHG would overcome barriers of time and space, thereby diminishing dependency, improving communication for those with interpersonal difficulties, encouraging participation of reluctant members, and establishing relationships (Finn & Lavitt, 1994).

The differences between an ESHG and an ESG such as the ADSC are considerable. The ADSC group is facilitated by an MSW, has an expert panel available for questions, operates within the structure of the Alzheimer's chapter, and receives the support of and advice from the chapter and the university. The ADSC's placement on the Cleveland FreeNet provided visibility as well as credibility. Those differences, however, should not be interpreted as forcing a choice between one or the other. ESHGs are an appropriate companion to ESGs in the same way that agencies provide face-to-face self-help groups along with facilitated, closed support groups for people who have similar problems but who need different levels of service.

IMPLICATIONS OF ESGs FOR THE RURAL ELDERLY

Electronic support groups will become a standard feature for all rural agencies at some time in the future. ESGs will become an accepted tool in much the same way as telemedicine became accepted: Widespread resistance and a high level of disbelief will give way to rapid adoption once successful examples receive publicity in the profession.

As a result of their adoption, ESGs will lead to improved access, increased quality of social work, and better management of costs, similar to the improvements foreseen for the use of IT in public health (Harris, 1995). ESGs will help address the problems caused by distance of service providers, the lack of community-based services, and the lack of transportation services. An ESG can bring services right into the home at a time that is most convenient to the client, increase awareness of community services, and reduce reliance on transportation. The resulting improvement in the quality of social work may well be indicated by an increase in rates of participation in mental health services of the rural elderly with emotional problems. Finally, agencies will be better able to manage their costs by using ESGs. For example, the use of ESGs as an intake buffer to aid in assessment and improve scheduling are being considered by health care providers and may be adopted by managed care organizations. ESGs used following treatment can provide psychosocial benefits to aid in recovery or maintain resistance to recidivism in addiction work.

USE WITH INDIVIDUALS, ORGANIZATIONS, AND SOCIETY

The previous two sections described the challenges and opportunities for rural practitioners at the group and community level in ESW. Some brief observations on changes at the individual, organizational, and societal levels are highlighted in the following sections.

Impact on Individual Rural Elderly People

The impact of IT on people in American society may be underestimated. For example, Turkle (1996) suggested that "we are moving from modernist calculation toward postmodernist simulation, where the self is a multiple, distributed system" (p. 20). Kelly (1994) used the term "neobiological civilization" to mean a society in which both the technology and the user are the relevant unit of life and in which assessment and interventions must be designed for both the person and the machine. As a result of the growth of technology, the next generation of rural elderly may well have new psychosocial problems and exhibit a much higher tendency to self-diagnose and access electronic assistance.

One current effect of IT on the rural elderly is the use of e-mail to communicate with relatives and friends. E-mail can be an especially useful tool in bridging the barrier of physical distance between the rural elderly and their family members without the financial costs associated with trying to maintain regular phone contact.

Another type of computer-mediated communication that has great potential for rural practice is the use of videoconferencing technologies. Presently, videoconferencing on the public telephone system is expensive because of long-distance charges. As videoconferencing moves to the Internet, the drop in cost will bring affordable enhanced visual contact with family and friends to elderly people. In addition, small video cameras can allow family members to monitor the personal care and home environment conditions of their older parents. This monitoring may allow the rural elderly to stay in the community for a longer period of time while keeping the risk of accidental harm at a lower level.

Another IT application that has the capacity for enhancing the lives of the rural elderly is the use of Internet shopping and entertainment services. This provides people in rural America with access to goods, services, and entertainment that is comparable to the access of their urban counterparts. This change will enhance the quality of life for the rural elderly and enable them to maintain their independence later into life.

Impact on Organizations and Agencies

Some home health agencies presently use videoconferencing to maintain daily blood pressure and health monitoring services with patients living in rural areas. IT is likely to produce analogous major changes in the structures, systems, and strategies of social work organizations. The "virtual organization" is now a commonplace term in the for-profit sector. The changes brought about by IT in society over the past 25 years are likely to diffuse among rural organizations quickly and, possibly, in a disruptive manner. In the short term, this change is likely to result in increased coalition-based activity, increased participation in the development of standards and practices by formerly isolated specialized professionals, and an improved responsiveness of agencies as a result of better data analysis, archives, and communications links. Eventually, IT-driven re-engineering of social service organizations will allow reinvention of bureaucratic organizations and perhaps the development of a postbureaucratic organizational structure.

Impact on Society

Changes in IT may change society and civic life even more than IT changes organizations. The implications are potentially powerful for location-bound rural elderly. The rural elderly someday could participate in the democratic process from their living rooms through videoconferencing or interactive television technologies (for example, participation in community forums). In the future, the rural elderly should be able to vote from their homes and not be isolated from the electoral process. Given this enhanced ability to participate, the increased numbers of elderly, and the concerns in society regarding the health and welfare of the elderly, the political power of the rural elderly may grow, and with it the patterns of funding and programs in rural areas.

THREE BARRIERS TO ESW

Three major barriers exist to achieving the benefits of ESW in rural areas. The first barrier is the lack of universal access to the Internet and to interactive interface devices, such as personal computers. The second problem, a larger one, is to find a way to assist the rural elderly to take advantage of changes in IT. The third, most challenging barrier and the key to the first two, is addressing needed changes in social work education, continuing education, and the profession.

The 1934 Communications Act first established universal access to electronic communications as a goal (Communications Act of 1934). The 1996 Telecommunications Act reaffirmed the basic value of universal access, applied it to Internet access, and included the concept that this access would need to be affordable even to low-income families (Telecommunications Act of 1996). Currently, the convergence of different communications technologies toward a single mechanism lends credence to the belief that all rural residents will eventually have access to the Internet.

Similarly, the cost of interconnect devices for the home is dropping rapidly; prices for a personal computer with Internet capability are under $1,000, and new and refurbished machines are available for a few hundred dollars. In the past, local communities were challenged to provide the rural poor with running water, electricity, a telephone, and a refrigerator. The current challenge is to add Internet access and a computer-based machine capable of interfacing with the Internet. Doing so will surely cost no more than implementing current policies regarding universal Internet access to schools and students.

CSN success will depend on adaptation to the new environment by the rural elderly and the social work service community. In some ways, this may prove easier for the rural elderly than for the professional community. A significant number of older citizens have already accepted the challenge of learning how to access the Internet: The American Association of Retired Persons indicates that more than 2 million computer users are among its membership (Dickerson, 1995). SeniorNet, a non-profit organization committed to helping older citizens take advantage of IT, provides computer training at more than 130 learning centers throughout the United States, many at local senior centers (SeniorNet Learning Centers, 1998).

Many of the elderly living in rural communities, however, will not have easy access to learning centers. Social workers serving the rural elderly will need to see as one of their responsibilities the development in their clients of the necessary competencies to take advantage of CSNs. For this to happen, all social workers must take as their ethical responsibility the development of sufficient knowledge and skills to be able to help clients develop IT competencies. In addition, many social workers will need to develop the skills to be able to professionally mediate an ESG.

Beyond individual social workers, social agencies will have to develop the capacity to create and maintain various aspects of the CSNs in their areas, including the development and operation of ESGs, content for CSNs, and a range of computer-mediated communication avenues to serve their clients. Agencies may need to expand the range of staff expertise to include those with Internet or other network experience.

CONCLUSIONS AND RECOMMENDATIONS

Four conclusions can be drawn from the preceding discussion. First, the interaction between IT and all five levels of society will greatly change rural society, including the nature of client problems and the resources available to address those problems. Second, those changes will offer opportunities for new practice approaches; two of those approaches, CSNs and ESGs, are already available and being used. Third, significant problems that may arise from these changes (for example, loss of local resources to nonspatial networks). Finally, social work practice itself must change to deal with the impending changes in rural society.

These conclusions direct attention to several areas in which the social work field should change, both for the benefit of practitioners and elderly clients in rural areas and for social workers in other settings.

Social work education has been as slow to adjust to IT as it was to adjust to earlier innovations, such as telephone, radio, television, and cable. In earlier times, however, technological change was slower, had less detrimental impact on clients, and offered less potential for direct benefits to clients and for social change. Today, technology is bringing rapid changes in society, significantly affecting clients and increasing the potential for both direct client benefits as well as social change. As a result, social work education's out-of-date perspectives on IT not only handicap students but also curtail the profession's potential.

Baccalaureate and master's programs must enable students to practice ESW in the classroom and in fieldwork. Most programs still focus on the instrumental aspects of IT, such as how to send an e-mail, but fail to assist students in obtaining a broader perspective (for example, the role of CSNs and ESGs in rural communities). Social work programs should be aggressively creating laboratory experiences for student to gain skills. Students have numerous opportunities for electronic practice in current fieldwork settings, yet faculty and field liaisons typically direct them away from IT and thus needlessly limit their progress at a time when fieldwork students and new graduates should be the leaders in helping agencies adjust to ESW.

In a similar manner, continuing education has failed to keep pace with changes (for example, the amount of practitioner-centered content regarding ESW at conferences is limited). Continuing education settings that relegate IT-oriented activity to separate conferences or tracks rather than encourage integration may hinder rather than help.

Ultimately, practitioners will need to adapt to IT, just as they adapted to telephones and computers for data processing. Practitioners should not depend on IT technicians to design and implement social work interventions that use IT, when current technology can be used by most practitioners with a reasonable amount of training and a suitable level of motivation.

Social work should recognize these issues and take action. The standards and expectations of the profession will need to be altered to take the demands of ESW into consideration. The Council on Social Work Education standards, those of bodies accrediting agency practice, certification standards used by the National Association of Social Workers, and the standards used by state boards all must examine the demands of ESW.

Above all, we should reflect back a century to Hull House. There, social workers struggled to build community and help clients. Today, we face a similar, albeit electronic, opportunity in rural areas. Numerous variations of CSNs operate today: America Online, Blacksburg's electronic community, electronic home shopping malls, and huge electronic structures such as the federal government's Web sites. In the midst of this virtual forest of examples, why can't we use CSNs as electronic Hull Houses, stocking them with a full range of computer-mediated communication tools that will work to build community and benefit clients? The rural areas of this country offer an excellent opportunity that also would provide an example for social work educators, continuing education, and the discipline. The future appears likely to reward social work boldness, creativity and new approaches regarding IT, whereas the consequences of hesitation, lack of vision, and traditionalism may be much more severe than during previous technological transitions.

REFERENCES

Blanchard, A., & Horan, T. (1998). Virtual communities and social capital. *Social Science Computer Review, 16*(3), 293–307.

Brennan, P. F., & Moore, S. M. (1994). Networks for home care support: The ComputerLink Project. *Caring, 13*(8), 14–27.

Brennan, P. F., Moore, S. M., & Smyth, K. A. (1992). Alzheimer's disease caregiver's uses of a computer network. *Western Journal of Nursing Research, 14*(5), 662–673.

Brennan, P. F., Schneider, S. J., & Tornquist, E. (1997). *Information networks for community health.* New York: Springer.

Bryant, A. D. (1994). *Creating successful bulletin-board systems.* Reading, MA: Addison-Wesley.

California senator introduces "smart communities" bill. (1998, July). *Government Technology, 11*(7), 2.

Carlton, L. (1991). Some considerations of the rural elderly black's underuse of social services. *Journal of Gerontological Social Work, 16*(1/2), 3–17.

Communications Act of 1934, 47 U.S.C.A. §151.

Coward, R. T., & Dwyer, J. W. (1998). The health and well-being of rural elders. In L. H. Ginsberg (Ed.), *Social work in rural communities* (3rd ed., pp. 213–232). Alexandria, VA: Council on Social Work Education.

Dickerson, J. F. (1995). Never too old: Millions of senior citizens are getting connected to the Net. *Time, 145*(12), 41.

Ferguson, T. (1996). *Health online: How to find health information, support groups, and self-help communities in cyberspace.* Reading, MA: Addison-Wesley.

Finn, J., & Lavitt, M. (1994). Computer-based self-help groups for sexual abuse survivors. *Social Work with Groups, 17*(1/2), 21–46.

Godwin, M. (1994, June). Nine principles for making virtual communities work. *Wired, 2*(6), 72–74.

Harris, L. (Ed.). (1995). *Health and the new media: Technologies transforming personal and public health.* Mahwah, NJ: Lawrence Erlbaum Associates.

Hiltz, S. R., & Turoff, M. (1993). *The network nation: Human communication via computer* (Revised). Boston: MIT Press.

Jones, S. G. (Ed.). (1995). *CyberSociety: Computer-mediated communication and community.* San Francisco: Sage Publications.

Kelly, K. (1994). *Out of control: The rise of neobiological civilization.* Reading, MA: Addison-Wesley.

Lucas, H. C. (1996). *The t-form organization: Using technology to design organizations for the 21st century.* San Francisco: Jossey-Bass.

Office of Technology Assessment. (1990). *Losing a million minds: Confronting the tragedy of Alzheimer's disease and other dementias* (Report No. OTA–BA–323). Washington, DC: U.S. Government Printing Office.

Rheingold, H. (1993). *The virtual community: Homesteading on the electronic frontier.* New York: Harper Perennial.

Rapaport, M. (1993). *Computer-mediated communications: Bulletin boards, computer conferencing, electronic mail, and information retrieval.* New York: John Wiley & Sons.

Ripich, S., Moore, S. M., & Brennan, P. F. (1992). A new nursing medium: Computer networks for group intervention. *Journal of Psychosocial Nursing, 39*(7), 15–20.

Rogers, E. M. (1983). *Diffusion of innovations* (3rd ed.). New York: Macmillan.

Rogers, E. M. (1986). *Communication technology: The new media in society.* New York: Free Press.

SeniorNet Learning Centers. (1998, June). *Inside SeniorNet.* Available: http://www.senior-net.org/ inside/ceners.html

Smyth, K. A., & Harris, P. B. (1993). Using telecomputing to provide information and support to caregivers of persons with dementia. *Gerontologist, 33,* 123–127.

Spense, S. A. (1991). The black elderly and social services. *Families in Society, 72,* 371–374.

Spense, S. A. (1993). African Americans and service delivery: A study of health and social service needs and service accessibility. *Journal of Gerontological Social Work, 20*(3/4), 187–202.

Sumner, L. (1998). Limited access: Health care for the rural poor. In L. H. Ginsberg (Ed.), *Social Work in Rural Communities* (3rd ed., pp. 277–290). Alexandria, VA: Council on Social Work Education.

Sussman, G. (1997). *Communication, technology, and politics in the information age.* Thousand Oaks, CA: Sage Publications.

Telecommunications Act of 1996. 47 U.S.C.A. §254.

Turkle, S. (1996). *Life on the screen: Identity in the age of internet.* New York: Simon & Schuster.

Ward, R. (1977). Services for older people: An integrated framework for research. *Journal of Health and Social Behavior, 18,* 61–70.

Waring, M. L., & Kosberg, J. I. (1980). Life conditions and use of social welfare services among aged blacks in North Florida. *Journal of Minority Aging, 5,* 233–241.

Weinberg, N., Schmale, J. D., Uken, J., & Wessel, K. (1995). Computer-mediated support groups. *Social Work with Groups, 17*(4), 43–54.

Wright, S. D., Lund, D. A., Pett, M. A., & Caserta, M. S. (1987). The assessment of support group experience by caregivers of dementia patients. *Clinical Gerontologist, 6,* 35–59.

SECTION VII

PREPARING SOCIAL WORKERS
FOR RURAL PRACTICE:
EDUCATION AND TRAINING

Social workers are often ill prepared to practice in rural communities and small towns. Although many of the issues in rural areas are the same as those in urban centers, the ways in which social workers intervene to help to address those problems is different. Being aware of a community's history and methods of problem solving is critical to effective social work practice. In this section, the authors present information that addresses the importance of specific education and training.

In chapter 23, Mary Ann Yevuta discusses the need to be a creative and innovative social work educator when working in rural communities. Focusing on the field experience, the author examines the way in which one student in a rural county in West Virginia developed a field placement in the local community by drawing upon community needs that the board of education could not meet with existing resources. The case serves as a model for other schools facing similar shortages of opportunities for student learning.

Susanne Mosteller Rolland discusses in chapter 24 the "clash" between Appalachian university students and their faculty. The author wanted to understand the students' perceptions of the faculty's respect for their culture, so she posed two questions: (1) "Do you think the faculty values your culture?" and (2) "In what areas, if any, do you experience cultural conflict between faculty and students?" Although the responses were mixed, the author notes that some of the students have an uneasy relationship with the faculty who teach them. The author concludes that training in cultural sensitivity might be valuable for all faculty working in a culturally sensitive rural area such as eastern Kentucky.

In chapter 25, Michael Daley and Freddie Avant discuss the importance of com-

313

petent service delivery in rural areas. They focus on the development and retention of professionally qualified social workers to provide and administer services in rural areas. The authors highlight retention issues within a rural region of East Texas, where the active involvement of a social work program has had a positive effect on the development of a cadre of professionals in the service delivery community. They use data on the social work labor force over a 10-year period to illustrate changes that have occurred in the region.

In chapter 26, Patricia P. Plaskon and Jay Bishop present a brief overview of the development of a dual-degree program in social work at two universities in eastern Maryland. Because few African American social workers were available to work in this rural section of Maryland, a majority school and a historically black university created a collaborative social work program. A survey of graduates who hold this degree revealed that 80 percent found work in the field. Few graduates pursued rural social work practice, however.

In chapter 27, Lena Williams Carawan, Lessie L. Bass, and Shelia Grant Bunch, all rural social work educators at a major school of social work, discuss ways of teaching competent and sensitive rural social work practice. They focus on the importance of modeling the collaborative process by inviting community residents to share with students their personal accounts of everyday life experiences in rural settings. These authors note that bringing rural narratives into the classroom helps develop a greater awareness of interpersonal dynamics in rural communities.

CHAPTER TWENTY-THREE

Nitpicking in Rural West Virginia:
The Small Stuff Does Matter

Mary Ann Yevuta

The issues that arise in the practice of social work in small towns and rural settings are in many respects the same as those found in an urban area, but the solutions often are not. In small towns and rural areas, services too often are difficult to access and expensive to implement. The social worker him- or herself is often a major resource. Practitioners are called upon to use all of their skills in meeting community needs. Plans must draw on a variety of sometimes seemingly unrelated elements in order to develop into a comprehensive whole. The same can be said of a social work student attempting to complete a field placement. Opportunities are limited, and one must, like the magician, be able to pull rabbits from hats and coins from thin air. Like the magician, the illusion is that something came from nothing; however, the reality is that the magician's talent, like the artist's, is in making the audience see things in a different way.

In every community in the nation, organizations have developed over time to meet local needs. This chapter examines the way in which one student in a rural county in West Virginia developed a field placement in the local community for the 1997–98 school year. The placement set out to fill needs that could not be met by the board of education with existing resources but which were identified as being important to the children served. A social worker had not previously been employed by the board of education, so the job description was developed jointly with the student and the school superintendent, along with input from county school principals. Additionally, the job changed over the course of the 10-month placement.

The student, by necessity, used a generalist approach to the problem and performed a variety of projects, including direct practice as well as community organization tasks. The placement basically consisted of three main projects. The first was a head lice prevention effort, focused primarily on some of the worst offenders from the previous school year; second was the development of an after-school child care program directed toward meeting the needs of working parents for quality child care following school hours; and third was to work with a group of underachieving middle school children in a group setting. None of the projects along would have constituted a full placement, but taken together, they provided a wide variety of new and challenging experiences for the student. A student who is willing to engage in a less-traditional learning environment could replicate this experience in any number of areas. Additionally, the community benefited from receiving services that had not been previously available.

SETTING

Wetzel County, West Virginia, probably resembles many other rural counties in the Appalachian region. It sits at the base of West Virginia's northern panhandle, having as its western border the Ohio River and as its northern border the Mason–Dixon Line. The county has a population of 19,258 and covers an area of 360 square miles (Holmes, 1995, p. 801), putting it in the midrange of the state's 55 counties in both categories. Of the county's population, 55.3 percent are rural; the racial makeup of the county is almost entirely white (Wetzel County Family Resource Network, 1997, p. 6). The industries in the county consist of petroleum and natural gas wells, glassmaking, sand and gravel production (from dredging the Ohio River), lumber, and small-scale farming. Many of the residents work in chemical plants, coal mines, or power plants in surrounding counties. The largest single employer in the county is the board of education, which operates four elementary and four secondary schools. The county has no large industries interested in sponsoring new resources in the county, and the population centers of the county are geographically isolated from one another because a poor highway infrastructure makes travel difficult. The county seat, New Martinsville, is one of the two largest towns in a multicounty area.

Rivalry exists among the population centers; residents of the smaller areas sometimes express intense resentment and jealousy toward those who live in the county seat. Other than New Martinsville, which has drawn many "outsiders" who work in the industries across the river or in neighboring Marshall County, most residents have lived here for generations. It is commonly said of Wetzel Countians that "if your grandparents weren't from here, then you aren't from here either." They and their kinfolk form close-knit communities, which are both a boon and a burden, depending on what one is trying to accomplish. The residents are generally conservative, with a small dose of labor liberalism thrown in because of the unionization of the residents who work in industry. The terrain consists of steep, wooded hillsides with a creek, a railroad, and a two-lane highway occupying the narrow valley bottoms and is thus typical of the terrain in much of Appalachia.

The county's problems, too, are typical. A partial list, compiled by the Wetzel County Family Resource Network (a collaborative organization of the major providers of social services in the county), includes the following:

- an unemployment rate of 11.2 percent (the state average is 8.4 percent)
- of the five counties in the northern panhandle, the highest percentage of births to mothers with less than a 12th grade education

- an increase in the proportion of teen births from 60.4 percent in 1980 to 65.9 percent in 1991
- an increase in the percentage of births to unmarried teens of 140.2 percent between 1980 and 1991, placing Wetzel County 45th out of 55 counties in the state
- an increase in the number of children living in poverty of 94 percent between 1980 and 1991; both per capita and median incomes for families are below the state average
- a lack of child care services (Wetzel County Family Resource Network, 1997, p. 6).

In addition, according to the Wetzel County Family Resource Network (1997), services are "categorized, fragmented, and at most times not known to our consumers, or by other service providers. . . . Organizations find themselves protecting turf and in competition for decreasing dollars while attempting to address dramatic increases in community and family needs" (p. 6).

It is in this setting that the story of the field placement for a student in West Virginia University's MSW program began. No master's-level personnel were working in the county office of the Department of Health and Human Resources (DHHR), where the student worked, and only one or two people with MSW degrees even lived in the county. Developing a field placement that did not involve a great deal of travel time to a larger population center with established social service agencies would take a great deal of creativity and collaboration.

PROCESS OF COLLABORATION

The seeds of this field placement were sown several years before its development. In 1994, the West Virginia legislature passed legislation aimed at improving the way in which the service needs of communities were met by encouraging local assessment and planning. The legislation allowed single- or multiple-county cooperatives to incorporate into Family Resource Networks, or FRNs, which could use funding streams from a variety of state agencies in new or creative ways (that is, blended funding), apply for grants, and administer grant-funded services as an umbrella organization for all the service agencies in the county or region.

The Wetzel County FRN began as a small project to bring together organizations serving at-risk students in the county. Spearheaded by the board of education, this effort also included the department of health and human resources, the department of vocational rehabilitation, the department of employment security, and Northwood, the local community behavioral health center. From this beginning, a core group of representatives from some key agencies worked for the next several years to reach out to and organize all the services in the county, develop by-laws and an organizational structure, become incorporated as a nonprofit organization, and obtain funding to run the organization and establish needed community projects. Gradually the health department, Community Resources of Wetzel County, Wetzel County Hospital, and other providers were brought in, and their representatives have served on the board of directors or on various committees. Non–service providers were also included in the process; this group included representatives of parents, senior citizens, business, industry, higher education, retirees, and most important, clients. The clients, incidentally, were the most challenging component of the partnership to recruit and keep active; this group had difficulty participating as equal partners, a graphic illustration of the perceptions of the public toward service providers that still needs a great deal of effort to overcome.

Before the collaboration, the agencies in the county worked together on an "as needed" basis, only getting together when an individual case demanded it. Little understanding existed of the scope of each other's services, other agencies' legal mandates, who to contact for necessary services, or even which service agencies were available. It seemed reasonable to presume that if the helping professionals did not know this basic information, then surely the general public was likely to be in the dark as well. Each provider could recite anecdotes describing clients' and other agencies' mistrust of their agencies; relationships existed on a very formal basis, sometimes only through telephone contacts. Working together on a project such as putting together an FRN allowed the representatives of the various agencies to develop personal and professional relationships that would not have been possible otherwise.

DEVELOPING THE FIELD PLACEMENT

A major stumbling block to the development of this field placement was the lack of an agency that employed an MSW who could function as a field supervisor. A woman with an MSW who taught part time at the local community college agreed to do the supervision if it could be arranged with an agency and if the University was willing to accept such an arrangement. Although the arrangement would have inherent problems, it was recognized that finding an ideal placement in such a rural area was difficult at best, and a commitment was made to find a way to resolve the problems. The most obvious problem, of course, was one of access. Since neither the student nor the supervisor worked for the same agency, it would be difficult to see each other on a regular basis for consultation or supervisory conferences. Neither person was familiar with the policies of other agencies that might provide a possible placement opportunity. Finally, the placement would require a strong commitment of time from both the student and the supervisor along with a concomitant balancing of personal lives. As a first step in overcoming those problems, the supervisor agreed to meet on Saturdays at her home. The other problems would have to be dealt with after more was known about the nature of the placement.

Because of the development of the FRN, it was apparent that an opportunity for a field learning experience was available in the county school system. Discussions had occurred early in the process of developing the FRN about the utility of a school social worker, but funding was not available. It seemed that many of the projects with which the schools had been involved for several years were not directly involved with education per se, but rather were aimed at dealing with social problems that often interfere with the learning process. Some of the initiatives included preschool interventions that involved working with the families; postgraduation planning, handled in a much more involved way than had been done in the past; and working with at-risk students. Other possibilities existed because so many service gaps existed, and a placement with the FRN itself might have been arranged. Personal preference and the willingness of the school system to accept the student's offer of a half-time volunteer for an entire school year eventually determined the choice.

The superintendent of schools was approached with an offer of a part-time school social worker for the1997–98 school year, which she accepted. In discussions between the workers and the superintendent, it was noted that only a few years earlier, the student would not have approached her, nor would she have accepted such an offer. It was through their previous collaborative efforts on the Family Services Network and the development of a personal relationship that the potential for mutual benefit in this arrangement was recognized. The student, supervisor, and school superintendent then met to discuss how such a placement might work and what roles each party would play. They needed to have a strong plan in place to present to the board of education for its approval as well as to the field instruction coordinator at West Virginia University.

PLANNING THE PLACEMENT

A great deal of planning was necessary before the placement could be approved. The first step had already been taken by discussing with the school superintendent her ideas for how the county's schools could best be served. It was decided to target the elementary and middle school children, rather than the students in the high schools; the greatest opportunity for change existed with younger children, whose attitudes toward school may have been more amenable to change than those of the older children. It was also decided to target at-risk students, meaning those who had the potential to drop out of school as they got older for whatever reasons. The aim was not to duplicate existing services, but rather to reach children whose problems were not addressed by other agencies or school programs. Inquiry into what school social workers did in the few counties in the state that had them revealed that often they were actually attendance directors; however, this placement was to be more than that.

One of the superintendent's first suggestions was to work with families whose children had chronic head lice. She also suggested working with families of kindergarten students to make sure that they had all of the necessary documentation for the first day of school and working with students who were not motivated to complete homework and were in danger of failing, possibly as an after-school program. These ideas were written up for presentation to the board of education by the superintendent and were included in the field placement application to WVU. Two of the ideas, the head lice project and the project to work with underachievers, became major parts of the field placement experience.

The next step was to talk with the four elementary school principals in the county. The four schools are New Martinsville School, Paden City School, Long

Drain School, and Short Line School. After discussion with all the principals, it appeared that each attendance area had unique needs.

Short Line School already had an after-school and summer program in place. The principal was helpful in outlining what the school already did and in offering suggestions about what to expect, what might be accomplished, and what to look for in developing a program for any other school. She was receptive to the idea of having someone work with families on the chronic lice problems but thought that her school's existing after-school program was working well without any need for additions or changes.

At Paden City School, the principal reported that there had not been any severe lice problems at the school that year, nor had there been a real problem with getting children enrolled as a result of a lack of birth certificates, immunization records, and other documentation. She suggested that having a before- and after-school child care program would be helpful. A number of children came to school early in the morning, before the school was open (a lack of resources prevented a before-school program), and she suspected that there might be a need for child care for children of working parents after school as well. The principal and the student discussed the need for a survey of students' families in order to determine what kind of child care program would be helpful.

At New Martinsville School, the principal was receptive to having someone help with the chronic lice problems. He thought that an after-school program might be difficult because of space problems and upcoming renovations to the building. Additionally, a previous effort to provide an after-school program had not been an entirely positive experience, so he was not anxious to repeat past mistakes. Although he was not enthusiastic about a formal child care program that would be available every day to families based on request, he was interested in a supplemental program for a few students who were referred by teachers because of poor academic performance.

At Long Drain School the principal was pleased about having someone work with the families with lice problems. He, like the principal at Paden City, was interested in the possibility of providing before- and after-school child care. He indicated that he, too, had noticed a number of children whose parents would bring the children to school early, despite the lack of formal supervision.

It appeared then that the field-placement activities would differ at each school. At New Martinsville, Short Line, and Long Drain, work would be done with some families in which head lice seemed to be a chronic problem, while at Paden City and Long Drain, the project would be to work with the principals on a child care program. The latter project would involve compiling surveys, completing the applications for the child care grants, recruiting and training staff for the programs, and supervising the provision of care. At New Martinsville, with the help of the principal, another project would be to determine the kind of program that would be most beneficial for a group of underachieving students, define the criteria for referrals, and provide the service.

In essence, the above description is the skeleton of the field placement that evolved. It evolved as conditions changed or as new knowledge was acquired. The structure of the placement was rather loose, and although this characteristic caused some organizational problems, it was also an advantage, in that there was freedom to make changes as the need arose without having to navigate as many bureaucratic channels. In this sense, the placement was an ideal laboratory for a generalist practice.

All of this planning had occurred before the placement was even approved. The importance of being fully prepared cannot be overemphasized. The approval of the placement by all the parties whose agreement was necessary (WVU, the board of education, the school principals, the school superintendent, the employer, and the field instructor) depended on good planning. Even after the placement was approved, work needed to be done before the placement actually started. To meet the deadlines for the School Day Plus grant, which was the grant to fund the before- and after-school child care programs at Paden City and Long Drain, it was necessary to start working a full month earlier than the start date for the field placement (July 1997). More meetings with the principals were needed before the end of the 1996–97 school year in order to get referrals for the head lice project, since work with the families was projected to begin in the summer. A student unwilling to make this commitment in time and effort could not succeed in this kind of alternative placement. The commitment seemed to be worth the extra time and effort, however, in the payback. Not only did it allow for a placement close to home, the efforts also resulted in services to the local community and strengthening of the professional relationships that had begun during the development of the FRN.

NITPICKING BEGINS

The starting point for the placement was the school child care project because the grant for the 1997–98 school year was due before the end of the 1996–97 school year. Activities related to the School Day Plus program continued throughout the summer: forming an advisory board, recruiting staff, developing policies and procedures, and the countless small things that need to be done when instituting a new program. This initial work was done on weekends, evenings, and any time during the week that could be taken. Once the placement actually started, the routine became one of working every Friday and Saturday and doing paperwork on weekday evenings. Occasionally it was necessary to work on Sundays.

In addition to School Day Plus, other summer activities focused on contacting the families who had been referred as having chronic head lice infestations during the past school year. Referrals were received from the principals at New Martinsville School and Long Drain School. The principals at the other two schools reported that lice had not been a prevalent problem for them during the previous school year. Nine families were on the lice project caseload, and every Friday was set aside for field visits for the purpose of introducing the project, explaining the social worker's role, and beginning to assess each family for the individual problems leading to their children being constantly infected with head lice. Unfortunately, school teachers and principals are unable to address problems such as chronic lice infestation on an individual basis. The common strategy when children are discovered with lice is to contact the parents to come get the child. Parents are told to treat the child, to thoroughly clean the house, and to use pesticide sprays. Regardless of the care that is taken to treat the parents respectfully, there is inevitably resentment, shame, and resulting denial on the part of parents. A stigma of dirtiness is attached to having head lice, and although most of the families in this project did have dirty homes, some of them made every effort to keep their homes and their children clean under adverse circumstances, including the lack of water, transportation, money, laundry facilities, and social support. Indeed, it can be very expensive to treat lice; as lice become more and more resistant to pesticides, the problem becomes increasingly complex for families with limited resources.

It is thus not surprising that initial efforts were met with polite resistance. Families were generally not hostile; in fact, they often expressed gratitude toward those contacting them, but for the most part they made it clear that they would not willingly accept additional assistance. A monthly newsletter was sent to the families with information about lice and how to combat them, and repeated home visits were made. The families invariably reported that their children were fine or that the school or other children were at fault. Of course, during the summer when the project was initiated, the families were not in crisis, and after the principals made the initial referrals, they became distracted and forgot to report further instances of infection after school started in the fall. Several weeks in September and October were spent under the misconception that the initial efforts were going so smoothly that the problem had been resolved with just a minimum of effort! Of course, it could not be that easy.

In November the principals were contacted again. Many of the children had been sent home with lice, and neither the principals nor the families had reported it. It is difficult to confront families if no immediate crisis exists, and being notified immediately tremendously helps efforts to deal with a problem. Five of the families with head lice problems in the New Martinsville area were related by blood or marriage. In at least one of the families, perhaps two, the recurring infections were a result of the children's interaction with their cousins. The mother was extremely frustrated with her relatives, because just when she would get her children free of lice and nits, they would be reinfected. With the consent of the families, a group meeting of all the parents was convened. It was agreed beforehand that the meeting would be nonjudgmental. During the meeting, the families agreed that when any of the children were found to be infected, all the families would be willing to help with the treatment efforts by applying pesticide shampoos, cleaning, and taking on the tedious and difficult job of picking nits. Only when notification occurred on the same day that the children were found to be infected was it possible to make inroads with the families. Often, efforts consisted of sitting with the parents and picking nits together while discussing the problem. Some families continued to resist offers to provide such concrete assistance and never became willing to do more than talk.

Some administrators had become so frustrated in continually dealing with the same families that a mutually respectful relationship was impossible. The hostility between the school and the parents was such that a main part of the social work role was to act as an advocate for the parents. A continued punitive stance, especially in families with very small children, bodes ill for the long term and simply serves to stiffen the resistance. The relationship between one parent and the school had become so bad that the mother and the principal could hardly be in the same room together without harsh words and shouting. The progress that was made with that family for the entire school year was mainly to establish enough trust to allow direct confrontation with the mother about the need to consider that she and the children's father had to be treated in addition to the children if the lice were ever to be successfully overcome. This breakthrough came about when, after three or four months of working together, the social work student asked the mother to check her head for nits, since she was working with so many children and was concerned about becoming infected herself. After checking the social worker's hair, the mother's anxiety and shame about the possibility of infection was reduced, trust was strengthened, and she asked the worker to check her hair. In the first half of the school year, the children had missed up to 20 school days because of lice. Conversely, after intervention was begun, they missed only one day because of lice during the second half of the school year. Although this progress was remarkable, uncertainty remains about the long-term gains in the parents' being able to resolve the problem on their own because of a lack of follow-up. This situation illustrates a major problem with the providing services in a field placement such as this one, which is not an established program.

One advantage of not being notified about the head lice infestations immediately was that more time could be devoted to the other projects. The proposal that was submitted for the School Day Plus program was approved, but the funding was less than one-half of what had been expected. Since revisions were required to the projected programs in light of the reduced funding, the start date was delayed from the beginning of the school year until November 1, and only after-school care was provided. Unfortunately, the attendance at Long Drain School never approached what had been expected from our initial survey of the parents. It may be that the delayed start caused parents to make other arrangements for their children, or the lack of trust that rural people have of "outside" services kept them from the program. Eventually, because of layoffs among the parents, attendance dropped off altogether and the program had to be discontinued. Attendance grew steadily at Paden City, however, and the program there was a remarkable success. In fact, a decision was made by the principal and the school superintendent that even without a social worker to administer the program they would continue it the following year.

At New Martinsville School, a plan evolved for a project to help underachieving students. The focus was on helping seventh- and eighth-grade students be more prepared for the transition to high school. The makeup of the group changed each six weeks, depending on the grades of the students. The students worked with an assistant principal one day per week on homework assignments and with the social worker in a process group another day of the week to motivate them to think about why they were failing and what they could do to help themselves. It had been decided that this group would consist of students who had the ability to make passing grades and were not eligible for special education services. Many of the students had significantly dysfunctional families or had suffered emotional trauma in the past. Most of them were in the group for only one grading period, and it was not determined whether this group or other factors helped them get better grades; however, it did seem that the experience of talking about their problems was helpful to them. In fact, some students requested to be allowed to continue in the group despite improved grades. Their need for a forum in which they could safely talk about their problems was evident. Unfortunately, it was not possible to allow their continued participation because of the need to limit group size and the possible impact on the group dynamics for the new participants each grading period. It would probably be helpful for those students to have a support or process group in order to deal with some of their issues on a long-term basis.

CONCLUSION

What does it mean to have gone through a field placement experience such as this one? Because the activities of the placement were developed to meet specific personal and community needs, the answer inevitably varies. Like the placement itself, the key lies in looking at the many different parts, both within one's self and within the environment as a whole. There is meaning to the community in the services offered that were not previously available; there is meaning to the student in the knowledge, experience, and credentials gained; and there is meaning to the educational institution in the development of an innovative way of meeting a requirement of the MSW program.

For the community, although the after-school child care program failed at one of the schools, it was a resounding success at Paden City School and has continued despite the absence of a school social worker to run the program. The schools adopted many of the concepts used in the head lice prevention project. For example, for the following year it was the intention of the superintendent to have the school nurse make home visits to the families with chronic infestations and to use the assistance of Community Resources of Wetzel County. The value of support services for students who are struggling academically was also recognized.

For the MSW student, the placement's activities indeed offered a wide variety of experiences for a generalist approach to social work. The after-school child care project required her to act as a community organizer and as an administrator. She was required to do two surveys, organize meetings with key participants to get input, develop the program, write a grant, attend a child care conference, and administer the program. The head lice prevention project required the direct practice skills of assessment, advocacy, concrete assistance, and education. The intervention with underachieving students required direct practice skills as well: assessment, counseling, and group facilitation. The placement required organizing the various projects, developing documentation systems, documenting activities, and advocating for approval of the placement and its various activities.

Seen as a whole, the placement was a job with a variety of tasks; if funding were available, it would be a desirable position for the board of education to make permanent. If the position were permanent, even more projects or tasks could be performed, such as acting as liaison with child protective services when children are reported abused or neglected; developing additional support groups within the schools, including the high schools; overseeing and coordinating grant-funded programs; writing grants for new programs; working with other special populations of students and families (such as with the head lice project); and many others.

Anticipating the placement, it truly did appear as if it would require pulling a rabbit from a hat in order to make it work and was a bit overwhelming. To say that the time and work that was put into this field placement was well worth the effort, however, is an understatement. Certainly, some things could have been done differently; that is the nature of a learning process. That something new was created, or perhaps more accurately, something new was synthesized from existing pieces of many elements was the beauty of this field placement. The field placement could be replicated by students in other rural communities, allowing them to work in an exciting and creative way while meeting local and personal needs.

REFERENCES

Holmes, D. E. (Ed.). (1995). *West Virginia Blue Book.* Charleston, WV: State of West Virginia.

Wetzel County Family Resource Network. (1997). *Handbook for Board of Directors, Section 2.* Wetzel County, WV: Author.

CHAPTER TWENTY-FOUR

Valuing Rural Community: Appalachian Social Work Students' Perspectives on Faculty Attitudes Toward Their Culture

Susanne Mosteller Rolland

Educators whose college or university serves rural populations have the opportunity to participate in preserving and strengthening rural communities through educating their students to assume constructive leadership positions in the rural communities from which they come and to which many of them return. If they are to do this conscientiously, however, educators themselves must value rural society. Finding educators who do so may be especially problematic when the particular rural society from which their students come, and to which they return, is one that the larger society gives permission to scorn, as in the case of Appalachia.

In "politically correct" society, where it is generally unacceptable to cast aspersions on the basis of ethnic group membership, the "hillbilly," the product in good part of European American stock, remains an acceptable subject of derision. Assignment to the category is based primarily on region of birth. Hillbillies are not found in the mountains of New Hampshire or Vermont or in the American West. They are mostly a subspecies of a larger group, that of the white American southerner, whom intellectual circles find somewhat acceptable to view with contempt.

In a recent popular and well-regarded book, humorist Bill Bryson (1998) discussed his long trek along much of the Appalachian trail. He encountered mostly sane and sensible folk along the northern reaches of the trail, but that was not the situation as he first set out along the trail in north Georgia. His description of what I regard as the pleasant small town of Hiawassee, Georgia, located on the North Carolina border, was as follows:

> And then we were alone with our packs in an empty motel parking lot in a dusty, forgotten, queer-looking little town in northern Georgia. The word that clings to every

hiker's thoughts in north Georgia is *Deliverance,* the 1970 novel by James Dickey. . . .
It concerns, as you may recall, four middle-aged men from Atlanta who go on a
weekend canoeing trip down the fictional Cahulawassee River (based on the real,
nearby Chattooga) and find themselves severely out of their element. "Every family
I've ever met up here has at least one relative in the penitentiary," a character in the
book remarks forebodingly as they drive up. "Some of them are in for making liquor
or running it, but most of them are in for murder. They don't think a whole lot
about killing people up here." Early in the book Dickey has his characters stop for
directions in some "sleepy and hookwormy and ugly" town, which for all I know
could have been Hiawassee. . . .

Dickey's book, as you might expect, attracted heated criticism in the state
when it was published, but in fact it must be said that people have been appalled by
northern Georgians for 150 years. One nineteenth century chronicler described
the region's inhabitants as "tall, thin, cadaverous-looking animals, as melancholy
and lazy as boiled cod-fish," and others freely employed words like "depraved,"
"rude," "uncivilized," and "backward" to describe the reclusive, underbred folk of
Georgia's deep, dark woods and desperate townships. Dickey, who was himself a
Georgian and knew the area well, swore that his book was "a faithful description."
(pp. 64–65)

Dickey was, indeed, a Georgian, but he grew up in the prosperous Atlanta district
of Buckhead, and his perspective on north Georgia was that of a city person. A native
of Hiawassee would likely describe that town quite differently than does Bryson, who
goes on to discuss his adventures in Hiawassee in the spirit of Dickey. How fortunate,
for the population with whom I am concerned, that neither Dickey nor Bryson wrote
about eastern Kentucky, the quintessential home of the Southern hillbilly! Many
other outsiders, however, have concerned themselves with eastern Kentucky, some to
poke fun, some to exploit its resources, but others in the spirit of helpfulness.
Appalachia has long been considered a major problem area. After many other southern mountain regions have found some prosperity, eastern Kentucky continues to be
one of the poorest areas of the entire country. It is an area in need of help.

ORIGINS OF THE STEREOTYPES

When my students in eastern Kentucky speak of being humiliated and derided
by outsiders, however, it is not so much the obvious caricaturists of hillbillies at
whom they are upset as it is those who seek to illuminate area problems. They speak
with special annoyance of media portrayals of Kentucky during the War on Poverty
of the 1960s and 1970s, a time when the nation at large discovered the poverty of
eastern Kentucky, West Virginia, and the nearby counties of generally prosperous
Ohio. Students from the counties visited by presidents and newscasters speak of
their humiliation at seeing the worst of unpresentable poverty in their areas portrayed as typical and the most embarrassingly deprived of their fellow citizens presented as representative. The world, they complain, views them as they are at their
worst and ignores them as they are at their best. Even the people who come to help

have in mind helping the caricature of themselves, the hillbilly of outsiders' imaginations.

The caricature has at least a 100-year history. Henry Shapiro (1978) reported that between 1870 and 1900 visiting writers convinced the remainder of the country that Appalachia was "a strange land inhabited by a peculiar people" (p. xiii). He contends that American perceptions of Appalachia are not and never have been based on reality. David Hsiung (1997, 1998) explained that two different outlooks developed in the course of the 19th century within the region itself. One was that of inhabitants of the broad valleys and towns with a regional and national outlook, who saw their region as falling behind and sought to "extend their connections to other people and places"; the other was that of people more isolated in rugged terrain, who sought land and "more intimate ties with a much more narrow range of people" (1997, p. 187). Within the region, some people separated themselves from others.

The history of Appalachian stereotypes is closely intertwined with the economic history of the region. Altina Waller, who has studied late 19th-century Kentucky feuds in general (1995), and the Hatfield-McCoy feud in particular (1988), pointed out that it was precisely at the moment in the late 19th century when outside capital began pouring into eastern Kentucky and neighboring West Virginia to exploit the mineral and forest wealth of the area that the mountaineer began to be portrayed as a savage. A *New York Times* editorial of 1885 characterized Appalachians as more savage, degraded, and lawless than other Americans or even other southerners. Waller (1995) made it clear that the late 19th-century Appalachian conflicts characterized as feuds were firmly rooted in political and economic contests over the course of economic development. She concluded that

> Appalachian history can reveal something of the complex dialectic that operates between subordinate and dominant societies to create cultural hierarchies and stereotypes. In Appalachia that process has for one hundred years obscured the struggle for control of Appalachia's economic riches by trivializing and mythologizing its people's struggle to accommodate, adapt, or resist. (p. 370)

Paul Salstrom (1994), who has studied Appalachian economic history, commented that Appalachia "since the middle of the nineteenth century has increasingly been relegated to the periphery of America's market economy" (p. xiv). Among the bulk of the population, "which had little more than its labor to invest in development, the growth of capitalist relations did not inspire much adoption of capitalist values. . . . Capitalist relations and local mentality were related, of course, but often in Appalachia they were related antithetically" (p. xvii).

EASTERN KENTUCKY TODAY

Present-day eastern Kentucky is a place in economic decline. Employment in mining has decreased steadily and dramatically. The area farmers worry as their principal crop, burly tobacco, is increasingly threatened. According to the 1990 census, of the 28 poorest counties in Kentucky, 27 are in eastern Kentucky. Owsley County, which has an official poverty rate of 52.1 percent, is the sixth-poorest county in the nation. Nineteen counties, all with more than one-third of their residents living in poverty, are among the 100 poorest counties in the nation (Websdale, 1998, p. 42).

Rural Kentuckians have a long-standing pattern of "making do" in such circumstances: the practice of voluntary reciprocity within family groups, described by its practitioners to an anthropologist as "the Kentucky way" (Halperin, 1990). Members of family networks exchange goods and services regularly without attention to record keeping or reporting. Employed members of family networks, who may be in urban settings, may share monetary resources with those back in the hills who carry on unremunerated agricultural work. "Putting all your eggs in one basket" is not considered a wise thing to do. Barter and informal exchange are central to the system, which has as its goal the maintenance of the entire network of participating kin.

Eastern Kentuckians generally accept the designation of "hillbilly," even if they find it annoying, but their view of the culture of the mountains is far different from that of outsiders. Eastern Kentuckians, along with other Appalachian people, value their world of close extended family, "who stick together through thick and thin"; local church, where they find "a universal and freely chosen Christian love"; and interactive local community (Bryant, 1981, pp. 130–133). They see their world as different from that of most of late 20th-century America, and they value that difference. They do not leave their mountain homes lightly, but over the years many have left in the quest to make a living. A sizable percentage of those who leave yearn for the hills, may come home to retire or, in greater number, are buried at life's end on top of familiar hills (Schwarzweller, Brown, & Mangalem, 1971).

Eastern Kentuckian Chris Holbrook begins the title story of his short-story collection, *Hell and Ohio,* with eastern Kentucky small-town barber Marvin speaking to his customers: "I believe if I owned both Hell and Ohio, I'd rent out Ohio and live in Hell," says Marvin (Holbrook, 1995, p. 1). The "Hell" of the particular story relates to the tormented aftermath of a tragedy in eastern Kentucky, but the sentiment expressed by Marvin is a widespread one in eastern Kentucky. Better to remain in poverty and even pain than to go off to the alien world of Ohio.

Eastern Kentucky families frequently do not rejoice when family members go off to the regional university. To seek higher education, even locally, is akin to leaving for Ohio. As relatives watch students enter a larger world, remove themselves to a certain extent from the close-knit family and its demands upon them, and shift their speech patterns closer to those of the outside world, they may see these students as rejecting and betraying. They are "getting above their raising," as they say in eastern Kentucky. Although university professors may hope, as do many of their students, that those students will remain at home to the enrichment of the area, educators must prepare them for Ohio. In doing so, they must introduce students to values alien to their upbringing and insist while students are in their midst that they adhere, at least to a certain extent, to alien mores and patterns of communication.

Faculty members serving Appalachian students, of course, have a great deal of leeway in regard to how much they support regional culture or how much they insist on its rejection. Faculty vary greatly in how sensitive they are to regional culture and how much they value it. Some, such as social work faculty, are trained to be culturally sensitive. Others have no education whatsoever in this area. To the sensitive faculty member, the dilemma is obvious: If our students are to be successful by late 20th- and 21st-century American standards, they must give up something of what they value. To eastern Kentuckians, the demand that they give up something of their culture in order to earn a living is not a new one, even for those who stay at home. Many of them, while part of a rural world, are also part of industrial Appalachia. Their families have been making compromises to earn a living for a long time. The world of higher education brings its own demands that they do so.

EXPLORING STUDENT PERCEPTIONS

With two colleagues, I explored the issue of faculty-Appalachian student culture clash in 1997 at the annual spring institute on instruction at Hazard Community College, which brings together faculty of Appalachian Kentucky institutions of higher learning to explore common issues. As part of that undertaking, I asked undergraduate social work students some questions and found their answers interesting enough that I decided to question a broader range of students. For the present study, I included graduate students in a social work master's degree program of the University of Kentucky offered at Morehead State University as well as two new groups of sophomores and seniors. In expanding to graduate students, I was interested in exploring whether cultural issues and concerns remained the same over the education process or shifted. Participating in the more recent study groups were 19 sophomores, 14 seniors, and 25 graduate students. Students in all three educational groups were about equally divided between students of traditional college age and older students, often in their forties.

Almost all the students in the study had grown up and still lived in eastern Kentucky or the contiguous mountainous regions of West Virginia and Ohio. Exceptions were some students who grew up in the neighboring Bluegrass region, a few who grew up in the Cincinnati urban sprawl, and an interesting few who had grown up at military posts around the country and the world and who, with one exception, defined their culture more broadly than did their peers.

All students were asked to respond in writing, anonymously and without consultation with each other, to two questions: "Do you think the faculty value your culture?" and "In what area(s), if any, do you experience cultural conflict between faculty and students?" Most were also asked to respond to a third question: "How do you define your culture?" They were asked additional questions about their age and where they had grown up.

The substantive questions were deliberately vague. No mention was made of Appalachian, mountain, or eastern Kentucky culture, leaving students free to specify their own cultural milieu. With few exceptions, however, in both the 1997 and the 1998 samples, students assumed that they were being questioned about the relationship of faculty to eastern Kentucky mountain culture, and they themselves saw that as their culture. Culture for them clearly was defined by *place*. This finding is not surprising, given that eastern Kentuckians are self-conscious about their supposed differences from other Americans and even other Kentuckians.

Some examples from sophomores of how they defined their culture:

> I feel that my culture is related to living in eastern Kentucky my whole life. Like any other area, people from eastern Kentucky have their own set of values, morals, etc. [a 20-year-old southeastern Kentuckian from the coal field area]

> My culture is the place in which I grew up. Culture to me is my beliefs and ways due to the place where I grew up. [another southeastern Kentucky 20-year-old from the coal fields]

> I view my culture as being that of where I came from, my race, religion, *language* [italics in original], and beliefs. I feel that it is the area in which I gained my beliefs and knowledge. [another 20-year-old from the same region]

Interestingly, three of 19 sophomores specifically mentioned language or accent as part of what defined culture for them. Two of the three were of traditional student age, but a third was in her late forties. I have thought about this finding and think that it likely reflects the pressure that Appalachian students who have recently embarked on higher education feel to bring their spoken and written language into conformity with that of the larger world. This is a serious cultural issue for them, because to abandon traditional speech patterns is to be seen as "putting on airs" and distances them from the people of their home communities. Additional complexity is added to the issue by the fact that for social work students who intend to remain and work in their home communities, it is not necessarily wise to abandon traditional speech. I urge my own students to develop the ability to talk more than one way, to be colloquial when it will be appreciated and to be formally correct in their speech when that seems more appropriate.

Seniors joined sophomores in defining their culture by place, but they tended to be much more thoughtful and introspective about it:

> Backward, outspoken . . . very threatened by outsiders that seem to look down on hillbillies.

> My culture is complicated, complex and paradoxical. Coming from Southeastern Kentucky, I find myself attempting to be laid back, trying to take it easy, whereas my professors are saying speed up the pace. This causes great frustration in an attempt to achieve goals that are more rapid paced.

Graduate students, who were no doubt influenced by the fact that all of those questioned were currently enrolled in a cultural diversity course, tended to see culture in more complex terms while also seeing themselves as Appalachian:

> Appalachian, rural, Christian, heterosexual, conservative, white, rural, law-abiding.

> Appalachian woman—strong attachment to the land, family ties, liberal perspective, traditional values.

Some of them also showed a strong awareness of negative outside views of Appalachian culture and had come to terms with their perception of how they were viewed. For example:

> Appalachian and proud of it. Many refer to Appalachians as "hillbillies." Well, if so, that's me.

> Appalachian culture, but not necessarily as outsiders see it, but rather as a family person who has found my own way regardless of what other family siblings think.

Thus, students came to view culture in increasingly complex and individual ways as they proceeded through social work education, but the sense of place—that place being Appalachia—did not leave them.

What did students have to say about whether professors valued their culture? Among the three sophomores with a broad view of their culture that resulted from living around the world and who had no strong Appalachian perspective on it, none reported conflict with their professors. Three students who viewed their culture in an Appalachian context also reported no conflict. Four other students felt that most professors valued their culture, but they could name some exceptions, who did not particularly bother them. However, nine of 19 sophomores, almost one-half of the sophomore group, including both traditional and older students, had some strong negative feelings about faculty valuation of their culture. Some comments from students with negative feelings included the following:

> On the whole I don't think faculty value our culture. I've even had teachers act as if they were better because of where they originated.

> I have experienced negative stereotyping from faculty.

> Many faculty see Eastern Kentucky origins as a disability. Some professors make negative remarks about the area. Some professors compare our educational backgrounds negatively to other places.

Three comments that specifically included speech as an aspect of cultural conflict were the following:

> Many professors see a southeastern Kentucky accent as indicating that a person is not as smart as other students.

> I have heard many students say that they don't participate in class discussions because of previous experiences. I'm currently taking a voice and articulation class to lose my dialect so I'm never placed in that situation again.

> No, my Eastern Kentucky accent lives a hard life. When asked to talk in class I am very uncomfortable because I am afraid they will make fun of me.

I have presented all three remarks about speech because I found them particularly interesting. I learned something from these remarks about why it is so difficult to get my sophomores to talk in class. It is clear that these sophomores perceive that some professors view them, as well as their culture, as inferior and unworthy.

Although sophomores were angry at perceived mistreatment based on culture, seniors were more thoughtful and analytic about faculty failings. Some comments of seniors:

> I think about half of the faculty value my culture. Some faculty who are from different areas don't get in touch with our culture. . . . It is essential for faculty to value our culture because our culture is just as important to us as our education.

> Eastern Kentucky people are considered by a lot of people as being dumb and some professors also believe this.

Speaking thoughtfully of a particular faculty member seen as not valuing the culture:

> In our culture we tend to be defensive and maybe we are looking at his observations as insults when, in fact, they may be just observations.

Seniors singled out particular professors as respectful or disrespectful of their culture, rather than lump faculty together. They generally thought that most faculty members were respectful of their culture but that some were not. They could be quite angry at particular professors over this issue, but were not nearly as angry as sophomores about cultural issues in general.

SUMMARY

If seniors were significantly less angry and more thoughtful about cultural issues than sophomores, graduate students seemed to have come to some terms with cultural issues. They saw their professors as valuing their culture and supportive of it. Their professors were, of course, social work professors, people trained in cultural sensitivity. Among sophomores, there was a contrasting of social work faculty with professors in some other disciplines, in whom students did not find equivalent sensitivity. Graduate students with social workers as their entire faculty reported positive student–faculty alignment. As one student said, "Faculty have the responsibility of equality, professionalism, and sense of diversity. They are more aware than students give them credit for. Cultural sensitivity is very common and encouraged." Social work faculty would, of course, be expected to be culturally sensitive, coming as they do from a profession that values cultural sensitivity highly.

Although Appalachian social work students appear to come to terms with their culture and to be less bothered by its detractors as their education progresses and they mature as students, we should note that among students at the undergraduate level, some strong feelings were expressed, indicating that many faculty are perceived by their students as sharing in the larger culture's bias toward southern mountain "hillbillies." About one-half of the responding students saw the faculty's relationship to their culture as a "mixed bag," with some faculty viewed as quite culturally sensitive and others not. A number of students made a distinction between university departments in talking about faculty appreciation of their culture.

This survey and its predecessor indicate that some Appalachian students in a geographical area that has experienced considerable exploitation have an uneasy relationship with the faculty who teach them because of a perception of cultural contempt on the part of some faculty. Social work students perceive social work faculty—faculty trained in diversity issues—as more accepting of their culture than faculty from some other disciplines. Training in cultural sensitivity might be valuable for all faculty working in a culturally sensitive rural area such as eastern Kentucky, if faculty are to play a positive role in strengthening rural community and preserving its cultural continuity. Awareness of the history of such an area and, in the case of Appalachia, its long, uneasy relationship with the larger society could also be valuable.

REFERENCES

Bryant, F. C. (1981). *We're all kin: A cultural study of a mountain neighborhood.* Knoxville: University of Tennessee Press.

Bryson, B. (1998). *A walk in the woods: Rediscovering America on the Appalachian trail.* New York: Broadway.

Geertz, C. (1973). *The interpretation of cultures.* New York: Basic Books.

Halperin, R. H. (1990). *The livelihood of kin: Making ends meet "the Kentucky way."* Austin: University of Texas Press.

Holbrook, C. (1995). *Hell and Ohio: Stories of southern Appalachia.* Frankfort, KY: Gnomen.

Hsiung, D. C. (1997). *Two worlds in the Tennessee mountains: Exploring the origins of Appalachian stereotypes.* Lexington: University Press of Kentucky.

Hsiung, D. C. (1998). "Seeing" early Appalachian communities through the lenses of history, geography, and sociology. In D. C. Crass, S. D. Smith, M. A. Zierden, & R. D. Brooks (Eds.), *The southern colonial backcountry: Interdisciplinary perspectives on frontier communities* (pp. 162–181). Knoxville: University of Tennessee Press.

Salstrom, P. (1994). *Appalachia's path to dependency: Rethinking a region's economic history, 1730–1940.* Lexington: University Press of Kentucky.

Schwarzweller, H. K., Brown, J. S., & Mangalam, J. J. (1971). *Mountain families in transition: A case study of Appalachian migration.* University Park: Pennsylvania State University Press.

Shapiro, H. D. (1978). *Appalachia on our mind: The southern mountains and mountaineers in the American consciousness, 1870–1920.* Chapel Hill: University of North Carolina Press.

Waller, A. L. (1988). *Feud: Hatfields, McCoys, and social change in Appalachia, 1860–1900.* Chapel Hill: University of North Carolina Press.

Waller, A. L. (1995). Feuding in Appalachia: Evolution of a cultural stereotype. In M. B. Pudup, D. B. Billings, & A. L. Waller (Eds.), *Appalachia in the making: The mountain south in the nineteenth century* (pp. 347–376). Chapel Hill: University of North Carolina Press.

Websdale, N. (1998). *Rural woman battering and the justice system: An ethnography.* Thousand Oaks, CA: Sage.

CHAPTER TWENTY-FIVE

Attracting and Retaining Professionals for Social Work Practice in Rural Areas: An Example from East Texas

Michael Daley and Freddie Avant

One of the most critical needs that must be met in order to deliver social work services effectively in small towns and rural communities is to alleviate the shortage of professionally qualified people to provide those services. It has often been noted that one of the most salient characteristics of social work practice in small towns and rural communities is the scarcity of services needed to serve clients (Barker, 1995; Ginsberg, 1993; Southern Regional Education Board, 1993). A significant factor that has contributed to this service shortage is the lack of an adequate number of professionals to deliver these services. As Weber (1980) indicated, the number of professional social workers who live and work in rural areas is clearly inadequate to meet the needs of the one-third of the population who call rural America home. Yet, whereas the issue of service shortage has been given considerable attention, the scarcity of professionals to deliver these services has been given relatively little.

Currently many small towns and rural communities are faced with a shortage of social welfare services to meet the needs of their communities, and the services that do exist are further diminished by the lack of professional training of the service delivery staff (Ginsberg, 1993; NASW, 1994). Rural service agencies often are forced to use higher proportions of baccalaureate-level and nonprofessional staff than is typical in nonrural areas (Johnson, 1980), and it is common for workers to be isolated from direct professional supervision.

An important issue for delivering social welfare services in rural areas is thus the development and retention of more professionally qualified social work staff to provide and administer these services. This chapter discusses development and retention issues for professional social workers within a rural region of East Texas, where the active involvement of a school of social work has had a positive effect on the development of professional social work in the service delivery community. The chapter uses data on the social work labor force over a 10-year period to illustrate changes that have occurred in the region. Hopefully, the development and retention strategies discussed can prove useful to other rural regions of the country in strengthening their social welfare services delivery systems.

DEVELOPING A PROFESSIONAL SOCIAL WORK
LABOR FORCE IN RURAL AMERICA

Social work scholars, agency administrators, and community representatives have known for some time that rural areas face a serious shortage of professionally educated workers to deliver services to their communities. The structural factors that produce this shortage are complex, and interventions to remedy the problem are likely to be neither easy nor quick.

To develop a labor force that is adequate to their needs, small towns and rural communities must first address the problems inherent in the educational system that produces professional social workers. Historically, social work has developed from urban roots and has paid relatively little attention to the issues and concerns related to rural populations (NASW, 1994). Most social workers receive little information on rural social work as a part of their professional education.

The general lack of preparation in rural content in social work educational programs creates a major barrier for rural communities across the nation in developing the professional social work labor force needed to address social problems. It is difficult to attract workers who lack knowledge of the rural environment and lifestyle and equally difficult to keep them. It is even more difficult to attract and retain workers with advanced education. Most authors agree that generalist preparation is the best approach for rural practice (Daley & Avant, 1996a, 1996b; Davenport & Davenport 1995; Ginsberg, 1976), yet the specialized nature of most advanced content at the graduate level tends to force students away from this approach.

To increase the number and percentage of professional social workers, rural communities have two options: recruit workers from outside the region or "home grow" them. The former has been attempted in many rural areas for a number of years but with limited success. Social workers who have limited knowledge of rural communities and rural lifestyles are unlikely to find living and working in a rural area attractive. Although some people view rural communities as idyllic, many others may view those communities as dark, foreboding places (Davenport & Davenport, 1995) or as dull and uninteresting.

Ginsberg (1993) identified several positive aspects of working in rural communities that may serve to attract social workers to rural communities. The positive aspects include independence, rapid advancement, tangible results, personal rewards, and recognition. Yet, even if the rural community is successful in recruiting social workers, it may have difficulty in retaining them. If the social worker is unprepared for the demands of rural practice and is not able to learn about what makes rural practice different, the worker will have difficulty finding acceptance and success. Specifically, authors such as Davenport and Davenport (1995), Farley, Griffiths, Skidmore, and Thackeray (1982), Ginsberg (1976), and Martinez-Brawley (1990) referred to the rural practice environment as one in which social workers work in a much more informal context than in urban areas and must be more concerned with horizontal relationships within the community than with vertical relationships outside the community. Home-grown and other rural social workers may be lost because they are forced to relocate to urban areas to seek the opportunity provided by advanced education.

In many ways, the home-grown approach offers many advantages to that of outside recruitment. Several authors speak to the need to educate social workers specifically for rural practice in order to make them more effective (Ginsberg, 1993; Locke, 1991; Zlotnik, 1998). Social workers who receive training in rural social work are more likely to want to work in that environment, should be more successful, and should be more likely to stay.

The traditional objection to the home-grown approach has been the small number of social work educational programs in rural areas. With recent increases in the number of BSW and MSW programs, however, many more rural communities have university-based professional education as a resource. Unfortunately, the development of rural social work curricula has lagged far behind the development of new programs. Just because educational programs are located in rural communities does not mean that the programs prepare their graduates for rural practice. Programs located in rural communities must develop strong rural social work content to prepare their graduates for rural practice.

The question arises, What kind of organization should take the lead in developing a strong professional social work labor force in rural communities? University-based social work education programs can play an important role in this development. Weber (1980) stated that "providing and preparing social work manpower for practice in rural social systems is the responsibility of social work education." Zlotnik (1998) stressed the importance of university–community partnerships as a means of addressing the needs of service delivery agencies. Universities, especially schools of social work, should position themselves to be able to affect the personnel employed in rural communities, a strategy that is particularly important for educational programs located in rural areas. Social work education should take the lead in developing social workers who are well prepared for rural practice, because local agencies and service providers in rural communities are often too isolated and overwhelmed with service demands to be able to effectively address their social work staffing needs in a comprehensive way.

SOCIAL WORK AND SOCIAL WELFARE SERVICES IN RURAL EAST TEXAS

The university housing the school of social work is a regional, state-supported institution located in East Texas and which has a student body of approximately 12,000 students. It is in a small town of about 30,000 and has a service area of 36 rural Texas counties, which border the neighboring states of Arkansas, Louisiana, and Oklahoma.

Based on U.S. Census data, this service region has approximately 1.5 million residents living in an area of 28,227 square miles, an area roughly the size of the state of West Virginia with a slightly smaller population. The region averages only 50.2 residents per square mile versus 65.6 for the state of Texas; it includes four counties classified as metropolitan, but there are only two cities with populations greater than 50,000.

The East Texas region is geographically isolated from surrounding urban areas. Most of the population of the area lives more than 100 miles from an urban community, and transportation is a significant issue. The region has a limited number of bus, rail, and airline connections and virtually no mass transit. The primary mode of transportation is the private automobile. The primary racial groups in the region are white, 78 percent; African American, 17 percent; and Hispanic, 4 percent. Approximately 25 percent of the population for the region is over age 55, versus only 17 percent statewide.

From a social welfare perspective, the region is somewhat typical of many rural areas. The region has high poverty and unemployment rates, a shortage of low-income housing, little diversity in the economy, and limited health care and mental health resources. Services to meet these needs are both limited and scattered. Often physical distance and lack of transportation make inaccessible the services that do exist.

The region has a high poverty rate, particularly for racial and ethnic minorities; rates vary from a high of 28 percent to a low of 17 percent, and almost 40 percent of the African Americans live in poverty. The average income for those who work is less per capita than the state average. Almost 80 percent of the counties have unemployment rates higher than the state average, and most of them have only one or two major industries. Nearly half of the counties in the region have no state employment office, and unemployment recipients take three to five weeks longer than average to find a job. A shortage of low-income housing exists, and large numbers of people wait two years or more for public housing. Regional educational levels are below the state average.

Serious medical deficiencies exist in the region. For every county in the area, at least part of the population is considered medically underserved. For example, women in many East Texas counties do not receive any early prenatal care. This lack, coupled with the high teen pregnancy rate, contributes to the region having one of the highest percentages of low birthweight babies and the highest infant mortality rate in the state.

Mental health services fare no better. Seven of the 36 counties have no services at all delivered within the county. Three of the regional mental health authorities in the area have the longest waiting periods for services in the state.

Access to services is a serious problem, one that is caused by the geography of the region. The agencies tend to maintain offices only in the larger communities. Some, such as children's protective services, extend services into the rural areas through workers who periodically visit the smaller communities. The more rural areas in the region, however, often do not receive the same level of service as the larger towns.

REGIONAL SHORTAGE OF PROFESSIONAL SOCIAL WORKERS

The East Texas region has fewer social workers per capita than many other regions of the state with similar populations. Additionally, the East Texas region has low numbers of MSW social workers and high percentages of both BSWs and nonprofessional "social workers" compared with other regions in the state. The smaller number of social workers, the general level of professional education for those social workers, and the low population density limit not only the availability but also the quantity and quality of social welfare services available to residents of the region.

Data from the Texas State Board of Social Worker Examiners (personal communication with a representative from the Texas State Board of Social Worker Examiners, June 1998) comparing East Texas and another Texas region of similar population may help illustrate the shortage of professional social workers in East Texas. Everyone engaged in the practice of social work in Texas is required to obtain a license based on categories that correspond to the educational qualifications of the social worker.

A small amount of error exists in the actual numbers reported because of previous grandfathering provisions in the law, but currently the correspondence between licensing category and social work degree is quite high. Based on Texas State Board of Social Worker Examiners data (personal communication with a representative from the Texas State Board of Social Worker Examiners, June 1998), 693 social workers were licensed in the East Texas region in 1992. Of these, 398 (57.4 percent) were licensed in the BSW category, and 295 (42.6 percent) were licensed in one of the MSW categories. Moreover, 38 percent of the counties in the region have two or fewer MSW-level social workers to serve the entire county. Of real concern are the 237 social service providers licensed in the nonprofessional category, who are delivering social services and who do not have social work degrees.

The Dallas region, as identified by the Texas State Board of Social Worker Examiners (personal communication with a representative from the Texas State Board of Social Worker Examiners, June 1998), was used for comparison because it has a similar population and offers the contrast of a large urban community. The Dallas region (which includes the city of Dallas) has a population slightly larger than that of East Texas (1.8 million) but has almost three times as many licensed social workers. In the Dallas region, only 25 percent of the social workers are licensed at the BSW level, and 75 percent are licensed at the MSW level; only 115 social service providers are licensed in the nonprofessional category. The region is only about 10 percent of the size of the East Texas region, and Dallas County, where the bulk of that region's population is located, covers only 880 square miles.

Thus, rural East Texas has only about one-third the number of social workers that the Dallas region has to serve a population of similar size. In Dallas, 75 percent of the social workers have advanced education, whereas the percentage for East Texas is only 43 percent. Furthermore, in East Texas more than one-third of the social workers are associate social workers; they have no education in social work, and few professional social workers are there to supervise them. Comparisons between other rural regions and urban areas in Texas reveal similar shortages of social work professionals.

What effect does this professional shortage have on services? Consider the case of children's protective services in East Texas. In 1992, In the southern half of this region, of 121 social workers, 16.6 percent of the workers and none of the supervisors had a professional degree in social work; none had an MSW.

Undoubtedly, the shortage of professional social workers in the region is a result of the relative scarcity of resources for professional education. Within the region are only two institutions that offer the BSW through programs accredited by the Council on Social Work Education. The enrollment in each of those programs was relatively small until recently. Before 1990 both programs combined did not exceed 41 BSW graduates per year.

One of the institutions has new MSW program that has just entered candidacy, but otherwise the geographic location of MSW programs outside the region is such that access to the programs for area residents is difficult without relocating. In contrast, the Dallas region has four BSW programs, a large MSW program, and a doctoral program in social work that are all in close proximity to each other.

The question arises, What can be done to address this shortage of professional social workers that is all too common for rural areas? The following pages discuss the interventions by an East Texas school of social work and the outcomes that relate to social work labor force development in that region.

WORK FORCE INTERVENTIONS

Social work program "S" in the region was actively involved in the development of the region's labor force. (This is not to suggest that the other program in the region was not involved in some development, only that the data reported here are for just one of the two education programs.) Program S is located in the southern half of the East Texas region, and from 1988 to 1998, it produced approximately 74.5 percent of the BSW graduates for this region (611 students). The other social work program is located more than 150 miles away and is in the northern part of the region. The most obvious contribution for Program S to the region is the production of professionally educated social workers. Additionally, the graduates from Program S tend to become employed in rural settings.

In a 1994 survey of graduates from the program, it was determined that 88.6 percent of the program's graduates were employed in social work. Detailed data are not available on the specific location where the graduates were employed, but about 60 percent reported that they worked in communities with a population of less than 50,000. A comparison of the graduation rates of both programs with the number of licensed BSWs in the region reveals that the increase in the number of BSWs in the labor force over the past five years is equivalent to 40 percent of the number of graduates. Taking into account that some BSWs are probably taking positions as replacements for social workers who have retired, moved out of the area, or left social work, a conservative estimate would be that 50 to 55 percent of the BSW graduates remain in the region.

Another way in which Program S has been involved in professionalizing the social welfare labor force is through active job development. As is frequently the case in rural areas, social welfare agencies in East Texas employ large numbers of non-professionals in service delivery agencies. In those agencies it is quite common for the administrators or staff to resent BSWs and to resist hiring them, thus creating a difficult environment for professionalizing the labor force.

A common characteristic of rural communities is that people tend to be identified in terms of who they are, as opposed to what they are (Davenport & Davenport, 1995). Thus, professionals gain acceptance and credibility from what people know about them, rather than from their qualifications. Social work professionals who are new to the community find difficulty in securing employment. In addition, it is common for agency staff who have developed their knowledge base from on-the-job experience to resent and to discount the BSW, who in their view only has academic experience or "book learning."

Program S has effectively used selective field-instruction placements to overcome much of this resistance. As a result of those interventions, more and a wider range of positions are open to professional social workers in the area. For example, school social work was virtually nonexistent in the region five years ago, and most districts were reluctant to hire a social worker for any kind of student services position. Program S then worked to develop field-instruction placements within two local school districts. When the placements were developed, strong students with a clear interest in school social work were placed in the districts, and Program S provided supportive supervision. Several districts in the area now employ a social worker, and one is close to developing a social work department. This type of endeavor has worked effectively in several service delivery agencies.

Yet another way in which Program S has helped develop the professional labor force is by serving as a central point of contact for job information. The nature of rural areas is such that agencies are widely dispersed and rarely have a large labor pool from which to draw. Thus, finding qualified applicants for positions is difficult and time consuming. A university-based social work program is an attractive point of contact because it offers both a central location and a high concentration of potentially qualified applicants. What is essential on the program's part is that it maintains close contacts and good working relationships with the agencies so that they are knowledgeable about and comfortable with contacting the program to discuss their needs. A good working relationship between the university and the community can be developed through a strong field-instruction program.

CHANGES IN THE REGIONAL WORK FORCE

One way to illustrate the changes this activity has produced is to examine data for the social work labor force in East Texas. Data from the Texas State Board of Social Worker examiners (personal communication with a representative from the Texas

State Board of Social Worker Examiners, June 1998) was collected for the 10-year period 1988 to 1998. Because everyone who practices under the title "social worker" is required to obtain a state license, this data is the best available on social workers in the region.

In 1988 Texas required social workers to be certified rather than licensed, but in 1993 the state requirement changed from certification to licensing. Fortunately, the levels of certification/licensure and the categories for licensure did not change in the shift from certification to licensing. Thus the data from 1988 to 1998 are comparable. Important changes did occur between 1988 and 1993, however, which should be kept in mind when interpreting this data.

In 1988 Texas had only recently adopted a competency examination for obtaining a certificate *or* license. In addition, in 1988 Texas did not require that an applicant have a professional degree in social work to qualify for certification or licensure at either the bachelor's or master's level. Many people could become licensed in those categories with a related degree and experience. Thus, the pool of social workers in 1988 included much higher percentages of nonprofessional social workers than in later years. By 1993, the state laws and regulations had changed to require a professional degree in social work from a CSWE-accredited program in order to obtain a license.

To simplify the presentation of data, the numbers of social workers by category for the East Texas region are reported at five-year intervals. Because of the consistent trends within each category, the intervals accurately reflect the changes in the social work labor force in the region. Additionally, five-year increments avoid the idiosyncrasies of annual changes.

The licensing categories reported by the state are those in current use. The SWA stands for Social Work Associate and is a preprofessional category. It requires either an associate or bachelor's degree that is not in social work and requires additional experience. The LSW is the first professional category. It stands for Licensed Social Worker and requires a BSW from a CSWE-accredited program. The LMSW stands for Licensed Masters Social Worker and requires an MSW from a CSWE-accredited program. AP (advanced practice) and ACP (advanced clinical practice) are advanced categories; both require the LMSW as well as two years of additional experience with approved supervision. All categories require applicants to pass a competency examination.

Table 25-1 reports data on the number of certified/licensed social workers in the East Texas region and shows that the greatest increase in the number of social workers was in the bachelor's-level LSW category. In fact, increases in this category over the 10-year period far exceed the increases for all other categories combined (320 versus 208).

Since 1988 the percentage of BSWs in the region's social work labor force has gone from 32 percent to 49 percent, while the percentage of MSWs (LMSWs, APs, and ACPs combined) has gone from 47 percent to 28 percent; the percentage of preprofessional SWAs has remained fairly constant at between 20 and 22 percent. Perhaps more striking is the fact that growth in the LSW (BSW) category accounts for 61 percent of the total increase in social workers in the region for the 10-year pe-

Table 25-1

Certified/licensed social workers in the East Texas region, 1988, 1993, and 1998

	1988	1993	1998
SWA	73	166	202
LSW	117	234	437
LMSW	70	92	124
AP	20	21	20
ACP	84	106	109

riod. This data clearly indicates that the region has experienced significant growth in the number of social workers, but primarily in the number and percentage of BSW social workers.

The explanation for this growth is fairly straightforward because the region has two institutions producing BSW graduates and, until very recently, no MSW programs. Between 1988 and 1993, the growth of LSWs in the region occurred at a rate equivalent to 27.6 percent of the graduates of both BSW programs. From 1983 to 1998, this growth rate jumped to the equivalent of 40.4 percent of the graduates of those programs. This increase in the percentage of BSWs relative to graduates within the region may be a result of an increased acceptance of the value of professional social work that occurred within this rural area.

Although specific data are not available, it appears that a large percentage of the region's BSW graduates remain in the region. In addition to expanding the number of BSWs, many of the graduates undoubtedly replaced social workers that retired or left the profession. Thus, it appears that the two BSW programs within the region are the primary sources for providing social workers for the region's labor force.

The comparison of the BSW and MSW data suggests that the practice wisdom of many agency administrators in the area is correct. They state that it is difficult to attract social workers from outside the region and believe that the few professionals who leave the region to get advanced professional education seldom return. In short, home-grown social workers are the only answer to meeting the needs of the region's service agencies.

SUMMARY AND CONCLUSIONS

Small towns and rural communities are faced with serious shortages of professionally educated social workers to deliver vital social welfare services. Given that services are both scattered and in short supply in most rural areas, this shortage of trained personnel makes it even more difficult for rural agencies to meet the needs of their communities. Rural service agencies face great difficulty in recruiting and retaining social workers and cannot solve the problem alone. The assistance of social work education is needed.

Social work education programs have an excellent opportunity to assist rural America in meeting the need for professional social workers. Many observers would add that meeting this need is not only an opportunity but also a responsibility. Through educational programs that focus on generalist practice, which is particularly well suited for rural social work, graduates will be better prepared to be successful in rural communities. Social work programs, however, must also prepare their graduates with course content in rural communities and lifestyles to help them better adapt to and work in rural communities and with rural people.

Recent developments in social work education offer hope for the development of additional rural social work professionals. The growth in the number of both BSW and MSW programs gives rural America better access to this valuable resource of trained professionals. Moreover, the Council on Social Work Education standards that require the teaching of the generalist method in the professional foundation give graduates the appropriate preparation for rural practice.

Although these developments are encouraging, they are not sufficient. Too few programs prepare their graduates for rural practice at either the BSW or MSW level. BSW programs, especially those located in rural areas, should offer preparation for rural practice, but all too frequently this preparation is either omitted or is not adequate. At the MSW level, students receive preparation for generalist practice in the foundation year but rarely receive any advanced rural content. The number of MSW programs that provide either advanced generalist or rural preparation for practice is still quite small.

The preparation of social workers for rural practice represents one of the great challenges that social work education faces in the 21st century. With strong curriculum development in the areas of rural social work, rural behavior and environments, generalist practice, and advanced generalist practice, social work education can effectively address this important unmet need. In addition, educational programs should be actively involved in the rural community in terms of job development and in working collaboratively with agencies to help them to employ professional social workers.

This chapter has provided data that suggest social work education can make a difference in terms of meeting the need for rural social workers. Although the result from one program's experience is promising, more data are needed. Hopefully, other social work programs will explore how they can address this need and enrich our knowledge base in this area. Perhaps we will then be able meet this important challenge.

REFERENCES

Barker, R. L. (1995). *The social work dictionary* (3rd ed.). Washington, DC: NASW Press.

Daley, M. R., & Avant, F. L. (1996a, August). *Reconceptualizing rural social work practice.* Paper presented at the 21st National Institute on Social Work and the Human Services in Rural Areas, Kalamazoo, MI.

Daley, M. R., & Avant, F. L. (1996b, November). *Reconceptualizing rural social work practice.* Paper presented at the NASW Meeting of the Profession, Cleveland, OH.

Davenport, J. A., & Davenport, J. (1995). *Rural social work overview.* In R. L. Edwards (Ed.-in-Chief), *Encyclopedia of social work* (19th ed., Vol. 3, pp. 2076–2085). Washington, DC: NASW Press.

Farley, W. C., Griffiths, K. A., Skidmore, R. A., & Thackeray, M. G. (1982). *Rural social work practice.* New York: Free Press.

Ginsberg, L. (1976). An overview of social work education for rural areas. In L. Ginsberg (Ed.), *Social work in rural communities: A book of readings* (pp. 1–12). New York: Council on Social Work Education.

Ginsberg, L. (1993). An overview of social work education for rural areas. In L. Ginsberg (Ed.), *Social work in rural communities: A book of readings* (2nd ed., pp. 1–17). Alexandria, VA: Council on Social Work Education.

Johnson, L. C. (1980). Human service delivery patterns in nonmetropolitan communities. In H. W. Johnson (Ed.), *Rural human services* (p. 69). Itasca, IL: Peacock Publishers.

Locke, B. L. (1991). Research and social work in rural areas: Are we asking the right questions? *Human Services in the Rural Environment, 15*(2), 13.

Martinez-Brawley, E. E. (1990). *Perspectives on the small community.* Silver Spring, MD: NASW Press.

National Association of Social Workers. (1994). Social work in rural areas. In *Social work speaks* (pp. 244–248). Washington, DC: Author.

Southern Regional Education Board, Rural Task Force Manpower Education and Training Project. (1993). Education assumptions for rural social work. In L. Ginsberg (Ed.), *Social work in rural communities: A book of readings* (2nd ed., pp. 18–21). Alexandria, VA: Council on Social Work Education.

Weber, G. K. (1980). Preparing social workers for practice in rural social systems. In H. W. Johnson (Ed.), *Rural human services* (pp. 209–210). Itasca, IL: Peacock Publishers.

Zlotnik, J. (1998). Preparing human service workers for the 21st century: A challenge to professional education. In J. Zlotnik & S. Jones (Eds.), *Preparing helping professionals to meet community needs: Generalizing from the rural experience.* Alexandria, VA: Council on Social Work Education.

CHAPTER TWENTY-SIX

Increasing the Numbers of African American Social Workers in Rural Areas: An Example from Maryland's Eastern Shore

Patricia P. Plaskon and Jay Bishop

Small towns and rural areas often have had difficulty attracting professionally educated social workers, and attracting social workers who are members of minority groups has been even more difficult. Several approaches have been used to attract professional social workers to rural areas, including advertising jobs in metropolitan newspapers, recruiting from urban social work educational programs, and making linkages with rural social work educational programs. In this chapter we report on a rural undergraduate social work education program designed to encourage African American students to practice in the local area.

In recent years, the social work community has become increasingly concerned about ethnic and racial incongruence between clients and staff. The issues include whether clients are comfortable enough with workers of another culture to build therapeutic working relationships and whether interventions are culturally appropriate (Gould, 1995; Gwyn & Kilpatrick, 1981; Latting & Zundel, 1986). Questions are also raised about the factors contributing to the shortage of African American social workers at all levels of the profession, including doctoral programs (LeDoux, 1996) and positions of leadership. Efforts have been made in the 1990s to involve more women and people of color in the profession, especially in supervisory and leadership positions (NASW, 1997a); however, little has been written recently about recruiting and retaining racially and ethnically diverse social workers in rural areas.

A LOCAL APPROACH

Local field agencies and employers on the Eastern Shore (which includes rural parts of Maryland, Delaware, and Virginia) have faced a number of traditional challenges to rural service provision, including a shortage of qualified professionals, geographic distance, social and professional isolation, multiple job demands, and limited funding. Social workers also have encountered personal challenges as a result of a history of racism in the region and local conservative political views that sometimes conflict with social work values. The Salisbury State University (SSU) social work program's professional advisory committee (PAC) was formed at the inception of the social work program to bring together agency representatives to address many of these issues. The committee has met regularly to share problems and solutions regarding field placements, employment issues, agency policies, and funding issues. The university faculty members have been able to offer "expert" advice or technical assistance. Perhaps the most important function of the PAC, however, is the partnership between practitioners and academicians that keeps each group focused on the relevant, practical issues in the local area that are often outside the scope of government agency regulations or Council on Social Work Education (CSWE) standards.

In the mid-1980s the PAC identified a need for more African American social workers in local agencies. The agencies' current employees and applicants were mostly white, and a racial imbalance existed between the staff and the local populations served. The few staff who were African American were more likely to have a high school diploma than a college degree, leaving little room for visibility and advancement. Those who had completed an undergraduate degree usually did not have a bachelor's degree in social work. The African American staff's career options were limited because Maryland law requires a social work degree as a minimum qualification for a social work job.

Workers who had non–social work undergraduate degrees who wanted to get an MSW and advance their careers faced several obstacles. In addition to the distance involved in traveling to graduate school, the cost and time of going to graduate school while working and raising a family were great obstacles. Ineligible for advanced standing, they faced two full years of graduate work at a campus up to three hours away. Some workers would choose a master's degree program in a related field requiring fewer credits at a more convenient location, which would take less time and money in the short term. This approach still limited the number of African American workers able to get licensed and achieve managerial social work positions.

In an effort to recruit more African American students in the BASW program at SSU, where less than 10 percent of the students were African American, the committee approached a nearby historically black university, the University of Maryland Eastern Shore (UMES). The UMES student body was 70 percent black and 30 percent white, Latino, Asian, and of international origin. A substantial number of students were enrolled as sociology majors and were interested in jobs in human services.

PAC representatives and faculty met with the presidents of both universities to make the situation known and suggest ways to allow the students on the UMES campus to enroll in SSU social work classes and earn a social work degree while remaining enrolled at UMES. The advantages included more opportunities for students, an increased pool of well-trained, career-oriented graduates for employers, and increased availability of African American professionals for clients. Political obstacles, such as protections against any loss of tuition or additional costs for either institution, made negotiations delicate. Furthermore, UMES students who were proud of the black heritage of their school would not be eager to leave their school and their identity to become SSU students.

After long negotiations, the chancellor of the University of Maryland system (from which both institutions received state funding) approved the new program (known as the SSU/UMES Dual Degree in Sociology/Social Work). The program was approved by CSWE as an alternative program under the Salisbury State program's accreditation, and a full-time faculty person was hired by UMES as faculty and coordinator for the program. Beginning with six students, enrollment in the dual-degree program has increased steadily to more than 120 students enrolled as of 1998.

The social work dual-degree program became a model for further collaboration between the two campuses; there are now dual-degree programs in biology, environmental/marine science, and engineering and collaborative programs in education, business, and art. A shuttle bus service between campuses and development of a universitywide collaborative coordinating council has enabled more interaction between students and faculty and helped reduce the racial and cultural isolation common in some rural areas. In 1998 SSU and UMES were recognized by the TIAA/CREF Theodore M. Hesburgh Certificate of Excellence for their collaborative efforts. The success of the dual-degree program in social work, however, would ultimately depend on the outcomes of its graduates. Surveys were planned to follow alumni progress in their social work careers and to gain their insights about modifying the program if needed.

LITERATURE REVIEW

Several approaches have been taken to increase diversity in the social work profession. Some attempts have aimed at the recruitment of social workers with certain ethnic and racial backgrounds or gender. Others have addressed multicultural sensitivity. Agencies have developed training to make current (nonminority) workers more culturally sensitive to clients and peers, have increased access to educational and employment opportunities, and have built supports for workers already in the system to ensure more opportunity for retention and promotion of women and people from ethnic and racial groups. Similarly, efforts by universities have included increasing recruitment of students from ethnic and racial groups, hiring more diverse faculty members, including more content on racial and ethnic issues, and pursuing more research on experiences of "nondominant" groups.

Berger (1992) found that at City University of New York, where 70 percent of the students were classified as minority, the two factors that were the most significant in predicting whether students would complete the social work program were their life stage and their previous GPA. Berger found that people between ages of 35 and 44 seemed to have competing family responsibilities and that people with low GPAs were not always able to compensate once they started taking upper-level required courses. These students, therefore, were more likely to drop out of school and forego becoming a social worker. Berger's findings suggest that students may need more creative options for fitting in course work and study time in order to become successful social work graduates.

Several authors have suggested specific steps to assist students of color in becoming successful graduates. Those steps address issues of retention. Hodges and Balassone (1994) created an orientation program for MSW students of color to provide emotional support and information to sustain them through the challenges of graduate school. The key of the program was to foster sustaining relationships with other diverse students, faculty, and practitioners. The goal was for the students to build a level of comfort in their social and academic environments. The authors have warned, however, that because students may have faced isolation and biases, creating a "special" program for students of color can create more stigma and should be planned carefully.

Gitterman (1991) noted that white college instructors need to be more sensitive to the learning styles of African American students and address the racial conflicts and taboos that can otherwise deter African American students from completing a degree once they have matriculated. At most CSWE-accredited schools, African Americans are minorities at predominantly white institutions. Gitterman felt that attention must be given to the needs and comfort level of black students if they will be truly encouraged to complete the program.

To help students learn to be effective social workers, Jayaratne and colleagues (1992) suggested designing curricula on minority issues that would be as relevant for minority students as it was for traditional white students. They point out, for instance, that pat formulas for working with African Americans can themselves be condescending and racist. They advocated for inclusion of all aspects of diversity even before CSWE standards called for an infusion of diversity into social work curricula. Their hope was to make all students more sensitive and effective when working with any client who is from another culture.

Other models for recruiting and retaining diverse and nontraditional students have tried to make college courses more accessible and convenient (Miller, Williams, & Lusk, 1993). Examples of this approach include distance learning, video courses, and courses that can be taken over the Internet. Although their primary focus had not been specifically on recruitment and retention of diverse professionals, the National Health Services Corps and Area Health Education (AHEC) models have been matching professionals in rural areas as preceptors for student professionals. The premise is that because the student will be endeared to the area, and the area endeared to the student, the graduate may return to do practice in a rural area. (He or she may also practice there in return for the training.) Statistics on the outcomes of the approaches specific to social work students from ethnic and racial groups are lacking (personal communication with E. Layman, Eastern Shore Area Health Education Center, University of Maryland, July 14, 1998).

Little has been documented on the direct outcomes of many of these approaches because of the complicated nature of the issues. Women and people from ethnic and racial groups continue to be underrepresented in decision making and administrative positions in the field (NASW, 1997b). In a recent survey of its membership, NASW reported that only 5 percent of its current (active) members were African American (NASW, 1998). Although the membership of the National Association of Black Social Workers seems to be growing, the percentage of African American social workers among rural social workers is difficult to capture and compare with previous years in the literature.

Overall, tracking of students from ethnic and racial groups in social work at the undergraduate level has received less attention than at the graduate level. Statistics on African American social workers in undergraduate programs in rural areas are even scarcer. Yet for many, an opportunity to enter an undergraduate degree program in social work is a crucial factor in choosing social work as a profession and going on to earn an MSW (Berger, 1992).

Even if more African American students were to become social work majors and graduate, the need for racially (and ethnically diverse) social workers in rural areas may not be necessarily resolved. In their closing address to the 20th Annual National Institute on Social Work and Human Services in Rural Areas, Mermelstein and Sundet (1995) pointed out that most graduate schools prepare students for clinical practice, which contrasts with the need for generalists in rural areas who can truly participate in regional and community planning. The survey reported in this chapter is just one step of many needed to study the career tracks of African American social workers in rural areas.

METHOD

The study described here examined the graduation and postgraduation outcomes of African American students who earned a BASW in the dual-degree program. Of interest was whether students remained in the field of social work, whether they found jobs or continued their education at the graduate level, and whether they were working in a rural setting. The graduates were also given an opportunity to give feedback on the program to help refine it for future students.

Surveys were sent to all dual-degree students who graduated between 1992 and 1997 ($N = 44$). Seventeen surveys were returned completed. Through random follow-up telephone interviews, data was gathered from 12 additional respondents for a total response rate of 66 percent.

The survey form requested nominal and Likert-type scale responses to questions and included room for optional comments. Questions were asked about demographic information, such as gender, income, current geographic location, and geographic origin before attending college; employment; attendance at graduate schools; and evaluation of the dual-degree program.

Eighty-three percent of the respondents ($n = 24$) were female, which was representative of the graduates of the program. At the time of the survey, the respondents ranged from age 23 to 40; the average age was 26.7. Fifteen respondents identified themselves as being from a rural area or small town.

FINDINGS

Twenty-two of the respondents were employed full time; the rest were either in graduate school or not employed. Seven females and one male had already completed an MSW program. Four females and one male were currently enrolled in graduate social work programs. All but four of those employed were currently employed in a human service setting. Their reported income levels were spread evenly among categories of earned income ranging from $15,001 to $30,000.

Ten alumni reported that they had been hired for their first social work job upon graduation, whereas 11 were unable to locate a social work job at first. Those who found social work jobs reported that the job search took from one week to four months. Seven of the 11 respondents who stated that their first jobs were not in social work reported that their current jobs were either directly or somewhat related to social work. Six respondents were licensed as social workers, and two others had recently applied.

Although 15 alumni were originally from the Eastern Shore region, only seven reported seeking social work employment in the local area. Of the seven, one did not find employment and moved out of the area; another took a non–social work job in a day care center as a teacher. Five were currently working in social work jobs in the local area.

As for satisfaction with the dual-degree program, little if any criticism was received. Of those who found social work jobs, nine said that the program provided excellent preparation for their job, seven viewed the program as giving good preparation, and one saw it as adequate preparation. All alumni who entered graduate programs responded that the program provided good or excellent preparation.

Alumni who attended the program after the shuttle service between campuses was started commented positively about the convenience of taking courses on either campus. Some also relied on the shuttle as part of their transportation to field placements. However, a number of students who did not have cars thought that additional transportation was needed in order for them to have access to a better variety of quality field placements.

DISCUSSION

The central purpose of the survey was to determine whether the dual-degree program was meeting its mandate to recruit, educate, and retain African American social workers. The results were encouraging in that 18 of the 29 respondents were employed in social work jobs, and 11 had either completed or were enrolled in graduate social work programs. Only seven, however, reported looking for a job in the local area, and only five were actually employed locally. Several respondents commented that the lack of jobs or lack of "good-paying" jobs, graduate programs, and opportunities for socialization with peers influenced their decision to leave the area. Most of these graduates were younger and did not have partners or family obligations to tie them to the area.

Since almost one-half of the students were not originally from a rural area, one cannot assume that all dual-degree students are potential candidates for rural practice. Many students report coming from large cities to attend UMES because of factors such as safety and lower cost compared with other institutions, rather than an affinity for its rural setting.

The alumni made several suggestions on how the program might be strengthened. Surprisingly, only a few of those changes involved curriculum; most would require community efforts. Suggestions were made to facilitate contacts between local African American professionals and the students. Several alumni commented that information on career advancement, mentoring by other professionals, and more speakers, especially African American professionals, in classes or in social work club meetings would be helpful—not only at the college level but beginning at the high school or junior high school level. This approach may lead to more interest among local students to stay and practice in the area.

As for curriculum, additional content on rural practice might increase understanding and interest in practicing in the local area. The local AHEC may be able to assist faculty in finding ways to build appreciation of rural experiences, as it already does so with medical students.

Another suggestion is noteworthy for administrators of BASW programs. Because experience in field placement can favorably or unfavorably influence a student's impression of the area and of the professional community, field experience also may be a key issue in determining a student's pursuit of rural employment upon graduation. Placing African American students in agencies where African American role models are available or where African American students are made to feel especially welcomed and valued for their input is critical.

Even those graduates who wanted to stay in the local area reported having difficulty finding a social work job at first. What is not known is the extent of the current need for African American workers among human service employers. A few graduates did not feel welcome at agencies or with clients, who were mostly white. An updated survey of local agencies may help assess the attitude of the staff and community.

Currently, the PAC is working with the University of Maryland–Baltimore to pilot a part-time MSW program on the Eastern Shore, which would help BASW workers complete a degree locally that would offer them more advancement. It is the committee's hope that the availability of a graduate program will encourage more African American social workers to remain in the area.

SUMMARY

Even if dual-degree alumni leave the area once they graduate, the program provides several benefits to both the students and the local community. Local residents benefit from African American students' involvement in agency field placements and club activities. Clients have the opportunity for more culturally appropriate interventions. Clients who are children benefit from interaction with African American students, who serve as role models and mentors.

Another advantage of the dual-degree program recognized by faculty and students alike is that the predominantly white SSU students gain a better understanding of African American culture. They also have the opportunity to register for classes on the UMES campus, and many have taken a variety of courses there. This has afforded them closer interaction with people from another culture who have similar interests.

In contrast to these benefits, the small number of African Americans who go into rural practice remains an issue worthy of further study. Advocacy for higher pay in rural agencies, the continuing battle against racist perceptions, and the need for more social opportunities for young professionals are issues the faculty, the PAC, and the rural community at large need to address.

As the program continues to develop, racial stereotypes, communication styles, and expectations of students, faculty and administrators, and the public continually need to be addressed. The two campuses are constantly learning how to encourage integration without forcing assimilation of the African American students to the white culture of the SSU campus. The same comfort level must be achieved in the community agencies if graduates are to feel valued and welcomed as new employees. The legacy of UMES as a historically black institution can be celebrated in the community, bringing recognition and appreciation of the community leaders who received their education there.

Finally, at the same time that local employers are recruiting African American workers, a growing Latino population will present new challenges for expanding the diversity among professionals on the Eastern Shore. New programs to address recruitment and retention of Latino and Spanish-speaking social workers can be built on the experience gained from the collaboration of campus and community that has made the dual-degree program successful. The real challenge will be to secure enough resources to serve both communities well rather than place them in competition with each other.

REFERENCES

Berger, R. (1992). Student retention: A critical phase in the academic careers of minority baccalaureate social workers. *Journal of Social Work Education, 28,* 85–97.

Gitterman, A. (1991). Working with difference: White teacher and African American students. *Journal of Teaching in Social Work, 5,* 65–79.

Gould, K. H. (1995). The misconstruing of multiculturalism: The Stanford debate and social work. *Social Work, 40,* 198–205.

Gwyn, F. S., & Kilpatrick, A. C. (1981). Family therapy with low income blacks: Tool or turnoff? *Social Casework, 62,* 259–266.

Hodges, V., & Balassone, M. L. (1994). Planning and implementing a support program for students of color. *Journal of Teaching in Social Work, 9*(1/2), 85–106.

Jayaratne, S., Gant, L. M., Brabson, H. V., Nagda, B. A., Singh, A. K., & Chess, W. A. (1992). Worker perceptions of effectiveness and minority-relevant education as a function of worker and client ethnicity. *Journal of Teaching in Social Work, 6,* 93–116.

Latting, J. E., & Zundel, C. (1986). World view differences between clients and counselors. *Social Casework, 67,* 533–541.

LeDoux, C. (1996). Career patterns of African American and Hispanic social work doctorates and ABDs. *Journal of Social Work Education, 32,* 245–252.

Mermelstein, J., & Sundet, P. A. (1995). Rural social work is an anachronism: The perspective of twenty years of experience and debate. *Human Services in the Rural Environment, 18,* 5–12.

Miller, K. A., Williams, M. S., & Lusk, M. W. (1993). Offering a part time bachelor of social work degree in a rural area: A sixteen year retrospective. *Human Services in the Rural Environment, 17,* 26–31.

National Association of Social Workers. (1998, May). Member survey: Here's looking at you. *NASW News,* 3.

National Association of Social Workers Delegate Assembly. (1997a). Affirmative action policy statement. *Social work speaks* (4th ed.). Washington, DC: NASW Press.

National Association of Social Workers Delegate Assembly. (1997b). Racism policy statement. *Social work speaks* (4th ed.). Washington, DC: NASW Press.

Queralt, M. (1996). *The social environment and human behavior: A diversity perspective* (pp. 259–305). Boston: Allyn & Bacon.

CHAPTER TWENTY-SEVEN

Using Narratives in Educating Social Workers for Rural Practice

Lena Williams Carawan, Lessie L. Bass, and Shelia Grant Bunch

Experience in preparing social work students for practice in small towns and rural areas has convinced us that students can benefit from exposure to a variety of people who live and work in such communities. Belief in the importance of first-person accounts of everyday life and working from the question of how to capture the "lived" experience(s) in a rural community is the foundation of this approach to social work education. Embracing the voice of rural residents by bringing them into the classroom to tell their stories helps students learn to respect other ways of knowing. This approach is based on the premise that each story of rural life comes out of a cultural context which, when recognized and respected, can enhance social work practice in rural communities. In this chapter, we will use the terms "narrative" and "storytelling" interchangeably. (Riessman, 1993, p. 1). As we work with our students, it is our expectation that including narratives as part of the classroom experience will result in our students being better able to assist rural people in social action and community work. "Rural people have the right to expect human service personnel to understand their situations, to design work methods that are attuned to local people" (Collier, 1984, p. 18).

We have been drawn to the use of narratives in our teaching from our own history, our own stories and desires. In collaboration with rural people in our classrooms and in the community, we explore our own past, since we were born in small, rural communities. As professors working in a university situated in a rural area, we reflect on what ruralism has meant for our mothers, fathers, siblings, and our extended families. As Harding (1986) pointed out, people are not simply defined by an ideological construct of what they should be but negotiate conflicting discoveries in the context of their own life activities and desires.

As three female academics who grew up in rural eastern North Carolina, we began to encounter students in our classes who did not appear to recognize or appreciate the richness and diversity of social work practice in rural areas. Administrators of rural social service agencies visiting the rural class often spoke of their frustration at not being able to attract credentialed social workers to their areas. Since relatively few books about rural social work have been published (Collier, 1984), we began inviting rural residents into the classroom to add to the existing knowledge base by telling their stories. We have found that the narratives tell us much about the inner lives of rural people and give us a more contextual picture of what goes on in various small towns and rural communities.

The visit of two women from commercial fishing families, for example, provided one of our richest classroom experiences. Through their narratives, these women greatly expanded classroom knowledge about the work and achievements of commercial fishing families and their current fears of losing their livelihood and culture. These women shared their thoughts, feelings, and experiences in a way with which students were able to immediately identify. The women shared their anger at governing boards that make sweeping decisions about their livelihood but have few, if any, representatives from fishing communities. They said, "We need rules and regulations, but we are against people making decisions who do not understand our industry. Scientific data doesn't take care of families."

The women from fishing families told stories of how they had become socially active and had earlier in the year marched on the state capital in an attempt to influence the legislature's decision making to favor the fishermen. The women told of their fear, not only about loss of income but also about the possibility of losing their way of life. They spoke of growing up in fishing families and marrying fishermen and of their part in what they considered a family business. Although the women were sisters who had grown up in the same family, they had taken different paths in their earlier lives. One married shortly after high school, becoming a stay-at-home wife and mom and later home-schooling her two children. The other graduated from college, then married and began a career. Both women felt that they contributed in a large way to the family business; their contributions ranged from buying boat parts to managing and investing the family money. The women also explained their understanding of what was happening along the North Carolina coast regarding the declining fish population and the sustainability of the region. The students were moved by the strength and emotion that the women brought to the classroom.

When the visitors left, the students spoke with concern and enthusiasm about issues of social justice and action as well as loss of culture. It was enlightening to experience students who wanted to be active in a social cause. In the spirit of advocacy and joining, they spoke of marching with the fishing families to increase public awareness and legislative responsibility.

WHAT IS NARRATIVE?

The term "personal narrative," as used in this chapter, refers to talk organized around consequential events. A teller in a conversation takes a listener into a past time or "world" and recapitulates what happened then to make a point, often a moral one. For our rural social work students, talk is the vehicle for the work, and long stretches of talk take the form of narrative accounts. According to Howard

(1991) and Sullivan (1977), the study of narrative does not fit neatly within the boundaries of any single scholarly field. Narrative is inherently interdisciplinary. As realist assumptions from natural science methods prove limiting for understanding social life, a group of leading U.S. scholars from various disciplines is turning to narrative as the organizing principle for human action (Bruner, 1986; Sarbin, 1986). "Narratives structure perceptual experience, organize memory, and build the very events of a life" (Bruner, 1986, p. 15). Narrative is a recapitulation of every nuance of a moment that has special meaning for the storyteller. Telling stories about past events seems to be a universal human activity, one of the first forms of discourse we learn as children. "So natural is the impulse to narrate that the form is almost inevitable for any report of how things happened, a solution to 'the problem of how to translate *knowing* into *telling*'" (White, 1989).

The narrative/story permits an understanding of how different groups see their world and their community. The key feature guiding cultural studies is the uniqueness of socially constructed meaning. The narrative supports the notion that communities are not rational entities governed by universal laws or truths. Storytelling as an instrument for understanding the dynamics of relationships and community allows for the expansion of the theoretical base of inquiry. Storytelling is not restricted to predetermined hypotheses (Glaser & Strass, 1967). Having rural individuals come to the classroom provides an opportunity for students to critique stereotypical views of what it means to be rural.

Storytelling within a narrative framework may be an opportunity to integrate experiences into personal identity, and the stories families tell may reflect family identity (McAdams, 1989). Miller and Moore (1989) suggested that the family environment is rich in narrative opportunities. The recent work of attachment theorists has shown that the coherence of a parent's narrative may be related to attachment relationships with the child (Crowell & Fellowman, 1991; Main & Goldwyn, 1984). Storytelling and self-narratives organize experience in a way that will fit with the storyteller's understanding of the world (Sarbin, 1986) and identity (McAdams, 1989).

Vitz (1990) suggested that narratives (stories) are a central factor in a person's life development. Others have suggested that narratives and narrative thinking are especially involved in how empathy (Hoffman, 1987), caring and commitment (Gilligan, 1982), interpersonal interaction (Haan, 1985), personal character, and personality (Coles, 1986; Hogan, 1973; Rushton, 1980; Staub, 1979) lead to moral development. Narrative presents concrete human and interpersonal situations in order to demonstrate their particular validity. It is a description of reality, and it is a way of seeing that aims at a fundamental and true value. Narrative is an attempt to depict realism. The following are excerpts of student comments from two different classes:

> Although this diversity class lasted for a short time, my life is richer because I have known the individuals and families that told their stories. Just like the "rabbit" [referring to *The Velveteen Rabbit*], I am learning that becoming "REAL" is a process. Thank you class and presenters for being a part of my process. I shall always remember this class, for you have written your stories on my heart. ("Human Difference" class, 1997)

That was a tremendous learning experience for me. It was first hand [*sic*] knowledge of the area issues and problems. The compassion and dedication from you and all those guest speakers is truly phenomenal. (Student evaluations, "Rural Course," 1997))

The story mode requires imagination, understanding of human intention, and an appreciation of the particulars of time and place. Narratives focus on people and on the causes of their actions, intentions, goals, and subjective experiences. Goal seeking and searching are basic, innate attributions of human mental life. We believe that the narrative can be used as a valuable part of rural social work education. Stories are narratives through which events, sometimes major and other times trivial, become charged with symbolic significance (Gabriel, 1991). Turning facts into stories is a distinctly human activity, as is listening to stories, reconstructing them, embellishing them, and censoring them. Many people have the ability to transform their lives and their experiences easily into stories.

Bringing rural narratives into the classroom helps us build on our current development process of discovering interpersonal dynamics in rural communities and expectations in community environments. Students experience, compare, and contrast skills within the narrative perspective as the rural storytellers reveal the rural community psyche, other community cultures, and subcultures, as the storytellers feel warranted. For example, the students' ability to look through the cultural lens of rural people can assist them in exploring emerging themes in order to interpret and understand the reality of rural life. As themes become visible, questions and considerations may emerge around differences and similarities of communities of similar size located in different regions.

From first-person narratives, we can experience firsthand the conditions of a rural person's life. According to student evaluations, the classroom narratives of rural people add a richness to the learning environment that is invaluable in the learning process. Accounts of rural people's lives, their own memories, the ways they frame their life choices, and the way they are viewed by observers are all issues for discussion in the classroom. Students must be prepared to connect the experiences of clients with the problems that bring them to seek help, such as job training, substance abuse, depression, hunger, housing, or school absence. As teachers, we ask students to consider the conditions under which the rural story is shared, both from a historical perspective and in terms of the dominant issues of the day. We also ask them to consider the relationship between speaker and audience. If Collier (1984/1993) was correct in his belief that the major job for rural workers is interpreting, analyzing, and constructing, then this kind of respect and collaboration can provide a method for future rural work that we believe can play an important role in preserving and strengthening small towns and rural communities.

WHAT IS RURAL?

A review of written material on rural social work includes work from the 1930s to the present. Much of the early work appears judgmental and stereotypical. The books from the 1930s are only helpful insofar as they give a historical perspective of rural social work. As illustrated in the following passage, the material presents and reinforces negative imagery around rural life:

> Both public officials and private citizens have viewed with alarm the large sums of money spent annually by their counties upon dependent families whose conditions appears not to be improved but to be made worse thereby. They see the same families asking for help year after year, receiving the same monthly doles and becoming more and more dependent, their homes dirtier, their children more neglected and often delinquent. (Brown, 1933, p. 4)

Writings about rural social work after the 1930s continue to be specific and descriptive. Much of American writing on rural areas is about farm families in particular and provide little information that actually analyzes rural relationships, behavioristic experiences, and expectations. According to Collier (1984), "In being specific and descriptive, the literature on human services fails to analyze why rural and remote people are the way they are" (pp. 17–18). Whose definition of rural does one use when looking at the literature and considering the concept? Many professionals agree that the definition of rural is more complex than the normative definition of land mass, population, and density.

Of North Carolina's 100 counties, 85 are considered rural, based on the Rural Economic Development Center's definition of rural as county with a population density of less than 200 people per square mile (Department of Agricultural and Research Economics, 1994, p. 4). The U.S. Census Bureau classifies as rural those communities with populations below 2,500. In Canada, however, areas are considered urban when there are 1,000 or more people living in continuously built-up areas and when the population density is at least 400 per square kilometer (Big & Boolean, 1994).

Criteria-based definitions offer a variety of suggestions in describing and explaining what is rural. An important criterion in Ginsberg's (1976) list is a look at rural government. Ginsberg believes that although rural areas' officials may be elected, the local wealthy citizens may have a relatively more powerful influence on what occurs at the local level than in urban areas. He also suggests that rural living is less impersonal than urban living. Ruff (1991) included consideration of the economic base of the rural community Ingerbrigtson (1992), however, perhaps best captured the essence of what to consider when trying to understand a rural community. She listed factors including isolation, poverty, distance, environmental stresses, one-industry towns, differing views about future directions for the area, and high labor turnover.

Rural human service administrators who have visited our classes often speak of the difficulty in recruiting and retaining professionals with social work degrees. Distance becomes a primary transportation issue, with services being clustered in the largest town or county seat. In addition, the lack of available and affordable health care is a major problem confronting rural residents.

A METHOD TO ENHANCE RURAL PRACTICE

In the early 1980s and 1990s, the use of stories as a method of systematic inquiry was viewed as a relatively new discovery (Martin & Powers, 1982). The method that evolved from our classroom experience led us to the use of systematic inquiry, more collaborative teaching, and learning that included working in the direction of gaining a voice for all of the participants. Validation for other ways of knowing, raising levels of consciousness around oppression, and facilitating empowerment were the anticipated outcomes for learning.

Bringing rural community into the classroom through the use of narrative helps social work students use stories as a method of systematic inquiry (Hansen & Kahnweiler, 1993). The use of systematic inquiry helps students develop critical thinking skills in their exploration of the nature of rural life. In *Women's Ways of Knowing: The Development of Self, Voice and Mind* (Belenky, Clinchy, Goldberger, & Tarule, 1986), the authors talk of connected teaching (pp. 214–230) as a more collaborative model of teaching. Their work speaks of allowing students to see the imperfect process of the teacher's thinking (p. 215) and of teachers having the courage to risk gaining a voice (p. 16) for both themselves and their students. The classroom then becomes the place to explore all voices (that is, the voices of the rural community, the students, and the teachers). This approach can be seen in the following student comment about the use of speakers in the rural course:

> Another helpful aspect of this class was the guest speakers. They were able to provide important information related to practice. I also thought that they felt free to truly express their personal feelings and experiences. The ladies from the fishing community provided much information that I had never before thought about. They inspired me to look more closely into the problems of the fishing communities. I also feel that much of the same fervor can be applied to other industries within rural communities such as tobacco farming, and factory work. Many of these families face similar difficulties as those faced by the fishing community. (Student evaluations, "Rural Course," 1997)

It is important that we create a safe place for students to unveil themselves so that learning and collaboration can occur on all systemic levels. The classroom process attempts to model respect, equality, and validation for other ways of knowing.

The examination of culturally diverse rural communities should occur in the social work classroom. As social work instructors, we are always seeking ways to raise levels of consciousness around difference and oppression. Friere (1973) used his form of education (praxis) as a method to combat societal oppression. Through education the disenfranchised learn to think for themselves, to tell their own stories, and name their reality as a first step in identifying how change should or could occur in their lives and communities. Reflecting and then acting is an important aspect of empowerment; it is based not on the whim of politicians but instead on belief based on ones' own reality:

> The speakers, I feel, were one of the strongest aspects of the course. I enjoyed them because they are the experts of the area where they live and more can be learned from them, I feel, than just reading about them. (Student evaluations, "Rural Course," 1997)

In addition, our goal is to help students understand the role that the larger society plays in maintaining oppression. Social work students may not carry considerations for the more subtle forms of psychological wounding by denying the importance or value of the client's culture. The range of cultural wounding that occurs as a result of oppression, devaluation, or stigmatization in the lives of rural people reveals itself in the client's story (Rodwell & Blankebaker, 1992).

Storytelling can allow students to understand the feelings and behaviors of oppressed persons and develop a new level of empathy, thereby allowing them to consider a different type of problem-solving effort. Riessman (1993) pointed out that culture speaks through an individual's story. Thus, cultural storytelling is more than an intriguing portrayal of reality. It can affect the processes and outcomes of individual, family, and community performance:

> Tremendous power exists in telling one's own story, and personal power becomes political power if minority members share their stories with one another, join their voices, and mobilize to demand a meaningful role in societal decision making. In order for the fishers of North Carolina to play a meaningful role in determining their own future, they will need the support of social workers and other allies who might support greater autonomy in their communities. (Student evaluations, "Rural Course," 1997)

A need exists to extend storytelling and its use in the classroom as a community tool to build group commitment to neighborhood and community work. From a practitioner perspective, research is lacking that evaluates the effectiveness of stories as a classroom teaching instrument for learning about rural community and culture. Intuitively, stories seem to be a powerful means of measuring various components of a rural community or culture. Furthermore, stories may help professors, students, schools of social work, community leaders, and communities gain insight into their own perceptions of culture (Hansen & Kahnweiler, 1993, p. 1402). As rural communities experience the possibility of cultural transformation brought on by changes stemming from global expansions of industry and governmental regulation, it seems especially important to gain a better understanding of how stories may influence community development and sustainability (Hansen & Kahnweiler, 1993).

The narrative method actualizes this thinking by inviting rural people into the classroom to tell their stories. Again, it models for the student respect for rural people and other ways of knowing. When students in one of our courses that used the narrative method were asked to evaluate their experience, every one of them rated the visits of rural people to the classroom as their most exciting learning experience. Based on this feedback, we have begun to incorporate the use of the narrative into other classes. In so doing, we have found that the individual's perspective takes precedence over any other definitions of the situation and is the central theme of the life of the rural person, community, or neighborhood.

TEACHING STUDENTS TO USE NARRATIVE IN RURAL SOCIAL WORK PRACTICE

By using the narrative approach, we want students to be open to new learning and unlearn old stereotypes, myths, and prejudices about rural people. We want them to learn how to enter the world of rural peoples, to understand their world view so that their interventions will have cultural relevance and meaning.

What are the structural conditions (inequality and social injustices) that affect and inform the choices of rural peoples? We want students to understand economic oppression, that is, how a changing economy affects their lives. For example, we want students to learn from fishing families how changing economic conditions are affecting the culture of fishing communities. Another example is how the influx of others into rural areas usually is accompanied by the exploitation of rural resources (both land and people—cheap labor). Students must be prepared to connect with and at the same time increase sensitivity to the negative and positive experiences of clients in order to not engage in or propose simplistic interventions. In other words, we want our students to really learn empathy. Empathy is the ability to move from the worker perspective to the client perspective. We want our students to be sensitive to the lives of the people and to learn to respect tradition by patiently listening to the stories.

The ability to be empathic to rural peoples affirms the client's identity and culture. The clients define their own reality in storytelling. The narrative has the ability to move the client from the margin to the center of analysis. We want the social work student to experience humility in order to relinquish his or her "expert power." What we really hope for is that the students' thinking about rural practice will be transformed by hearing the stories of rural people. Professionally, this transformation can lead to the development of skills in understanding, analyzing, and interpreting the lives of rural people. When students leave our courses, we want them to be different in the sense that we want them to be better able to see the world of rural people through the cultural lenses of these people. Such transformation, according to Hoffman (1987), is based on direct interpersonal identification and the development of understanding and empathy with the rural community. For social work students to begin to challenge their own understanding of the rural experience and culture, they first must engage in a self-discovery process rooted in empathy. Exposure to narratives from rural people helps in this process. As the story unfolds, the character of the rural client becomes a catalyst for direct interpersonal identification between the community worker and the client.

Stories appear to have a vast and untapped potential for understanding, explaining, and enhancing the effectiveness of that elusive entity known as community (Hansen & Kahnweiler, 1993). Stories frequently serve as a means of transmitting behavioral expectations for rural community relationships. One example comes from our human behavior theory class where "C" came to support a friend and join in a class storytelling event:

> C was born to rather successful parents, by the community's standards. She and her sister, the only children to this couple, experienced considerable difficulty in familial relationships. C made the decision to propose to a foreign man who needed citizenship. She proposed that she marry him in order to meet his need and that he marry her in order to rescue her from her family. They would then work on love and loving each other. Before the proposal, C had been diagnosed with an incurable cancer at the age of 20. She did not tell her parents that she was married, and she

also did not reveal the diagnosis of cancer. C wrote a check for medical treatment, and the parents learned that she was married and sick simultaneously. The parents immediately terminated their support for C, including the use of their car, which hindered medical treatment processes because of the ruralness of the region. C borrowed cars from people in their community who seemed to understand the dilemma; the new husband worked overtime and two jobs in order to purchase a used car.

C shared with the class many strategies for maintaining her self-esteem and therefore maintaining health. C believed that her greatest ally in the life process was her humor. When she and her husband assessed their relationship after two years, they agreed that they truly loved each other. C related in her story to the class much of the pain of familial separation and rejection; attempts to build family relationships where relationships did not exist; a small, rural community response to one family's troubles; and the complexities of how rural communities struggle to support relationships when family code and rule dictate the life condition of one of its members.

In the case of C, the class became her community. After the class presentation, the students joined C, who continued the story while they ate lunch together. C felt comfortable communicating with the class after she returned to her home community.

Some practitioners view the heart of effective multicultural practice as listening carefully to the person's story and bringing to awareness the themes and values that the storyteller is using by giving meaning to the events of personal experience. As rural people tell their stories, social work students begin to understand how living in small towns and rural communities has affected, influenced, or shaped the community. Students develop this understanding by treating stories as symbolic reconstructions of the history, rather than as accurate accounts of past events (Allaire & Firsirotu, 1984). The truth, value, and meaning for the rural client is embedded in the story, which may be the most effective method of expressing what the client wishes to communicate. The narrative method teaches students to turn facts into stories from the feelings and meanings that are generated. One may seek to convert the story into a piece of data. By asking questions one can establish details and search for themes, such as looking for constants in family stories.

The narrative may help students learn and feel empathic injustice (Hoffman, 1987, p. 56). For instance, if students compare highly disadvantaged rural and oppressed people with rural people who are more privileged, the students may feel empathic injustice. Students in a human difference class were able to connect with Mr. and Mrs. "S." Their story is a wonderful example of how the structure of opportunity in a rural area affected their lives. The narrative becomes a conduit for the student transformation from nonempathic listening to empathic understanding.

In this particular human difference class, many students who believed that all members of society have the same chance in life had those beliefs challenged. When Mr. and Mrs. S shared their story of rural farming life, the students were able to begin to identify the societal racial barriers in the story. The S story was one of growing up African American in a southern rural sharecropping system. Storytelling thus holds the power to reveal both the historical and the present-day infrastructure of rural life for people.

> Mr. S told of the professional options available to him as an African American male in rural sharecropping America. He knew that he could not work in "that tobacco field in the hot sun for the rest of [his] natural life," he said. "I wasn't sure what I would do, because the only options that seemed to be open to me were to preach or teach. I decided to go to college, and that is where I met my wife. We both currently teach in rural school systems. Though we live in town, it is a rural town," and he laughs. "We probably live in an area where blacks and whites get along best."

A student in the class asked why Mr. and Mrs. S believe they live in a rural community with less prejudice and racism than in other communities. Mr. and Mrs. S described the racial and ethnic mix of their community. Most of the residents are retired-military or active-military families. They believe that the exposure of residents of their community to world communities, various ethnic experiences, the military culture, and the experience of many other world views has shaped their community. Not only were the students curious and comfortable, but they were able to use systematic inquiry in the kinds of questions they asked, such as "How does racism exist from your perspective?"

SUMMARY

The use of narrative in classroom teaching helps students examine their desire and commitment to work in a rural community. One student talked of his human difference class and how the storytelling affected his decision to return to his urban hometown to practice social work. He felt that the class and his rural internship forced him to draw on all of his learning and experiences. The intern stated that although his awareness and sensitivity towards rural social work was enhanced through the storytelling method, he in the end chose to return to urban social work. Another student felt that the visits of rural residents to the class increased the students' sensitivity to the unique needs of clients living in rural areas. In a recent conversation with this student, she stated that as a mental health social worker in a service-starved rural region, she can relate, interact, merge, and collaborate with the community.

Using storytelling in our teaching is a multi-tiered approach. By modeling a method of teaching that allows a more level playing field for all participants—the rural storyteller, the student, and the instructor—we are at the same time modeling a process that can move into the community. By attempting to create in the classroom a safe and nonjudgmental place for all voices to emerge, we are at the same time attempting to validate each other and other ways of knowing. Respect for difference and the difference that difference makes is at the core of our teaching and learning for both the classroom and rural community. It brings together the "we" as opposed to the "us" and "them." This method also provides us with another opportunity to teach about difference other than using race as the defining cultural factor. In the rural South, where black and white relations historically have been complex, stories can provide the bridge to cross cultural lines by collective sharing and empathy.

Our work with narrative, rural people, and students has been an exciting process. As we continue to search for creative and promising teaching methods that engage and respect all participants, we expect that our method will change as our learning, experiences, and knowledge expands. We believe that the use of the narrative method and of inviting rural residents into the classroom can be an effective tool in areas other than the rural South. Regardless of where a social work educational program is located, we believe that students will benefit from being exposed to the narratives, the stories, and the real-life experiences of rural residents.

REFERENCES

Allaire, J. H., & Firsirotu, S. (1984). Theories of organizational culture. *Organization Studies, 5 (3):* 193–226.

Belenky, M. F., Clinchy, B. M., Goldberger, N. R., & Tarule, J. M. (1986). *Women's ways of knowing: The development of self, voice, and mind.* New York: Basic Books.

Biggs, B., & Bollman, R. (1994). Urbanization in Canada. In Thompson Educational Publishing (Ed.), *Canadian social trends* (pp. 67–72). Toronto, ON: Thompson Educational Publishing.

Brown, J. (1933). *The rural community and social case work.* New York: Family Welfare Association of America.

Bruner, J. (1986). *Actual minds, possible worlds.* Cambridge, MA: Harvard University Press.

Coles, R. (1986). *The moral life of children.* New York: Atlantic Monthly Press.

Collier, K. (1984). *Social work with rural peoples.* Vancouver, British Columbia: New Star Books. [Original work published 1984]

Crowell, J. A., & Fellowman, S. S. (1991). Mothers' working models of attachment relationships and mother and child behavior during separation and reunion. *Developmental Psychology, 27,* 597–605.

Department of Agricultural and Research Economics (1994). *The rural economic index.* Raleigh: North Carolina State University.

Fellowman, S. P. (1990). Stories as cultural creativity: On the relation between symbolism and politics in organizational change. *Human Relations, 43,* 809–828.

Friere, P. (1973). *Education for critical consciousness.* New York: Continuum.

Gabriel, Y. (1991). Turning facts into stories and stories into facts: A hermeneutic exploration of organizational folklore. *Human Relations, 44*(8), 857–873.

Geertz, C. (1983). *Local knowledge: Further essays in interpretive anthropology.* New York: Basic Books.

Ginsberg, L.H. (1998). Introduction: An overview of social work education for rural areas. In Ginsberg, L. H. (Ed.). *Social work in rural communities* (3–21). New York: Council on Social Work Education.

Gilligan, C. (1982). *In a different voice: Psychological theory and women's' development.* Cambridge, MA: Harvard University Press.

Glaser, B., & Strass, A. (1967). *The discovery of grounded theory.* Chicago: Aldine.

Haan, N. (1985). Process of moral development: Cognitive or social disequilibrium? *Developmental Psychology, 21,* 996–1006.

Hansen, C. D., & Kahnweiler, W. M. (1993). Storytelling: An Instrument for understanding the dynamics of corporate relationships. *Human Relations, 46*(12), 1391–1395.

Harding, S. (1986). *The science in feminist theory.* Ithaca, NY: Cornell University Press.

Hoffman, M. L. (1987). The contribution of empathy to justice and moral development. In N. Eisenberg & J. Strayer (Eds.), *Empathy and its development* (pp. 47–80). New York: Cambridge University Press.

Hogan, R.T. (1973) Moral conduct and moral character: A psychological perspective. *Psychological Bulletin, 85,* 76–85.

Ingerbrigtson, K. A. (1992). Rural and remote settings: Characteristics and implications for service. In M. Tobin & C. Walmsley (Eds.), *Northern perspectives: Practice and education in social work* (pp. 7–16). Winnipeg, MB: Manitoba Association of Social Workers.

Martin, J., Feldman, M.S., Hatch, M. J., & Sitkin, S. B. (1983). The uniqueness paradox in organizational stories. *Administrative Science Quarterly, 28,* 438–453.

McAdams, D. P. (1989). The development of a narrative identity. In D. M. Buss & N. Cantor (Eds.), *Personality psychology* (pp. 160–174). New York: Springer-Verlag.

Main, M., & Goldwyn, R. (1984). Predicting rejection of her infant from mother's representation of her own experience: Implications for the abused–abusing intergenerational cycle. *Child Abuse and Neglect, 8,* 203–217.

Peters, T., & Waterman, R. H., Jr. (1982). *In search of excellence: Lessons from America's best run companies.* New York: Harper & Row.

Riessman, C. K. (1993). *Narrative Analysis.* Newbury Park, CA: Sage.

Rodwell, M. K. & Blankebaker, A. (1992). Strategies for developing cross-cultural sensitivity: Wounding as metaphor. *Journal of Social Work Education, 28(2),* 153–165.

Ruff, E. (1991). The community as client in rural social work. *Human Services in the Rural Environment, 14*(4), 20–25.

Rushton, J. P. (1980). *Altruism, socialization and society.* Englewood Cliffs, NJ: Prentice-Hall.

Sarbin, T. R. (1986). The narrative as a root metaphor for psychology. In T. R. Sarbin (Ed.), *Narrative psychology: The storied nature of human conduct* (pp. 3–21). New York: Praeger.

Staub, E. (1979). *Positive social behavior and morality: Vol. 2. Socialization and development.* New York: Academic Press.

Sullivan, E. V. (1977). A study of Kohlberg's structural theory of moral development: A critique of liberal social science ideology. *Human Development, 20,* 352–376.

Vitz, P. C. (1990). The use of stories in moral development: New psychological reasons for an old education method. *American Psychologist, 45*(6), 709–720.

White, M. (1989). *Selected papers.* Adelaide, South Australia: Dulwhich Centre Publications.

SECTION VIII

Organizing for
Social Change

Social workers help people and communities cope with problems. Exacerbating the normal stresses and strains of daily living are issues of powerlessness and disenfranchisement. Social workers serving small towns and rural communities often must help the residents of those communities come together for positive social change. Sometimes this assistance involves taking risks or taking unpopular stands; sometimes it involves helping people deal with relationships among different racial or ethnic groups, bringing about changes in attitudes; and sometimes it involves helping to change conditions within the community.

Each of us as individual social workers and all of us together need to work hard to help create a climate that empowers people and that brings about a more participatory democracy. Although in serving small towns and rural communities, social workers need to be generalists, they must be particularly skilled in creating and working with coalitions. In addition, they must be knowledgeable about the political system and how to affect power structures and be willing and able to confront sexism, racism, and homophobia wherever they are found.

The closing plenary speaker at the 23rd Annual National Institute on Social Work and Human Services in Rural Areas was Si Kahn, Executive Director of Grassroots Leadership, Charlotte, North Carolina, who spoke eloquently of the "Habits of Resistance" that all of us need to develop in ourselves and foster in others. Si is a singer, songwriter, community organizer, and widely read author. His presentation at the institute was in the form of a song-speech, and everyone in attendance was deeply moved. In chapter 28, we are pleased to be able to share the song-speech with you in written format.

CHAPTER TWENTY-EIGHT

Habits of Resistance[1]

Si Kahn

In the city of Warsaw such a long time ago
Two hundred children stand lined row on row
With their freshly washed faces and freshly washed clothes
The children of Poland who never grow old

In the orphanage yard not a child remains
The soldiers have herded them down to the trains
Carrying small flasks of water and bags of dry bread
To march in the ranks of the unquiet dead

With their small Jewish faces and pale haunted eyes
They march hand in hand down the street—no one cries
No one laughs, no one looks, no one turns, no one talks
As they walk down the streets where my grandparents walked

Had my grandparents stayed in that dark bloody land
My own children too would have marched hand in hand
To the beat of the soldiers, the jackbooted stamp
That would measure their lives till they died in those camps

The cries of my children at night take me back
To those pale hollow faces in stark white and black
Only the blood of the children remains
It runs in the streets—and it runs in our veins

In the spring of 1993, I returned to this country from a 10-day visit to the Netherlands. I went there not for political but for family and musical reasons. I went with my then–14-year-old son Gabriel to visit his brother, my then–22-year-old son Jesse, who was studying in Europe for a year, and also to record a live album of my songs for a Dutch label called "Strictly Country Records."

But although I did not go to the Netherlands seeking to encounter history and memory, I also knew that I would not be able to avoid them. So I prepared myself for what would be my first visit ever to a concentration camp. The knowledge and

369

imagination of the Nazi death camps have haunted my dreams, shaped and mis-shaped my consciousness since I was a child. They are a destination I have antici-pated and dreaded, imagined and avoided since I became aware of them. But that spring, a few days before my 49th birthday, I finally went with my two younger chil-dren to deal with the past and to confront myself.

I am not going to talk to you about numbers. The statistics are there for those who want to know them. But I want you to know how we stood in the long line and silently filed through the Anne Frank house, where for two years in the secret annex concealed only by a revolving bookcase (which in the end was not enough to save her from betrayal, capture, and death in Auschwitz), in a room today marked only by the yellowing pictures of movie stars she pasted on the walls more than 50 years ago, this young Jewish teenager poured her intelligence and her heart into a diary which is an immortal testament to life and hope. In the small farming town of Vlagtwedde, in the house where Gabriel, Jesse, and I slept, we stared at the ceiling joist where on June 15, 1940, with a lead pencil, another Jewish teenager, Wiardus G. Kosses, had written his weight and height before he too vanished into the smoke of history and hate.

I want you to know how we walked in the woods near the small village of Westerbork, where a Nazi concentration and transportation camp once stood. Where each Tuesday morning, a train carrying nearly a thousand human beings, pushed and packed into the barred and bolted cars, left the Netherlands for places from which most of them would never return. Week after week, month after month, year after year; until almost every one of them had vanished into the air, had become smoke and ashes, as surely as the coal that powered the train.

In the little museum adjoining the camp, we stared through the glass at the small, hand-painted wooden toys that these prisoners of hatred were forced to make as the price of staying alive a little longer. For whose children were these toys sawed and shaped and sanded, polished and painted by these enslaved artisans, whose only crime was that they were Jews and whose own children, whose own parents, whose own selves and souls would soon vanish as if they had never been?

And I thought, too, of my own country's history of genocide and slavery, of some hunted to death in their own nations, of others captured and transported, bought and sold, into a slavery whose impact still persists after almost 400 years.

> *My hands are as cracked as an August field*
> *That's burned in the sun for a hundred years*
> *With furrows so deep you could hide yourself*
> *But I ain't chopping cotton no more this year*
> *I'll just sit on the porch with my eagle eye*
> *And watch for a change of wind*
> *The rows are as straight as a shotgun barrel*
> *And long as a bullet can spin*
> > *You know how hot it gets*
> > *In Mississippi*
> > *You know how dry it gets*
> > *In the summer sun*

The dust clouds swirl
All down the Delta
I just hope that I don't die
'Fore the harvest comes
Black clouds gathering on the edge of town
But no rain's gonna fall on us
Hoes rise and fall in a distant field
Earth takes a beating for all of us
I thought I heard the angel of death overhead
But it's only the cropduster's plane
Hoes rise and fall like the beating of wings
Lord, send us freedom and rain
   You know how hot it gets
   In Mississippi
   You know how dry it gets
   In the summer sun
   The dust clouds swirl
   All down the Delta
   I just hope that I don't die
   'Fore the harvest comes

But there is another side to the story of the Netherlands during those years of occupation and war—a story that has important lessons for those of us who are trying to deal with issues of hatred and violence against people of color, against women, against lesbians, gays, and bisexuals.

In a square in Amsterdam called the Jonas Daniel Meyerplein, right outside the largest synagogue in the world—the Portuguese synagogue completed in 1645—is a statue by Mari Andriessen called "The Dockworker." This statue of a solitary worker in baggy pants, peaked cap, and peasant blouse commemorates and celebrates the resistance of the people of the Netherlands to the occupation of their country by the forces of Nazism and fascism. But most specifically, the statue commemorates the moment on February 25, 1941, when workers throughout Amsterdam walked out in a general strike against the Nazis to protest the first deportation of Jews from that city. This was the first antipogrom strike in the history of Europe.

However, this was only one moment in a movement of resistance to fascism that was immediate and profound, whose recorded history begins the day after the surrender of the Netherlands to the invading German army, when a Dutch schoolteacher wrote and distributed the first of what would eventually be 1,200 underground newspapers, and whose history only ends with the Nazi surrender to the Allied forces five years later.

I want to explore this history a little longer before turning to conditions in this country because I believe that embedded within it is a secret that can be of great value to us in America as we struggle to confront our own internal forces of racism and fascism, of sexism and homophobia. This is a secret that I believe can be both learned and taught, a secret I have come to think of as "the habit of resistance." To me, the habit of resistance is a deep, clear, abiding sense and philosophy about right and wrong, about good and evil and, of equal importance, a reflexive ability to take direct and immediate action when confronted with injustice or to consciously refuse to act when confronted with an unjust choice.

There is a museum in Amsterdam dedicated to this particular element of the human spirit, to this "habit of resistance." It is called, as you might imagine, the Resistance Museum, and it records the history of the Dutch Resistance during the years from 1940 to 1945. This museum records and celebrates the hundreds of habits of resistance that sustained people during those years. These include such acts as

- copying underground newspapers by hand, page by page, reading them, hiding them, passing them on hand-to-hand for others to read, copy, hide, and pass on
- writing poems that marked important events in the life of the Resistance, such as Jan Campert's "Song of the 18 Dead," a title which is tragically self-explanatory, printing the poems up on mimeograph machines powered by bicycles, and selling them to raise money to feed hidden Jewish children
- listening to illegal radio broadcasts on concealed radios and crystal sets
- sponsoring secret concerts and readings behind locked doors in private homes so that artists in hiding could earn a living
- concealing, at the risk of one's own death, those others who had been marked for death and were being hunted by the Nazis. These included Jews, of course, but also Catholic priests and Protestant ministers who spoke out from the pulpit against the occupation and its brutality, railroad workers who struck to paralyze Nazi military transport systems, students who refused to sign the Nazi loyalty oath, artists who refused to join the Nazi "Chamber of Culture," and medical doctors who refused to join the Nazi "Chamber of Doctors."

So many hid and were hidden that by the end of the war, in 1945, out of a small nation which even today numbers less than 15 million people, 300,000 were in hiding within the country from the occupying Nazi forces.

With the profound exception of Native Americans, we in the United States have for more than 100 years had the extraordinary good fortune neither to have fought nor to have lost a war against an invading army nor to have lived under the domination of a foreign power. Nevertheless, many millions of our citizens are not free from daily hatred and violence that endangers their lives, their safety, their security, their self-esteem, their sense of themselves, or their sanity. Unfortunately, there are in the United States today systems of belief and action that are based on hatred of and deadly violence toward certain groups of our citizens because of who and what they are.

> *There's war in South Africa*
> *War in the Balkans*
> *War in Peru*
> *War in Jerusalem*
> *They tell us all wars*
> *Are far off and foreign*

In the United States
There's a war against women
  Take to the streets
  Lift up your voice
  Fight for your life
  While you still have a choice
    Tell them, nobody's body but mine
    This is nobody's body but mine
    Nobody's body but mine
    This is nobody's body but mine
They bow down to laws
That protect private property
While a woman's not safe
In the home or the factory
They say the hallways of justice
Are solemn and sacred
But in front of the law
Only women stand naked
Though manners and banners
Are often expedient
The most civil act
Is to be disobedient
Just like in South Africa
Or in Mississippi
No jail, no law
Will lock up our bodies

So what then are these habits of resistance that we can learn and teach, which will help us help others and ourselves as we struggle against the forces of hatred and violence in our society? What are these habits of resistance that will help us as we work to build organizations that are not only diverse but also just?

Let me give you an example from the daily work that I do. My "day job" is as a staff member of a small nonprofit organization called Grassroots Leadership. Grassroots Leadership is a team of African American and white organizers whose job is to help poor and working people in the American South learn the skills of citizenship, such as how to stand up against injustice and how to use the strength of numbers against the power of money and position. Grassroots Leadership helps build community organizations of poor and working people that can represent those people and help them work and fight for what they want and need.

One of Grassroots Leadership's most important programs is called "Barriers & Bridges." The goal of Barriers & Bridges is to help people build organizations that are more effectively multiracial and multicultural by helping them learn how to confront the barriers of race, gender, class, or sexual orientation that so often divide us from each other. Barriers and Bridges strives to help people learn to build bridges that connect them to each other across these barriers.

As part of Barriers & Bridges, Grassroots Leadership has developed two-person, biracial teams, African American and white, female and male, who work together in communities across the South. Three days after my return from the Netherlands, I went to spend a day with one of these teams in the small town of Winnsboro, in the middle of rural Fairfield County, South Carolina.

Fifty years ago, people in Winnsboro who weren't farming mostly worked in the mills. There's a famous old song about Winnsboro and the mills called the "Winnsboro Cotton Mill Blues":

> Old man Sargent sitting at the desk
> The durned old fool won't give us a rest
> He'd take the nickels off a dead man's eyes
> To buy a Coca Cola and an Eskimo Pie
>   I got the blues, I got the blues
>   I got the Winnsboro cotton mill blues
>   Lordy, Lordy, spooling's hard
>   You know and I know, no need to tell
>   You work for Tom Watson got to work like hell
>   I got the blues, I got the blues
>   I got the Winnsboro cotton mill blues
> When I die don't bury me at all
> Just hang me up on the spinning room wall
> Put a bobbin in my hand
> So I can keep on working in the Promised Land

In Winnsboro today the cotton mills are long gone, but there's a Mack truck plant organized by the United Auto Workers Union, usually known as the UAW, and a shirt factory organized by the Union of Needletrade, Industrial and Textile Employees, known as UNITE.

By the time I got to Winnsboro it was late Friday afternoon. I finally found a parking space on the main street of town right in front of the Fairfield County Courthouse. A few blocks down the street, at the UAW union hall, about 70 workers from the shirt factory had crowded into the back room. It was a pretty mixed crowd. There were blacks and whites, women and men, kids just out of high school, and folks who looked like they'd been working in the factory since it opened more than 30 years ago. There were teenagers and folks in their twenties, male and female, wearing T-shirts and shorts, blue jeans and ball caps. There were older women, black and white, in cotton print dresses, and older men with work boots and overalls.

Every one of them was, as we say, "madder 'n hell." They were in a "fired up, ain't gonna take it no more" mood. A few days before, out in the factory parking lot, a white worker had walked up to a black worker sitting in his car and had slugged him. Now both of these workers, black and white, had been fired for fighting. That action by the company had broken loose everyone's feelings about what was wrong in the plant: sexual harassment, racial discrimination, favoritism, unclear rules, and unfair treatment. But folks weren't just talking about these issues, they were shouting about them. They were on their feet arguing, pointing their fingers, waving their arms, interrupting, shouting each other down, stomping out of the room, slipping back in.

Up at the front of the room was the Barriers & Bridges team from Grassroots Leadership. They were trying to bring order out of chaos, trying to get people to stop interrupting and start listening, trying to get the louder people to leave some space somewhere so that the quieter ones could speak, trying to get everyone to starting thinking and working together so they could figure out what all of them wanted to do and not just what some of them wanted to do.

In one corner, wearing a *kufi* cap and a shirt with the red, black, green, and gold colors of black liberation, was Kamau Marcharia. An African American man from South Carolina, Kamau was born and raised just down the road from Winnsboro in another small crossroads town called Saluda. He learned his organizing skills during the 10 years he spent in a maximum security prison in New Jersey. He won his release in a historic lawsuit that for the first time in this country's history established the rights of prison inmates to what is now known as "contract parole." After his release from prison, Kamau went home to Saluda to work, first with young African Americans and then eventually with black people of all ages and with poor and working-class white folks, too, all over South Carolina.

In the other corner, wearing blue jeans and a white blouse, was Cathy Howell, a white working-class woman born and raised in the historic steel mill town of Homestead, Pennsylvania. Cathy's paternal great-grandfather was one of the striking steelworkers who in 1892 fought a pitched battle with Pinkerton detectives armed with high-powered rifles that the company floated down the river on barges to attack the workers camped on the shore. Her great-grandfather survived the gun battle, only to die later in an industrial accident in the mill. She had learned her organizing skills on the job while working as a caseworker for the Pennsylvania Department of Social Services. After leaving Pennsylvania, Cathy had put those skills to good use all over the country, organizing in Arkansas and Oregon, helping build this country's reproductive rights movement as a staff member of the National Abortion Rights Action League and in 1982 coming to the Carolinas to help make a difference in those states.

As you can imagine, it was a long meeting. A lot of good things got said, as well as some that weren't so good. What I remember most clearly happened right at the end of the meeting, after Kamau and Cathy had finally cleared the space so that every single person there had the chance to say what it was they wanted and needed to say, and when all 70 people in the room—black and white, female and male, young and old—had decided together what they were going to demand and what they were going to do.

The crowd had quieted down. The folks were ready to go home to supper and kids and Friday night. But Kamau asked them to stay just a minute so that he and Cathy could say a few last words. Their words teach us a lot about habits of resistance that we can use to help preserve and strengthen the small towns and rural communities, as well as the organizations, in which we live and work.

Kamau told them:

> It's not about black against white or about women against men. It's not about any of you against any others of you. The issues we've been talking about aren't between

one worker and another, but between all of us as workers on the one hand and management on the other hand. So it's up to us as workers not just to stick together, but to stand up for each other. If you're a man and you see another man sexually harassing a woman, if you don't stand up and say something, then you're as guilty of sexual harassment as he is, because you're letting it happen.

And Cathy said:

The same thing goes for white people. If you hear a white worker refer to a black worker by some racial slur and you don't say something to that white worker, then you're no better than they are.

She said:

You know, it's not easy to do this. You may risk losing that other white worker as a friend. The person you're defending may not be someone you like. They may even be someone you can hardly stand for reasons that have nothing to do with race. That's not the question. The question is not whether you can stand them, but whether you're going to stand up for them.

Standing at the edge of the crowd, backed into the far corner of the union hall right next to the trash can, whose contents now seemed to be fermenting in the continually increasing heat and humidity, still only hours away in time from the monuments and memories of the Netherlands, I thought how extraordinary and rare it is when human beings act with such unassuming courage and clarity. And I thought how wonderful it would be if such extraordinary ways of thought and action were in fact so ordinary that all of us did whatever was called for, whenever it was needed, without even thinking about it.

I believe that over the years of working side by side with ordinary people who were in danger and who were at risk, and of working side by side with each other, these two co-workers of mine—Cathy Howell and Kamau Marcharia—developed the habits of resistance, or, as Elie Wiesel once put it, the quiet courage "to speak truth to power," even at significant risk to themselves.

Far from the battlefields of World War II and the killing fields of the Holocaust it is such quiet courage and such habits of resistance that give us hope for the future.

> *From the beachhead at Anzio*
> *To the cities of the plain*
> *The veterans of the "last good war"*
> *Are gathering again*
> *They stand in circles like*
> *The wooden soldiers in a store*
> *Only they can tell the sergeants*
> *From the privates any more*
>
> *They are dressed up like civilians*
> *You and I could never tell*
> *The times like their old uniforms*

No longer fit them well
They are listening to a different drum
From others in the crowd
They were heroes to each other
Tell me, who's a hero now

They are fading like the smoke
From all the bridges that they burned
Fifty years, how many wars
You wonder what we've learned
From the sisterhood of struggle
To the brotherhood of war
Is living well or dying well
More worth fighting for

So how, then, in this troubled and troubling world do we fight not only to live well ourselves but to help others create the space and freedom to live well themselves? How do we learn the habits of resistance that will help us stand firmly and act justly?

We learn the habits of resistance just like one learns to play the piano—by practicing daily.

Those of us in America who are white, who are male, who are so-called straight need to understand and recognize that the leadership in challenging the barriers in our society that have been established in reaction to race, gender, and sexual orientation comes first from those who have suffered the most because of them. People of color, women, lesbians, and gays have for a long time learned and practiced the habits of resistance as a matter of survival.

It is up to those of us who are white to challenge other whites who express racism on their racism. . . . It is up to those of us who are men to challenge others on sexual harassment, on rape, on spousal abuse, on all forms of violence. . . . It is up to those of us who are so-called straight to challenge other straight people who express hatred of and violence toward lesbians, bisexuals, gays, and transgendered people. . . . To blame people of color for racism, to blame women, lesbians, and gays for the many forms of hatred and violence directed against them, makes as little sense as blaming those of us who are Jews for what the Nazis did to us in the Holocaust of World War II.

It is up to those of us who have any degree of power and access in this society to make sure that our access and power are used to open doors and not to close them to those who are not as privileged as we are. It is up to us to refuse to cooperate with injustice, to refuse to lend our names, our reputations, our presence, our work to those institutions, events, and processes that refuse to share power and access equitably. It is up to all of us to teach our own generations and those generations that will follow the habits of resistance so that we are never unsure of how and when to act justly and quickly, even in the face of fear.

In the homes in which my children and I stayed during our visit to the Netherlands, there were refrigerator magnets which, translated into English, said

"Racism is not an opinion—Racism is a crime." Beside a canal near the Anne Frank house there is a series of triangles built of pink marble, which is a monument not only to the lesbians and gays who were murdered by the Nazis but also to the international struggle for the liberation of gays and lesbians everywhere. And, at the foot of the Dockworker statue next to the old Portuguese synagogue, I saw a bunch of tulips bound by a green and white ribbon with gold letters that said "In eternal gratitude"—in German.

I hope, I expect, I believe that these small and large public symbols are in no way accidents but are instead the flowering of attitudes and ways of being that have been carefully cultivated. I believe that the lessons of the Dutch resistance to the Nazis between the years 1940 and 1945, because they have been carefully preserved and taught, have nurtured the public and private habits of resistance that I encountered among so many people in the Netherlands. These are the same habits of resistance that I encounter among committed antiracist and antisexist organizers and activists like Kamau Marcharia and Cathy Howell. These are also the habits of resistance that I hope and believe are being learned, practiced, and taught by many of you who are here today. These are the same habits of resistance that are necessary to preserve and strengthen our small towns and rural communities and all who live in these communities.

In a world racked by violence and hatred, such habits of resistance are only a beginning. But in a world racked by violence and hatred, we can only begin.

> *Good friends, from whom we now must part*
> *Where are we bound*
> *Your hands and voices lift my heart*
> *Here is my home*
> > *Come darkness, come light*
> > *Where are we bound*
> > *Come morning, come night*
> > *Here is my home*
> *For those who sing in harmony*
> *Where are we bound*
> *Can learn to live in unity*
> *Here is my home*
> > *Come darkness, come light*
> > *Where are we bound*
> > *Come morning, come night*
> > *Here is my home*
> *If we can join ourselves in song*
> *Where are we bound*
> *Our hearts will live when we are gone*
> *Here is my home*
> > *Come darkness, come light*
> > *Where are we bound*
> > *Come morning, come night*
> > *Here is my home*

The spirit that finds music here
Where are we bound
Will sing forever in the air
Here is my home
    Come darkness, come light
    Where are we bound
    Come morning, come night
    Here is my home

The first draft of this songspeech, 18 pages in length, was completed on Yom Hashoah, the day of remembrance of the Holocaust, April 18, 1993. That week also marked both the opening of the Holocaust Museum in Washington, DC, and the 50th anniversary of the Warsaw Ghetto uprising by Jewish resistance fighters. During the time I was writing it, my then–25-year-old son Simon, who was born on February 25, the same date as the Dutch general strike against the Nazis in 1941, was in Poland as a member of the U.S. government delegation to the Warsaw Ghetto tribute.

RECOMMENDED READINGS

Kahn, S. (1991). *Organizing: A guide for grassroots leaders* (Rev. ed.). Washington, DC: NASW Press.

Kahn, S. (1994). *How people get power* (Rev. ed.). Washington, DC: NASW Press.

Kahn, S. (1995). Community organizing. In R. L. Edwards (Ed.-in-Chief), *Encyclopedia of social work* (19th ed., Vol. 1, pp. 569–576). Washington, DC: NASW Press.

Index

Note: Material presented in figures and tables is indicated by italicized letters *f* and *t* following page numbers.

About The Editors

Iris Carlton-LaNey, PhD, is Associate Professor in the School of Social Work at the University of North Carolina at Chapel Hill, where she also serves as Director of the Advanced Standing Program. Her research interests include aging in rural communities and African American social welfare history. She has served as guest editor for special issues of the *Journal of Sociology and Social Welfare* and the *Journal of Community Practice* and has authored a monograph entitled *Elderly Black Farm Women as Keepers of the Community and Culture.* She has served on the editorial boards of several journals and has published articles in *Generations, Social Work, Social Service Review, Arete,* and the *Journal of Sociology and Social Welfare.* Currently, she is completing a book entitled *African American Leadership in Social Welfare: An Empowerment Tradition.*

Richard L. Edwards, PhD, ACSW, is Dean and Professor at the University of North Carolina at Chapel Hill's School of Social Work. His research and teaching interests include public and nonprofit management and fundraising for nonprofit organizations. He was editor-in-chief of the *Encyclopedia of Social Work—19th Edition* (1995) and the *Encyclopedia of Social Work—1997 Supplement.* He also is a former president of the National Association of Social Workers. He is senior author of *Building A Strong Foundation: Fundraising for Nonprofits,* and senior editor of *Skills for Effective Management of Nonprofit Organizations.* He has published articles in a number of journals, including *Social Work, Human Services in the Rural Environment, Arete, Administration in Social Work, Nonprofit Times,* and *Professional Development.*

P. Nelson Reid, PhD, is Professor and Chair of the Department of Social Work at the University of North Carolina at Wilmington. His research focuses on the development of social welfare and the influence of social ideals, the character of the social work profession, and social service organization and management. He is coeditor of *The Moral Purposes of Social Work* and *Professionalization of Poverty: Social Work and the Poor in the 20th Century.* He is a contributor to the *Encyclopedia of Social Work—19th Edition.* In addition, he has published articles in a number of journals, including *Social Work, Journal of Social Welfare, Social Service Review, International Journal of Contemporary Sociology, Journal of Social Service Research, Journal of Education for Social Work,* and *Arete.*

About the Contributors

Mary Altpeter, MSW, MPA, ACSW, is Associate Director for Operations at the University of North Carolina's systemwide Institute on Aging and is Research Assistant Professor in the Department of Social Medicine in the School of Medicine at the University of North Carolina at Chapel Hill. She is also a doctoral candidate in Social Work at Memorial University of Newfoundland, Canada. Her research has focused on testing community-based health interventions in rural, eastern North Carolina. She has been lead or coauthor of numerous community provider education or community health promotion grants from private foundations and state and federal entities. She is coeditor of *Skills for Effective Management of Nonprofit Organizations* and she has published in a number of journals.

Freddie Avant, MSW, ACSW, LMSW-AP, SSWS, is Baccalaureate Program Director and Associate Professor, School of Social Work, Stephen F. Austin State University, Nacogdoches, Texas. His research interests are rural social work, social work education, school social work, and multicultural social work.

Lessie L. Bass, DSW, is Assistant Professor, School of Social Work, East Carolina University. Her professional career has be devoted to the child welfare arena, with several years experience in the area of foster care. She has a particular interest in working with children and their families within their own communities. Her interest in narratives and storytelling has grown out of her work in foster care and community projects.

Kathleen Belanger, MSSW, is the Director of the Child Welfare Professional Development Project, School of Social Work, Stephen F. Austin State University, Nacogdoches, Texas. She has taught social work at SFA for 12 years in both graduate and undergraduate programs. She has done consultation and program evaluation for Child Protective Services and has helped build numerous programs to meet the needs of rural communities.

Jay Bishop, PhD, ACSW, LCSW, is Assistant Professor and Coordinator of the Dual Degree Program in Sociology and Social Work at the University of Maryland Eastern Shore and Salisbury State University. He has received numerous grants from state and regional government sources. His research interests include homelessness, substance abuse and HIV/AIDS prevention and treatment.

Robert Blundo, PhD, is Associate Professor in the Department of Social Work at the University of North Carolina at Wilmington. His research interests and publications have focused on applying postmodernism, social constructionism, the strengths perspective, and ethnomethodology to a range of topics in social work. These topics include social work pedagogy, power and agency, as well as diversity, oppression, and social work practice.

Shelia Grant Bunch, MSW, is a lecturer at the School of Social Work, East Carolina University and a doctoral candidate in sociology at North Carolina State University. Her research and teaching interests include cultural diversity, social justice/equality, and direct practice with children and families.

Natasha K. Bowen, PhD, is a Research Associate at the School of Social Work, University of North Carolina at Chapel Hill. She is interested in school social work and the application of risk and protective factor theory to the development and evaluation of interventions for child and adolescent behavior problems. She has been a frequent contributor to professional journals.

Fran Cissna Butler, MSW, is a direct service provider with North Care Mental Health Center's Ardmore office serving rural communities in southern Oklahoma. She was previously State Coordinator for Healthy Families Oklahoma and has been involved in a broad range of social services and legislative advocacy activities affecting the rural population with an emphasis on family and child welfare.

Lena Williams Carawan, MSW, is an Instructor in the School of Social Work at East Carolina University and a doctoral candidate in Social Work at Memorial University of Newfoundland, Canada. She is interested in the use of first-person storytelling and narrative in the classroom. Her research interests include social work with rural people with an emphasis on commercial fishing families, as well as children and families who reside in mobile home parks.

Joanne Chezem, MSW, is an Instructor in the School of Social Work, College of Education, Southern Illinois University at Carbondale. She is the former Executive Director for the Federation of Community United Services (FoCUS) of southern Illinois. Her primary area of expertise is in human services with special emphasis on rural areas. She has served as a consultant to the Governor's Task Force on Human Services Reform, the Governor's Task Force on the Future of Rural Illinois, and the Lieutenant Governor's Task Force on Rural Health. She has conducted numerous studies on rural health and social service issues.

Rosemary Arrowsmith Clews, MA (Social Work), MSocSci (Social Services Management), is an Assistant Professor of Social Work at St. Thomas University, Fredericton, New Brunswick, Canada. She is a doctoral candidate in Social Work at Memorial University of Newfoundland, Canada. After working as a social worker, a social work educator, and a social services manager in multicultural urban and rural communities in England for over 20 years, she moved to Canada in 1993. She was a faculty member at the University of Regina in the rural prairie province of Saskatchewan for three years before relocating to New Brunswick

H. Stephen Cooper received his MSW degree from Stephen F. Austin State University, Nacogdoches, Texas, with a concentration in Advanced Rural Generalist Social Work. His work experience includes two and a half years in mental health related services with children and young adults. His law enforcement background includes four and a half years as a certified peace officer in the State of Texas.

Ellen L. Csikai, PhD, MPH, is an assistant professor in the School of Social Work at Stephen F. Austin State University, Nacogdoches, Texas. She has several years of social work practice experience in child welfare services and in medical social work. She is also engaged in collaborative research in conjunction with the School's Child Welfare Professional Development Program.

Michael R. Daley, MSW, PhD, ACSW, LMSW-AP, is Associate Dean and Director, School of Social Work, Stephen F. Austin State University, Nacogdoches, Texas. His research interests are rural social work, social work education, social work administration, and children's protective services. He has served as President and Treasurer of the Texas Chapter of the National Association of Social Workers.

Judith A. Davenport, PhD, LCSW, is Professor and former Director of the School of Social Work at the University of Missouri—Columbia. She has been a director of BSW programs at the University of Georgia and the University of Wyoming. She has extensive practice, research, and teaching experience in rural social work in the United States and has begun examining rural social work/community development in developing countries.

Joseph Davenport, III, PhD, ACSW, is a consultant to agencies and organizations addressing social problems in rural areas, especially those facing rapid change. He has taught at several universities and has prior practice experience with a United Way agency and with the U.S. Indian Health Service. His many publications include coauthoring with his wife, Judith, the overview article on rural social work in the *Encyclopedia of Social Work—19th Edition* (1995).

Paul K. Dezendorf, PhD, CSWM, CHES, is Lecturer, School of Social Work, East Carolina University in Greenville, North Carolina. His background includes cable television operations and management consulting. His research interests include the interaction between information technology and social work practice particularly in health care and aging and the integration of information technology into the social work education curriculum and programs.

Ellen Russell Dunbar, PhD, is Professor and Director at the Social Work Department, California State University, Stanislaus. She was formerly professor at Eastern Washington University School of Social Work and has many years of experience in administration as executive director of the California Chapter of NASW, and Program Director in a Los Angeles agency. She has previously published on rural mental health service delivery. Her research interests include equity in service delivery and history of Spanish poor laws.

Eugenia Eng, MPH, DrPH, is an Associate Professor and Director of the Masters Degree Program in the Department of Health Behavior and Health Education in the School of Public Health at the University of North Carolina at Chapel Hill. Over the past 15 years, she has developed a body of community-based research that is recognized, both nationally and internationally, for its contributions to public health practice. She has assisted practitioners and researchers alike in the U.S. and other nations on the design and conduct of the *Action-Oriented Community Diagnosis,* which is a community assessment procedure that combines the principles of community organizing with those of the social ecological framework for health promotion.

Thomas W. Fuhrman, PhD, is a clinical instructor at the Behavioral Healthcare Resource Program of the Jordan Institute for Families in the School of Social Work at the University of North Carolina in Chapel Hill. Previously, he served as the Director of Managed Care at Crossroads Behavioral Healthcare, one of 40 area mental health authorities in the state of North Carolina. He is currently drawing upon his background in public and private sector service delivery and administration to provide training and consultation to behavioral healthcare professionals.

Anne-Linda Furstenberg, PhD, is Associate Professor and Chair of the Doctoral Program in the School of Social Work at the University of North Carolina at Chapel Hill, where she teaches in the Aging Concentration. Her research interests focus on the health problems of older people, particularly hip fracture, and their experiences in the health care system. She also explores the meanings that older people attach to old age. She was principal investigator and project director for The Carolina Companions Project, which provided an opportunity to collaborate with community agencies in designing and evaluating an intervention affecting both mental health consumers and the companions who met with them.

Denise L. Gammonley, PhD, is an Assistant Professor in the School of Social Work at Florida International University. She collaborated in the development of the Carolina Companions Project, and was the Research Director for the project. Dr. Gammonley has also studied care of ing populations in Central America.

Ronald K. Green, MSW, MPA, JD, ACSW, is Professor of Social Work and Chair, Department of Social Work, Winthrop University, Rock Hill, South Carolina. He has served as a faculty member and in administrative positions at the Mandel School of Applied Social Sciences at Case Western Reserve University and at the University of Tennessee College of Social Work. He has contributed to the literature related to both information technology and practice and rural practice starting with the coediting of the first rural reader, *Social Work in Rural Areas,* in 1978.

Bill Horner, DSW, is the Program Director of BASW education at Eastern Washington University. His current research interest focuses on what people with BSWs actually do in social service agencies and the fit between what they do and CSWE's generalist emphasis. He has also done research on child protective and child mental health service systems.

Si Kahn, PhD, is Executive Director of Grassroots Leadership, based in Charlotte, North Carolina, a team of African American and white organizers working with communities and organizations throughout the South. He is a singer, songwriter, and community organizer who has worked in the South for more than 25 years on issues of social justice and human rights. His books include *How People Get Power* and

Organizing: A Guide for Grassroots Leaders. He has recorded eight albums of original songs plus a collection of traditional civil rights, women's, and labor songs recorded jointly with Jane Sapp and Pete Seeger. Si frequently appears in concerts and major folk and labor festivals throughout North America and Europe.

Raymond S. Kirk, PhD, is a Clinical Associate Professor and Senior Research Associate in the School of Social Work at the University of North Carolina at Chapel Hill. He has held teaching and administrative positions in academe and government, and has worked extensively with private sector organizations and foundations on program design and program evaluation. He is currently involved with the evaluation of North Carolina's Intensive Family Preservation Services Program, technical assistance and training on the development of self-evaluation capabilities for child welfare reform sites funded by the Annie E. Casey Foundation, and the development of the North Carolina Family Assessment Scale. Additionally, he is co-principal investigator to evaluate the effectiveness of the Enhanced Employee Assistance Program, a project funded by the Robert Wood Johnson Foundation.

Ameda A. Manetta, PhD, LCSW, is an Assistant Professor in the Department of Social Work at Winthrop University in Rock Hill, South Carolina, where she is responsible for coordination of field students and continuing. She serves on several community boards and is a member of the American Association of Suicidology.

Kathleen Marks, BA, works in North Carolina with The Conservation Fund's Resourceful Communities Program and provides assistance to other nonprofit organizations on community development and communications projects. She has a deep appreciation for North Carolina's unique resources—its people and its special places. Working with programs that address both local citizens' needs and resource protection provides her with the opportunity to help find sustainable, practical solutions to many problems facing rural communities.

Clyde O. McDaniel, Jr., PhD, is Professor in the Department of Sociology and Anthropology at the University of North Carolina at Wilmington. His areas of concentration are applied research, social problems, and community organization. He has directed research centers in school systems and universities, has served in various university administrative capacities, and had consulted and presented papers throughout the country and abroad. His publications include more than seventy-five journal articles and four books. Until recently, he wrote a weekly newspaper column and hosted a weekly radio talk show.

Judson H. Morris, MSW, has worked in a variety of rural communities in California, Oregon, Washington, and South Carolina. He is particularly interested in rural community development, self-sufficiency, and empowerment. His photos have appeared in *Human Services in the Rural Environment.*

Lynne Clemmons Morris, PhD, is an Associate Professor of Social Work in the School of Social Work and Human Services at Eastern Washington University. Her teaching responsibilities include courses in the areas of research and rural community development. Her recent research has been focused on the impact of managed care on rural mental health systems and the design of gender-friendly distance education for rural communities.

Edith Parker, MPH, DrPH, is an Assistant Professor in the Department of Health Behavior and Health Education, University of Michigan School of Public Health. She is currently involved with several community-based health intervention research projects in Michigan funded by the Centers for Disease Control and Prevention, the Center for Environment and Children's Health, the National Institute for Environmental Health Sciences and the Environmental Protection Agency, and the U.S. Public Health Service. She teaches courses on program planning and development, community-based health interventions, and patient education.

Patricia P. Plaskon, PhD, ACSW, LCSW-C, has been an Assistant Professor at Salisbury State University and a practitioner in rural health care settings for 15 years. She has been active in the leadership of the NASW Maryland Chapter, serving on the state licensing task force and on several nonprofit boards. Her research interests include health care and hospice.

Robert O. Rich, PhD, is a Professor in the School of Social Work at Eastern Washington University where he has primary responsibility for the graduate level mental health practice and policy curriculum. His research activity in recent years has been directed toward the impact of mental health reform and managed care on rural mental health systems, providers, and consumers. He has practiced in public mental health programs in Washington, Kansas, and California.

Amelia C. Roberts, PhD, is an Assistant Professor in the School of Social Work at the University of North Carolina at Chapel Hill, where she teaches in the Mental Health Practice Concentration. She has held supervisory, administrative, and consultant responsibilities in the areas of child welfare and substance abuse. Currently, she serves as a co-principal investigator for a project funded by The Robert Wood Johnson Foundation to evaluate the effectiveness of the Enhanced Employee Assistance Program initiative.

Susanne Mosteller Rolland, PhD, is an Assistant Professor in the Department of Sociology, Social Work, and Criminology at Morehead State University in Kentucky. Her research interests are in the areas of domestic violence, family change and adaptation, and cultural values and cultural change. Her publications have appeared in several journals.

T. Laine Scales, MSW, PhD, is currently Assistant Professor of Social Work and Associate Director of The Center for Family and Community Ministries at Baylor University, Waco, Texas. Her research interests are in the areas of rural social work, church social work, and social welfare history.

Anna Scheyett, MSW, CCSW, is a Clinical Instructor and Program Coordinator of the Behavioral Healthcare Resource Program, in the Jordan Institute for Families at the University of North Carolina at Chapel Hill School of Social Work. There she develops and provides training and technical assistance on a wide range of behavioral healthcare topics including managed care, case management, and services to people with severe and persistent mental illness. She is editor and contributing author of *Making the Transition to Managed Behavioral Healthcare: A Guide for Agencies and Practitioners.*

Sharon B. Templeman, PhD, LMSW-ACP, ACSW, teaches in the Undergraduate Program at the Stephen F. Austin State University School of Social Work. She has also worked in the area of Children's Services for over 25 years and continues to conduct research in this arena.

Martin B. Tracy, PhD, is Professor and Director of the School of Social Work in the College of Education, Southern Illinois University at Carbondale. He has been involved in several community capacity-building projects in Iowa and southern Illinois and has conducted policy analyses on a variety of issues related to social security and income support systems in economically developing countries in Asia and Eastern Europe and on social cohesion in industrial nations. He is a consultant to the International Social Security Association, Geneva, Switzerland.

Patsy Dills Tracy, MSW, PhD, is a Clinical Associate Professor at the School of Social Work in the College of Education, Southern Illinois University at Carbondale. She has a particular interest in research and service issues related to community, child welfare, and social cohesion in a cross-national context, as well in rural areas in the Lower Mississippi River Delta region. She was a Visiting Lecturer at the Centre for Rural Social Research, Charles Sturt University, Wagga Wagga, New South Wales, Australia, in the summer of 1999.

Cheryl Waites, PhD, ACSW, is an Assistant Professor in the Department of Social Work at North Carolina State University, Raleigh. She previously taught at the University of North Carolina at Pembroke, where she was the Coordinator of Field Education. She has extensive experience in child welfare and has worked as a program administrator, supervisor, family therapist, protective services worker, and planning social worker. She has published in the areas of child welfare, African American adolescents, multicultural social work practice methods, and social work education.

Kenneth R. Wedel, PhD, is Professor at the University of Oklahoma School of Social Work, Norman. His major areas of research and teaching include social policy, social program planning, and evaluation. He is co-principal investigator on a research project involving the impacts of welfare-to-work programs on rural public transportation demand in Oklahoma.

Craig White, MSW, works throughout North Carolina and Appalachia as a consultant to nonprofit organizations and a facilitator of rural community development and conservation efforts. Currently, he serves as a facilitator of the New River watershed planning process under the President's American Heritage Rivers Initiative. He is also an adjunct faculty member in the School of Social Work at the University of North Carolina at Chapel Hill.

Frank Wilson is Mayor of Bolton, North Carolina. A lifelong resident of Bolton, he comes from a long line of African American leaders in this region.

Smith Worth, MSW, LEAP, is a Clinical Instructor in the Jordan Institute for Families at the School of Social Work, University of North Carolina at Chapel Hill. Drawing upon her nine years working as an Employee Assistance Program counselor and addictions specialist in the private sector, she has been involved in developing North Carolina's Enhanced Employee Assistance Program model.

Mary Ann Yevuta, MSW, has worked for the West Virginia Department of Health and Human Resources for over 18 years, primarily as a worker and supervisor in Family and Children's services, but also as a supervisor of Adult Services. In addition to her responsibilities at WVDHHR, she is a part-time faculty member at West Virginia Northern Community College. She has served on the Board of Directors of United Way, and the Wetzel County Family Resources Network.

Deborah J. Zuver, MA, LMFT, RDT/BC, is a mental health consultant at the North Carolina Division of Mental Health/Developmental Disabilities/Substance Abuse Services, Child and Family Services Section. She was the coordinator for Project HOPE, the long-term crisis-counseling program that responded to Hurricane Fran survivors in North Carolina. She is licensed as a marriage and family therapist and has served as a board member of the National Association for Drama Therapy.

RECENT TITLES FROM NASW PRESS

Preserving and Strengthening Small Towns and Rural Communities, *Iris B. Carlton-LaNey, Richard L. Edwards, and P. Nelson Reid, Editors.* This volume defines the issues and crises of the surprisingly diverse populations of small towns and rural communities and illustrates the myriad of solutions and interventions available to the social worker in these contexts. Contributors analyze the strengths, obstacles, and societal mores found in these communities and present sensitive approaches. *Preserving and Strengthening Small Towns and Rural Communities* offers a much-needed generalist approach to practice in the rural environment, where the dynamics of family and community create a unique opportunity for positive change.

ISBN: 0-87101-310-X. Item #310X. $36.95

Clinical Intervention with Families (Companion Volume to *Clinical Practice with Individuals*), *Mark A. Mattaini.* Written for social workers in family practice as well as for instructors and advanced-level students, *Clinical Intervention with Families* is a state-of-the-art treatment guide for family practice. This essential resource provides a coherent conceptual framework and an in-depth discussion of the processes of shared power. It also presents a detailed outline of three core intervention strategies, including the latest guidelines and techniques for applying them. This is an essential volume for those who want to understand the extrinsic factors affecting the theory and practice of family social work!

ISBN: 0-87101-308-8. Item #3088. $32.95

New Directions for Social Work Practice Research, *Miriam Potocky-Tripodi and Tony Tripodi, Editors.* This book helps readers put their fingers on the pulse of research into social work practice—past, present, and future. Contributors from the United States and the United Kingdom, all of whom are prominent researchers of social work, offer a variety of critical assessments of practice research. They provide a wealth of new data on the current status of research and clearly lay down their own vision of the agenda for future studies.

ISBN: 0-87101-305-3. Item #3053. $28.95

Multicultural Issues in Social Work: Practice and Research, *Patricia L. Ewalt, Edith M. Freeman, Anne E. Fortune, Dennis L. Poole, and Stanley L. Witkin, Editors.* This volume outlines new strategies for helping diverse groups and communities find their voices and enhance their capabilities. This book will help readers develop an understanding of changes in multicultural practice skills now required by the revised NASW *Code of Ethics;* learn subtleties in cultural patterns and political circumstances in diverse immigrant populations that affect practice approaches; and enhance skills for responding to new public policies that reflect victim blaming, cost containment, and cultural intolerance.

ISBN: 0-87101-302-9. Item #3029. $41.95

The Social Work Dictionary, 4th Edition, *Robert L. Barker.* With nearly 8,000 terms, *The Social Work Dictionary* is an essential tool for understanding the language of social work and related disciplines. Here—in a single user-friendly resource—are all the terms, concepts, organizations, historical figures, and values that define the profession. These terms were gathered from the social work literature and primary texts in related disciplines, then revised for brevity, clarity, and accuracy and reviewed by an international editorial board. The resulting reference is a must for every human services professional, regardless of level of experience or field of practice.

ISBN: 0-87101-298-7. Item #2987. $34.95

(Order form on reverse side)

ORDER FORM

Title	Item #	Price	Total
__ Preserving and Strengthening Small Towns and Rural Communities	310X	$36.95	_____
__ Clinical Intervention with Families	3088	$32.95	_____
__ New Directions for SW Practice Research	3053	$28.95	_____
__ Multicultural Issues in Social Work	3029	$41.95	_____
__ The Social Work Dictionary, 4th Edition	2987	$34.95	_____
		Subtotal	_____
	+ 10% postage and handling		_____
		Total	_____

❑   I've enclosed my check or money order for $ _____.

❑   Please charge my   ❑ NASW VISA*   ❑ Other VISA   ❑ MasterCard

_____   _____

Credit Card Number   Expiration Date

Signature _____

Use of this card generates funds in support of the social work profession.

Name_____

Address _____

City _____ State/Province _____

Country _____ZIP _____

Phone _____ E-mail _____

NASW Member # (if applicable) _____

(Please make checks payable to NASW Press. Prices are subject to change.)

NASW PRESS
P. O. Box 431
Annapolis JCT, MD 20701
USA

Credit card orders call
1-800-227-3590
(In the Metro Wash., DC, area, call 301-317-8688)
Or fax your order to 301-206-7989
Or order online at http://www.naswpress.org

Visit our Web site at http://www.naswpress.org   EDWBI99